Culture and Power in Banaras

Culture and Power in Banaras

Community, Performance, and Environment, 1800–1980

EDITED BY

Sandria B. Freitag

UNIVERSITY OF CALIFORNIA PRESS

Berkeley Los Angeles London

University of California Press
Berkeley and Los Angeles, California
University of California Press, Ltd.
London, England

Library of Congress Cataloging-in-Publication Data

Culture and power in Banaras: community, performance, and environment, 1800–1980/edited by Sandria B. Freitag.
p. cm.
Bibliography: p.
Includes index.
ISBN 0-520-06367-8
1. Vārānasi (India)—Civilization. 2. Power (Social Sciences)
I. Freitag, Sandria B.
DS486.B4C85 1989
954′.2—dc19 88-21092
CIP

Printed in the United States of America

1 2 3 4 5 6 7 8 9

CONTENTS

LIST OF ILLUSTRATIONS

MAPS

FIGURES

CONTRIBUTORS

David Arnold holds the chair in South Asian history at the School of African and Oriental Studies, University of London. He received his D. Phil. from Sussex University. He is the author of *The Congress in Tamilnad: Nationalist Politics in South India, 1919–37* (1977) and *Police Power and Colonial Rule: Madras, 1859–1947* (1986). His current research is on epidemics and famines in nineteenth- and twentieth-century India.

Diane M. Coccari recently completed her Ph.D. in the Department of South Asian Studies at the University of Wisconsin and is affiliated with that institution. Her dissertation is entitled "The Bir Babas of Banaras: An Analysis of a Folk Deity in North Indian Hinduism."

Sandria B. Freitag, academic administrator and adjunct lecturer at the University of California at Berkeley, recently completed a monograph, *Collective Activity and Community: Public Arenas in the Emergence of Communalism in North India.* Interested in general in the interaction between the British colonial state and collective activities, including protest and popular culture, she is currently working on collective crime.

Kathryn Hansen is an associate professor in the Department of Asian Studies at the University of British Columbia. Her publications include an anthology of translations, *The Third Vow and Other Stories,* by Phanishwarnath Renu (1986), a special issue of the *Journal of South Asian Literature* devoted to Renu (1982), and articles on Hindi fiction, Indian cinema, folk theatre, classical music, and South Asian women. She is writing a book on the Nautanki theatre tradition.

Christopher R. King received his training in Indian history and Hindi at the University of Wisconsin and now teaches Intercultural Communication and related subjects, as well as Hindi, in the Department of Communication Studies at the University of Windsor, Ontario. His previous work has included translations of Hindi literature into English, and studies in the social, cultural, and political aspects of language in modern north India.

Nita Kumar teaches South Asian history at Brown University. Her book *The Artisans of Banaras: Popular Culture and Identity, 1800–1986* has been published by Princeton University Press. She is working on a monograph, "Primary School Curricula in Twentieth Century India: The Social Construction of Meaning."

Philip Lutgendorf is an assistant professor in Asian Studies at the University of Iowa. His dissertation for the University of Chicago, completed in 1986, was entitled "The Life of a Text: Tulsidas' *Rāmcharitmānas* in Performance."

Scott L. Marcus has conducted extensive fieldwork on Indian folk and classical music in Banaras and the surrounding villages. His Ph.D. dissertation for the University of California at Los Angeles, based on fieldwork conducted in Egypt, is on the melodic modes (the *magamat*) of Arabic music.

Robert G. Varady obtained his Ph.D. at the University of Arizona, specializing in the nineteenth-century history of South Asian transportation systems. Since 1981 he has been a member of the faculty of the Office of Arid Lands Studies at the University of Arizona.

PREFACE

Several purposes informed the collaborative work behind this volume. First, it provides a sustained examination, from a variety of viewpoints, of one urban place. Banaras was chosen primarily because it had attracted a sufficient "critical mass" of new scholarship to be especially suggestive. (The extent to which it can be considered "typical" is examined below.) But even though the contributors sketch the outlines of north Indian urban history over the preceding two centuries, they do not claim that their essays provide a definitive picture.

Rather, the essays explore new vistas, either methodologically or topically. Our second purpose, then, was to suggest by these juxtaposed examinations new ways to approach the history of South Asia. The topical implications of such new approaches are discussed in greater detail below; here it will suffice to note that the authors have shared as a focal point the participation of nonelite groups in the developments, events, and political narrative that previously have constituted "history." As a collective effort to expand the methodologies and topics that constitute history, these studies are intended not only for South Asianist scholars, but also for scholars of other cultural regions interested in comparative discussions of what has been called "popular culture," as well as undergraduate students just learning about South Asia. (Given the limits of space, however, the volume does presuppose a rudimentary familiarity with the decline of the Mughal Empire, the initial infiltration of the East India Company into the subcontinent, and the general outlines of the South Asian political narrative for the nineteenth and twentieth centuries.)

The third purpose in putting together this collection of essays is suggested by the topics included. The authors have shared an interest in looking at everyday activities to see what these could tell us about shared values and motivations, processes of identity formation, and the self-conscious constructions of community that have marked the last century and a half in South Asia. Most of us shared as well a conviction that these elements of everyday life have significance on two levels: taken on their own terms, they identify the important building blocks of South Asian urban culture; and, related to the larger geographical, ecological, and political worlds in which they operate, they provide rational explanations for the actions of the ordinary person in these larger contexts.

The working title of the volume used a shorthand term, "popular history," to imply that we were interested in the role of popular participation in the processes of history. As a group, we also often used the term "popular culture" in our discussions, without worrying overmuch about the analytical problems the term has presented to scholars, or the debates that have emerged, particularly among Europeanists. Because the term is so imprecise, however, we ultimately decided not to use it. The analytical problems inherent in the concept may have been best expressed by Roger Chartier, who pointed out that "no one questioned the basic assumption, . . . namely, that it was possible to identify popular culture by describing a certain number of corpora (sets of texts, gestures, and beliefs). [But] . . . they made no critical examination of the categories and the intellectual distinctions on which they were based." Moreover, the study is often shaped by a dichotomous understanding of the uses made of these corpora; perhaps Chartier's greatest contribution to the discussion is his nuanced analysis of the ways in which printed matter, for instance, could be used by semiliterate, or even illiterate, consumers (Chartier 1984:229 et seq.).

Nevertheless, from the literature developed by Europeanists on so-called popular culture, two contributions emerged that have proved useful to this volume. Chartier's work makes clear the extent of overlap in the meanings imputed by those who participated from different levels in society. This provides a very helpful gloss on Peter Burke's discussion of popular culture as "majority culture," suggesting that the significance of such collective activities, while similar, need not necessarily have been precisely the same. In his definition Burke posited, as well, a withdrawal over time of the European literate elite into a "minority culture," which worked to distinguish itself from the common culture, previously shared, that had characterized activities in public spaces (Burke 1978:28, 270–81). As the essays included here make clear, this definition (particularly as nuanced by Chartier) is appropriate for South Asia in the late nineteenth and the early twentieth century as well, because it highlights the process by which the elite withdrew from a shared, or more precisely an overlapping, popular culture.

Similarly, a more recent definition of "popular culture," which emphasizes the underlying power relationships and social conflicts inherent in these work and leisure activities, has proved particularly helpful (Yeo and Yeo 1981). The collection of essays by the Yeos emphasizes the importance of focusing on change, power, and conflict—three characteristics that quickened the "cultural and associational forms" of English public life between the sixteenth and the nineteenth century. This volume, too, focuses on cultural activities in order to reveal power relations in a particular urban space and to see how these change over time.

Change is, indeed, at the heart of our enterprise, for it is through change in "popular culture" activities that adjustments to the power relationships in Banaras were accomplished. Each of the essays that follow deals with change differently. Taken together, however, they suggest how important a continuously evolving structure with a changing content can be for expressing popular convictions. As Chartier noted, popular religion (or culture, writ large) is "both acculturated and acculturating" (Chartier 1984:233). I mention here only a few of the structures examined here for change: these include the alterations in *Mānas* recitations to accommodate both changes in patronage and in the audience's own view of the *Mānas;* evolution of the *birahā* folk music form to a more professionalized genre with an appeal beyond a particular lower caste (but, significantly, retaining the ability to incorporate lyrics about recent and localized scandals and stories of great interest); changing perceptions of particular city spaces and the ceremonial (and historical) significance attributed to these; elaborations of certain associational forms—particularly *akhāṛās*—used to mobilize people who see themselves as connected. Each of these adjustments may also be used to chart changes in the nuanced power relationships in the city: culture and power are thus, as our title suggests, inextricably entwined in the history of Banaras.

To those familiar with the historiography of nineteenth- and twentieth-century India, this pairing of culture and power will also signify a very straightforward commentary on what previously has been treated as a dichotomy between studies of cultural activities and discussions of political developments. It may be argued that, in this juxtaposition of essays, we have tried to make one additional historiographical comment to distinguish this collective work from what has gone before. Many of us were concerned that our work demonstrate that both culture *and* environment made up a single, coherent whole. Beyond approaching both topics in several guises in the following essays, we wanted a dynamic way to organize the essays, in order to avoid the traditional division into ecological, cultural, and political topics: many felt that such an organization assigned more "reality" to either culture or environment, depending on the order. To solve this problem, the volume treats as a single whole the variety of topics that provided interest and order to everyday life in Banaras. The essays are organized around three related focii. In Part 1 the essays focus on performances that would have drawn audiences from throughout the city; these performances—by taking place in public spaces and attracting citywide patronage—express an essential aspect of Banarsi public life and thus reveal important aspects of the belief systems and world views of the city's residents. Part 2 turns to the more localized constituents of identity in an urban space—those of neighborhood, leisure, and work—to examine the processes by which urban residents use a sense of identity to make sense of life and to organize activity. Part 3 links these experiences within Banaras to the larger world. It is hoped that this different format will juxtapose subjects (that otherwise have been treated as discrete) in a productive and provocative way. The environmental setting, the material conditions of life, and the changes in both of these have figured as important pieces in the cultural puzzle we are trying to reconstruct historically.

As this summary of our discussions suggests, this volume—much more than is usually the case—has been a collaborative enterprise. The editor began by consulting widely to discover scholars working on Banaras and its environs. Thanks are due to all those who enthusiastically participated in this process. Special recognition goes to Nita Kumar, whose dissertation provided much of the original inspiration for the project, and whose suggestions proved particularly helpful in initiating the volume. Those invited to contribute agreed as well to begin by presenting, in different combinations, preliminary drafts at scholarly gatherings: these included the Southeastern Association for Asian Studies (Raleigh, January 1985); the South Asia Conference sponsored by the University of Wisconsin (Madision, November 1985); and the Association for Asian Studies (Chicago, March 1986). We wish to thank those in the audience and the commentators in each of those venues for their contributions to our individual essays and to the volume as a whole. Because of considerations especially of length, some of the essays originally prepared for the volume could not be included here. We thank those authors for their insights and participation in the discussion: their work contributed much to the collective whole. Special references to these papers are included where appropriate in the text.

Following on these preliminary presentations, contributors met for a weekend workshop (Berkeley, March 1986) to discuss one another's essays and to set certain guiding principles to inform their revisions. The most important of these, as was suggested above, involved the interplay between culture and environment and the fact that we wanted to emphasize what was "typically urban" about Banaras, rather than what was unique. On the basis of this latter decision, some subjects that would otherwise have seemed essential to a discussion of Banaras were ignored—including death specialists and dying, pilgrimage, and the like—and certain additional essays were solicited to illuminate processes and values essential to understanding an urban environment. This workshop was open to other interested scholars, and we thank them for their friendly participation in this process. As she worked on revising the volume, the editor continued to consult freely with appropriate contributors, particularly David Arnold, Philip Lutgendorf, Scott Marcus, and Kathryn Hansen, and appreciates their comments and responses to her drafts. It should be noted, however, that much of the introductory material that follows reflects her own work and interpretations and may not be shared by all the authors included herein.

Collectively, as our citations will attest, we also owe a great debt to the three scholars who sufficiently mined the field of classical and historical Banaras to enable us to concentrate on these refinements: Diana Eck for her elegant description of the Kashi of Hindu high culture philosophy and practice; Chris Bayly for his inspired vision of economic and political change in the region—we each found him there, before us, during moments of discovery; and Barney Cohn for his pioneering, still unmatched lucid insights into the processes that formed early colonial Banaras. We refer readers interested in these particular subjects to their work.

Finally, we wish to thank those who provided the green support necessary to make this collaborative project successful in an astonishingly short two years. The South Asia Council of the Association for Asian Studies provided seed money that not only covered the inevitable costs of communication and revision that go into creating a volume, but that also encouraged contributions from the University of California to support a weekend workshop. To cover the costs of the latter, we also thank three institutions located on the University of California–Berkeley campus: the Center for South and Southeast Asia Studies; its parent organization, the Institute for International Studies; and the Graduate Division. Tangible support beyond the green was provided by Steven Gilmartin, Barbara Howell, and Christine Noelle, for whose research assistance and wordprocessing skills we are very grateful.

NOTES ON TRANSLITERATION

VOWELS AND DIPHTONGS (NASALIZED VOWELS)

अ	a	आ	ā	(ã, ā̃)
इ	i	ई	ī	(ĩ, ī̃)
उ	u	ऊ	ū	(ũ, ū̃)
ऋ	ri			
ए	e	ऐ	ai	(ẽ, aĩ)
ओ	o	औ	au	(õ, aũ)

The nasalized versions of the diphtongs *ai* and *au* carry the tilde only on the second element: aĩ, aũ

CONSONANTS

Stops and Nasals

क	k	ख	kh	ग	g	घ	gh	ङ	n
च	ch	छ	chh	ज	j	झ,झ	jh	ञ	n
ट	ṭ	ठ	ṭh	ड	ḍ	ढ	ḍh	ण,रा	ṇ
ड़	ṛ	ढ़	ṛh						
त	t	थ	th	द	d	ध	dh	न	n
प	p	फ	ph	ब	b	भ	bh	म	m

Others

य	y	र	r	ल	l	व	v
श, ष	sh	स	s	ह	h		

Arabian and Persian Consonants

क़	q	ख़	ḳh	ग़	g̣h	फ़	f	ज़	z

ञ is printed with a tilde (ñ) when preceded by ज (j), as in *yajña*, "sacrifice."

GENERAL RULES

1. Personal names and place names are printed without diacritics; Tulsidas and Banaras. This applies as well to languages and scripts.
2. Diacritics are retained in book titles and newspaper names: *Kalyāṇ* (magazine), *Bhārat durdashā* (play).
3. Social and political movements, societies, festivals, months, places (e.g., of worship), and castes are in roman type, with an initial capital letter and diacritics: Sankaṭ Mochan Temple, Sanātan Dharm movement.
4. All other words not listed in Webster's Third Edition are in italics, with diacritics and no initial capital letters: *rāsdhārī, akhāṛā.*

EXCEPTIONS

As the Bhojpuri used in Chapter 3 differs somewhat from the Hindi for which the transliteration system is designed, certain exceptions have been made in that essay. Also, because the व in Bhojpuri is often a clear w rather than a v, Marcus has used the former where needed. Finally, the general transliteration of Awadh has used the w rather than the v; we have conformed to that usage.

Introduction: The History and Political Economy of Banaras

To place in context the essays that follow, we begin with an examination of the "political economy" of the city—that conjunction of political, economic, and social structures which provided the context for historical events and processes. Not least important, in this respect, was the city's location—occupying that auspicious niche of land where the Ganges and Varana rivers meet. We tend to see the significance of Banaras primarily in terms of auspiciousness, in its function, that is, as one of the premier pilgrimage sites in the subcontinent. At the same time, however, we must remember that it was also the largest urban center in the eastern Gangetic plain (see map 1). Thus the political economy of this central place affected a densely populated hinterland with a high level of agricultural production. Furthermore, as the center of the Bhojpuri cultural region, Banaras provided a focal point for a vernacularly based culture that encompassed what is now eastern U.P. (Uttar Pradesh) and western Bihar (see G. Pandey 1983a for an interesting discussion of the potential of this culture for mobilization).[1] Within the city itself the population grew rapidly in the last half of the eighteenth century, coming to number about 200,000 for much of the nineteenth and early twentieth centuries—a good-sized urban site in the days following the decline of Mughal imperial centers.

Although the history of Banaras reaches back into the mists of time, tempting the historian to follow,[2] our narrative begins with the eigh-

1. U.P. refers to that general area in the north Indian Gangetic plain and Himalayan foothills which underwent several name and boundary changes in this period. It was known variously as the two separate provinces of North-West Provinces (NWP) and Oudh; the combined provinces of NWP and Oudh; and finally the United Provinces. Since independence it has been known as Uttar Pradesh.

2. Diana Eck, for instance, begins with the sixth century B.C. (1982:43).

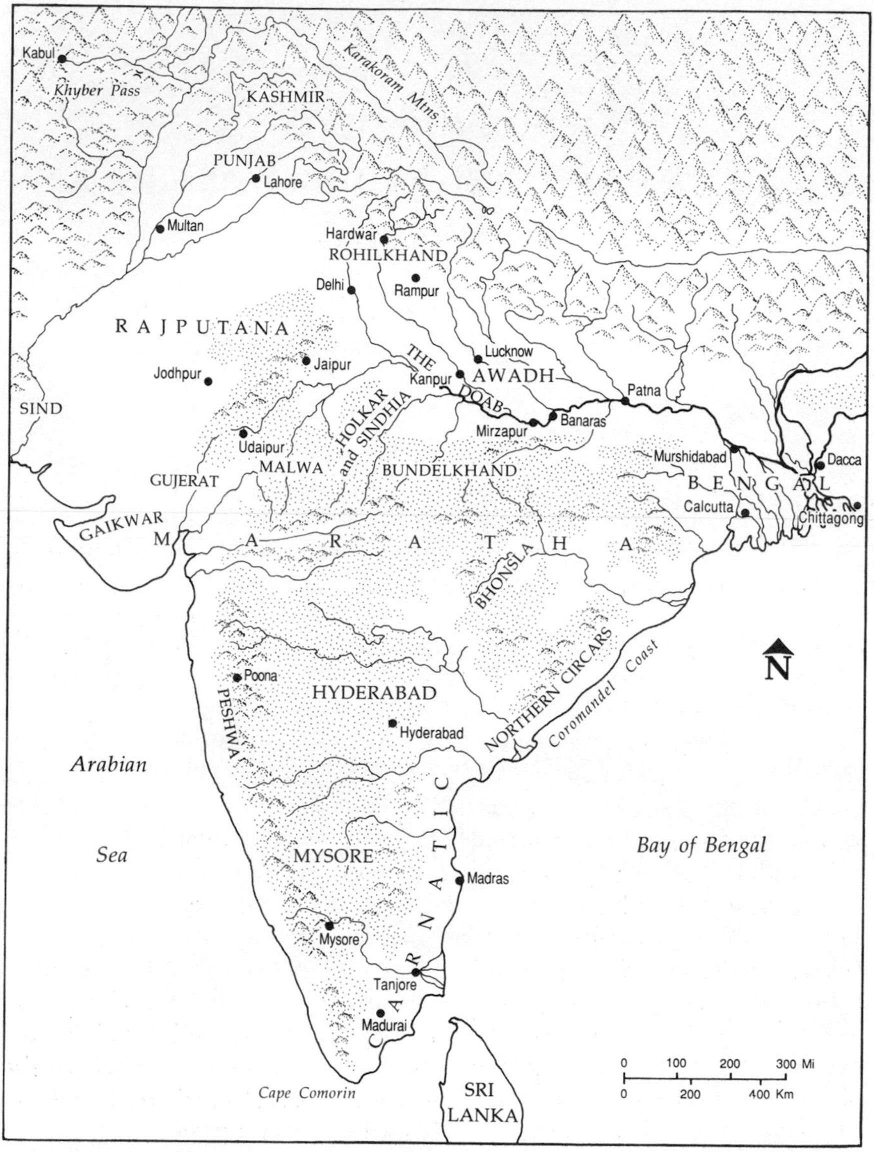

Map 1. South Asia about 1785.

teenth century: it is in this century that new politicocultural alignments emerged which have profoundly affected the processes and people analyzed in this volume. Physically, too, the period produced most of the architectural landmarks that anchor the contemporary city. Such widespread construction became possible, in part, because much of the reli-

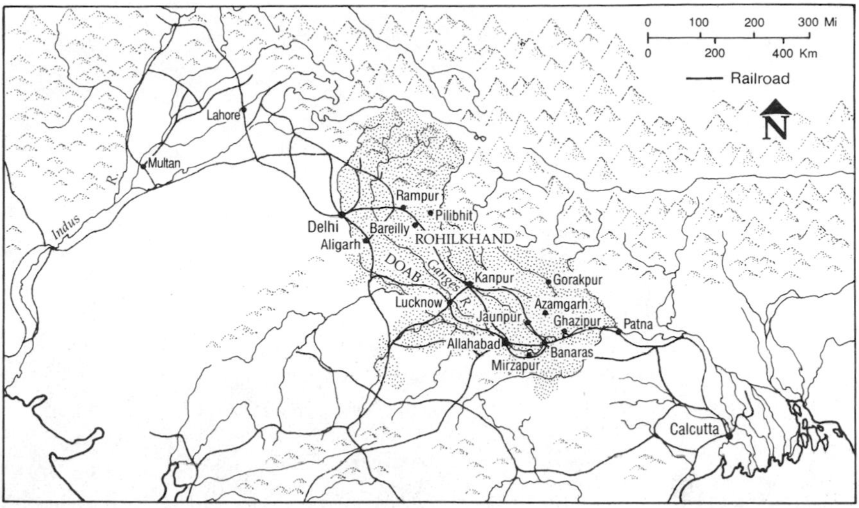

Map 2. North India about 1860. Stippled area indicates U.P. and Bhojpuri districts.

gious architecture of the city had been razed (c. 1660s) by the Mughal emperor Aurangzeb (1657–1707). Following the pattern of a good Muslim ruler, he observed the dictates to build mosques in every city—in the process superimposing an Islamic city on the site of Banaras, which he tried to call "Muhammadabad."[3] Neither the name nor the "qasba" cultural style took root, however.[4] Instead, an alternative cultural collaboration emerged between an upstart dynasty, merchant bankers, and mendicant soldier-traders. It is to the impact of this collaboration that we now turn.

NATIONAL, REGIONAL, AND LOCAL POLITICAL POWER

For our purposes, the most important elements of Banaras's political economy include its place within the larger political structures of the subcontinent (as these were expressed at the national, regional, and local levels); the composition of its economic cum social and cultural elite; and the characteristics of its population—as well as the relationships of these subgroups to each other. The significance of beginning with the eighteenth century as we establish a context for our studies stems largely from the fact that these elements of the political economy un-

3. Stephen Blake has described this process, as observed by Shahjahan, in his essay (1986).

4. See below; see also Bayly 1983 and R. Kumar 1977 for discussions of this *qasba* style.

Fig. 1. Drawing of the river festival of Ganesh (elephant-headed god especially popular with the Marathas). From Louis Rousselet, *India and its Native Princes* (1876).

derwent significant change then, prompted primarily by the ebbing of power and influence from the centralized Mughal Empire, which had dominated north India for two preceding centuries. Indeed, during the last half of the eighteenth century Banaras became "the subcontinent's inland commercial capital . . . [receiving] immigrant merchant capital from the whole of north India and [standing] astride the growing trade route from Bengal to the Maratha territories." Its strength came in large part from the integrated regional economy that had been achieved by the 1780s around holdings of the Raja of Banaras, based on a larger pattern for the period of "commercial development which arose within the agricultural society and then linked up with growing urban demand produced by the emergence of the new kingdoms" (Bayly 1983:104–6).

As the Mughal Empire declined, what Cohn (1960) has characterized as the "national level" political responsibility for Banaras came to rest, first, with the Nawab Wazir of Awadh and, by the end of the century, with the British East India Company. Just below this national level, actors at the regional level—what is usually referred to as the Mughal Empire's successor states—proved particularly important for our narrative. But contenders for control moved rather easily during this century between the national, regional, and local levels of power, often using resources accumulated at one level to build claims for power in the next. While neither the research nor the space available allow us to discuss these eighteenth-century changes in detail, we should note that the most important actors moving among the levels of power included the Maratha empire in the west; the nearby Nawabi of Awadh, with its capital at Lucknow; and the family that came to be known in this period as the Rajas of Banaras, whose zamindari (estate) eventually encompassed the present districts of Ballia, Banaras, Ghazipur, Jaunpur, and Mirzapur (see maps 1 and 3).

Much of our narrative refers to Awadh and Banaras. But we should not minimize the interests of the Marathas in the old urban centers of north India: the military collaboration of the Marathas with the Nawabi against the Rohillas (in the hills of the area; see map 1) included a condition that, in return for their military support, the Marathas would acquire control over Mathura, Prayag (Allahabad), Banaras, and Gaya (B. N. Singh 1941:27); all were urban centers significant for their prominence on Hindu pilgrimage routes. While this Maratha desire to exercise direct political control was thwarted when the British replaced Awadh as ruler of the area, the Marathas remained culturally important in the city of Banaras itself. Reflecting their intellectual as well as their trading interests there,[5] Marathas financed much of the eighteenth-century Hindu reconstruction of the city, which encompassed dharmshalas (rest houses) for pilgrims, temples and feasting to support Brahmin priests, and palaces for themselves and their local kin and agents (and see fig. 1).[6]

Without treating in detail the political history or functional realignments that marked the eighteenth century, we must recognize the significance of the emerging economic and cultural collaboration between the Raja, mendicant trader-soldiers (usually referred to as "Gosains"), and the merchant-banker families of Banaras (whose most prominent members constituted a tightly knit oligarchy called the Nau-

5. "Deccani pandits" had contributed substantially to Sanskritic studies from the sixteenth century on (B. N. Singh 1941:23); among the early documents prepared for the East India Company in the late eighteenth century was an unfavorable analysis of the trading deficit with the Maratha empire.

6. Maratha immigrants in Banaras came to number almost 30,000 people by the end of the eighteenth century and "included traders (naik and Sipahi Nagar bankers), Deccani Brahmins and the retainers of the many nobleman who temporarily or permanently resided in the city" (Bayly 1983:137). Maratha-sponsored construction included the present Visvanatha temple in 1777, as well as the temples of Annapurna, Kalabhairava, Sakshivinayaka, and Trilochanesvara. A large number of the bathing ghats along the riverfront—such as Amritrao Ghat, Ahilya Ghat, Scindia Ghat, Bhonsla Ghat—were also built by the Marathas (B. N. Singh 1941:28).

patti). Although full histories of all three of these groups of collaborators await closer scholarly scrutiny, we do know something about each.

The Gosains—the largest owners of urban property in Banaras in the late eighteenth century—have been identified as possessing several important characteristics. They formed a "religio-commercial sect, militarized to some degree, and organized according to the guru-chela principle,"[7] recruiting without regard to caste, and thus admitting "any person of abilities among them" (Kolff 1971:213–17). This combination of religion, trade, and military prowess may not be as peculiar as it seems at first glance. Moneylenders and merchants worked together to establish credit as well as transport for a particular shipment of goods to a far-flung urban destination; since "long distance trade needed armed protection, the dividing line between trading and soldiering must have been a thin one" (Kolff 1971:217; Gordon 1971:219). As the "principal merchants" dealing with the Maratha empire in the Deccan, these Gosains "resided at Benaras and transported their goods to Mirzapur, there to sell them to other members of their own sect who came annually from the Deccan to buy them" (Kolff, quoting Shakespear 1873:17–21). Thus the Gosains possessed a commercial edge on other merchants, able to utilize their pilgrimage networks for trading purposes. At the same time, they could amass the capital needed for trade through inheritance procedures, which permitted them to pass on a larger share to one chela (Cohn 1964:175–82). To these advantages, bestowed by their unique organization of resources, they added other significant characteristics. Numerous in Banaras, they could call on religious connections with other sadhus to be reckoned a major force in the city.[8] Indeed, they constituted "a body of brokers between different social groups. They attracted veneration from the mass of the people and also had a close hand in the running of the merchant communities" (Bayly 1983:181–84).

As for merchant-bankers, H. R. Nevill notes, in the gazetteer produced for Banaras early in the twentieth century, that "in the palmy days of Benares many large fortunes were accumulated, so that there is a good deal of money in the place." The banking family firms described in the *Gazetteer* include many whose histories are suggestive of the ways in which ties were established between Banaras and other trading centers, as well as the paths to political and social influence within Banaras itself. One was a Maratha family who benefited from

7. The term refers to a highly disciplined teacher-student relationship that implies much more: the chela is at once student, follower, and disciple of the guru.

8. The Magistrate in the early nineteenth century counted the Gosains as "one-fourth" of the city's inhabitants; to reach this figure he must have included all those who appeared to be mendicants. Boards Collections no. 7407:298.

the Deccan's elaborate trading, intellectual, religious, and political ties described above. Another, a family with "extensive dealings with the Bengali community," had originally owned the site of Fort William (the military center of the East India Company in Calcutta). Once settled in Banaras, this latter family proved to be important local citizens, giving land for the Grand Trunk Road, "proving their loyalty" during the Mutiny/Revolt of 1857, and becoming "noted for their public spirit and charitable works . . . the present heads being honorary magistrates and members of the municipal board." Another family came from Jhind, where they had held the hereditary office of *kanungo* (revenue official); they had followed the former Mughal royal family to Banaras and by the early twentieth century boasted both an honorary magistrate and a government treasurer. Yet another firm was started by brothers resident in Allahabad; their sons and grandsons had become "connected by marriage with most of the leading Benaras families." Two banking families were noted as well for their "dealings in silk and other costly fabrics" and as *chaudharī* (headman) "of the kincob merchants" (a type of silk fabric: see DuBois 1987). Other large bankers functioned as "considerable landowners" in the district (Nevill 1909a:53–55).

Such merchant-bankers were drawn to Banaras for the commercial opportunities provided by this trading center located on the main west-to-east trade route. They provided important connections with their constituent groups back home in Jhind, Allahabad, and the like. To regulate so complex a trading and banking world as that of Banaras, they further organized internally. Building on the Naupatti ("Society of Nine Sharers")—which had become "a self-perpetuating oligarchy of status which no aspiring family could enter"—other merchants and bankers grouped themselves in a structure whose pinnacle was occupied by the Naupatti families. The resulting linkages were based variously on organization within a particular trade, among those trading in a particular region, or among those performing a particular function in the trading structure. Most particularly, all shared conceptions of status and mercantile honor (Bayly 1983:177–80).

Especially important for us is the emergence of the Raja of Banaras as the regional ruler of the area.[9] Bayly notes that, particularly during this period of political flux, the establishment after migration of the great agricultural clans of Bhumihars or Rajputs led to the creation of new commercial centers. Building on the model sketched by Richard Fox (1969), Bayly suggests that a two-stage process linked economic development to the political emergence of a raja from the previously democratic clan organization. Working from a relatively small estate

9. See the model developed in Bayly (1983:95–96).

(zamindari), between the 1730s and 1750s, this Bhumihar family[10] used its position as tax official for Awadh to become zamindar for most of Banaras province, and to gain the title of Raja.[11] Functioning as the virtually independent regional-level ruler, it paid only a lump-sum tax or tribute to Awadh. What enabled the family to preserve this distance from Awadh was its own ability to profit from the changing economic and legal circumstances affecting control of land—particularly that introduced by the British (see Cohn 1960 for details)—as well as the interdependent relationship the family developed with the Banaras merchant-bankers for meeting Awadh's demand for tribute.

These histories of successful banking families, and the evolution of a landlord family into local dynasty, personalize the larger trend of shifting economic and political structures which marks out the eighteenth century. If, as Bayly argues, the intermediate economy emerging in the eighteenth century rested on "the distribution of local political power expressed in revenue assignments" (Bayly 1983:52), then this ability of the banker-merchants to command resources located deep in the countryside gave them "considerable, if covert, political power within the state." It was not only that they had the capacity to float huge loans to the Raja when his tribute was owing to Awadh. It was also that they possessed important rural connections to generate such resources, mobilizing "shadowy groups of substantial rural men of capital."[12]

THE NINETEENTH-CENTURY CULTURAL PATTERN AND POWER RELATIONSHIPS

Local political power became intimately connected, as well, to cultural patronage (discussed in more detail in Part 1). The merchants and the Raja figured prominently in this patronage, which expanded at the re-

10. The caste name is usually transliterated in British sources Bhumihar or Bhuinhar. (We have ignored Platt's transliteration of Bhunhar, which may be based on a different regional pronunciation.) This twice-born caste enjoyed high status throughout north India; exercising much influence, particularly in the rural areas, its members were prominent landowners and tenants with very favorable terms. The family that became Rajas was headed, first, by Mansa Ram (1730–38) and then by his son Balwant Singh (1738–70). The longevity of Balwant Singh was doubtless significant in consolidating the power of the family. Chait Singh succeeded to the gaddi (throne, seat of authority) in 1770. The power of the dynasty also helped to entrench the power of the Bhumihar clan in the area.

11. This was elevated to Maharaja in reward for loyalty during the 1857 Mutiny/Revolt.

12. For examples of occasions when he required large amounts of money, see IOL & R L/PS/10, vol. 173 for 1910, file 876; Winter to Dane, p. 2. (These "rural men of substance" had emerged from commercial development that linked consolidation with agricultural society to "growing urban demand produced by the emergence of the new [successor state] kingdoms"; Bayly 1983:104–7.)

gional and local levels as the Mughal Empire faltered. In part, such patronage conveyed legitimation for these emerging power-holders. Most important, the devolution of the locus of cultural patronage from the national to the regional and local levels, together with the ability to mobilize the intermediate economy, provided significant linkage between the newly emerging Hindu merchant elite, the regional political figure of the Raja of Banaras, and the artisans and others who made up the lower classes of Banaras.

The interaction of these power and culture relationships developed in ways unique to Banaras.[13] In the early eighteenth century, like many of the other "celebrated holy places such as Prayag (Allahabad) and Ajodhya," Banaras had been a "mughalizing city," owing much to the cultural patterns established first by the Mughals and then fostered by the Nawab of Awadh's court. The physical world of Banaras certainly reflected this mughalization—in its Muslim buildings, the establishment of *muḥalla*s (neighborhoods: see below), and the dotting of Muslim shrines. The social world, too, had been mughalized, with configurations of such urban functionaries as the "service types, sufi orders, pirs . . . and scribal groups." No doubt this mughalized style accounted, in part, for the strong ties established early in the career of the Banaras dynasty with the Muslim lower-caste groups such as the weavers.

Nevertheless, the pattern in Banaras, unlike that in other mughalizing urban centers in north India, changed so that, by the early nineteenth century, a Hindu tradition had been "reinvented"[14] to serve certain goals cherished by the triumvirate of power-holding groups in Banaras. More will be said, below,[15] about the importance of this reinvented Hindu style for the Raja of Banaras. Here it will suffice to point to the other actors in Banaras who could also respond to this reinvention, including the Marathas, the immigrant Bengalis, and those from the eastern U.P. countryside. The nexus of culture and power in nineteenth-century Banaras, then, was located in a reformulation of Hindu culture that drew together a disparate group of power holders. Such a style, nevertheless, made room for the substantial numbers of (generally lower class) Muslims resident in the city as well.[16] Equally important, this special amalgam that marked Banaras also protected it, to a surprising degree, from British intrusions, particularly in the early nineteenth century and again after 1910.

13. I am indebted to Chris Bayly for calling my attention to the importance of explicitly emphasizing this point. The formulations quoted in the paragraph that follows are from a private communication dated 17 May 1987.

14. In this term, Bayly is drawing on vocabulary and concept developed in Hobsbawm and Ranger, 1983.

15. And in chapter 7.

16. For a discussion of how this was accomplished, see below and chapter 7.

In recognition of the virtual independence of the Raja of Banaras, the British did not attempt to rule the area directly when they took Banaras over from the Nawab in 1775, but simply replaced Awadh as the national-level authority. Indeed, as a special mark of favor, the East India Company Governor-General, Warren Hastings, gave further rights to Raja Chait Singh, allowing him to coin money and administer penal justice ("A History," 1873:100–7). Hastings established a Resident there but did not interfere directly in the administration of Banaras until the pressures of war with France led him to make extortionate money demands on the Raja, who "rebelled" in 1781. Even then, the British simply replaced Chait Singh with his young relative, Mehip Narayan, whose claim to the throne was at least as compelling as Chait Singh's own. The rights to the mint and judicial functions were withdrawn, however, and by 1795 the Resident's administrative power had expanded greatly. This was symbolized by his permanent revenue settlement of the area and was officially recognized when the young and perhaps epileptic Raja signed away his independent authority to the East India Company in 1794.[17]

Consequently, during the nineteenth century the British administered the Banaras region directly, with the ruling Bhumihar family occupying a vague position somewhere between that of large landlord and the ruler of a princely state.[18] While the government officially maintained the distinction in status between Banaras and the other "native princes" ruling elsewhere in the subcontinent (these enjoyed legal status under the doctrine of "internal" or "limited sovereignty"), India Office administrators debated in the 1870s whether or not the characterization of Banaras as a "mere zamindary" was grossly misleading ("A History," 1873). Earlier studies have suggested that nineteenth-century direct rule by the British represented a collapsing of the levels of political authority from three to two; that the British came to represent both the national and the regional level of authority.[19]

17. His successor (Udit Narayan Singh, 1795–1835) unsuccessfully attempted to have the agreement set aside (Nevill 1909a:116).

18. For a delineation of the rights accorded to the Raja, and how they exceeded those available to ordinary large landholders, see documents submitted by the provincial government to the Government of India, beginning in 1905. IOL & R L/PS/10, vol. 173 for 1910, file 876; Winter to Dane, pp. 6–7.

19. Cohn 1960:430. Cohn's analysis reflects scholarly preoccupation at that time with the need to analyze the political impact of the British on their empire. The new interpretation of the political history of the Banaras region sketched here reflects a shift of focus from overtly political arenas to those expressed by cultural activities. This shift enables us to make different measurements about the extent of power and influence exercised by the dynasty within the political economy of the area. As a result, we argue that the Raja maintained an important politicocultural influence that kept alive the intermediate "regional" function within local society. See also chapter 7.

But in 1910–11 the British government took the unusual action of creating a new princely state of Banaras,[20] investing the Maharaja with "full ruling powers" over the area encompassed within his zamindari.[21] While retaining direct British rule in the city of Banaras, the British nevertheless recognized the Maharaja's cultural influence there by allowing him to retain his capital at Ramnagar (situated directly across the Ganges River, and the only other town of any size in the district). This decision to re-create the princely state was informed in part by early-twentieth-century British political concerns.[22] The move also, however, officially recognized the ongoing politicocultural influence possessed by that triad of collaborators—the Bhumihar dynasty, the Gosains, and the merchant-bankers. In turn, it also perpetuated this influence: in its unofficial and then official role as princely state, Banaras provided important patronage for Indian artists and intellectuals, as well as opportunities for talented Indian administrators. The Maharaja's council, for instance, reflected the confluence of mercantile, landowning, caste, and educational elite possessing what we refer to here as "Hindu merchant-style" culture (see below). Together the triad shaped this culture so successfully that it integrated those who resided in the city in a way that came to be virtually unparalleled in urban north India.[23]

The preeminent ceremonial expression of this integration—we might even say the cultural expression of the city's political economy—was the Ramnagar Rāmlīlā.[24] This observance, performed under the aegis of the Bhumihar dynasty, is discussed from several different viewpoints in the essays that follow; here we will look at the symbolic expression of civic identity it embodied as it came to be elaborated over

20. See L/PS/10/173 file 876 for references to other unsuccessful attempts in the late nineteenth century to re-create princely states from areas acquired and ruled directly by the British.

21. He was to receive a 15-gun salute, and could be received and visited by the Viceroy. (*List of Leading Officials, Nobles and Personages* 1925:1.)

22. Administrators, particularly those at the center, perceived the princes as an important political counterweight to emerging nationalist agitators. To support the case that the Maharaja should be deemed a Native Chief, the Government of India remarked to the Secretary of State for India that "responsible as we are for the maintenance of peace and the checking of the seditious movement in India, which now causes us such grave anxiety," [we are] "deeply impressed" with the Maharaja's ability to keep "conservative Hinduism at Banaras on our side." L/PS/10/173 file 876, p. 2.

23. Delhi represented a similar phenomenon, but one perhaps much more dependent on the strength of the Mughal political power (see Frykenburg 1986). Lucknow presented a regionally focused phenomenon closer to Banaras, but, ultimately, shorter-lived (cf. Oldenburg 1984).

24. See also Hess 1986 and chapter 1 in this volume, relating to this subject, as well as N. Kumar 1984, and Schechner and Hess 1977.

two centuries. Cosponsored by the Maharaja and the Hindu merchant "corporation" of the city, this staging of the Rāmlīlā stands out for its length and performance elaboration even among the large number of Rāmlīlā observances staged annually in Banaras and its environs (see Mathur 1978, 1979 for brief histories and descriptions of the wide range of Rāmlīlās staged in the various *muḥalla*s of Banaras). For our purposes, it possesses several key attributes, most notably its expression of the "relationship between government, Maharaja and ordinary people" (Schechner and Hess 1977:54). This is symbolized particularly by the Maharaja's mythical roles as king and as representative of Siva ("the lord of ancient holy Kashi"):

> The identification is so complete that everywhere the Maharaja goes he is hailed with the name "Mahadev," a name for Siva. And while the Maharaja is cheered as a god in the Ramlila, Rama is cheered as a king. . . . Usually the Maharaja on his elephant forms one of the spatial limits of a scene, with Rama forming the other. Both Maharaja and Rama are elevated, and the audience is on ground level, assembled between them" (Schechner and Hess 1977:69, 74).

Indeed, as the story unfolds over the thirty-one days, "the boundaries between Rama's world and the Maharaja's world" dissolve. This is facilitated by the extensive patronage provided by the Maharaja's family. Support for Rāmlīlā by the Bhumihar dynasty has always represented a substantial investment, although the burden of support has been shared with the merchant community. Even today—when the state of Uttar Pradesh underwrites about a third of the cost—the authors estimate that the year-round related expenditures total more than Rs. 350,000 (Schechner and Hess 1977:66, 73). Why did the Maharaja's family invest so substantially in this event? One response has been that it was done to "restore the lost glory to the Hindus." The Maharaja himself recognizes the importance of his family's patronage: "My ancestor who started the dynasty also began a renaissance of Hinduism," he notes.

While the emphasis on Hindu values and legitimizing myth have played an important role in fostering the Rāmlīlā (see chapter 1), the emphasis on the Maharaja as kingly expression of the entire community moves this beyond a Hindu framework. Given the close interrelationship of upper and lower (frequently Muslim) classes in Banaras,[25] this vehicle of high Hindu culture was rendered palatable, even essential, through the predominant role played by the local ruler, with whom all Banarsis could identify, through whom all communities became symbolically integrated. This cause was doubtless helped by that

25. See N. Kumar 1984.

strain in Tulsidas which emphasized social equality among those devoted to god (Hess 1987).

Given the communities involved, this was a particularly significant accomplishment. The ordinary denizens responsible for the main "industries" or production activities operating in Banaras included artisans, religious specialists, and scholars. Most of the literature on Banaras emphasizes the latter two,[26] but artisans were the most numerous group; their wares included, particularly, silk products, brass ware, and wooden toys. Of these various producers, we may judge the weavers, virtually all Muslim, to be the most important, in part for their numbers (more than a quarter of the city's population), and in part for the collective role they have played in the life of the city (see N. Kumar 1984 and chapter 5 in this volume).

We may also use the weavers to illustrate social and cultural integration in Banaras. On the one hand, since the weavers were independent artisans, their production schedule was their own—a form of "freedom" they prized highly. On the other hand, both for their supplies of yarn and for marketing their goods, they depended heavily on Hindu merchant middlemen or agents. From the early nineteenth century on, observers have pointed to this close relationship when explaining why the weavers of Banaras are not more confrontational in behavior. (Indeed, their collective behavior differs dramatically from that presented by Julāhās, or Ansaris, as they wished to be called, in other urban sites of north India [see G. Pandey 1983b for an inventory of historical references to "bigoted Julahas" rioting or protesting to protect their perceived rights].) In 1931 an observer could still write:

> It should be explained that in Benares the Mahomedan population is nearly entirely dependent upon the Hindus. With the exception of a few members of the old Mahomedan aristocracy, who are now in straitened circumstances, the entire community lives a hand to mouth existence . . . . The weavers are without exception dependent on the good will of their Hindu employers. The two communities are therefore closely bound to each other by economic ties.[27]

Beyond this indicator of economic interdependence, we also have evidence to suggest that Muslim weavers actively participated in the public ceremonials expressing a shared Banarsi civic culture, including "the marriage of the Laut" (Bhairava), Bharat Milāp, and the day-to-day observances related to particular figures and shrines (see chapter 7

26. See Eck on scholars and priestly groups. Jonathan Parry's work on the death specialists of Banaras adds another entire dimension to the literature; see, for instance, Parry 1980, 1981, 1982.

27. IOL & R. L/P & J/7/vol. 75 for 1931, p. 573.

for more details). Moreover, even Muharram fit into this larger pattern. An observance during the first ten days of that month, this event commemorated the martyrdom of the Prophet's grandson, Husain, massacred in a battle over the appropriate line of succession. This memorial functioned in early-nineteenth-century Banaras as a ceremonial expression of "Islam" in which many members of the city participated, nevertheless. Some 90 percent of the Muslim participants were Sunni not Shi'i (the group for whom the event had historical importance), and very substantial numbers were Hindu.[28] Like the style of observance in other areas where the crowd preponderantly featured non-Shi'i participants, the ceremonial emphasis in the Banarsi Muharram focused on its processional elements, while popular participation encompassed a range of behaviors that permitted participation by Hindus and Muslims, disinterested in the original martyr motif, to join in fully. In all these characteristics they closely resembled other, ostensibly "Hindu" observances of the city's shared ceremonial life.

Thus the style of Muharram observance carried the implication that the Muslims in Banaras pursued, through ceremonials, simultaneous goals of reiterating their Islamic identity and reinforcing their ties with other Banarsis, particularly those power holders interested in the reinvented Hindu culture that came to characterize Banaras. This fits with other evidence now emerging, particularly from Nita Kumar's fascinating examination of schooling among the Banaras Muslims. In a recent presentation she pointed to the history of the Jnana Vapi Mosque perpetuated among Muslim students by such texts as a geography prepared by Abdus Salam Nomani (1963). Denying attribution of the mosque to Aurangzeb, the text maintained: "This is wrong. The foundations of this mosque were laid by the great grandfather of Badshah Alamgir, Akbar, and Alamgir's father, Shahjahan, had started a madras in the mosque in 1048 hijri."[29] That is, in legitimizing their claims to space—and, implicitly, to a presence and role in the city—Banaras's Muslims turned particularly to rulers known simultaneously for establishing Muslim rule and for developing a distinctly integrative, syncretic Indo-Muslim culture.[30]

28. As late as 1895, the local vernacular press could comment, "Mohurram passed off without disturbance. . . . when it is Hindus who mostly celebrate this festival, what fear can there be?" *Bharat Jiwan*, 8 July 1895, p. 1, quoted in N. Kumar 1985:316.

29. Quoted in N. Kumar, "History and Geography as Protest: The Maintenance of 'Muslim' Identity in 'Hindu' Banaras, c. 1880–1987," p. 33. Paper presented to the panel on Protest and Resistance, American Historical Association, December 1987.

30. N. Kumar has called attention in chapter 5 in this volume to her differing interpretation of these relationships. She argues that not enough credence is given here to the Muslim and lower-class point of view. I suggest, instead, that this viewpoint cannot be fully understood unless it is viewed from a comparative perspective that places this view-

To this cultural claim, moreover, the Muslims of Banaras added that of power in numbers. That Muslims were a coherently organized group capable of bringing pressure to bear on the municipal government, and that, therefore, their civic integration was prized as much by municipal power-holders as by weavers, is indicated in the 1909 gazetteer's reference to the impact of the famine of 1897. While Banaras district "fared moderately well" in this famine, "the city population, however, suffered considerably, as must inevitably happen when prices rise to famine level and when trade is dull." Money raised locally and contributed by the municipality was distributed in three ways: in the form of doles to "respectable poor"; as "gifts of clothing to paupers" (which created a demand for cloth); and as "advances to the weavers for making cloth, which was afterwards purchased for distribution in the city and elsewhere." That this reflected the priority placed on placating the weavers is clear, for "the weavers were among the first to feel the pinch of scarcity, and on the 15th of September 1896 they made an organized demonstration, complaining against municipal taxation and the octroi duty [presumably that levied on imported yarn]: they were informed that their demands could not be complied with, but that relief would be afforded them should the necessity arise" (Nevill 1909a:48–49).

Evidence suggests that other artisan and low-caste service groups proved similarly important in the political economy of the city—particularly butchers and Ahirs (or Yādavs, as they prefer to be called). This should not surprise us for, as Bayly notes,

> both Hindu and Muslim writers imply that the provision of services by a large client population is a guarantee of an appropriate religious [and civic] existence. Thus the city (*nagar*) for some Hindu theorists was where the system of castes reaches its most perfect expression and the greatest number of ritual specialists and *jajmans* are on hand for the protection of *dharma*. Similarly, for Muslims the city is the "flower of earthly existence" because this is where the faithful can find the basis of social life—the mosque, running water for purity, learned *qazis* to settle disputes, and the Sultan to protect the *umma* [community of believers]. (Bayly 1986:223)

The essays in this volume provide additional insights on the central role played by service and artisan groups. To understand the civic roles

---

point next to that expressed in other, nearby cities. Her argument that the popular culture activities in Banaras express a shared set of lower-class values that she designates "Banarsipan" cannot be convincing without references that make clear what distinguishes lower-class culture in Banaras from that expressed in other north Indian urban sites. Nothing noted in her essay or earlier work suggests that such a distinction exists. Instead, what distinguishes Banaras from other central places is the nuances of the nexus of cultural expressions and social power, as elaborated in this volume.

played by these groups, we must understand the nature of an urban site in nineteenth-century north India.

BANARAS AS URBAN CONTEXT

As a municipal-level site for much early experimentation in self-government, the city of Banaras provided many outlets for the civic interests of its merchants and other intellectual and economic elite of the area. References in the gazetteer to merchant-bankers as municipal commissioners and honorary magistrates suggest some of the avenues pursued by this elite. These positions provided more than symbols of power, for local government had access to increasingly significant resources over the nineteenth and into the twentieth century. For instance, new forms of taxation were sought almost immediately by the British to cover the costs of administering the city once they had taken direct control. A local tax to support neighborhood police *(chaukidarī)* was introduced at least by 1795; perhaps because this *phatakbandi* was levied by the neighborhoods themselves, who also appointed and paid the *chaukidar*s, residents voiced few objections. In 1810, however, the British attempted to introduce a form of house tax; the protest in Banaras proved so vehement that the administration had to retreat to the *phatakbandi* (see chapter 7 for a further discussion of what this protest revealed about power relationships in the city); this arrangement remained in effect until 1867, when the provisions of the Municipalities Act of 1850 were applied to the city.

Under the Act a new municipal committee collected revenues for a police force, conservancy, and other "general improvements." Ultimately the octroi tax on imports became the "backbone" of municipal income (B. N. Singh 1941:79), providing more than half the revenues; other revenue derived from taxing pilgrims, as well as from assessments for water, light, and (eventually) houses; these were supplemented by income from rents and licenses. Initially, the District Magistrate functioned as the president of the committee. The municipal board became increasingly representative after 1884, however, and by 1904 it consisted of twenty-eight members, twenty-one of whom were elected. Interest continued high in civic participation; in contrast to the district committee governing the rural areas, Nevill noted that "the elected members [of the *municipal* committee] exhibit great interest in the work, and the attendance at meetings reaches a high average" (1909a:168). Indeed, in 1941 a local scholar could comment that "with the exception of political events [i.e., nationalist agitation], the general public is more interested in Municipal administration" than in any other topic (B. N. Singh 1941:95).

The ostensibly familiar veneer of these modern-style interactions should not mislead us, however, for it covers a process in which the idiom was much more indigenous. It was a process that had begun much earlier. "The early colonial period," Bayly tells us, "saw the further consolidation of a merchant and service class between the state and agrarian society. It was as much the product of the slow commercialisation of political power which had gathered pace in the late Mughal period as of the export of trades and land market of colonial rule. . . . But as an indication of the persistence of an indigenous social change [begun in the eighteenth century], it was no less important because its idiom remained 'traditional'" (1983:344–45).

This idiom proved particularly strong in Banaras. We may explain this best by briefly examining the place of Banaras in the "indigenous social change" to which Bayly refers. Begun in the eighteenth century, this was rooted in the development of urban places in north India. That is, at the same time that certain urban centers emerged during the late eighteenth century, a new set of intermediary groups emerged within them: these have been designated by Bayly as "corporations." We will examine the implications of the rise of this form of collective decision-making at the local urban level in more detail below.

The word "town," Bayly notes, can be applied to a number of different levels in the hierarchy of central places in India. The lowest level was *hath*, or "humble periodic market, which had no urban features at all." Above this was the *ganj*, the small, fixed-market centers founded "by the agents of regional political authority, and the fortress lineage-center of the local zamindar or petty ruler. . . . A congregation of fixed markets sometimes became, in effect, a small town. But the most obvious bottom rung of the urban hierarchy proper was the country town or *qasbah* which generally supported a population of more than 3,000" and possessed distinguishing characteristics in terms of social, legal, and economic status (Bayly 1983:110–12). As R. Kumar has noted, such a center was "urban in the sense that its residents, by and large, were not directly engaged in agricultural production. . . . Besides the revenue officers and the men of commerce, the *qasbah* was also the seat of the petty landlords of the locality, just as it was the base of artisans and craftsmen who produced goods for a wider market" (R. Kumar 1978–79:202).

Finally, with a population of over 10,000, were the cities proper, of which there were more than sixty serving many different functions in 1770.[31] Of the very largest centers in the province, the three great cities

31. "These functions ranged from retail centers and bulking points, through transit points for longer-distance high value trades, to service centers for regional rulers or their 'great lieutenants'" (Bayly 1983:110–12).

under the Mughals—Delhi, Agra, and Lahore—had lost their primacy as well as much of their population (from 400,000 in 1700 each had declined to 100,000 a century later). By 1800, however, cities like Banaras and Lucknow—as centers of regional successor states—had acquired a comparable dominance in their own regions, with populations of about 200,000 each. Though the number of cities in the next lower level, that is, those holding populations of 10,000–100,000 did not change greatly in this century, there was much movement of population among them, prompted particularly by Jat and Rohilla conquests in the west of the province and by consolidation of the commercial economy in the east. Even among "cities proper," then, there were a number of sites whose size of population shifted in the eighteenth century in response to economic and political stimuli.

Consistent behind this movement of peoples, however, stood commonly held notions of urban organization, including, particularly (1) neighborhood social organization; (2) policing and peace-keeping functions and the dispensation of justice; and (3) an "intermediary" role developed and filled by "corporations" of leading citizens. Each of these will be discussed in turn.

Not enough work has been done on the *muḥalla* (neighborhood) as the basic unit of urban social organization and what we may call associational activity. The key to understanding this may be the work of Stephen Blake, which traces an eighteenth-century shift in the organization of residential space in Shahjahan's capital city. The pattern, begun as an outgrowth of the emperor's camp organization, featured neighborhoods centered on the *hawelī* (great house, palace), in which service and other client groups lived in domestic configurations clustered around their patrons (courtiers or large merchants). But in the eighteenth century, as the Mughal Empire declined, this pattern shifted to one in which residence units, instead, clustered caste or craft groups together in specific *muḥalla*s (Blake 1974). The shift, though substantial, may never have been complete: evidence can still be found throughout the nineteenth century of the *hawelī*-centered pattern (see Bayly 1978). How the *muḥalla* served as an organizational base for local community identity and activities is examined in more detail in Part 2. Here it will suffice to note that the shifting pattern of neighborhood may also have reflected social (and power) shifts that emerged over the nineteenth century. That is, from the patron-client structures of the inner city, city power bases may have moved outward, thus accommodating the caste- and occupation-specific *muḥalla*s located at the outer edge of the city (and see chapter 7).

The role played, respectively, by the qadi and kotwal in policing urban centers and dispensing justice provided another central characteristic of the north Indian city. Indeed, the essential element in defining an urban space in the Muslim cities of the plains had been the presence of the qadi, or Islamic judicial official. "As a 'censor of morals,' the kazi was to enforce public righteousness when public opinion, embodied in periodic religious and caste assemblies, had proved unable to do so." This "strong moral, even religious sanction," applied to the "smooth working of city life," extended to the role of the kotwal as well. He "was supposed to work through the faithful and public-spirited citizens, 'engaging them in pledges of reciprocal assistance and binding them to a common participation of weal and woe'." Chapter 7 suggests what happened when this "framework of institutions and moral ideas" began to decay within "at the same time as their functions were reduced by the power of corporations or landed gentry" (Bayly 1983:308–11). That is, qadi and kotwal were affected by a process begun in the eighteenth century under indigenous pressures. Although qadi and kotwal were left in place, the impetus of moral action shifted to the triad: merchant-bankers, mendicants (Gosains), and the new ruling dynasty. It remained in the nineteenth century for the British empire to co-opt the kotwal completely and, ultimately, to abolish the position of qadi in about 1865.[32]

Perhaps most important for our purposes was the emergence, in this period of shifting urbanism, of "corporations" of Hindu merchants or Muslim learned men to provide a new organizational focus for urban life. The contributor of this concept, Bayly, defines "corporation" to mean "an occupational or religious organization which transcended the bounds of 'caste' in the sense of jati. It would therefore include commercial or priestly associations . . . as well as certain types of ascetic [groups] . . . which integrated urban or rural society and acted as self-regulating entities de facto. . . . [Thus] Indian society produce[d] dynamic, multi-caste institutions in the context of growing monetisation and the weakening of central state power" (1983:163n.).

It is to these corporations that we must look for the most significant change wrought in the eighteenth century, the development of "more stable patterns of local power [that] were slowly being precipitated between the state and agrarian society. There emerged a unified merchant class wielding covert political power, and a locally resident gentry [Muslim or scribal Hindu] of literate service families." It is these two groups—(predominantly Hindu) merchants and (predominantly Muslim) landlords with courtly connections—who, performing intermediary roles, developed attendant cultural patronage styles during the

32. See, for example, documents on abolition in NWP Judicial A Proceedings no. 48–108 for 19 January 1865.

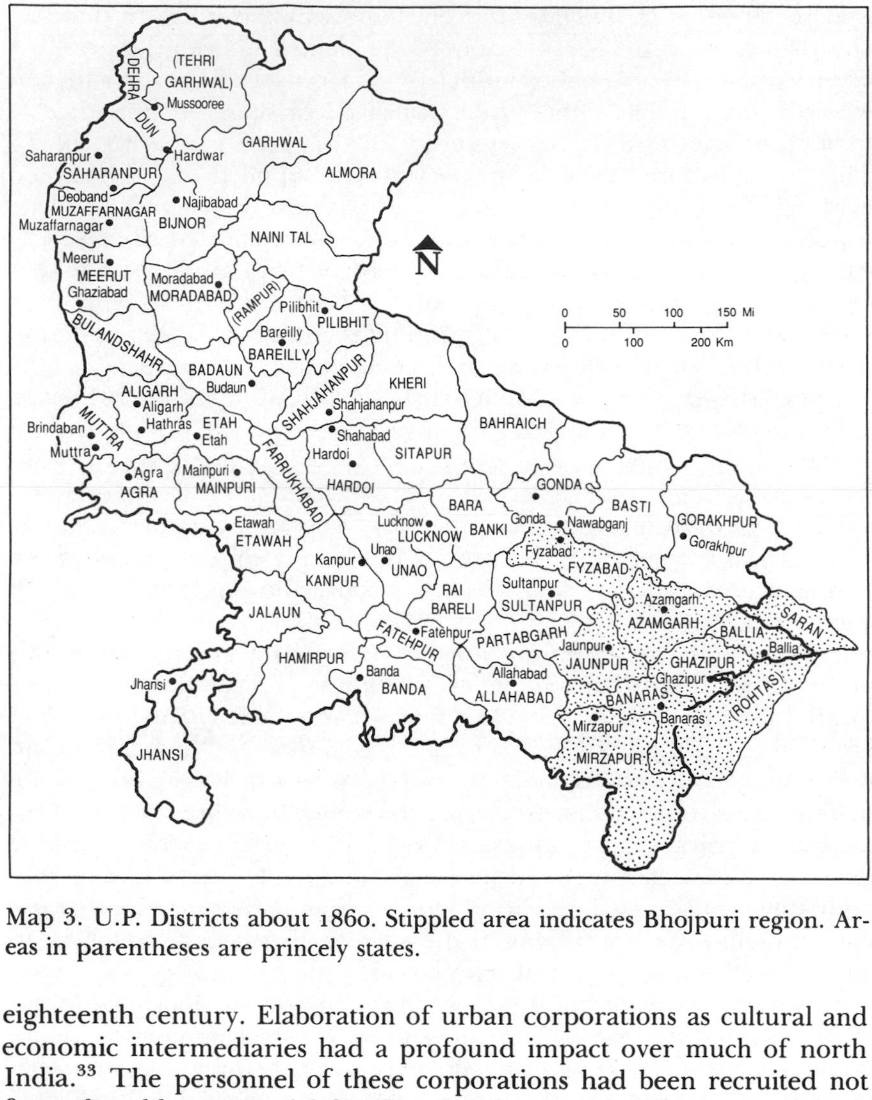

Map 3. U.P. Districts about 1860. Stippled area indicates Bhojpuri region. Areas in parentheses are princely states.

eighteenth century. Elaboration of urban corporations as cultural and economic intermediaries had a profound impact over much of north India.[33] The personnel of these corporations had been recruited not from the old commercial families, for these were definitely in decline along with the Mughals, but from "communities with their feet firmly in the villages and small towns who made the adaptation with least pain . . . and often, local groups from outside the bounds of the traditional merchant communities" (Bayly 1983:161–62). Implications of this pat-

33. It also established precedents of appropriate behavior which would prove very important for institutions of self-governance in the late nineteenth and the early twentieth century.

TABLE 1 Population of U.P.'s Largest Central Places

City	*1911*	*1941*	*Percentage increase*
Lucknow	260,000	387,000	49
Banaras	209,000	263,000	26
Agra	182,000	284,000	56
Kanpur	174,000	487,000	180
Allahabad	168,000	260,000	55

SOURCE: *Census of India* for years indicated.

tern were as important for city-hinterland connections as they were for urban residents themselves (see Part 3).

The emergence of such urban corporations is important for us in this study of the urban site of Banaras, for

> corporations of townsmen, merchants and religious specialists had developed a new coherence and autonomy which in some cases amounted to a virtual civic self-government. These changes were not frustrated by caste fragmentation or the passivity of Hinduism: on the contrary, caste and religion provided the building-blocks out of which mercantile and urban solidarities were perceptibly emerging. . . . [Although the growing European presence in India doubtless enhanced this process,] the commercialisation of politics and the rise of the corporations were by origin intrinsic changes within the economy and culture. War and political change, far from destroying towns and trade, had actually galvanized them into greater independence. (Bayly 1983:175)

Two major forms of such corporations had evolved by the end of the eighteenth century, shaping cultural expressions particular to each; the style of an urban site depended on whichever was dominant in that central place. The first emerged from the *qaṣbas* (or country towns) founded by Mughal service gentry; the Indo-Persian style that characterized this form emphasized "continuous connection with the rulers, dependence on service income," and Urdu literacy. It was expressed in what we may call the dominant economic "institution," the *qaṣba* landowner. The second emerged from the *ganjs* (small market centers), fostered by "a group of entrepreneurial castes with common professional practices who were also linked together through a system of hierarchically organized markets"; it was expressed through the economic institution of the Hindu family firm (Bayly 1983:370).

Each type of corporation fostered a particular cultural style. Interaction between these Indo-Persian and Hindu merchant cultural styles provides much of the background for developments in colonial Indian history. Largely as a result of the impact of the hold of the Mughal Empire after its decline, as well as the influence of Muslim successor states,

Indo-Persian cultural activities and values figured largely in urban and colonial political events in the late eighteenth and the early nineteenth century. But the history of late colonial India becomes increasingly dominated by the values and interests of the Hindu merchant elite; as this culture came to the historical forefront the influence of the smaller towns of north India in which it was rooted increased (Bayly 1983; Freitag 1989).

The culture emerging from Hindu merchant patronage had a number of identifying characteristics. For our purposes, the most important were Sanskritizing in nature, and included patronage of religious personnel, buildings (especially the construction, maintenance, and elaboration of temples), and ceremonials. Also important were reformist activities that frequently exhorted the lower castes to adopt Sanskritizing values and modes of behavior; perhaps most significant, these often became linked to political movements.

What the increasing dominance of Hindu merchant culture meant for the largest urban centers emerging in U.P. in the nineteenth century is especially interesting. Of the five major urban centers in U.P. (see table 1, showing population figures for 1911 and 1941)—Lucknow, Banaras, Allahabad (which became the provincial capital of U.P. under the British), Agra (an old Mughal capital), and Kanpur (a British-created inland industrial center)—four found it necessary to balance the traditions fostered by these two differing styles of corporate organization, for their populations reflected residents accustomed to each. Only Banaras lacked the strong presence of an Indo-Persian literary elite. That lack, coupled with the strength of the collaboration that had emerged among Maharaja, merchants, and Gosains, gave Banaras a very different urban style. It is aspects of that politicocultural style which we examine in the chapters that follow.

PART ONE

Performance and Patronage

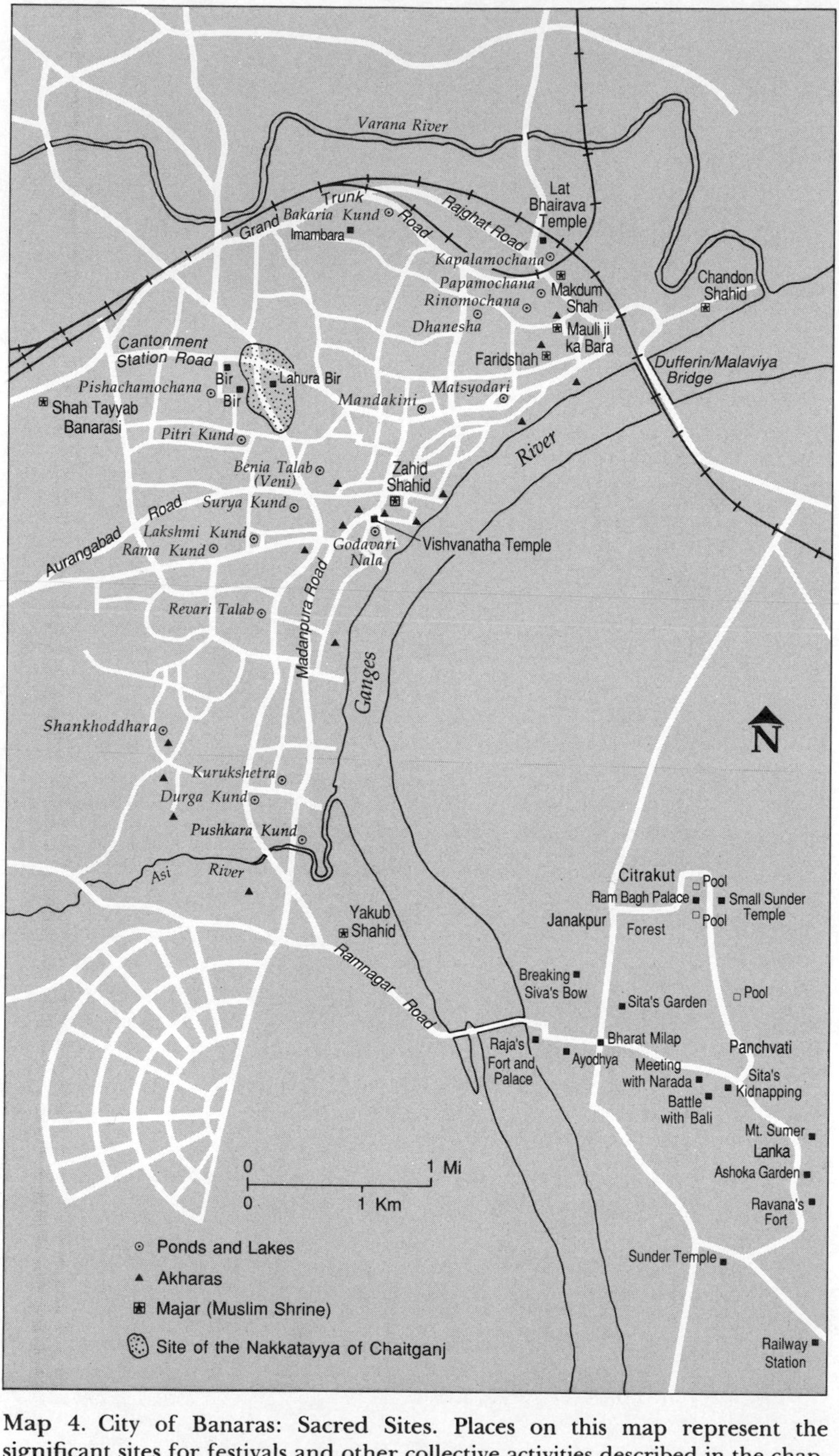

Map 4. City of Banaras: Sacred Sites. Places on this map represent the significant sites for festivals and other collective activities described in the chapters of this volume. Sources used for the map include Eck 1982, Kumar 1984, Schechner and Hess 1977, and the chapter authors.

Introduction to Part 1
Performance and Patronage

Our study of Banaras begins here by looking at a variety of performance genres enacted in the public spaces of that urban site. In many respects, collective activities in public spaces constitute the heart of shared urban cultural experience (see map 4). Analysis of such events thus enables us to examine more closely the relationship between the interests of the lower classes and castes and those of the intermediary "corporations" of power-holding elite in Banaras. Moreover, these activities form the intersection between the concerns and values of individuals (and expressions of the communities they accordingly construct) and the larger movements and events treated as "history." Thus Part 1 provides a logical connection point linking, functionally as well as analytically, the discussions that follow of the constituent identities of Banarsis (Part 2) and the larger Indian world within which Banaras fits (Part 3).

Analysis of these performance genres enables us to see how values are perpetuated to upper and lower castes, as well as to examine the incorporative aspects of collective activities. The significance of such activities for our purposes is suggested by a preliminary study conducted by Linda Hess, in which she analyzed with her informants several of the basic values inculcated through the performance of Tulsidas's *Rāmcharitmānas* in the Rāmlīlā. The extent to which cultural norms can be transmitted and shared in a society with large numbers of illiterate people is particularly important to keep in mind. As Hess has noted, if you are a resident of a north Indian town,

> you don't have to be able to read to know Tulsidas. Your grandmother will tell you Ram's stories, your neighborhood will have a Ramlila that dramatizes the epic every year, a visiting *vyas* [specialist in *Rāmcharitmānas*

> discourse] will lecture with gusto, chanting verses and pouring forth commentary with a skill that combines a preacher's drama and fluency with a professor's urbanity and wit [see chapters 1 and 4]. Singers will perform beautiful Tulsi-*bhajans*, lyric verses by the poet set to music in every imaginable style. Images of Ram, Sita, and Hanuman will live in your house, as familiar and unregarded as your uncles and cousins, yet at times brought forth for special veneration. If you do read, you are likely to be a reader of the *Manas*, whether occasionally or as a daily practice.

Indeed, the characters of the narrative are held up as exemplary models of appropriate behavior: Sītā for young girls, Rām for boys. Moreover, as Hess notes, "Whatever your age or sex, you are likely to have an archetype in your head of social and political perfection—the perfect state ruled by the perfect leader—and that archetype will be called *rāmraj*" (Hess 1987:2–3).

Another important point made by Hess in this essay relates to the tension inherent in Tulsidas's original text as well as the performances that emanate from it. This tension connects what Hess calls "bhakti and orthodoxy." By bhakti she means the "grass-roots movement, protesting against religious formalism and priestly domination" that insisted "on the accessibility of God to everyone [and stressed] the importance of inner experience" in the Hindi region between the fifteenth and the seventeenth century. As Hess notes, this "leveling tendency" was accompanied also by the rise of vernacular literature (see chapter 6 for the implications of this pattern). By contrast, Tulsidas's writing also includes an "allegiance to the old Brahmanical social order," stressing hierarchical relationships, including the reverence to be paid to Brahmins, and recognition of the lowliness of Shudras (such as Ahirs, the subject groups of chapters 3 and 4), and the subservience of women. As Hess notes, "these two sides of Tulsidas—egalitarian and hierarchical, liberal and conservative—can be traced in intricate and sometimes baffling detail throughout the *Ramcharitmanas*" (Hess 1987:172).

While the two elements in contention are clearly present in the text, it does appear (from Hess's and Lutgendorf's work) that a "tilt" in the interpretation emerged as bhakti changed from a countercultural phenomenon to one underpinning general devotional religion. This tilt made bhakti more consistent with orthodoxy (thus de-emphasizing social equality of women and untouchables). The historical timing of the tilt in interpretation of Tulsidas's text seems especially significant when placed next to the emergence of the triumvirate of power holders in Banaras who espoused Hindu high culture. Their patronage of *Mānas* activities—from Rāmlīlā to the *kathā* discussed by Lutgendorf—becomes explicable particularly when seen not only as an auspicious act of charity, but also as an investment in a form of didactic instruction for the lower-caste residents of the city dominated by these power holders.

The collective activities expressing these values tended to be of three types: public performances, collective ceremonies, and collective protests.[1] If arranged in order according to degree of direct participation by the public, the first type would be *public performances,* by which we mean such activities as street theatre, musical performances, even the recitation and exegesis of religious texts available for "consumption" by the general public. These form the subject matter of this part. As the following essays make clear, audiences for these public performances were not passive: as consumers, they shaped the style and value content of street theatre (chapter 2); they interacted with the speaker (chapter 1); they functioned as final arbiters in deciding who had "won" a musical contest (chapter 3). Participants thus played an active role in shaping these public-space performances, and we therefore may characterize such activities as "collective."[2]

At the workshop, contributors discussed other genres that, like those analyzed here, fit within this first category. Perhaps most influential was the form of public debate that emerged around the advent of Western missionaries. Evolving from informal confrontations—often staged on street corners, pitching those who preached the gospel against local defenders of South Asian sects and belief systems—these became highly ritualized, well-publicized formal performances by charismatic spokesmen for each religious tradition (Christian, Hindu [usually Arya Samājī], Muslim). Analyses of these confrontations suggest not only that it was important that all religions be represented, but that each speaker paid virtually no attention to the others, directing his remarks not at a general audience but at his own supporters. As a consequence, each participant could assert that he had "won." In the process, the genre became an important elaboration of a formally constituted mode of conflict, in which participants followed commonly accepted rules and castigated the "Other" located outside a religiously constructed community, through a rhetoric of abuse that was shared as well.[3]

Collective ceremony, the second type of public activity, is the genre in which collective experience is the most regular, sustained, and repetitive. As such, it tends to set the patterns, and often the symbolic rhetoric or vocabulary, for all public activities. Processions, especially,

1. This typology represents an interpretation of the editor, much enriched by the ideas of workshop participants. The concept, however, was never discussed directly by them.

2. This volume presents the only sustained effort attempting to tie discussions of South Asian performance genres to larger historical developments. The body of analysis is much greater for European history; see, for instance, the volume edited by the Yeos (1981).

3. Cf. presentations by Barbara Metcalf, Ken Jones et al., at 1985 panel at Association for Asian Studies on such debates with Christian missionaries.

presented forms of collective ceremony that brought together in public spaces a congeries of people who may have mobilized on the basis of very different kinds of identities, particularly those of *muḥalla*, caste, and occupation, or voluntary associational ties. Once assembled, however, the liminality of participating in shared public ceremonials created a temporary shared identity or sense of community.[4] Moreover, by extension, the very space in which these ceremonials occurred took on sacredness and thus gained important new connotations. The dynamic was captured by an observer of Agra's Juljhulni festival (honoring Krishna) in the late 1880s:

> When the chief street is reached all is changed: the aspect of the houses with roofs, windows and balconies crowded with spectators, animates the worshippers, the throng in the streets becomes denser, the enthusiasm increases, the shouts of the multitude round the car are answered by the crowds on the houses, and as amidst the triumphant clamour of voices the great mass of human beings passes up the street, the organizers of the festival feel that their god has been honored, and that their management has been a success.[5]

The third type, *collective protest*, resembles ceremonial actions in many important respects. Once again, people were generally mobilized on the basis of some shared origin, occupation, or neighborhood. Their actions underscored, through their choice of targets, the issues that had prompted their unease. Such actions also enacted symbolic statements expressing a perception of shared values. Moreover, the construction of identity that resulted from such action was one that frequently defined the actors together, against an "Other." At the same time, the use of public space constituted an important statement about their centrality in urban life.[6]

Keeping in mind this broader context of collective action in public spaces, then, the following three chapters examine several different kinds of performance genres. While their audiences ranged from middle to lower classes, and their patterns of development differed to some extent, taken together they provide a clearer picture than we have had

4. See Victor Turner 1974 for a discussion of this process, which he terms "communitas." Also important to remember is his point that, while "communitas" stops just short of its antithesis ("structure"), it cannot emerge without structure, which is needed to create the appropriate occasions. See also an extended discussion of communitas and South Asian ceremony in Freitag, 1989.

5. Report of A. Cadell, Officiating Commissioner, Agra Division, to Chief Secretary to Govt, NWP & O, dated 4 October 1888. IOR NWP & O General Proceedings (Progs) for June 1890. Progs no. 3, serial no. 2, paragraph 23.

6. See chapter 7 for further discussion of the analytical relationship among these categories of collective activities.

hitherto of the nature of public performance and of the relationship between these and larger historical movements.

Seen against the backdrops provided by Parts 2 and 3, these three essays also suggest the outlines of a historical process of great import; it will be useful to provide a brief sketch of the process here. An initial expansion of collective activities in public spaces can be documented for urban north India in the late nineteenth century (see Freitag 1989; N. Kumar 1984). Particularly for performance genres, this increased activity reflected both the involvement of a wide range of urban dwellers and shifts in patronage supporting that expansion. The pattern of changing patronage is explored in more detail below.

As chapter 2 suggests, however, the very success of these expanded activities led, in turn, to increasing uneasiness among the "corporation" of leaders in Banaras about the nature of many of the activities occurring in the city's public spaces. Eventually, for reasons suggested below, this led to a separation between activities sponsored and attended by the educated elite and those of the lower classes/castes. This process, begun as early as the 1880s, culminated in the late 1920s and early 1930s. Reformism—possessing both religious and "secular" attributes—played a key role in this separation. In view of the separation, it is particularly interesting to find that at least since the 1950s another period of expansion has been under way, one that has affected the activities examined in Part 2, including annual temple *shringārs*, the proliferation of neighborhood shrines, and the expansion of neighborhood-sponsored versions of public ceremonials (see chapter 4). Although this process may have developed apace, if separately, for both middle- and lower-class activities, most of the evidence presented in this volume relates to the expansion of activities supported by the lower classes. More evidence is needed, but it may be that this process actually documents a movement *only* among lower-class groups, in which they are staking out cultural power in a world discretely their own.

URBAN CONSTITUENCIES: AUDIENCE AND PATRONS

The key to understanding this collective activity in public spaces, particularly that of performance genres, has been the changing nature of patronage. Originally such patronage fell within the purview and privilege of the royal courts and those involved in courtly culture. Related to the shifts traced below, during the eighteenth century merchants began "purchasing the perquisites of kingship and local lordship," including that of patronage (Bayly 1983:194–95). Not until the 1850s did mercantile patronage in other parts of U.P. completely replace courtly consumption; and, as we have seen, this pattern was mitigated in Banaras by the continued presence of the courtly culture fostered by the Maharaja of Banaras.

Nevertheless, one result of the process, even in Banaras, was an increase in activities expressing what we have called "Hindu merchant" values in public venues—activities that were perceived by their sponsors as reflecting orthodox religious beliefs, and that included such examples as *Mānas* recitation and exegesis (*kathā*), or Rāmlīlā performances. Through a kind of ripple effect, however, even these orthodox efforts indirectly patronized activities more popular in appeal: *birahā* performers were incorporated into annual renewal ceremonies for temples (*shringār*s); street theatre formed a prelude or followed Rāmlīlā enactments; the originator of the *birahā* style even performed at *kathā* events. When we speak of urban culture as it was expressed through collective activities in public spaces, then, we are referring to a culture that encompassed overlapping (though not identical) values, world views, venues, and occasions for both literate elite and lower-class patrons.

The impact of the expansion of print technology may also have figured importantly in this cultural overlap. Both Hansen and Lutgendorf note the influence of printed versions of their subject matter: Hansen suggests that street performances whetted the appetite of viewers, who would then purchase printed copies of the plays they had witnessed. In turn, we may assume, the existence of such printed copies could have encouraged local troupes to perform these same versions and thus perpetuate the messages contained therein. Lutgendorf, too, sees the accessibility of the printed *Rāmcharitmānas* as important in making *kathā* a popular audience activity. (For further implications of the expansion of print technology, see also chapter 6 on linguistic definition.) Perhaps the most important aspect of the interplay between oral performance and these new, easily accessible printed versions, has been explicated by Roger Chartier:

> Cultural consumption, whether popular or not, is at the same time a form of production, which creates ways of using that cannot be limited to the intentions of those who produce. This perspective gives a central place to the "art of doing" and "doing with," as Michel de Certeau wrote, and it gives cultural consumption a new status—it is no longer seen as passive or dependent and submissive but as creative, and it sometimes resists suggested or imposed models. [See the discussion in the introduction to Part 2 on the Ahir interpretation of Tulsidas.] (Chartier 1984:234)

Thus the expansion of patronage, from the courtier to the merchant, carried with it implications for a further expansion, from the merchant to the lower-class members of the audience.

This second wave of expansion of public-venue activities, which we have dated in these essays to the 1920s and 1930s, can be traced primarily to the influence of reformism. Motivated by Hindu merchant values, a vernacularly literate elite (supported by the merchant "corporation") worked simultaneously to purify public performances and to withdraw from those they deemed inappropriate (see N. Kumar 1984; chapter 7 in this volume). This self-conscious redesign of urban ceremonial life had a profound impact. In some cases it led to a sanitizing of popular festivals. The Nakkatayya festival staged by the Chaitganj *muḥalla* in Banaras provides an important case in point: focused around the Ramayana story in which the nose of a demoness is cut off, the Nakkatayya, by including a procession representing the forces of the demoness, had become a festival of reversal. Participants dressed and behaved in ways that, in all other contexts of urban life, would have been deemed unacceptable. This license to rowdiness doubtless contributed to the wide appeal of the festival, until the reformers purged it of its more "offensive" elements and, at least temporarily, substituted nationalist motifs for those deemed unacceptable (N. Kumar 1984:267 et seq.). Other festivals simply disappeared, either through periodic cancellations (see chapter 7) or through permanent withdrawal of elite patronage.

While some public ceremonials continue to be shared events (the Ramnagar Rāmlīlā being the most celebrated example), the impact of the reformist impulse led, once more, to a shift of the burden of patronage, this time to the lower classes themselves. In this case, the very organizational forms responsible for sustaining the public expressions of lower-class culture gained new significance. That is, the structures supporting leisure and work patterns—such as occupational *chaudharīs* (headmen), *muḥalla* organization and *akhāṛās*—also have taken on the tasks related to organizing collective ceremonials. It is they who often canvass for small contributions, they who organize each unit that goes to make up a citywide procession. Closer to the audience as well as to participants, these structures are able to respond much more directly to lower-class values and enthusiasms. (During the workshop discussion, contributors noted recent innovations in staging—for instance, the incorporation of strings of electric lights to adorn street-corner performance pavilions, and the public use of VCRs, often in lieu of live performances.)

The nature of neighborhood in providing an organizational base will be discussed in greater detail in Part 2. Another important structure, the timing of the emergence of *akhāṛās*, as a significant form of sustenance and patronage for popular activities, fits the process of shifting patronage described above. This shift has been documented especially for classical music and medicine: "The great scholars and artists, particularly those of Delhi, had depended on patronage from the royal court and from nobles associated with it. With the end of this patronage they adopted new strategies to sustain themselves. . . . In the second half of the nineteenth century, at exactly the same time and for the same reasons that the gharanas of musicians became important, physicians focused more centrally on their origins and their past" (B. Metcalf 1986:301). By encompassing new organizational forms within the structure expressed in familial terms and the teacher-disciple relationship, *akhāṛās* could lay claim to a legitimacy for what would otherwise have been perceived as striking innovation. Further exploration of the significance of *akhāṛā* organization will be pursued in Part 2. It is worth noting here, however, that *akhāṛā* organization, while not limited to lower-class activities, nevertheless provided an alternative mode for organizing activities frequently supported by the lower classes. It also provided an alternative avenue of mobility and form of patron-client bond between such participants and the leaders of the *akhāṛās*.

This examination of performance genres suggests one final point: the integral role played by competition in the structuring and presentation of these various activities. A "conflict mode" of expression forms the central dynamic underlying the methods of mobilization, processes of identity formation, and constructions of community that provided form and substance to collective activities. Hansen and Marcus both suggest the ways in which competition among *akhāṛās* animated the performers and shaped the rhetoric by which they appealed to the gods for assistance as they did artistic "battle."

Perhaps most important, competition functioned to bring the audience, as participants, into the confrontation—both to pronounce the "winners" and to express symbolically their positions in the competition through the very act of attendance. Thus popular patronage became a conscious, public act taken in a competitive context to further one's own, chosen group against an "Other." Workshop participants felt that the extent to which this formulation of relationships affected perceptions can be gauged by the adversarial relationship expressed in the "court scene" vignette that opens chapter 6.[7] Since, in other literary contexts contemporaneous with that scene, Urdu and Hindi were not seen as so profoundly antithetical,[8] the "conflict mode" that developed

7. Implications of this active role for audiences, as self-conscious statements of identity that become political statements as well, are explored in more depth in Freitag 1989.

8. Hansen noted, for instance, that the texts of the dramas presented by street theatre troupes often incorporated conventions from both literary traditions and even were printed in both scripts.

in urban cultural activities helps to explain this style of exchange between representatives of such constructed communities.

While competition provided the basic motivating force underlying these public performances, we should not lose sight of the fact that all players—including the audience—nevertheless shared much in common. Their very understanding of the rules by which competition should be expressed is not the least of these shared perceptions. (This may also help delineate the ways in which Hindu power-holders and Muslim lower-class groups participated in the same cultural world, since their understandings of the signification and organizational modes would have overlapped.)

That public performances expressed shared concepts thus makes all the more significant the increasing separation of middle- and lower-class culture, which ultimately developed by the 1930s. These implications are examined in greater detail in Part 3. For the moment, we turn to the performances themselves for what they can tell us about the constituent elements of urban culture, the connections between middle- and lower-class activities, the nature of voluntary social organization, and the significance of these for larger historical events.

ONE

Rām's Story in Shiva's City: Public Arenas and Private Patronage

Philip Lutgendorf

Infinite is the Lord, endless his story.
All good people in diverse ways tell and listen to it.

The captivating deeds of Ramchandra
Cannot be sung even in ten million aeons!

RĀMCHARITMĀNAS, 1.140.5,6

THE PERFORMANCE

The setting is a *maṇḍap,* a brightly canopied enclosure for festive observances, erected in a small square in the heart of Banaras (see fig. 2). The ground within is spread with cotton rugs on which hundreds of people are seated, men and women on opposite sides of a central aisle. At the far end of the enclosure stands a lofty dais draped with rich brocades, on which an oversized book, covered with flowers, is enshrined on an ornate stand. A dignified looking man, immaculately clad in a crisply pleated dhoti and silk *kurtā,* reverences and then mounts the dais, whereupon he is garlanded by another man. Closing his eyes, he composes himself in a brief meditation and then begins murmuring an invocation. He salutes Shiva, primal guru of the world and special patron of this city, Valmiki, the first singer of Rām's deeds, and Tulsidas, who brought the divine song into the language of ordinary people; he also venerates his own teacher, and Hanuman, the beneficent patron of all retellers of the *Rāmāyaṇ.* Finally he opens his eyes and begins to chant: "Sita-Ram, Hail Sita-Ram!" The crowd takes it up after him, beginning many rounds of antiphonal exchange, until the speaker senses that the proper atmosphere of devotion has been created. Then at last he begins to speak, reciting from the book that lies before him, though he never opens its petal-strewn cover. The listeners know that he has no need to read from this book, for he has studied it so deeply and internalized it so completely that he has it, as they say, "in the throat"[1]—he has himself become its living voice. Now he invites his listeners to enter the special world of this book, an entry that may be made at any point, since the whole story is a divine revelation charged with the pro-

1. *Kaṇṭhastha,* the Hindi idiom for "memorized."

Fig. 2. The podium and a section of the crowd at the *Mānas-kathā* festival held annually at Gyān Vāpī (November 1982). Photograph by Philip Lutgendorf.

foundest significance. Selecting a single line, the speaker begins to muse and expand upon it; to "play" with it as a classical Indian musician might play upon a raga. But here the improvisations consist not of musical tones but of words and ideas, images and anecdotes, folk sayings, scriptural injunctions, and snatches of song from great devotional poets, all interspersed with numerous chanted quotations from the book itself. The speaker has no single theme, constructs no systematic argument; instead he evokes a succession of moods and invites his audience to savor them. His purpose is less to analyze than to celebrate, and when a fresh insight occurs to him he "digresses" to explore it.

As he performs he engages his audience in numerous ways: making a particularly striking point, he turns to certain listeners near the front of the crowd to solicit their approval and is rewarded by exclamations of delight; chanting a well-known verse from the book, he stops midway and motions for listeners to supply the last few words, evoking a rhythmic and enthusiastic response. A particularly poignant anecdote brings tears to many eyes, but these give way in the next moment to hearty laughter over an earthy recasting of the story and its divine characters. Narrating dialogue, the speaker assumes the various parts and acts them expertly, with vivid facial expressions and gestures.

The speaker's verbal tapestry envelopes the crowd for nearly an hour, and then with expert timing he ends it with a resounding benediction: "Hail Sita's bridegroom, Ramchandra!" just as a priest appears before the dais bearing a brass lamp, which he waves in worship before the book. The listeners rise to sing a hymn in its praise, and when this concludes many come forward to place an offering on the book, to touch the speaker's feet reverently, and to receive from him a blessing of *prasād* in the form of sacred *tulsī* leaves from a sprig that has been resting on the book.

Performances resembling the one just described have been an important part of life in Banaras for many centuries. They are hardly unique to that city, of course, for similar forms of oral exegesis, perhaps differing in certain details or based on other texts, are found throughout much of India.[2] But Banaras has a special connection with the "book" in the present example, the Hindi epic *Rāmcharitmānas*—commonly called the *Mānas,* or simply the *Rāmāyaṇ* (since most Hindi speakers have no direct knowledge of the older Sanskrit work by this name) and generally acknowledged as the most popular text of north Indian Hinduism—for it was in this city that Gosvami Tulsidas (1532–1623) was said to have completed his epic and to have personally initiated its public performance through *kathā* (oral exegesis) and *līlā* (dramatic enactment).[3] During the eighteenth and nineteenth centuries the religious and political elite of Banaras enthusiastically cultivated these traditions, establishing patterns of *Mānas* patronage and performance that were emulated in other areas of northern India. While the annual cycle of Rāmlīlā plays has been the subject of a number of studies, the rhetorical art of *kathā,* which occurs throughout the year, has received little scholarly notice, perhaps in part because its performances are less conventionally "theatrical." Yet such programs are held in virtually every neighborhood of Banaras, and a number of large-scale ones have in recent years become important events for the whole city. This chapter will outline the development of this performance tradition, giving particular emphasis to the cultural and political context of its patronage.

ORIGINS OF THE TRADITION

While the term *kathā* is often understood to mean simply "a story," this translation tends to overly nominalize a word that retains a strong sense

2. That is, the *harikathā* of Maharashtra and Karnataka, the *burrakathā* of Andhra, and the *kathākālakshepam* and *pirachankam* of Tamil Nadu. Most of these genres have been little studied. On *Harikathā,* see Damle 1960:63–107.

3. All quotations from the *Rāmcharitmānas* refer to the popular Gita Press version edited by Poddar (1938); numbers indicate *kāṇḍ* ("canto"), *dohā* ("couplet"), and individual line in the "stanza" preceding the *dohā.*

of its verb root. In India a "story" is, first and foremost, something that is *told,* and the Sanskrit root *kath,* from which the noun is derived, means "to converse with, tell, relate, narrate, speak about, explain" (Monier-Williams 1899:247). *Kathā* might thus better be translated a "telling" or "narration"; it signifies a performance and suggests a milieu. To tell a story means that there must necessarily be someone to *hear* it, and in Hindu performance traditions the role of the "hearer" (*shrotā*) is generally a participatory rather than a passive one.

The roots of *kathā*-style performance lie in ancient Brahminical traditions of teacher-disciple dialectic and oral exposition upon existing sacred text; a milieu that can be glimpsed, for example, in the teaching dialogues of the Upanishads and in the terse structure of the sutra, which often presupposes the presence of a living expounder. The development of storytelling as a form of mass entertainment, however, was first reflected in the Sanskrit epics, the traditional narrator of which was the Sūta, originally a charioteer and royal herald (Rocher 1985:2.1.2). While the Sūta's social status appears to have been relatively low, at least in the eyes of Brahmin legalists, the "tales of wonder" with which he entertained priests and kings during breaks in sacrificial cycles came in time to be seen as powerful religious narratives, which could even claim a sanctity on a par with that of the Vedas themselves. Significantly the *Mahābhārata* provides evidence of the growing involvement of Brahmins with the epic, as its memorizers, performers, and elucidators (e.g., *Mahābhārata* 1.1.50).

The role of the oral mediator of sacred text increased in importance with the emergence of devotional cults advocating the worship of Vishṇu and Shiva and offering hope of salvation to faithful devotees regardless of sex or social status. The message of this new religious movement was set in the form of the "old story" (Purana), and while its language was still the Sanskrit of the twice-born elite, its intended audience explicitly included the lower classes, women, and Shudras.[4] To reach this largely illiterate audience, the Puranas ceaselessly advertised the merits of their own recitation and exposition, and even offered detailed directions for the staging of such performances (Bonazzoli 1983:254–80). The performer was called by a variety of names: *paurāṇika* (puranic specialist), *purāṇajña* ("knower" of the Puranas), *vyākhyātri* (expounder), and *vyās.* The latter term, denoting one who "separates" or "divides," recalls the archetypal expounder Veda-Vyas, who "divided" the one Veda into four in order to make it more readily comprehensible to the men of this Dark Age, and who was also credited with the authorship of the *Mahābhārata* and of many of the

4. An explicit statement to this effect is found, for example, in the *māhātmya* of the *Bhāgavata Purāṇa; Shrīmad Bhāgavata Mahāpurāṇa* 1964, 1:36.

Puranas themselves.[5] The puranic *vyās* was viewed as a spiritual descendant or even temporary incarnation of Veda-Vyas (himself an avatar of Vishṇu) and was privileged to speak from a *vyās-pīṭh:* a "seat" of honor and authority in the assembly of devotees.

This assembly too had a special designation: *satsang* or *sant-samāj*—"fellowship with the good." Although such congregational expression of religious feeling must have become common quite early in the puranic period, the establishment of Muslim hegemony in northern India in the late twelfth century helped create conditions favorable to the spread of this tradition. Unlike the Vaishnava royal cults of an earlier period, devotional expression through *satsang* required no elaborate superstructure of temples and images that could become targets for the iconoclasm of the new rulers, and storytellers and expounders were often wandering mendicants whose activities were difficult to regulate. Moreover, the bhakti message of devotional egalitarianism made a strong appeal to those of low status and served to counter the social appeal of Islam; this factor may have encouraged the patronage of wealthy twice-born Hindus who were alarmed at the conversion of low-caste and untouchable groups.[6] A related development was the composition of new "scriptures" in regional languages, in order to carry a devotional message—and any appended social messages—to the widest possible audience, regardless of whether it had access to the Sanskritic education of the religious elite.

The importance of oral exposition of scripture during the sixteenth century is amply attested by the *Mānas* itself, for Tulsidas's epic, set as a series of dialogues between gods, sages, and immortal devotees, invariably characterizes itself as a *kathā*, "born, like Lakshmi, from the ocean of the saints' assembly" (*Rāmcharitmānas* 1.31.10), and it constantly admonishes its audience to "sing," "narrate," and "reverently listen to" its verses.[7] The hagiographic tradition depicts Tulsidas himself as a *kathāvāchak* ("teller" of *kathā*), and the poet's frequent references to himself as a "singer" of Rām's praises seem to accord well with the traditional image. It is noteworthy, however, that while the *Mānas* appears to have rapidly acquired a singular and far-flung reputation among

5. The link between "division" and creative "elaboration" becomes clearer if we recall that, in Hindu cosmogonic myths, the act of creation is often accomplished by means of a primordial separation or division. See, for example, *Rig Veda* 10.90, *Brihadāraṇyaka* 1.2.3, and *Manu* 1.12,13.

6. Damle makes this argument with reference to the Maharashtrian *harikathā* tradition, which he feels became systematized during the period of Muslim rule (Damle 1960:64).

7. Such admonitions occur particularly in the *phal-shruti* verses at the end of each *kāṇḍ;* for example, 3.46a; 5.60; 7.129.5,6.

Vaishnava devotees[8] and among sadhus of the Rāmānandī order, it does not seem to have initially won the allegiance of the religious and political elite of Banaras. Although the legends of the epic's miraculous triumph over Brahminical opposition may lack historical veracity,[9] the process which they implicitly suggest was undoubtedly a real one: the slow and grudging acceptance by the religious elite of an epic composed in "rustic speech" and cherished by the uneducated classes and by the casteless mendicants of what was, at the time, one of the most heterodox of religious orders (Burghart 1978:124).

THE RISE OF ELITE PATRONAGE

The historical developments that were to lead to present-day styles of *Mānas* performance can be most clearly traced from the eighteenth century onward. The great political event of that period in northern India was the collapse of Mughal hegemony over much of the region. The rapid erosion of centralized authority which followed the death of Aurangzeb in 1707 facilitated the rise, especially in the eastern and southern Ganges valley, of a number of regional kingdoms, some of which were again under Hindu rulers.

In 1740, when Balwant Singh, the son of an ambitious local tax-farmer, assumed the title Raja of Banaras, he did so as a client of the Nawab of Awadh, who was still the paramount political power in the region, and who in turn still displayed a nominal allegiance to the weak Mughal regime at Delhi. As Bernard Cohn has pointed out, the Banaras ruler was essentially a "middle man" within a complex system in which authority was parceled out at many levels and in which the division of power was constantly being renegotiated.

> The Raja's obligations to the Nawabs were the regular payment of revenue and provision of troops when requested. The Raja of Banaras at every opportunity tried to avoid fulfillment of these obligations; and on several occasions the Nawab sent troops to try to bring his subordinate to terms, if not to capture and kill him. On these occasions, Balwant Singh would retreat with his treasure and army to the jungles of Mirzapur. After a time the Nawab, distracted by similar behavior in other parts of his

8. Thus in Nabhadas's hagiographic classic, *Bhaktamāl,* thought to have been composed in Rajasthan in the late 1500s, Tulsi is already acclaimed as a reincarnation of Valmiki (Rupkala 1909:756, *chhappay* 129).

9. The best-known story, which occurs in the controversial *Mūl qosāī charit* attributed to Benimadhavdas (1630?), recounts the "trial" of the *Mānas* in the inner sanctum of the Vishvanath temple; placed on the bottom of a pile of Sanskrit scriptures when the temple is locked for the night, it is found in the morning to be at the top of the pile, with the words *satyam, shivam, sundaram* ("truth, auspiciousness, beauty") inscribed on its cover.

> state or by his intervention in imperial politics, would compromise with Balwant Singh and withdraw, at which time Balwant Singh would resume his control of the zamindari. . . . A balancing of relative weakness appears to have been central to the functioning of the system. The Nawab could not afford the complete chaos which would result from the crushing of the Raja. (Cohn 1962:315)

If the Nawab was dependent upon the Raja because no one else was capable of guaranteeing the collection of revenue in the region (even if relatively little of it actually reached the Nawab's treasury), the Raja was in a similar relationship of dependency upon and intermittent conflict with his subordinates: numerous petty rajas, jagirdars, and talukdars who likewise controlled revenue and troops and were the primary intermediaries between the Raja and the peasants (Cohn 1962:316–17).

That the Nawab of Awadh was Muslim and the Raja of Banaras, Hindu, may at times have given an ideological edge to Balwant Singh's ambitions, though we should recall that some of the Raja's most intractable enemies were Hindu petty chieftains and that the Shi'a Nawabs were often highly catholic in religious matters.[10] What was at issue was less a matter of communal identity than of royal legitimation, for this was precisely what the Nawabs initially provided to the Banaras rulers: a legitimation that ultimately derived from the increasingly transparent premise of Mughal dominion. The Monas Rajputs of Bhadohi, for example, who were staunch rivals of Balwant Singh, held their land under an imperial grant from Shahjahan, and even after defeating them the Raja could not annex their territory until he had received the permission of the Nawab, the nominal Mughal representative in the region.

> Power the Raja had, but he needed authority as well. Even though the Rajas' goal in relation to the Nawabs was a consistent one of independence, they could not afford to ignore the ground rules and had to continue to seek the sanction, even if it was *ex post facto,* of their superordinates, the Nawabs. (Cohn 1962:315)

The glories of the Indo-Persian cultural synthesis had long exerted a powerful influence upon the tastes of the Hindu elite in north India, but by the mid-eighteenth century the Mughal legacy must have seemed increasingly bankrupt. Delhi itself was devastatingly looted in 1739 by a Persian adventurer who carried off the legendary throne of Shahjahan. Urdu poets like Mir, who fled east to Awadh, sang of the downfall of the capital, its deserted streets and ruined bazaars (Russell and Islam 1968:19–20, 259–60). Within the century the reigning motif

10. Note, for example, Asaf ud-Daula's patronage of one of the Rāmānandī subsects (Wilson 1862:57).

of Indo-Persian culture would become one of decline and lamentation over lost glory—a theme of little appeal to ambitious kings in search of positive and victorious symbols.

I suggest that the Banaras rulers' growing involvement, in the latter part of the eighteenth century, with the Rām tradition—a preoccupation which they shared with other petty Hindu kings in the region—reflected among other things their need to cultivate an explicitly Hindu symbol of royal legitimacy, and thus to achieve ideological as well as political independence from the Nawabs. In seeking to revive a Vaishnava ideal of divine kingship and harmonious but hierarchical social order, they turned not to the figure of Krishna (whose legend had, during preceding centuries of Muslim ascendancy, come to be almost exclusively focused upon a pastoral and erotic myth),[11] but to that of Rām, whose myth had retained a strong martial, imperial, and sociopolitical dimension, expressed most clearly in the vision of Rāmrāj, or the golden age of Rām's universal rule, and in the hero's role as exemplar of *maryādā,* a term that implied both personal dignity and social propriety. Moreover the Rām tradition's emphasis on social and political hierarchy, and on the properly deferential behavior of subjects and subordinates, could serve as chastening examples to the Rajas' rebellious underlings. That all these ideals had found expression in a brilliant vernacular epic which had already won a vast following throughout the region only enhanced the ideological utility of the tradition. Accordingly, it was to Rām and to the *Mānas* that the Rajas turned for a validating model of religiopolitical authority. The resulting trend toward elite patronage of the epic turned many courts of the period into centers of *Mānas* performance and scholarship. Not surprisingly, the prospect of generous royal patronage had the effect of awakening greater interest in the Hindi epic among Brahmins, who began increasingly to claim the privilege of authoritatively expounding its verses.

A further motive for the Banaras kings' patronage of the Rām tradition may have been their desire to maintain amicable relations with the economically and militarily powerful Rāmānandī order (Burghart 1978:126, 130; Thiel-Horstmann 1985). A mobile population that was difficult to monitor, these mendicants or sadhus often traveled in armed bands, served as mercenaries in royal armies, and controlled the trade in certain commodities (Cohn 1964:175–82); given the unstable conditions of the period, aspiring kings may well have been concerned to remain on favorable terms with them. The Banaras kingdom was in relatively close proximity to three important Rāmānandī centers: Chitrakut in the southwest, Janakpur in the northeast, and Ayodhya in the

11. David Haberman suggests that the de-emphasis on heroic and royal Vaishnava myths in favor of the legends of Krishna Gopal paralleled "a gradual (Hindu) retreat from the Muslim-dominated sociopolitical sphere" (Haberman 1984:50)

northwest. It was in part through conspicuous patronage of the Rāmānandīs—especially at the time of the Rāmlīlā festival, when thousands of sadhus were invited to set up camp in the royal city and were fed at the Raja's expense—that the Banaras rulers succeeded in turning their upstart capital, on the "impure" eastern bank of the Ganges, into a major center of pilgrimage, a move that must have conferred positive economic benefits even while it served to advertise their prestige and piety.

The troubled reign of Chait Singh (1770–1781), whose succession to the throne was disputed by the Nawab and who was eventually deposed by the British, nevertheless saw the commencement of an ambitious building project: an enormous temple with a one-hundred-foot spire visible for miles around, flanked by a vast tank and an expansive walled garden containing several small pavilions. The temple's iconography shows a deliberate blending of Vaishnava and Shaiva motifs,[12] and its construction may be interpreted as a major ideological statement on the part of the fledgling dynasty, which was concerned with its status in the eyes of the conservative Shaiva Brahmins across the river.[13] Possibly intended as the principal temple of a new royal capital, the structure eventually acquired the name Sumeru, after the mythical world-mountain, and came to be utilized as one of the settings for the royal Rāmlīlā pageant.

The greatest flowering of *Mānas* patronage at the Banaras court began during the reign of Balwant Singh's grandson, Udit Narayan Singh (1796–1835). By his time, real political power in the region had passed to the East India Company,[14] but this fact only reminds us that the symbols used to legitimate authority can serve equally well to compensate for its loss. Moreover, the imposition of de facto British rule brought a respite from the military rivalries which had preoccupied earlier kings, and freed Odita Narayan to devote his time and energy to *Mānas* patronage, to which he was in any case strongly inclined. During his long reign, *Mānas* manuscripts were assiduously collected and copied at the court, and the most eminent *rāmāyanī*s (experts on the epic) were invited to expound before the Maharaja, or present ingenious resolutions to *shankā*s ("doubts" or problems) concerning the text. The king encouraged some of these scholars to produce written

12. On this temple's connection to the Rāmlīlā, see Shrimati Chhoti Maharajkumari 1979:43–45.

13. By caste the Rajas were Bhumihars, a cultivator group that claimed Brahmin status.

14. The Company assumed control of the civil and criminal administration of Banaras city and province after 1781 and confined the Maharaja's authority to a separate "Banaras estate" in 1794; *Imperial Gazetteer,* pp. 134–35.

*ṭīkā*s ("commentaries"), which would preserve their profound interpretations. One of those who enjoyed Udit Narayan's patronage, Raghunath Das "Sindhi," wrote that the Raja in fact sponsored three *ṭīkā*s, only one of which, Raghunath's own *Mānas-dīpikā* ("Lamp of the *Mānas*"), was in written form. The other two "commentaries" were a magnificently illuminated manuscript of the epic, and the local Rāmlīlā itself, which was expanded into a month-long pageant, and for which Udit Narayan transformed his capital (now dubbed Ramnagar—"Ram's city") into a vast outdoor set (Avasthi 1979:57).

The fact that "commentary" was understood to refer to more than merely written works was characteristic of the *Mānas* tradition, and even the textual *ṭīkā*s produced during this period were usually derivative of the oral performance milieu. Such works often developed from the *kharrā*, or "rough notes," made by expounders in the margins of their *Mānas* manuscripts to serve as reminders to themselves in performance. Some were deliberately enigmatic, such as *Mānas-mayank* ("Moon of the *Mānas*"), composed by Shivlal Pathak (c. 1756–1820), a protégé of Raja Gopal Saran Singh of Dumrao and a frequent guest at Ramnagar. Pathak's "commentary" was in the form of *kūṭ*, or "riddling" verses, and depended upon his own verbal explanations; the key to understanding it is said to have been lost at his death (Sharan 1938:912). Indeed some of the most famous *rāmāyaṇī*s are said to have refused all requests to "reduce" their interpretations to writing. The legendary Ramgulam Dvivedi of Mirzapur (fl. c. 1800–1830) was believed to have obtained his extraordinary oratorical gifts and profound insights into the epic as a boon from Hanuman, who expressly forbade him ever to compose a written *ṭīkā* (B. P. Singh 1957:429).

Anjaninandan Sharan, a scholarly sadhu of Ayodhya who wrote a brief but valuable history of the *Mānas-kathā* tradition,[15] has recorded a story concerning Ramgulam that is richly suggestive of the virtuosity and prestige of expounders during this period. It is said that the Maharaja of Rewa, Vishvanath Singh (1789–1854), a friend and contemporary of Udit Narayan and himself the author of a commentary on Tulsi's song-cycle *Vinay patrikā,* once met Ramgulam during the Kumbh Mela festival at Allahabad. When the great *rāmāyaṇī* graciously offered to speak on any topic of the king's choosing, the Raja immediately quoted the first line of the famous *nām vandanā* ("Praise of the Name") in the first canto of the *Mānas,* stating that he had great curiosity concerning its meaning: "I venerate *Rām,* the name of Raghubar, / the cause of fire, the sun, and the moon" (1.19.1). Ramgulam agreed to ex-

15. See Sharan 1938; he was the compiler of the twelve-volume *Mānas-Pīyūsh* (Ayodhya, 1925–1932), an encyclopedic commentary that incorporated the insights of many eighteenth- and nineteenth-century expounders.

pound this verse on the following afternoon from 3:00 to 6:00 P.M. Then, according to Sharan,

> [he] went on for twenty-two days, with ever new insights, expounding this one line; and whatever interpretation he would put forth on one day, he would demolish the next, saying it was not right. Finally on the twenty-third day the Raja, filled with humility, said, "You are indeed a fathomless ocean, and I am only a householder with all sorts of worries on my head. It is difficult for me to stay on here any longer. . . ." Then with much praise he requested leave to depart and returned to Rewa. (1938:921)

Mention must also be made of the sadhu known as Kashthajihva Swami ("wooden-tongued" swami, d. c. 1855),[16] who was a younger contemporary of Raja Odita Narayan and the guru of his son. An accomplished poet with a unique style, he composed more than fifteen hundred songs, several hundred of which concern problems in the *Mānas*. He was closely involved in the development of the Ramnagar Rāmlīlā, the performance script of which still contains a number of his songs. At the Raja's request he wrote a short *Mānas* commentary, *Rāmāyaṇ paricharyā* ("service of the *Rāmāyaṇ*"), which the king then expanded with his own *Parishishṭa* ("appendix"). These texts, however, like Shivlal Pathak's "riddling" verses, were written in an obscure style; to clarify them, Baba Hariharprasad, a nephew of the Raja, who had become a Rāmānandī ascetic, composed an additional commentary entitled *Prakāsh* ("illumination"). The composite *ṭīkā* with its grand title was published in 1896 and was held in high regard by expounders of the period.

The reign of Ishvariprasad Narayan Singh (1835–1889) has been called "the golden age of the *Mānas*" (S. Chaube 1976, 3:121), for under his patronage the Ramnagar court became the preeminent seat of *Mānas* patronage and scholarship. The king's legendary *rāmāyaṇī satsangs* were graced by the "nine jewels" of the court—the most eminent *Mānas* scholars of the day, including Kashthajihva Swami, Munshi Chhakkan Lal (principal pupil of Ramgulam Dvivedi), and Vandan Pathak, who was famed for his ingenious and even playful interpretations.[17] The king also sponsored a major revision of the royal Rāmlīlā,

16. There are various explanations of how this sannyasi got his peculiar name; see Sharan 1938:918, B. P. Singh 1957:450.

17. Pathak is said to have boasted that he did not concern himself with anything that was not mentioned in the *Mānas*. Once while he was performing, an old woman presented him with a clay dish containing a certain savory. Pathak quickly pocketed the gift, but someone in the crowd jokingly called out, "Maharaj, what does this have to do with the *Mānas*?" Pathak, who was renowned for his great presence of mind when expounding, instantly quoted a line from *Bāl kāṇḍ* (1.35.8), the last word of which made a pun on the colloquial name for the dish in which the woman had presented her gift (recounted by C. N. Singh, interview, Feb. 13, 1984).

allegedly under the direction of the Banarsi writer Harishchandra, who modernized and expanded the dialogues and set the production in the form in which it was to gain all-India fame (Avasthi 1979:81–88).

Although I have emphasized royal sponsorship, it should be noted that *Mānas* patronage was not confined to the court, for the king's fascination with the epic was shared by the nobles and wealthy landowners of the area. According to Vibhuti Narayan Singh, the present titular Maharaja, rajas and zamindars during the nineteenth century "vied with one another" in their efforts to promote the epic, and intimate knowledge of the text was regarded as a mark of cultural sophistication as well as piety.[18] The *Mānas* acquired the status not merely of a sacred book but of a cultural epic; hundreds of its verses entered popular speech as aphorisms, and its stanzas were set to seasonal melodies like *kajlī* and *chaitī* and performed by urban and rural folksingers.[19] By 1880 F. S. Growse would observe that Tulsi's epic "is in everyone's hands, from the court to the cottage, and is read, or heard, and appreciated alike by every class of the Hindu community, whether high or low, rich or poor, young or old" (Growse 1887:lv). And while their Indologist colleagues devoted themselves to the study of the Sanskrit classics, British administrators and missionaries, out of expedience, studied the *Mānas*. George Grierson was to recall: "Half a century ago, an old missionary said to me that no one could hope to understand the natives of Upper India till he had mastered every line that Tulsidas had written. I have since learned to know how right he was."[20]

THE BOOK IN PRINT

Other developments during the nineteenth century significantly altered the pattern of *Mānas* patronage and would in time affect even the structure of performances. One was the introduction of print technology, an innovation first sponsored by the British but quickly adopted by Indians. Among the first printed versions of the *Mānas* was an 1810 edition published in Calcutta, the city in which, partly due to the presence and patronage of the East India Company's College of Fort William, popular publishing in Hindi as well as Bengali had its start. Thereafter a steadily increasing number of both lithographed and typeset editions documents the westward expansion of publishing, and especially the dramatic rise of Hindi publishing in Banaras beginning at about mid-

18. Vibhuti Narayan Singh, interview, Aug. 11, 1983.

19. This genre has been described by N. Kumar (1984:178–236); see also chapter 2 of Lutgendorf (1987) and chapter 3, this volume.

20. Quoted in Gopal (1977:x); that knowledge of the *Mānas* was considered essential for a civil administrator was also noted by Growse (1887:lvi).

century.[21] The greatest expansion in *Mānas* printing occurred after 1860, however; during the next two decades at least seventy different editions of the epic appeared from publishing houses large and small, representing virtually every moderate-sized urban center in north India.[22] Especially notable are the Gurumukhi script editions which began appearing from Delhi and Lahore after 1870, versions with Bengali commentaries that were printed in Calcutta in the 1880s, and Marathi and Gujarati editions issued from Bombay and Ahmedabad beginning in the 1890s. Clearly the literate audience for the *Mānas* was growing during the latter part of the century and was spreading far beyond the traditional heartland of the epic and of its Awadhi dialect. Notable too is the steadily increasing size of the editions: whereas those published prior to 1870 had averaged four to five hundred pages and offered only the epic text, those issued in succeeding decades more typically ran to a thousand pages and included prose *ṭīkā*s, glossaries of archaic words, ritual instructions, *māhātmya*s (eulogies of the text), explanations of mythological allusions, and biographies of Tulsidas—all designed to serve the interests of a literate but geographically and culturally heterogeneous audience. The authors of the commentaries offered in these expanded editions were, like the editors of the earlier generation of unannotated texts, traditional scholars known for their oral exposition of the epic; the reputations of such famous *rāmāyaṇī*s as Raghunath Das of Banaras and Jvalaprasad Mishra of Moradabad were greatly enhanced by their association with such popular editions as those of Naval Kishor Press of Lucknow and Shri Venkateshvar Steam Press of Bombay (cf. numerous editions of Das 1873 and Mishra 1906).

The advent of mass printing eliminated the expensive and time-consuming process of scribal manuscript copying and made literature available to the middle classes. One consequence of this development was the fact that literate persons acquired the potential for a kind of participation in sacred literature that had formerly been the domain of a specialist elite. Books could be "read" of course, for private enjoyment and edification, but equally important, sacred books could now also be *recited* by nonspecialists. The meritorious activity of daily *pāṭh* (recitation), rooted in the ancient belief in the spiritual efficacy of the sacred word, was greatly facilitated by the ready availability of revered texts. By the end of the nineteeth century, many bazaar editions of the *Mānas* had begun to be annotated according to regular schemes of nine- and thirty-day recitation (*navāh pārāyaṇ* and *mās pārāyaṇ*) and in-

21. On the early history of printing in north India, see McGregor 1974:70–74.

22. The figure is based on my (still incomplete) file of early editions, drawn from the catalogues of the British Museum and the India Office Library, M. Gupta (1945), Narayan (1971), S. Chaube (1976), and several private collections.

cluded directions for accompanying rituals as well as descriptions of the spiritual and material benefits to be expected therefrom. Daily *Mānas* recitation became part of the household ritual of countless pious families, and one result was an audience that was both more knowledgeable with respect to the text and more discriminating with respect to oral exposition. The resolution of "doubts" (*shankā*s) concerning *Mānas* passages became an important duty of expounders, some of whom published *shankāvalī*s (collections of common textual problems with their "solutions");[23] these were among the tools utilized in the training of aspiring *rāmāyaṇī*s.

Two related developments also need mention here. The first, of special relevance to the Banaras region, was the rise of the Hindi language movement during the late nineteenth and the early twentieth century (see chapter 6). Although most advocates of Hindi and of Devanagari script favored the use of the Kharī Bolī dialect for prose purposes, the increasing association of Hindi with Hindu communal identity led to renewed interest in bhakti poetry among the university-educated elite, and to the founding of the Nāgari Prachāriṇī Sabhā in 1893, an organization for the promotion of Hindi, which soon undertook the preparation of a "critical edition" of the *Mānas* (Dvivedi 1903).

The second and contemporaneous development was the rise of what came to be known as the Sanātan Dharm movement—the self-identification of mainstream, socially conservative Hindus as adherents of an "eternal religion." During the second half of the nineteenth century, popular Hindu beliefs and practices came under increasing criticism both from Christian missionaries and from reform movements like the Arya Samāj and the Brahmo Samāj. There was a strong element of reaction in the Sanātanī stance, and a tendency for self-definition in largely negative terms: that is, those who were *not* Aryas or Brahmos, Christians or Westernizers, who did *not* advocate widow remarriage, initiation of untouchables, abandonment of image-worship, and so forth.[24] But one of the more positive identifications to which traditionalists could point was faith in the *Mānas,* the most accessible of scriptures and mainstream text par excellence—a bhakti work that still preached reverence for cows and Brahmins, claimed to be in accord with a comfortably undefined "Veda," offered a satisfying synthesis of Vaishnavism and Shaivism, and in the minds of many devotees, stood at one and the same time for fervent devotional egalitarianism, the

23. An early manuscript example is *Mānas shankāvalī* of Vandan Pathak (mid-19th cent.); printed examples include J. B. Singh (1918), Din (1942), and Ramkumar Das (n.d., 1950s).

24. On the antagonism between Aryas and Sanātanīs in Punjab, see Jones 1976: 108–12.

maintenance of the social status quo, and even a kind of nationalism in that it countered the British colonial ethos with an idealized vision of a powerful and harmonious Hindu state.[25] Sanātanī leaders, whose rhetoric was increasingly colored both by anti-British and by anti-Muslim sentiments, came to view the Hindi epic as an inspired response to a Dark Age particularly characterized by "foreign" domination of India.

Undoubtedly the most prominent Sanātanī spokesman in the early twentieth century was the Allahabad Brahmin Madanmohan Malaviya, who led the campaign for the establishment of a Hindu University in Banaras (Bayly 1975:215–17). A tireless advocate of cow protection and Devanagiri script, Malaviya also issued a call for *Mānas prachār*—the promulgation of Tulsi's epic:

> Blessed are they who read or listen to Gosvami Tulsidas-ji's *Mānas-Rāmāyaṇ*. . . . But even more blessed are those people who print beautiful and inexpensive editions of the *Mānas* and place them in the hands of the very poorest people, thus doing them priceless service. . . . At present *Mānas-kathā* is going on in many towns and villages. But wherever it is not, it should begin, and its holy teachings should be ever more widely promulgated. (Poddar 1938a:52).

One milestone for the Sanātanī movement in the 1920s was the founding of the Gita Press of Gorakhpur, publisher of the influential monthly *Kalyāṇ* (Auspiciousness). The Press answered Malaviya's call by churning out low-priced *Mānas* editions of every size and description,[26] sponsored contests to test children's knowledge of *Mānas* verses, encouraged mass recitation programs, and frequently published written exegesis by eminent *rāmāyaṇīs* like Jayramdas "Din" and Vijayanand Tripathi.

Tripathi deserves special mention, for he was the leading *Mānas* expounder in Banaras during the mid-twentieth century. The son of a wealthy landlord, he had no need to seek outside patronage for his *kathā*, and performed daily on the broad stone terrace of his house in the Bhadaini neighborhood, not far from Tulsidas's own house at Assi Ghat. His enthusiastic listeners are said to have included both Malaviya and Bankeram Mishra, the *mahant* (hereditary proprietor) of the powerful Sankaṭ Mochan Temple. Tripathi was much influenced by the conservative *Dasnāmī* ascetic Swami Karpatri, whose monthly magazine

25. Cf. Norvin Hein's observation that "[*Rāmrāj*] was one of the few vital indigenous political ideas remaining in the vastly unpolitical mind of the old-time Indian peasant" (Hein 1972:100). On the role of the Sanātan Dharm in fostering festivals, as well as the politicization of Rāmlīlā early in this century, see Freitag 1989.

26. Their popularity may be gauged from the fact that the *guṭkā* ("pocket edition") had gone through seventy-two printings as of 1983.

Fig. 3. The late Narayankant Tripathi, a venerable *Rāmcharitmānas* expounder, who performed daily at the Sankaṭ Mochan Temple in Banaras (July 1983). Photograph by Philip Lutgendorf.

Sanmārg (The True Path) he edited from 1936 to 1942, and his admirers liked to emphasize that his *Mānas* interpretations were strictly in accord with vedic and shastraic precept and with the *varṇāshram* system of social hierarchy. His three-volume *Vijayā ṭīkā* on the epic was underwritten by Seth Lakshminarayan Poddar, a wealthy merchant, and published by Motilal Banarsidass in 1955. Tripathi died soon afterward, but his influence continues to be felt through his many disciples, several of whom are presently among the leading *Mānas* expounders in the city.[27]

CHANGING STYLES OF PERFORMANCE

Even from the limited data available it is possible to make certain generalizations about the style and technique of *Mānas* exposition during the eighteenth and nineteenth centuries. The predominant mode of performance during this period was the sequential narration in daily

27. Among his pupils were Sant Chhotelal (d. 1983), Ramji Pandey (chief *rāmāyanī* of the Ramnagar Rāmlīlā), Baba Narayankant and Ramnarayan Shukla (resident expounders of the Sankaṭ Mochan Temple [see figs. 3 and 4]), and Shrinath Mishra.

installments of part or all of the *Mānas.* The special time for such *kathā* was late afternoon, from about 4:00 P.M. until the time of *sandhyā-pūjā* at twilight. The venue of the performance was usually a public place, such as a temple courtyard, a ghat, or the open veranda of a prosperous home. The speaker, who was usually called a *kathāvāchak* or *rāmāyaṇī,* recited from a manuscript or a printed text, though of course his performance was not strictly confined to the words before him; he could elaborate upon or digress from any line of the text, and the extent and ingenuity of his improvisation was limited only by his knowledge and training. That even early-nineteenth-century performances could feature very extended exposition of single lines is suggested by the story of Ramgulam's twenty-two-day tour de force; however, systematic exposition of a single *prasang* (episode), *kāṇḍ* (canto), or when possible, of the complete epic seems to have been the more usual practice.

Many expounders had their own characteristic interpretive approaches for which they were famous. Baijnath Kurmi (c. 1833–1885), a literary connoisseur and a *rasik bhakta* (a practitioner of the mystico-erotic path of devotion to Sita-Ram),[28] utilized the terminology of Sanskrit poetic and aesthetic theory, while the Kāyasth expounder Sant Unmani (c. 1830–1898), author of the commentary *Mānas tattva vivaraṇ* (Explanation of the Essence of the *Mānas*), interpreted the epic from the standpoint of yoga doctrine, and his *kathā* is said to have had special appeal for practitioners of hatha yoga (Sharan 1938:913, 918).

The economic rewards for such *nitya,* or "continuous" *kathā,* were generally modest. An expounder would usually be engaged by a patron—a landlord or the *mahant* of a temple—who provided nominal support in the form of meals and accommodation and became the official *shrotā,* or "listener," and beneficiary of the *kathā,* though the performances would also be open to the general public. In addition to the patron's support, the performer received the offerings in cash and kind which audience members made during the ceremonial worship at the close of each day's program. Performers were often hired on a long-term basis—for example, for an exposition of the complete epic, which might require two or more years. The ultimate completion of such an extended performance would be the occasion for a special celebration sponsored by the principal patron, who would then bestow a generous gift on the *kathāvāchak.* However, many illustrious performers are said to have had little interest in financial gain, and when, as sometimes happened, wealthy patrons rewarded their performances with

28. The only major study of this neglected tradition is B. P. Singh (1957).

lavish gifts, they chose to offer the money for pious purposes such as the feeding of sadhus.[29]

Daily *kathā* tended to focus closely on the narrative, and the performer might even choose to confine himself, in the *pramāṇs*, or "proofs," he cited for his interpretations, entirely to the *Mānas* itself, or to the other eleven works of Tulsidas, which acquired a kind of canonical status for the tradition. A common technique was to discuss each significant word in a verse in terms of its usage elsewhere in the epic. A gifted practitioner of this approach would delight his listeners by quoting line after line in which a given word was used, showing the different shades of meaning Tulsidas gave it in various contexts, and creating a sort of "oral concordance."[30] The appeal of such exegesis for an audience that knew the *Mānas* intimately and accepted it as the highest religious authority is suggested by the following comments made by a contemporary *kathā*-goer at Sankaṭ Mochan Temple, where sequential exposition of the epic is still presented each afternoon:

> When a man comes to hear *kathā* on the *Mānas,* he wants all the *pramāṇs* to be from that, because that is what he knows. What is the use for him if the *kathāvāchak* shows off his knowledge by quoting from here and there? It will only confuse him. In the old days they used to use the *Mānas* only, with maybe the *Vinay patrikā*—enough! Now they like to quote this and that, Vedas and shastras.[31]

The erudite quoting of "this and that," especially of authoritative Sanskrit texts, was a technique particularly associated with Ramkumar Mishra (c. 1850–1920), the leading expounder in Banaras at the beginning of this century, and it seems to have reflected a conscious concern among performers and audiences to demonstrate that the teachings of the *Mānas* were in accord with—approving of and "proven" by—the Sanskritic "great tradition." A pupil of the Kayasth expounder Chhakkan Lal and a favorite of Maharaja Prabhu Narayan Singh (1889–1931), Ramkumar has been credited with developing "the brilliant and fascinating (modern) style of *kathā* performance" (Jhingaran 1976:20). So great was his fame and so pressing the demand to hear him that Ramkumar began to travel about and give *kathā* in various places, staying only a short time in each. An annual performance series

29. Ramkumar Mishra is said to have summed up his attitude with the formula "Wear coarse cloth, eat coarse food; you are entitled to only enough [of the offering] to keep this body alive" (Sharan 1938:926–27).

30. On the use of a similar technique in Christian monastic discourse, see LeClercq 1961:79–83.

31. S. Singh, interview, Feb. 10, 1984.

Fig. 4. Pandit Ramnarayan Shukla expounding the *Rāmcharitmānas* during the *kathā* festival at Gyān Vāpī (November 1982). Photograph by Philip Lutgendorf.

in Banaras became a celebrated event, attracting crowds so great that the organizers were forced to make arrangements whereby people could reserve space in advance, to ensure getting a place to sit. A two-month exposition of the whole of *Sundar kāṇḍ* (the fifth canto of the *Mānas*) in the courtyard of Ayodhya's largest temple was said to have been such a success that other expounders in the city—a traditional center for daily *kathā*—found themselves without audiences for the duration (Sharan 1938:926–27).

In time regular "circuits" developed, frequented by other traveling expounders, who likewise began to give shorter programs. This in turn affected the economic aspects of the art; since performers were no longer maintained by an individual patron or community on a long-term basis, they began to accept set fees for their performances. The patrons of this kind of *kathā* were drawn less from the landed aristocracy than from urban commercial classes; indeed, one observer has termed the new style "Baniya (mercantile) *kathā*."[32] The underlying causes of this shift in patronage were the economic and political developments of the latter half of the nineteenth century, which precipitated the decline of the rajas and zamindars and the rise of urban mercantile communities such as the Marwaris.[33] Like the petty Rajputs and Bhumihars of the preceding century, the "new men" of the urban corporations found themselves in possession of wealth but in need of status, a dilemma which they resolved, in part, through conspicuous patronage of religious traditions.

Under mercantile patronage, *kathā* performances began to be held later in the evening—after 9:00 P.M., when the bazaars and wholesale markets closed. The leisurely and informal daily *kathā* of the late afternoon, in which the performer was assured of a regular audience and a steady if modest income, was replaced by a more elaborate form of performance, held on a few consecutive nights before large crowds, requiring more complicated arrangements such as *maṇḍap*s and lights, and at which the performer's talent might be rewarded with a considerable sum of money. Since the expounder—who was increasingly honored with the exalted title *vyās*—typically had only a single hour in which to display his talents, he abandoned systematic narration in favor of extended improvisation on very small segments of the text. The chosen excerpt became the basis for a dazzling display of rhetoric and erudition, backed up by citations of numerous Sanskrit works—a practice sure to win approval from the new class of connoisseurs. Such presentations, for which the performer typically prepared extensive notes in

32. C. N. Singh, interview, July 19, 1983.

33. On the economic changes of the period, see Bayly 1983:269–99; on the rise of a commercial community, see Timberg 1978.

advance, began to resemble academic lectures or speeches, although, like narrative *kathā,* they were still delivered extempore and were liberally interspersed with verses from the epic, which were usually sung or chanted. Storytelling survived largely in the form of anecdotes, and the term *pravachan*—"eloquent speech"—became the preferred label for such performances, rather than the more "story"-oriented term, *kathā.*

A subsequent and related development was the *sammelan,* or "festival": a large-scale, usually urban performance, which gave audiences the opportunity to hear, in one location, a selection of the most renowned *Mānas* interpreters of the day. The first such festival in Banaras was the Sarvabhauma *Rāmāyaṇ* Sammelan (universal *Rāmāyaṇ* festival) organized in the mid-1920s under the auspices of the Sankaṭ Mochan Temple, a shrine to Hanuman reputedly established by Tulsidas himself but which in fact rose to prominence only in this century. Additional financial backing came from Munnilal Agraval, a prominent Marwari businessman.[34] The festival began on the evening following the full moon of Chaitra (the traditional birthday of Hanuman) and continued for three nights, with a series of *vyās*es featured at each program. In addition to Banarsi expounders, well-known out-of-town performers were invited, their travel and lodging expenses were met, and they were given a cash *dakshiṇā*—the term applied to a gift to a Brahmin preceptor. The Sankaṭ Mochan festival became an annual event, and its prestige made it an important platform for aspiring *vyās*es. To be invited to perform there and to make a favorable impression on the discriminating Banaras audience could represent a major breakthrough into a successful performance career, and some performers today still fondly recall their "debuts" there.

The same combination of Sanātanī leadership and mercantile financing that supported this festival was to lead in time to the mounting of even more elaborate programs, the prototype of which was the Shrī Rāmcharitmānas Navāhna Pārāyaṇ Mahāyajña (Great Sacrifice of The Nine-Day Recitation of Shrī *Rāmcharitmānas*) organized in the mid-1950s at Gyān Vāpī, in the heart of the city.[35] The instigation for this festival came from Swami Karpatri, who had become a celebrated figure because of his vociferous denunciation of the "secular" policies of the Congress government and his founding of a political party that promised to bring back "the rule of Ram" (Weiner 1957:170–74). Financial backing came from the Mārwāṛī Sevā Sangh, a charitable trust organized by prosperous and socially conservative merchants.

34. Nita Kumar, writing on Rāmlīlā patronage, has discussed the typical collaboration of merchants and religious leaders in organizing such events (1984:274).

35. "Well of wisdom"; the site marks the location of a temple destroyed by Aurangzeb in 1669; see Eck 1982:127.

Fig. 5. One hundred and eight Brahmins chant the *Rāmcharitmānas* during an annual, nine-day festival held at Gyān Vāpī (November 1982). Photograph by Philip Lutgendorf.

The special innovation of this annual festival was that it was organized around a nine-day ritualized recitation of the entire *Mānas*, conducted on the model of a vedic *mahāyajña* ("great sacrifice"). An auspicious hundred-and-eight Brahmins, identically clad in ochre robes, sat in long rows in a huge *maṇḍap*, surrounded by a circumambulatory track, and mechanically chanted the *Mānas* for five hours each morning (see fig. 5), their voices echoing throughout much of downtown Banaras over a network of some three hundred loudspeakers. Other features included a diorama of opulently costumed clay images of *Mānas* characters, special performances to commemorate important events such as Rām's wedding and enthronement, and a climactic procession to the city's main ghat to immerse the images.[36] The public responded warmly, and merchant families vied with one another to engage in the meritorious activity of offering refreshments and gifts to the Brahmins—each donor's name being trumpeted over the public-address sys-

36. The use of *pratimās* (clay images) probably reflects the influence of Durga Puja observances, which have proliferated in Banaras during the past half century; see N. Kumar 1984:322.

tem.[37] As in a vedic *yajña,* the "breaks" in the sacrifice (in this case, the evenings from 7:00 P.M. on) were devoted to storytelling, that is, *kathā.* Lesser-known or aspiring *vyās*es were invited to speak during the early part of the evening when the crowd was still assembling, to be followed later each night by three featured performers. In certain respects, the Gyān Vāpī festival and its many spinoffs (by 1983 more than a dozen such annual programs were being held in Banaras) have come to resemble classical concerts or Urdu *mushairas* (poetry recitation festivals). As at these performances, a strict protocol is observed, with the most highly respected performers invariably appearing last, and prominent connoisseurs often not arriving until just before the most famous *vyās* takes his place on the dais. Dress is traditional and often opulent, the atmosphere is formal, and there is frequently an element of tension and competition among performers, especially younger ones who are still establishing their reputations. In 1982 and 1983, the Gyān Vāpī and Sankaṭ Mochan festivals each paid on the order of Rs. 250 per evening to featured performers, apart from travel and lodging expenses. This is a comparatively modest *dakshiṇā* for a successful *vyās,* but these festivals compensate by the prestige and exposure they offer, and so performers are willing to accept lower fees than they might command elsewhere.

One controversial development of recent years has been the advent of women performers, a number of whom have gained considerable renown (Upadhyay 1984:16–17). Several *kathāvāchikās* were trained by the Banarsi expounder Sant Chhote-ji (himself a pupil of Vijayanand Tripathi) and have begun to make careers for themselves despite the continuing opposition of some conservative males who argue that women lack the *adhikār* (spiritual "authority") to expound the epic. Women have probably always made up an important component of the *kathā* audience, and a recent article in a popular Hindi magazine notes:

> The ironic thing is . . . that there will often be a preponderance of women among the listeners. So those who are opposed [to women expounders] are clearly saying, "Yes, of course you can listen to *kathā,* you can recite the *Mānas* too; but you can never sit on the dais and give *kathā*!" (Jhingaran 1976:23)

Another trend, which has developed largely since the 1960s, is the increasing vogue among wealthy patrons for private performances, often in the patrons' homes or business institutions. The sponsors of this

37. So lucrative has the program become that there is intense competition for the 108 places. I was told that a reciter could expect to take home upwards of Rs. 400 in cash, plus gifts of food, cloth, and even stainless steel utensils; S. Pandey, interview, Feb. 23, 1984.

new form of "aristocratic" patronage include, appropriately enough, many of the "princes" of Indian industry, most notably the Birla family of Marwari industrialists, who manufacture everything from fabrics to heavy machinery and have also been conspicuous in the construction and endowment of temples and dharmshalas. The Banarsi expounder Ramkinkar Upadhyay, who is widely acclaimed as the greatest contemporary *vyās,* has enjoyed Birla patronage for roughly two decades, and each spring at the time of Rām Navamī (the festival of Rām's birth), he performs for nine evenings in the huge garden of "Birla Temple" ("Lakshmi-Narayan Temple"), a marble-and-masonry colossus about a kilometer west of Connaught Place, the commercial heart of New Delhi. The prosperous looking crowd includes thousands of office workers, many of whom bring cassette recorders to tape the discourse. Just before he takes his seat on an elaborate canopied dais that resembles one of the aerial chariots seen in religious art, Ramkinkar is garlanded by the patron and official *shrotā* of the performance, the head of the Birla family and chief executive of its vast corporate empire, who is dressed for the occasion in the dhoti and *kurtā* of a pious householder.[38]

Such munificent patronage has considerably upped the financial ante in the world of *kathā,* giving rise to the oft-heard complaints that contemporary performers "sell" their art, or that they have "turned it into a business" (Jhingaran 1976:21). But while there is a tendency among aficionados to idealize the great performers of the past for their alleged noncovetousness, many expounders readily concede that *kathā* is indeed a profession and speak willingly and even proudly of the fees they are able to command. An ordinary *vyās*—a local expounder who rarely or never receives invitations from "outside" (an important criterion of success in Banaras performance circles)—may receive as little as Rs. 11 or Rs. 21 for an hour's program, but not more than Rs. 100. Some daily *kathāvāchak*s still perform on a monthly stipend of only a few hundred rupees, supplemented by listeners' offerings.[39] The middle range of performers consists of those who receive Rs. 100–300 for a performance; a considerable number of well-known *vyās*es fall into this category, and if they perform regularly, as many of them do, their incomes may be substantial. However, the hourly fees of the highest

38. In 1983 the chief patron was Basant Kumar Birla, son of Ghanshyam Das Birla. His wife, Sarla, heads the Birla Academy of Art and Culture, which sponsors Ramkinkar's performances in Delhi and Calcutta and also publishes more than a dozen volumes of transcriptions of his *kathās*.

39. An example is the young *vyās* who performs each evening under the auspices of the Chīnī Kshetra Trust in a lane near Dashāshvamedh Ghat. He receives a monthly stipend of Rs. 150; V. Tripathi, interview, July 20, 1983.

ranking or "All-India" expounders (so called because of their frequent invitations to perform in such distant cities as Bombay and Calcutta) are considerably higher. Shrinath Mishra of Banaras, the principal pupil of Vijayanand Tripathi, has a normal minimum fee of Rs. 500 per hour, and often receives upwards of Rs. 1,000.[40] Ramkinkar Upadhyay is said to receive in the range of Rs. 1,500–3,000 for each talk. Given such financial incentives, the reported proliferation of performers in recent years seems understandable.[41]

One of the most significant effects of the new style of entrepreneurial backing of *Mānas kathā* has been to shift the geographical center of the art away from smaller centers like Banaras, where the springs of courtly patronage have long been dry, to such urban industrial centers as Bombay, Delhi, Kanpur, and Calcutta, where the wealthiest patrons now reside. This trend is lamented by some Banarsi aficionados, for while the city remains a major center for *kathā* and a training ground of performers, the most renowned exponents of the Banaras-based "Tulsi lineage" (the *paramparā,* or "tradition," which traces itself back, through Vijayanand Tripathi and Ramkumar Mishra, to Ramgulam Dvivedi and ultimately to Tulsidas himself)[42] can rarely be heard in the city these days, and indeed seldom appear even at public *sammelan*s, as most of their busy schedules are taken up with performances in the homes and institutions of their wealthy patrons. Expert *vyās*es, like virtuosi of music and dance, tend to go where they are best rewarded, and when they leave, their art departs with them. This fact serves to underscore the observation that *Mānas kathā* is much more than impersonal "commentary" upon a written text: it is an individual performance art that unfolds within a specific milieu.

CONCLUSION

The art of *Mānas* exposition is rooted in ancient Hindu traditions of oral mediation of sacred text, but it has undergone significant change during the past two centuries and is continuing to develop and change today. It is an extensive and multiform tradition, and much that has been said about it here has necessarily been in the nature of generalization, to which, in many cases, exceptions might be cited. If I have spoken of elite patronage of *kathā,* I could point out that there are still *vyās*es who neither solicit nor desire lavish fees and who narrate the

40. Shrinath Mishra, interview, Feb. 21, 1984.

41. Jhingaran wryly remarks: "How many *vyās*es are there in Kashi nowadays? Even if one were to have a census taken by Hanuman, that energetic seeker who found the herb of immortality, perhaps for once even he would fail in his efforts!" (1976:20).

42. A diagram of this *paramparā* is given by Sharan (1938:910).

epic in the humblest of settings. I have emphasized the stimulating effect of royal patronage, yet there were expounders even in the eighteenth century who, it is said, gave no importance to kings, because they recognized only one monarch: Ramchandra of Ayodhya.

Now I must hazard one more generalization and invoke the oft-used concept of "Sanskritization"—the acquisition or confirmation of status through an appeal to established standards of orthodoxy—which I suggest has been a process central to the evolution of the *Mānas* tradition. When Tulsidas boldly undertook the fashioning of a religious epic in the language of ordinary people, he presented himself as only a fourth-hand transmitter of a divine *kathā* first uttered by Shiva to Parvati, and he was careful to point out its fundamental consistency with authoritative Sanskrit scriptures.[43] An epic which, in the charming hagiographic allegory of its attempted "suppression" by the Brahmins of Banaras at the bottom of a pile of sacred texts, irresistibly "rose up" from folk popularity to command elite recognition,[44] the *Mānas* became, by the eighteenth century, the text of choice for the upwardly mobile and nouveau arrivé: the vehicle of legitimation for an upstart dynasty of Bhumihar tax collectors, the solace of rising mercantile communities, and the refuge of captains of industry seeking religious merit and good public relations. On a more modest scale, it continues to serve smaller institutions in similar fashion: thus the "All-India" *Mānas* Sammelans mounted by tiny neighborhood temples bidding for a wider clientele—oddly enough, even goddess shrines (where one might expect some more appropriate text, such as the *Devī bhāgavatam*), because "the *Mānas* is sure to bring in a crowd!"[45]

Even with the exodus of some of its most illustrious performers, *kathā* remains a flourishing business in Banaras, and despite the predictable nostalgia for the past ("Back in those days you heard the *real kathā*!"), successful contemporary performers concede that their status and fees have never been higher. People still flock to *kathā* festivals, and middle-class devotees now exchange Ramkinkar cassettes with the same enthusiasm with which they trade film videos. Yet there is another dimension to "Sanskritization," which could affect the future of the tradition: the tendency of a new elite to reinterpret a popular tradition and attempt to make it, narrowly, its own. The example of the Rāmānandī sadhus may be pertinent: for several centuries they were one of the most liberal religious orders in India, accepting women, untouchables, and Muslims into their fold; but when, in the early eighteenth century,

43. See, for example, the final *shloka* of the invocation to *Bāl Kāṇḍ*.

44. See note 9.

45. Interview with patron of *Mānas* festival at Kāmākshā Devī temple, Kamachchhā, Banaras, Jan. 24, 1983.

they became desirous of royal patronage, they had to adapt themselves to a different set of rules: restrict entry to twice-born males, apply caste-based commensality practices to communal meals, and appoint only Brahmins as their *mahants* (Burghart 1978:133–34; Thiel-Horstmann 1985:5).

The very existence of a brilliant Hindi *Rāmāyaṇ*—however "orthoprax" in its teachings—has remained so vexatious to some pandits that there have been repeated attempts to fabricate line-by-line Sanskrit versions and put them forth as the original "divine" *Mānas,* which Tulsidas had merely translated into vulgar speech—a "Sanskritization" so literal as perhaps to seem laughable, except that it is so doggedly implacable.[46] Now that Tulsi's language has come to be significantly at variance with the dominant spoken dialect, the tendency to "Sanskritize" his text takes on new meaning, and in the *yajñas* of Swami Karpatri and his followers perhaps more than simply words are being "sacrificed." For such ceremonies, the Gita Press prints instructions (in Sanskrit!) on the correct way to go about reciting the *Mānas,* and the assembled Brahmins go through the concocted rituals with customary expertise. The chanting of an epic which in other contexts has served as a cultural link between upper and lower classes is here transformed into a specialist activity and spectator sport, and the text, now venerated as mantra, rumbles out of three hundred loudspeakers as a kind of auspicious Muzak. In such exercises, the cultural epic that won recognition as the "Fifth Veda"—the proverbial Hindu euphemism for the scripture one actually knows and loves—seems to run the risk of becoming more like one of the original four, "recited more, but enjoyed less," as one of my informants wryly remarked. The same man complained of Swami Karpatri, "He has made our *Mānas* into a *religious* book—something people chant in the morning, after a bath. But in my family we used to sing it together at bedtime, for pleasure."[47]

The present vogue for *yajñas* is paralleled by the "Brahminization" of expounders[48] and the rise of private *kathā,* and all these develop-

46. These "duplicities" are mentioned by Sharan (1938:908). I too was sometimes told that "Tulsi only copied a Sanskrit *Mānas;* there are texts to prove it!" These claims recall similar efforts to "Brahmanize" Kabir (see Keay 1931:28); such attempts to "rewrite history" (as anti-Muslim propagandist P. N. Oak frankly labels his agenda) are perhaps more influential in shaping the popular conception of the past than either Indian or Western scholars realize.

47. C. N. Singh, interview, July 19, 1983.

48. The ranks of nineteenth-century expounders included many prominent non-Brahmins, such as Chhakkan Lal and Baijnath Kurmi. In recent years, however, there have been controversies over whether a non-Brahmin has the "authority" to sit on the *vyās-pīṭh.* Judging from my sources, mercantile sponsorship has tended to favor Brahmin performers, perhaps because the patrons represent status-conscious groups.

ments may be related to another process: the withdrawal of the new college-educated elite from what it perceives as "backward" or "rustic" entertainment forms such as *Mānas* folk singing and Rāmlīlā pageants (N. Kumar 1984:289). Although the epic continues to retain religious status for this elite, its performance forms are increasingly "refined" to limit personal participation, or are physically removed from the public arena. Thus in its newest transformation, the lively art of *kathā*—which has flourished for centuries on the streets and squares of Banaras and has offered at times a platform for social and political commentary[49]—seems to be becoming a sort of pious chamber music of the nouveau riche. But while this development may have significance for the future, it cannot obscure the present vitality and popularity of public *kathā*, which continues to draw enthusiastic audiences and to remain a highly visible and (thanks to amplification) audible part of everyday life in Banaras.

49. The political activities of *kathāvāchaks* have been noted by Bayly (1975:105) and by Pandey (1982:147–48, 168–69).

TWO

The Birth of Hindi Drama in Banaras, 1868–1885

Kathryn Hansen

The construction of the modern literary history of India has been informed by an elitism comparable to that identified by the Subaltern school of historians in regard to Indian nationalism. Like nationalism, modern Indian literature, particularly in its origins, has been conceived as "the sum of the activities and ideas by which the Indian elite responded to the institutions, opportunities, resources, etc. generated by colonialism" (Guha 1982:2). The birth of Hindi drama in nineteenth-century Banaras affords a compelling example. In the received view, modern drama originated with Bharatendu Harishchandra, "father" of modern Hindi literature, in response to the introduction of European models and the rediscovery of a Sanskrit dramatic tradition (itself a "response" to the activities of foreign Indologists). The preexisting theatre traditions of the region are seen to have had no bearing on the nature of this event, and they have been excised from literary history.

Writing on the development of modern Hindi literature, Shrikrishna Lal declared an "absence of Hindi dramas" before Bharatendu (Lal 1965:181). Following Somnath Gupta, and before him the influential critics Shyam Sundar Das and Ramchandra Shukla, he posited reasons for this assumed absence, ranging from Muslim rulers' opposition to the dominance of bhakti poetry. Folk theatre forms, while acknowledged at least by Lal and Gupta, were not seen to have contributed to the growth of drama, being inherently "undramatic" (*anāṭakīya*). Extant Braj Bhasha dramas from the eighteenth century and earlier were regarded as poems only. These discussions make clear

This chapter is based partially on research supported by grants from the Shastri Indo-Canadian Institute (1982), the Social Science Research Council (U.S.A.) (1984–85), and the Social Sciences and Humanities Research Council of Canada (1984–87). The generosity of all these agencies is gratefully acknowledged.

the wide acceptance of certain criteria of drama. A genuine dramatic text should be divided into acts and scenes, use different speech levels, and indicate entrances and exits (rules of Sanskrit drama); it should describe scenery and scene changes, develop complex characters, and build to climax (conventions of European stage); and it should not be predominantly poetic or musical or contain a self-referring narrator (as in Indian folk drama). These rules, as will become clear, were formalized by Bharatendu Harishchandra himself and were inherited together with Bharatendu's published canon of dramatic works, thus securing the "absence" of pre-Bharatendu drama and transforming it into a "problem." In the process, the popular theatre of the time was denied, lost to the pages of literary history, to the point where it is common to read, "Before Bharatendu, Hindi drama had no tradition of its own" (B. Shukla 1972:150).

My purpose in this chapter is twofold. If the value of studying popular culture, as Carlo Ginzburg suggests, lies in removing some of the silence imposed upon the nonelite groups by history, then, first, I would hope to give voice to the thriving, vital presence of popular theatre in Banaras at the time of Bharatendu's "invention" of modern drama.[1] I have used the evidence of recently discovered play texts published in Banaras, together with historical accounts of travelers, administrators, and local informants, supplemented by my own fieldwork on present-day folk theatre, to document the popular secular theatre traditions of Banaras in about 1880. Second, I would propose that Bharatendu's drama constituted an articulated, intentioned rejection of these popular traditions. The confrontation between Bharatendu's concept of a new elite theatre and the indigenous theatre is expressed in his theoretical writings on drama, and these, together with secondary biographical and historical data, constitute the sources for the second part of the chapter.

POPULAR THEATRE IN LATE-NINETEENTH-CENTURY BANARAS

Theatre was an important component of popular culture in nineteenth-century Banaras. Sacred spectacles like the annual Rāmlīlā native to Banaras or the seasonal Rāslīlās of the *rāsdhārī*s from Vrindavan were interwoven into the fabric of public religious life. The secular varieties of entertainment were probably just as numerous. These ranged in complexity from the street shows of solo disguise artists (*bahurūpiyā*s), acrobats, and animal trainers, to the elaborately staged musicals of the Parsi theatrical companies. Most of the forms found in

1. On the "silence" of the subordinate classes in history, see Ginzburg's valuable preface to *The Cheese and the Worms,* especially xvii–xxii.

Banaras were common to the region extending from the Punjab to Bihar. A shared system of cultural codes and symbols, including the lingua franca Hindustani, its specific meters and song genres, a common body of folktales, and a single musical system, enabled the actors, musicians, and dancers to communicate easily throughout this region. The personnel associated with popular entertainment were primarily professionals who led an itinerant existence, touring within a geographical range that varied with their fame and access to patronage.

While certain unifying characteristics existed within this multiplicity of forms, I focus the present discussion on two varieties of theatre that can be definitively documented in late-nineteenth-century Banaras. The first is the folk theatre tradition known in this period as Svāng or Sāng (lit., "mime"). Svāng is a musical form of theatre (often described as "operatic"), featuring full-throated male singers, loud, arousing drumming on the *naggāṛā* (kettledrums), and dancing by female impersonators. The tradition seems to have originated in the Punjab in the early nineteenth century, developing from recitations of ballads and oral epics. It then spread to Delhi, Meerut, and Banaras, where fledgling Devanagari printing presses reproduced its handwritten, illustrated librettos, known as Sāngīts, from the 1860s on.

In about 1890 the Svāng tradition was developed by certain folk poets of Hathras, who introduced a greater variety of themes, meters, and musical features into the plays. Further changes took place in Kanpur under the influence of the Parsi theatre, so that two distinctive styles (*hāthrasī* and *kānpurī*) are now recognized. At some time in the early twentieth century, Svāng came to be known as Nauṭankī, after a fairy-tale princess, Nauṭankī Shāhzādī; her story was a favorite in the theatre. In a state of decline since the 1940s, Nauṭankī shows are still found occasionally in the countryside as well as in the poorer neighborhoods of the cities, although its stories and tunes now imitate Bombay films rather than old ballads.[2]

Specifics of the nineteenth-century Svāng tradition can be ascertained in part by examining the Sāngīts in the India Office Library and the British Museum in London (Blumhardt 1893, 1902). Unlike much folklore, consigned to the oblivion of oral tradition, Svāng dialogues were copied down, probably for the actors' convenience, and circulated in manuscript form.[3] Beginning in 1860 or earlier, these handwritten manuscripts were lithographically printed, and typeset versions appeared in the 1890s. Sāngīts in pamphlet form can still be purchased from publishers' warehouses or on the street. The quantity of pub-

2. For a brief history of Svāng and Nauṭankī, see Hansen 1986.

3. Robson mentions obtaining the manuscripts of Khyāls owned by Maharajas in Rajputana, and Temple also consulted the texts in the possession of Svāng actors.

lished Sāngīts is very large. Dozens of local presses are engaged in the trade, and during the last century, four hundred titles or more have appeared.[4]

Eight Svāng plays (Sāngīts) published in Banaras between 1868 and 1885 are preserved in the British Museum. All except one are named for their heroes. Five of them concern famous devotees (*Prahlād, Gopīchand Bhartarī, Rājā Harichandra,* and two versions of *Dhurūjī*), while one is a fragment concerning a king reclaiming his throne (*Raghuvīr Singh*), and two are romances (*Rājā Kārak* and *Rānī Nauṭankī*). Four were published in Banaras (Kashi) by Munshi Ambe Prasad, three by Munshi Shadi Lal, and one by Lala Ghasiram, and the dates of publication range from 1875 to 1883. Except for the 1875 *Dhurū Līlā* and *Sāngīt Rānī Nauṭankī kā,* all of the texts had been published previously, in Delhi, Meerut, Agra, or Lucknow.[5]

Two of these Sāngīts, *Gopīchand Bhartarī* and *Prahlād,* had a long publishing history, with at least twenty-seven editions of *Gopīchand* appearing between 1866 and 1893, and sixteen of *Prahlād.* The Sāngīt version of *Gopīchand* even came to the attention of linguist George A. Grierson. "There is no legend more popular throughout the whole of Northern India," he wrote, "than those [*sic*] of Bharthari and his nephew Gopi Chand. . . . A Hindi version of the legend can be bought for a few pice in any up-country bazar" (Grierson 1885:35).

In five out of eight of these plays, the name and particulars of the author are mentioned within the text. The famous *Prahlād* and *Gopīchand* plays were both written by Lakshman Singh, alternatively styled Lachhman Das, but little is known of him. The author of *Raghuvīr Singh* was Hardev Sahay; he also wrote *Sāngīt Siyā Svayamvarā kā* and coauthored *Sāngīt Rūp Basant* with Lakshman Singh. In the text he describes himself as a Brahmin (*vipra*) and a pandit, and he appears to be the same Hardev Sahay who ran the Jnan Sagar Press in Meerut. Khushi Ram, the author of *Rānī Nauṭankī,* describes himself as a Brahmin from Faraknagar in Gurgaon district. Jiya Lal, the author of *Rājā Harichandra* as well as of *Rājā Mordhvaj,* provides the fullest self-introduction:

> I am head of the guards, a Jain scribe by caste.
> In the world my name, Jiya Lal, is famous.
> My name Jiya Lal is famous, my hometown is Faraknagar.
> In Chaproli I received this story already made.
>
> (Jiya Lal 1877:51)

4. For figures and statistics on the volume of popular publishing in Sāngīts and other genres, see Pritchett 1985:20–36, 179–90.

5. A list of Banaras Sāngīts published between 1868 and 1885 appears at the end of this chapter.

Internal evidence helps us to assign the texts to a single genre. All except one contain the word Sāngīt in the title, while the terms *sāng, svāng, sāngīt,* or *sāngīt bhāshā* ("musical play in the vernacular") are also present in many of the invocations and colophons. Two of the plays refer to themselves as *līlā,* and each of these, significantly, is focused on a saintly personage, in these cases Dhuru and Gopichand. Such dramas may have developed in imitation of the *līlā*s of Krishna and Rām, pointing to an earlier stage when Svāng was indistinguishable from popular religious theatre. However, these saint legends were more likely connected with oral recitations by ascetics and mendicant groups. The Gopichand story, which concerns the conversion of a king to the path of Guru Gorakhnath, was one of the legends popularized by the Kanphata or Nath Yogis, who wandered all over north India. Other legends associated with this sect are Guga (Zahir Pir), Puran Bhagat, Raja Rasalu, Hir-Ranjha, and Rani Pingla (Briggs 1938:183–241). It is noteworthy that Svāng versions of all these Nath stories exist in the old Sāngīt collections.[6]

The Banaras Sāngīts can be distinguished from legends, tales, and other types of dramatic texts by their poetic meters. The characteristic meters at this time are *dohā* (a couplet, line length 24 *mātrās*), *kaṛā* (a quatrain, line length 24 *mātrās*), and *chaubolā chaltā* (a quatrain, line length 28 *mātrās*). Songs in various *rāginī*s (modes or tunes) are also interspersed. These meters are specified in the text in full or abbreviated form (*do.* for *dohā, chau.* for *chaubolā*). The alternation of speakers is marked by headings, such as "reply of the queen to the king" (*javāb rānī kā rājā se*). These meters and printing conventions continue in the twentieth-century Sāngīt texts.

The connection of the Banaras Sāngīts to more recent texts is also illustrated by their subsequent publishing history. Lakshman Singh's *Gopīchand Bharthari,* for example, continued to be reprinted well into the twentieth century. A chapbook printed in modern type recently came to my attention in a Jaipur bazaar. On examination, the text turned out to be identical to the nineteenth-century version by Lakshman Singh, except for orthographic changes introduced to conform to current printing practices.

That Sāngīt texts were published in Banaras in the 1880s suggests that performing Svāng troupes had toured the area and established a

6. In further support of this point, Sherring records two groups of ascetics, Bhartharis and Harischandis, whose main occupation involves retelling the stories of the famed kings for whom they are named (Sherring 1872:261, 267). Similarly, K. Raghunathji mentions a group called Gopichandas, who "carry fiddles and sing in praise of Gopichand" (Raghunathji 1880:279). Given the prominence of Banaras as a gathering point for ascetics, we can assume that their lore became part of popular culture and was assimilated into theatre and other performance traditions.

reputation for popularity. This in turn created a demand for the texts of their plays to be circulated in print (see fig. 6). Such a process was explained in an "Announcement" on the back cover of a Sāngīt published from Kanpur in 1897:

> Let it be known to all good men that the entertainment (*tamāshā*) of the troupe from Hathras has been shown in various places in Kanpur, and many gentlemen have gathered for it and all their minds have been pleased. Seeing the desire of these good men, we have published the same entertainment . . . so that whenever they read it, they will obtain happiness and remember us. (Chiranjilal-Natharam 1897)

The publication of a play text subsequent to its performance is also confirmed by present-day practice (Pritchett 1983:47). Unfortunately, no details of Svāng performances in nineteenth-century Banaras appear to have survived. For information on the performative circumstances we must rely instead on accounts from other parts of northern India.

One source is Richard Carnac Temple, a British administrator who collected an impressive body of folklore from the Punjab in the late 1870s and early 1880s. His three-volume *Legends of the Panjab* contains texts of four Svāngs performed in Ambala district in 1881 and 1883: *Gurū Guggā, Shīlā Daī, Gopīchand,* and *Rājā Nal.* All of these were composed by a poet named Bansi Lal. In the preface to volume 3, Temple also lists a number of unpublished manuscripts in his collection, which include familiar Svāng titles like *Harichand, Amar Singh, Rājā Kārag, Dayārām Gūjar,* and *Rānī Nauṭankī.*

Temple was exposed to the Svāng tradition while attending the Holi festival at Jagadhri. He later called the actors in private and had a scribe copy down their verses as they recited. He also prevailed upon Svāng performers to give him their private manuscripts (Temple 1884, 1:ix). Temple's Svāng singers were Brahmins, of a higher status than other types of bards, and some of them were literate. They engaged in playacting as a profession (Temple notes they are "called in—on payment always"), but Temple gives no information on their backgrounds or features of their performance. His remark that the Svāng "is not strictly a play according to our ideas" seems to refer to the third-person commentary provided by the *rangāchār* (stage director) and by the characters themselves, and also to the absence of European conventions of scene divisions, curtains, and scenery (Temple 1884, 1:243). The metrical structure and other stylistic features of Temple's Svāngs link them clearly with the Sāngīts published in Delhi, Meerut, and Banaras in the same period.

Another account, from farther to the west in Rajasthan, is John Robson's *Selection of Khyals or Marwari Plays* (1866). (The term Khyāl was used in this period as a generic term for north Indian folk drama,

Fig. 6. The cover of *Sāngīt Rājā Harichandra kā,* by Jiya Lal (Banaras, 1877). Courtesy of The British Library, Oriental Manuscripts and Printed Books.

although nowadays Khyāl signifies a Rajasthani form and its language is Marwari or other Rajasthani dialects.) Robson, like Temple, describes a performance situation associated with the festival of Holi.

> In the principal cities and towns of that country, during the weeks following the Holi, crowds assemble night after night around elevated spots of ground or *chabūtras*, which supply a ready-made stage, and on which rude attempts at scenery are erected, and the players continue acting and singing accompanied by an orchestra of tom toms, on till late at night, or early in the morning, and for weeks and months afterwards, the favourite refrains and passages may be heard sung in the streets and markets. (Robson 1866:vi–vii)

Robson refers to a large body of Khyāls ("hundreds"), a history going back to 1750, and the low reputation of the form (Robson 1866:v–vi).

Descriptions of a performance of the drama *Prahlād* and the contents of a playbill of the "opera" *Pūran Bhagat* from Lahore in the late nineteenth century are contained in J. C. Oman's *Cults, Customs, and Superstitions of India. Prahlād* was sponsored by a "successful tradesman, who hoped to acquire some religious merit by having a moral drama produced for the benefit of his fellow-townsmen" (Oman 1908:195). Accounts of a number of other north Indian dramas, including *Prahlād, Hīr Rānjhā, Bīn Bādshāhzādī,* and Svāngs from the Punjab, such as *Gopīchand, Pūran Bhagat,* and *Hakīkat Rāī,* are found in William Ridgeway, *The Dramas and Dramatic Dances of Non-European Races,* which documents a slightly later period (Ridgeway 1915:181–99). The existence of Svāng *akhāṛās* in Saharanpur in 1910 is mentioned by Ramgharib Chaube in the *Indian Antiquary* (R. Chaube 1910:32). These reports do not satisfy our curiosity about the composition of Svāng troupes, the size and nature of the audience, caste of the patron, the costumes, makeup, stage appurtenances, presence of musicians and dancers, and countless other aspects of performance. However, they do establish the link between the Banaras Sāngīts and a Svāng theatre of considerable popularity, stretching from Punjab and Rajasthan to eastern U.P. in the late nineteenth century.

The manuscripts available indicate a transition from a simpler format, involving dramatic recitation of legends by two main characters, to a more complex structure involving a larger number of actors and more frequent turns of plot. Subject matter was gradually moving away from stories concerning saintly figures (*Gopīchand, Prahlād*) to romances (*Rānī Nauṭankī, Rājā Kārak*), shifting from otherworldly values to an emphasis on victory in love and war. The metrical varieties were becoming more sophisticated, suggesting a more complex musical repertoire and an evolving performing style. The later plays show more diversity of meters, and by 1892 the meter *daur̤* had joined the earlier *dohā* and *chaubolā* to form the stable ten-line stanza that constituted the metrical trademark of the genre.[7]

Assuming that the Svāng performance ethos changed little between the nineteenth and the twentieth century, we can infer its general character from more recent observation of the Svāng and Nauṭankī stage. Then as now, the performance venue was probably a public space accessible to many classes of people, such as a fairgrounds, crossroads, or market. Large crowds would gather, and social behavior reflected the spontaneity and looseness associated with impromptu open-air entertainment.[8] When private shows were commissioned, it was often in connection with a marriage or feast-day where an ebullient atmosphere prevailed. The reference in both Temple and Robson to Svāng festivals at the time of Holi, the spring bacchanalia, implies an affinity between seasonal rites of reversal and popular theatre.

In the techniques of theatrical presentation, an informality and openness characterized Svāng. Stage arrangements might include the erection of a makeshift platform where necessary or the use of an available porch or *chabūtra*. The employment of props, scenery, and stage devices was minimal, in part dictated by the itinerant lifestyle of the troupe. Plays had a loose, variable structure based on episodes, and a leisurely pace of presentation with little dramatic tension; performances lasted late into the night or until morning. During the performance the audience (and the actors) were free to eat, drink, smoke, chat, or be still (Gargi 1966:37).

Another important aspect of Svāng was its competitive, exhibitionistic impulse, a likely by-product of the *akhāṛā* system. The *akhāṛā* (lit., arena, gymnasium) was then and remains the organizational unit for many types of folk music and drama in northern India. Performers are linked by their allegiance to a guru or *ustād* to a particular *akhāṛā*, whose compositions are passed on to them; *akhāṛā* members form the primary personnel of the troupe. The various *akhāṛās* are in a perpetual state of competition with one another, which is acted out in each public appearance. The performance event is structured as a *dangal*, a

7. The text in which the meter *daur̤* first occurs is *Khyāl Pūranmal kā* (actually a Sāngīt in Khari Boli Hindi, not a Rajasthani Khyāl), published in 1892 by Ganesh Prasad Sharma in Calcutta. The play is significant because it appears to be the earliest published composition of Indarman, the guru of the first and most prominent of the Hathras *akhāṛās*, and because it is the first Sāngīt set in modern Devanagari type.

8. The ideology of "freedom" and "openness" has been discussed with reference to the artisans of Banaras by Nita Kumar (1984). A similar value system would seem to characterize the audience of nineteenth-century Svāng, many of whom (in the urban areas at least) were probably artisans of the type described by Kumar, although the audience was not limited to any one caste group.

tournament or contest between rival *akhāṛās*, with the object of outdoing the opponent and obtaining "victory."

The *akhāṛā* system entered the Svāng tradition through the institution of Turrā-Kalagī, a dialogic poetic genre traceable to eighteenth-century Maharashtra. In it, rival groups designated Turrā (representing the Shaivites) and Kalagī (Shaktas) directed questions and answers to each other on metaphysical themes, using the song type known as *lāvanī* (or *khyāl*) (Tulpule 1979:440). Later these troupes traveled northward, following the Maratha armies, and expanded their performances to include narrative material, giving rise to the folk drama forms Mānch in Madhya Pradesh, Khyāl in Rajasthan, and Svāng in U.P. (see fig. 7). By 1890, Svāng texts abound with references to the *dangal* situation. Most common is the invocation to the goddess to descend upon the poet and protect his honor by inspiring him during the poetic combat.[9] This competitive ethos resulted in a high degree of interaction between performers and audience, with an atmosphere of enthusiasm and partisanship akin to a sporting event. The *dangal* mode provided an alternative aesthetic structure to that of the Aristotelian plot, binding the performance event in a different tension.

Svāng shows, like most other public events that lacked an explicit religious function, were most likely off limits to women in the nineteenth century. Women did not participate as actresses on the Svāng/Nauṭankī stage until about 1920; before that all female roles were enacted by men. The fact that Svāng shows occurred in public space ensured that the audience would be primarily men. Women had comparatively less freedom to leave the home, because of *pardā* restrictions, and in lower-class families less leisure to do so, because of economic responsibilities. Upper-caste folk in general were admonished to avoid such entertainments; these were considered unsuitable, especially for those who were "by nature" morally weaker—for example, women and boys. Indications are that in the nineteenth century as in the twentieth, the popular stage was dominated by the "male gaze." Fulfillment of male fantasy and desire were among its main attractions, as they are in the popular cinema in India today.

This introduces perhaps the most often noted feature of Svāng, its allegedly "low," "lewd" character, which provoked exclamations of

9. In the *mangalācharaṇ* of *Khyāl Pūranmal kā* (1892), the poet invokes the goddess Bhavani:

> Come sit in my throat, goddess, and sing 3,600 ragas.
> . . . Protect the honor of your servant.
> Drink the blood of the wicked.
> Be gracious to me now,
> Uphold my respect today in the assembly.

Fig. 7. The cast of the drama *Bīn Bādshāhzādī,* a Svāng of the late nineteenth century. From William Ridgeway, *The Dramas and Dramatic Dances of Non-European Races,* 1915.

contempt from the foreign observer or high-caste Indian informant. Was the nineteenth-century Svāng indeed obscene? The Banaras Sāngīt texts, on the contrary, point to a highly moral universe, where good deeds and truthfulness are rewarded by the gods (*Rājā Harishchandra*), where kings yearn to become saints (*Gopīchand Bhartharī*), where even children are capable of exemplary devotion (*Prahlād, Dhurū*). When such instructive tales were posed in the common tongue, in an unbounded, exhibitionistic, male-oriented milieu, however, the message, at least for the elite observer, was reversed. (The allegations of obscenity were not made by the lower-caste spectators, or at least we have no record of their views.)

The opprobrium of the elite, I suggest, had less to do with the obscene gestures, the display of the female body, and the unruly crowd—all convenient pretexts—and more to do with the wider significance of the theatre in the cultural system. Parallel to festivals like Holi, Svāng provided an arena for staging symbolic inversions of the power structure of the society at large.[10] These inversions took place on stage, in the debunking of authority coded in the routines of clowns and transvestites.[11] Motives of mistaken or lost identity and disguise were very common, playing on the inversion of hierarchically ordered categories such as male-female, parent-child, master-servant. Virtually every text in our period reveals a significant element of status reversal—for example, king becomes an ascetic (*Gopīchand, Raghuvīr Singh*), king becomes an untouchable (*Harishchandra*), child becomes a preacher to adults (*Prahlād, Dhurū*). The text that set the fashion for future development in the genre, *Rānī Nauṭankī,* contains multiple incidents of cross-dressing and transformation of gender identity, both from male to female and from female to male.

Inversions were also manifest offstage, in crowd behavior expressive of loss of control and the absence of authority, ranging from noisiness, crude language, and drunkenness to actual physical violence. Such inversions were not written into the script, and they were not necessary to any given performance, but they were communicated in the larger text of the theatre: in the use of unbounded public space, in the open-ended time frame, in the competitive situation, in the absence of a controlling figure of authority, in the gathering together of spectators from all castes and classes. This was not a theatre of protest, and resistance to oppression was rarely an implicit or explicit message here.[12]

10. See Barbara Babcock's Introduction, 1978:13–36, for definition and discussion of the history and use of the concept of symbolic inversion.

11. A suggestive parallel to the clowns and transvestites of Svāng is provided by James L. Peacock in his study of these figures in Java, in Babcock 1978:209–24.

12. Political themes are not the norm in Svāng/Nauṭankī, a notable exception being a number of Sāngīts composed after 1920 on the incident at Jallianwalla Bagh (e.g., P. M. Shukla 1922).

Nonetheless, the very existence of such an arena outside of the direct control of the elite constituted a negation of their authority, and it was therefore perceived as a threat and condemned.

In the nineteenth century Svāng served all levels of society, and it would probably be fallacious to imagine its audience as composed entirely of lower castes and classes. Brahmins and high-caste poets were active in writing Svāng texts, and the widespread publishing of these texts suggests a sizable literate readership, who may well have included members of elite groups. The distinction between "popular" and "elite" that has been made so far is thus a somewhat idealized one; indeed, greater or lesser participation in "popular" entertainments by "elites" is observable throughout the period. However, in relation to the Parsi theatre we are about to describe, and even more so in relation to Bharatendu's theatre, Svāng manifested an overwhelmingly popular character. It was available to the laborers, artisans, and peasants and was part of their cultural universe, and it reflected their tastes, dreams, and beliefs. Svāng maintained its position distant from elite appropriation, and elite disapproval ironically ensured its survival.

In contrast, the Parsi theatre appealed to a relatively sophisticated, urban middle-class audience. The so-called Parsi stage of the second half of the nineteenth century was a broad-based commercial theatre whose appeal and influence extended far beyond the ethnic group for which it was named. It developed in about 1850 from Parsi-organized amateur groups in Bombay, like the Elphinstone Club, which were active in presenting English and Indian drama classics. Soon full-fledged professional companies were being floated by Parsi businessmen who were themselves theatre buffs. Many of the leading actors, also Parsis, held shares in these companies, and several of them went on to form their own companies. Khurshedji Balliwala founded the Victoria Theatrical Company in Delhi in 1877, and Khawasji Khatau, the "Irving of India," established the rival Alfred Theatrical Company in the same year. Dozens of companies sprang up across the subcontinent, attaching the phrase "of Bombay" to their names to associate themselves with this prestigious new theatre. Muslims, Anglo-Indians, and a certain number of Hindus joined the companies, but the organizational reins remained largely in Parsi hands.[13]

In a short time the demand for Parsi theatre fare spread to all parts of India. The major companies routinely toured between Bombay, Lahore, Karachi, Peshawar, Delhi and the Gangetic plain, Calcutta, and

13. Little original research has been done on the history of the Parsi theatre. The main secondary sources are R. K. Yajnik 1933; Somnath Gupta 1981; Ram Babu Saksena 1940; Birendra Narayana 1981; Annemarie Schimmel 1975; A. Yusuf Ali 1917.

Madras. The Parsi stage had a major impact on the emerging vernacular theatres in south as well as north India. Although Gujarati was the first language of the Parsi theatre, by the 1870s the large companies had adopted the practice of hiring Muslim *munshīs* (scribes) as part of their permanent staff, and Urdu became the principal language of the stage. In the early twentieth century, Talib, Betab, Radheyshyam, and others began writing plays in Hindi for the Parsi companies. The Parsi theatre was never a bastion of linguistic purity, and to entertain the widest cross section of society it favored the Hindustani forms of speech which were the most readily understood.

Much of the initial inspiration for the Parsi stage came from British-sponsored dramatic efforts in their colony. English-style playhouses were erected in Bombay and Calcutta in the late eighteenth century, and the native elite was invited to attend from time to time. Later the Parsi companies played in the same halls and took over the material culture of European theatre: the proscenium arch with its backdrop and curtains, Western furniture and other props, costumes, and a variety of mechanical devices for staging special effects. Artists from Europe were commissioned to paint the scenery, and the latest in "elaborate appliances" were regularly ordered from England, so as to achieve "the wonderful stage effects of storms, seas or rivers in commotion, castles, sieges, steamers, aerial movements and the like" (Yajnik 1933:113; Yusuf Ali 1917:95–96). The British example was also followed in matters of advertising and scheduling. Playbills boasting the latest Saturday evening performance were distributed throughout the city, and in the auditorium, spectators perused the "opera book" or program containing the lyrics of the latest songs (Yajnik 1933:111–15).

However, in several important respects, aside from language, the Parsi theatre revealed its Indian character: it employed Indian subject matter, and it included a great deal of music and dance. The first Indian-produced dramatic performance in Bombay is said to have been a Hindustani version of *Rājā Gopīchandra* written by Vishnudas Bhave. Hindu epic heroes and heroines—Harishchandra, Prahlad, Nala and Damayanti, Savitri, and Shakuntala—were extremely common on the Parsi stage, as were characters from the stock Islamic romances: Shirin Farhad, Laila Majnun, Benazir Badremunir, Gul Bakavali. The Parsi theatre's sizable repertoire of mythological and legendary plays drew upon the same stratum of north Indian popular culture that produced the nineteenth-century Svāngs. Of course Shakespeare was also very popular, usually dressed up in Indian guise, and some English comedies were adapted as well (Yajnik 1933:125–216; Yusuf Ali 1917:90).

The music and dance of Parsi theatre, while difficult to document, appear to have been liberal in measure and hybrid in manner. The "orchestra" often consisted of harmonium and tabla, played by accompanists who, sitting in the wings or pit, "also in many cases do duty as prompters" (Yusuf Ali 1917:96). The musical style has been described variously: "tuned to the traditional modes (Ragas)" and "in the chaste classical style," by Narayana (1981:40), but consisting of "slipshod Parsi and semi-European tunes," by Yajnik (1933:115). Partial manuscripts of two plays, *Jahāngīr Shāh aur Gauhar* of unknown authorship and Raunaq's *Benazīr Badremunīr,* do contain the names of classical and semiclassical ragas, such as Bhairavī, Soraṭh, Desh, Pīlū, Kālingṛā, and Kalyāṇ, at the headings of the *ṭhumrī*s, *ghazal*s, and other songs. An initial phrase is given in quotes, the opening line from an already well-known song, as an indication of the tune to be followed (S. Gupta 1981:Appendix 2, 40–50). In actual practice, this classical basis may have been considerably undermined in favor of novelty and catchiness.

When women were admitted to the Parsi stage in about 1880, an innovation commonly credited to Balliwala, they were recruited primarily from the ranks of professional singers and dancers. Their crowd-pleasing tactics were a big draw, and solo dancers "were rewarded by the audience with currency notes and coins amidst shouts of 'Encore'" (Narayana 1981:40–41). The better-known actresses, Khurshed, Mehtab, and Mary Fenton, achieved their fame at least partly on the basis of genuine talent. Boy actors gifted with sweet voices, good looks, and physical graces were also employed by many professional companies to play the heroines' roles and perform dance items, and "boy companies" became a popular item in certain regions (Yajnik 1933:109–10).

An idea of the literary style of the plays can be obtained from the available scripts, which show that a typical scene in a Parsi stage play consisted of a variety of songs and verses (in forms such as *ṭhumrī, ghazal, lāvanī, sher, musaddas, mukhammas, savaiyā,* or simply *gānā*) interconnected by prose dialogues. In the early plays even the dialogues were composed in rhymed metrical lines, and they were spoken with great emphasis to project the actor's voice to the back of the hall. Later, prose became predominant, although rhyme at the end of sentences was retained. In such stylistic matters, as well as in story content and music and dance, a great deal of mutual influence is visible between the north Indian folk theatre forms such as Svāng and the Parsi theatre in this period.

The first Parsi touring company to reach Banaras was the Victoria Nāṭak Maṇḍalī, which performed in 1875 (Anand 1978:54). After this, it can be assumed that visits by the Parsi companies became a regular part of the local entertainment scene. Several prominent playwrights of the Parsi theatre were from Banaras, including Raunaq, who published plays such as *Hīr Rānjhā, Lailā Majnūn,* and *Pūran Bhagat* in about 1880, and Talib, who was writing about twenty years later.[14]

Educated opinion in Banaras was uniformly disparaging toward the Parsi theatre. At a performance of *Shakuntalā,* several members of Bharatendu Harishchandra's party walked out of the theatre when Dushyant swaggered onto the stage, singing and dancing lasciviously (S. Mishra 1974:789). The Hindi journalist Mahavir Prasad Dwivedi warned novice playwrights against the quick path to fame afforded by "writing such trash" and reprimanded errant theatregoers: "Those who go to see *Indara Sabha* and *Gulabakavali* etc. presented by Parsi Theatrical Companies should think about their own good" (Narayana 1981:48).

Although the elite saw in the Parsi theatre vulgarity, sensationalism, and lack of aesthetic standards, the humbler sections of society thrilled to the mystique of English company names like the Corinthian, the Victoria, and the New Alfred. The allure was augmented by the sumptuous fittings of the Parsi stage, replete with elaborate painted scenery, fine costumes, exotic Anglo-Indian actresses, and tricks of stagecraft. Such shows may have been commonplace in the numerous theatre houses of the big cities, but in the provincial towns the spectacles no doubt overawed the populace. No wonder then that the Bombay companies were eagerly sought as the purveyors of all that was current and stylish in theatre practice—and were emulated and imitated wherever they performed. This was especially true in the cities of Uttar Pradesh like Banaras.

Despite its more elaborate organization and urbanized clientele, the Parsi theatre provided essentially the same stimulus to the reversal of social rules as did the simpler Svāng stage. Here too the crowd reveled in the public display of eroticism, in the extremes of pathos and melodrama, in the latest gimmicks and spectacles. Because of its closeness to middle-class popular taste, the Parsi theatre posed an even greater threat to elite standards of propriety than did the Svāng folk theatre. Here too the prevailing social codes seemed, however temporarily, to be turned upside down. What the Parsi theatre provoked by way of reaction—an elite theatre predicated on values of control, order, and refinement—will now be examined in the career of Bharatendu Harishchandra, its chief exponent.

14. At least four of some twenty-five plays of Raunaq's are in the British Museum collection; these were published in Bombay in 1879–1880 and are printed in Gujarati script. Also see S. Gupta 1981:62–71. For a discussion of Talib's works, including examples of his language, see Gupta 1981:71–85. Gupta indicates that Talib's plays were published by Khurshedji Balliwala, and he bases his comments on personally owned manuscripts.

BHARATENDU HARISHCHANDRA AND THE ELITE HINDI THEATRE

Bharatendu Harishchandra was born in 1850, the eldest son in a wealthy and socially prominent Agarwal family in Banaras.[15] Since the days of Shah Jahan his forefathers had been associated with various ruling families of northern India as moneylenders and bankers. Bharatendu's great-great-grandfather, Amichand (Omichand), amassed a large fortune in Bengal in the eighteenth century, acting as an intermediary between the British East India Company and the Nawabs at Murshidabad, but he was double-crossed by Clive and ultimately lost everything (Dodwell 1929, 5:141–51). After this debacle, his son Fateh Chand migrated to Banaras in 1759 and became financier to the Maharaja of Banaras while also continuing the friendly ties with the British which had proved his father's undoing. By the time of Bharatendu's grandfather Harsh Chand, the family had again become extremely wealthy. The Maharaja's treasury was kept in the vaults of Harsh Chand, and he led a life of ostentation, parading about the streets with large numbers of bodyguards and a martial band in attendance. Bharatendu's father, Gopal Chandra, protected the valuables of the British Residency during the unstable times in 1857 (Gopal 1972:4–10).

Bharatendu's literary talents and role as cultural patron appear to have been inherited from his father, who composed a number of poetic and dramatic works, including what some call the first modern drama in Hindi, *Nahush nāṭak.* In Bharatendu's generation the joint family continued its close ties with the Maharaja of Banaras, but their role as moneylenders eroded as Bharatendu squandered his fortune on literary and cultural activities as well as more hedonistic pursuits, such as the maintenance of his two mistresses, Madhavi and Mallika, and a harem of nautch girls. In his lifetime he was famous for emulating his namesake, King Harishchandra of the *Mārkaṇḍeya purāṇa,* who was so generous that he gave away his kingdom and sold his wife and son into slavery in fulfillment of a vow. Possessing little inclination for generating income or saving it, Bharatendu had no trouble devising ways of spending, and the lifestyle of the rakish, extravagant nobleman sat easily with him. He was a perfect representative of the wealthy Vaishya

15. The primary source for Bharatendu's biography is Shivnandan Sahay 1905, first published in Bankipur by Khadgvilas Press and reprinted by the U.P. Government Hindi Samiti in 1975. Sahay, a contemporary and friend of Bharatendu, records the many anecdotes and details which have been repeated in subsequent biographies. The chief English biography, Madan Gopal 1972, is not a scholarly work; however, it closely follows Sahay. R. S. McGregor's discussion (1974:75–85) is the best English-language treatment of Harishchandra's literary accomplishments.

class in Banaras in the 1860s, filling the place vacated by the Mughals and the Nawabs of Lucknow at the pinnacle of a feudal society where cultural consumption, in the form of patronage of music, poetry, and other arts, was simultaneously duty, occupation, and obsession.

Bharatendu's leadership in the literary field was a product of his own prolific energy, as well as of his fortuitous situation in the social hierarchy. His early education included training in Sanskrit, Hindi, Persian, Urdu, and English, and he was also fluent in Bengali in consequence of family ties to that region. He began composing poetry at a young age, and in his brief life-span of thirty-five years he produced many volumes of verse (almost all in Braj Bhasha), as well as eighteen plays and innumerable essays, which laid the foundation for a modern Hindi prose style. His activities in journalism involved the publication of two magazines, *Kavi vachan sudhā* and *Harishchandra chandrikā,* which spread his social, political, and literary programs to a new reading public. His network of friends and admirers extended beyond the upper echelons of Banaras society to Kanpur, Allahabad, and other northern cities, and these followers were his primary audience; several of them carried on his work in journalism and drama for a number of years after his death.

His reputation as "father of modern Hindi" was also based on his propagation of a language style that eventually became the accepted standard in the twentieth century.[16] This too was not unrelated to his social position. By virtue of not being a Brahmin, he was able to urge the adoption of a vernacular medium in place of Sanskrit. In the power structure of the time, the pandits were in fact dependent upon patrons like Bharatendu for their maintenance. (In 1870 Bharatendu organized the Banaras pandits to pay homage to the Duke of Edinburgh, and in return for publishing their poems and earning them honoraria, he received their lasting blessings and gratitude; Gopal 1972:37–42.) He appears to have been beyond the influence of their orthodoxy, at least in linguistic matters. However, as a devout Vaishnava he also opposed the infusion of Urdu expressions into Hindi, which was characteristic of the prose of Raja Shiv Prasad Singh. Shiv Prasad, who had taught Bharatendu English as a young man, became his lifelong rival, not only on the language issue but in the arena of favors distributed by the British and the Maharaja of Banaras.

This introduces the question of Bharatendu's relationship to both the British political presence in India and their social, educational, and cultural values. Bharatendu made manifest his loyalty to the British

16. Bharatendu's testimony before the Hunter Commission (1882) on behalf of the use of Hindi in the schools is recounted in Ramadhar Singh 1973 and reveals many aspects of Bharatendu's opinions on the language question.

Crown on a number of occasions, as when he played host to the visiting Duke of Edinburgh in 1870, publicly expressed his grief at the assassination of Lord Mayo in 1871, submitted poems to the Prince of Wales during his visit in 1875, celebrated the birthday of Queen Victoria each year, or commemorated in poetry her victory in Egypt in 1882. Bharatendu used the time-honored genre of panegyric verse to express an attitude that he shared with many of the people of India, who in his own words, "have a kind of superstitious reverence for their Sovereign, so much so that they regard their Sovereign but next in reverence to God only" (Gopal 1972:181). This attitude was not disinterested but was part and parcel of a feudal code of obligations that bound the subject and the sovereign to each other. Bharatendu, like his ancestors before him, undoubtedly expected a return on his loyalty to the ruling power, and after the Duke of Edinburgh's visit he was indeed rewarded by being appointed Municipal Commissioner and Honorary Magistrate at the unusually young age of twenty. Furthermore, the proffering of allegiance to the Crown was a technique of demonstrating his superior status in Indian society, a form of competition with local nobles such as Raja Shiv Prasad.[17]

Yet Bharatendu was given to satirizing the pomp and ceremony of British rule, especially when his rivals were the objects of British attention, as in the darbar held in Banaras in 1870 ("Levī prāṇ levī," V. Das 1953:938–40; Gopal 1972:102–5). He frequently tangled with local British officials and was under some sort of ban in 1880, apparently as a result of offensive editorials he had written (Gopal 1972:145). Later in his career his writings focused more frequently on the economic ruin of India, especially the outflow of cash for manufactured goods, as a result of British policies. He supported the Swadeshi movement and held that the imitation of English fashion and social behavior would lead to moral decadence as well as economic ruin for India. Despite his unsystematic and rather inconsistent political views, Indian historians have generally described him as a nationalist and social reformer, forerunner of the generation of leaders who founded the Indian National Congress (Verma 1974:377–87).

As could be expected from his education and socioeconomic class, Bharatendu's intellectual outlook was much influenced by his exposure

17. The theme of competition among the leading citizens of Banaras to demonstrate loyalty is alluded to by Gopal where he reports of Bharatendu, "None in Banaras could really surpass him in giving expression to loyalty to the British Crown" (1972:117). The competition with Shiv Prasad helps to explain perhaps some of the inconsistency in Bharatendu's position toward the British. When Shiv Prasad was in favor with the British, Bharatendu found fault with the rulers and accused Prasad of being their lackey. On other occasions he would court the British in precisely the same manner as his rival, for his own ends.

to several great literary traditions. His knowledge of Sanskrit classics (especially of the dramatic literature), coupled with his familiarity with English literature, helped produce the characteristic stance of the Indian Renaissance man—an urge at once to reclaim the past, reform the present, and progress into the future. Bharatendu was also close to intellectual currents in Bengal and derived many of his ideas and knowledge of Sanskrit and English literary works from Bengali writers.[18]

However, his education was not confined to these "high" sources. Bharatendu was a "bi-cultural" man, to use Peter Burke's phrase (Burke 1978:28). That is, he had access to a second Indian tradition of folk and popular culture in addition to the great traditions he had formally studied. He was well versed in the oral traditions of Hindi and Urdu poetry, and he composed in several genres typically associated with Banaras, such as *kajalī* and *holī*.[19] He is said to have sat in company with *lāvanī* singers on the pavement and learned their compositions, and his own *lāvanī*s were published as well (Gopal 1972:28). During festivals like the Burhwa Mangal, the riverboat festival patronized by his family, popular forms of music, dance, and poetry prevailed. Bharatendu's acquaintance with many forms of popular theatre is also apparent from his writings on drama, as we shall soon see.

But while Bharatendu participated in the popular cultural traditions of Banaras and no doubt derived relish from the activity, he seems never to have examined this cultural stream consciously or considered its role in society, except in one unusual essay. In "Jātīya sangīt" he recommends the dissemination of published booklets of folk songs written on themes of social reform as a technique of rural uplift, much as twentieth-century development planners use traditional media in the service of modernization (Das 1953:935–38). For Bharatendu, as for the European Renaissance man, the popular side of the culture was always available for recreation and amusement. Where serious thought or literary productivity were required, however, he turned to the high literary traditions. This attitude had a great deal to do with the shape that Bharatendu's activity in the theatre eventually took.

From early on, Bharatendu embarked on the enterprise of creating a Hindi theatre movement in Banaras. His father had composed "the first [Hindi] drama of literary scope in the modern period" in 1859, but

18. R. Stuart McGregor asserts, "The influence of Bengali literature and of views held in Bengal was clearly a dominant formative element in his work, and it is acknowledged in the prefaces to several of his plays" (1972:142). See also Mahesh Anand, who quotes Bharatendu as expressing a hope for the progress of Hindi, with the "help of her big sister Bengali, who is well-endowed and wise in years" (1978:53).

19. For a discussion of Bharatendu's Urdu poetry and his *lāvanī*s, see Ramvilas Sharma 1973:20–22. Gopal mentions Bharatendu's 79 *holī* verses (1972:142), and McGregor refers to his *kajalī*s (1974:82).

there is no record of any performance of his *Nahush nāṭak* (McGregor 1972:92). The first drama to be presented on stage was Shital Prasad Tripathi's *Jānakī mangal,* which was put on at the Banaras Theatre (also known as the *purānā nāchghar*) in 1868. The performance was sponsored by the Maharaja of Banaras, and Bharatendu himself made his acting debut as Lakshman in this play.[20] News of this performance was reported in the London-based *Indian Mail and Monthly Register,* and the item gives an idea of the ambience of the event:

> Benaras, April 4 [1868]. . . . Last night a Hindi drama named "Janki Mangal" was acted by natives in the Assembly Rooms, by the order of his Highness the Maharaj of Benaras. Our enlightened Maharaja who generally takes an interest in all the [*sic*] concerns the improvement of his countrymen, was present on the occasion, he was accompanied by Kunwar Sahib and his staff. The principle [*sic*] European and native citizens were invited to witness the performances. A few ladies and many military and civil officers were present, and many rich folks of the city. (Saksena 1977:128)

Bharatendu's own dramatic compositions date from the same year, with the publication of his *Vidyāsundar.* As with most of his early plays, this was a translation, from Bengali. After writing several such plays and then freer adaptations of classic tales from Sanskrit, such as *Mudrārākshas,* he began writing original dramas by the mid-1870s. Of his best-known plays, some employ totally contemporary settings, such as *Bhārat durdashā* (1880), his commentary upon the calamities that have befallen the Indian nation, and some treat historical themes highlighting India's past glory, such as *Nīldevī* (1881). Bharatendu attempted a number of styles, from romance to farce, and he used the generic classifications of Sanskrit drama to label his plays—for example, *bhāṇ, prahasan, nāṭikā, gītirūpak,* and so forth.

It is not known precisely how many of Bharatendu's plays were performed in his lifetime or, with a few exceptions, where and under what circumstances these performances took place.[21] However, there is

20. Bharatendu's on-the-spot memorization of his role is one of the most famous anecdotes concerning his acting talent. See Mishra 1974:24, 791; McGregor 1974:92. (McGregor erroneously records the author as Shital Prasad Tivari.)

21. Hindi criticism has taken the view that plays are meant primarily for reading, and hence most studies of Bharatendu consist of analyses of written texts. Not until recently has much emphasis been placed upon the performance dimension of Bharatendu's dramatic work. The problem is discussed by S. K. Taneja in his Introduction (1976:9–12). Nineteenth-century sources such as Sahay, however, do give some idea of the performance history of Bharatendu's plays. According to Sahay, five of the dramas *(Vedikī hiṃsā hiṃsā na bhavati, Satya Harishchandra, Nīldevī, Bhārat durdashā, Andher nagarī*) were performed in places such as Kanpur, Prayag, Baliya, Kashi, Agra, and Dumrao at that time. See Sahay 1905:160–211.

abundant proof that Bharatendu was actively involved in at least three aspects of theatre aside from his role as playwright: acting, organizing dramatic societies, and writing drama criticism. His biographers describe a flamboyant and exhibitionistic streak in his temperament, and he is said to have been fond of dressing up (Saksena 1977:138–39). After his youthful performance in *Jānakī mangal,* records show that he played the role of the madman in his own drama *Nīldevī,* and also performed in *Satya Harishchandra* and *Nīldevī* at Ballia with great histrionic skill (Taneja 1976:17; Anand 1978:60, description of his "overacting" by Gahmari).

Bharatendu expended considerable effort toward spreading his theatre movement among the educated elite. His organizational talents and probably his financial resources were instrumental in the founding of theatrical societies and literary clubs not only in Banaras but in other nearby cities. For example, Bharatendu was director of the Hindu National Theatre (Nāṭak Samāj) of Banaras, which consisted of a group of Bengali and Hindi speakers who met at Dashashvamedh Ghat, and it was for this society that Harishchandra wrote *Andher nagarī.*[22] He also organized the Kavitā Varddhinī Sabhā, which staged play performances at his own residence, and he founded the Penny Reading Club in Banaras, which engaged in regular play-reading and skit performances among its activities. In Allahabad, Bharatendu helped form the Āryā Nāṭya Sabhā, and a number of performances took place in the Railway Theatre. In Kanpur he inspired Protap Narayan Mishra to organize the Bhāratendu Maṇḍal; five dramas written by Bharatendu had been staged under its auspices by 1885. Similarly, Lucknow too had a theatre hall, the Vidyānt Nāṭyashālā. Patna had its own Nāṭak Maṇḍalī, as did Ballia, Muzaffarpur, and Agra (Taneja 1976:17–18; Anand 1978:54–55; McGregor 1974:92–93; Shivprasad Mishra 1974: 25–26).

These societies were sustained by a group of Bharatendu's disciples, who, like him, were at once amateur playwrights, actors, and organizers. Bharatendu's literary and personal influence was clearly marked on men such as Ambika Datt Vyas, Kishorilal Goswami, and Radhakrishna Das in Banaras, Pratap Narayan Mishra in Kanpur, Kashinath Khatri in Agra, Balkrishna Bhatt in Allahabad, and Keshavram Bhatt in Bihar. Within this circle they produced each others' plays, performed for each other, and criticized each others' performances in their journals, supported by members of the local elite who had the leisure and interest to engage in amateur theatre. Performances were

22. See Mishra 1974:25, 164. According to Taneja (1976:17) and Anand (1978:54), the National Theatre was founded in 1884, but the data of *Andher nagarī*'s composition is given as 1881 in Mishra.

held occasionally in members' residences or in the few auditoriums that existed. Many plays of the period were never performed on stage, although some of them have been used in play readings (McGregor 1974:93). In addition to the performances mentioned above, Bharatendu's own plays were performed at his residence and in the court of the Maharaja of Banaras (Anand 1978:54).

Another context for the dramas of Bharatendu and his colleagues was the boys' school. Bharatendu's preface to *Satya Harishchandra* indicates that it was written with the moral instruction of boys in mind. "My friend Babu Baleshwar Prasad, B.A., has asked me to write a play suitable for the education of boys, since the dramas which I have written in *shringār ras* [the erotic mood] are appropriate for adults but of no benefit to boys. At his request, I have composed this drama named *Satya Harishchandra*" (Mishra 1974:251). Similar plays compiled as school texts, to be read rather than acted, include Kashinath Khattri's *Tīn manohar aitihāsik rūpak* (1884) (McGregor 1974:93, 96). The popularity of dramatics both as an academic subject and as an extracurricular activity (no doubt inspired by British schoolmasters) is also confirmed by the early stages of modern theatre in Bengal and Bombay, where school and college clubs provided the first forum for plays in the vernacular.

The picture of Bharatendu and his theatre which emerges thus far contrasts sharply with the composite portrait of popular theatre drawn earlier in this essay. Far from being a "theatre of the common man," as some Hindi critics have claimed, this was an amateur theatre created by and for the leisured elite. The private space of the late-nineteenth-century drawing room was its distinctive setting, a closed environment that enjoined upon the spectators a refined, controlled mode of behavior. Access was limited to the socially privileged few, the private-club members and their friends. The frequent presence of British officers and their wives is another potent indicator of the degree of decorum and constraint that was observed.[23]

Furthermore, Bharatendu's theatre was still dependent upon the patronage of the court for its legitimation in the eyes of Banaras society, and courtly codes of conduct were naturally carried into the theatre milieu. The Maharaja of Banaras, Ishvariprasad Narayan Singh (1835–1889), was involved in many cultural ventures, but he was especially keen on the revival of the drama, as is testified to by his assistance to Bharatendu and his engaging a court poet to work specifically on be-

23. Mahesh Anand states, "The theatre invented by Bharatendu was a theatre of the common people (*jansamūh kā rangmanch*)" (1978:58). Shrikrishna Lal writes, on the other hand, "It may be said that these plays were written for a drawing-room theatre, whose viewers could only be the few, highly sophisticated scholars" (1965:195).

half of the theatre (Saksena 1977:140). On the model of his king, Bharatendu's charismatic leadership provided the backbone to the dramatic societies he founded. Through the figures of authority central to these occasions, the theatre event derived its primary significance to its audience—as an opportunity for the display and affirmation of social status.

That this elite theatre was being promoted in reaction to the popular theatre prevailing in Banaras becomes clear when we turn to Bharatendu's critical writings. The practice of drama criticism was yet another dimension of Bharatendu's zeal for theatre, and reviews of productions were regular features in the pages of his journals, such as *Harishchandra's Magazine.* From these sources, we find that Bharatendu had witnessed performances of the Parsi theatre groups and found them not at all to his taste. The Victoria Nāṭak Maṇḍalī's performance of *Shakuntalā* in Banaras in 1875 drew from him the comment that the players were "turning the knife at the neck of Kalidasa." Later he saw a Parsi production of *Gulbakāvalī,* "but unfortunately nothing occurred as I had hoped" (Taneja 1976:26–27). Similar denunciations issued from Balkrishna Bhatt's pen: "Nowadays the dance of prostitutes is considered a civilized form of entertainment." The Parsi theatre was "the sure ruin of the Hindu caste and nation," or in the words of Premghan, "equal to the arrival of Kāl (Death)" (Anand 1978:58–59). Still, Bhatt noted, at least the civilized members of society had the sense to avoid these shows: "When the spectacle is cheap, more rakes and loafers from the city congregate than do nobles and cultured people" (Taneja 1976:27).

It is not certain that Bharatendu saw any performance of the Urdu musical, the *Indarsabhā,* although the popularity of that drama was so well established that he could hardly have escaped it. Bharatendu published a parody of the *Indarsabhā* in the July 1879 issue of *Harishchandra chandrikā,* under the title *Bandarsabhā* (Assembly of the Monkeys). In the introduction to this piece he comments, "The *Indarsabhā* is a type of drama in Urdu, or the semblance of a drama, and this *Bandarsabhā* is in turn a semblance of it" (Mishra 1974:729). The imitation of the style of the *Indarsabhā* here reveals a familiarity with the work, possibly through reading of the text, but perhaps also through seeing it on stage. In any case, the parody makes clear Bharatendu's rejection of the *Indarsabhā* as a suitable model for his theatre.

Other references to popular theatre forms are scattered throughout Bharatendu's writings. One particular mention of the folk traditions of Bhāṇḍ and Bhagat appears in his opening verses written to accompany Shrinivas Das's play *Raṇdhīr Premmohinī.* Here he alludes to the former traditions of drama in the country as "full of stupidity," which has increased with the spread of troupes of "*bhāṇḍ*s, *bhagatiyā*s, and *ganikā*s" (jesters, actors, and courtesans). It is to rectify this deplorable situation that the present play was composed "full of all virtues" (Taneja 1976:104).

Bharatendu's rejection of popular traditions is most clearly stated, however, in his treatise "Nāṭak," written in 1883. The purpose of this essay is to redeem theatre as a respectable pursuit of the educated elite, a goal which Bharatendu considered essential to his campaign to establish a viable Hindi stage. The text alternates between defining typologies of dramatic species and constituent elements in the style of Sanskrit *shāstra,* sketching miniature histories of Indian and Western drama, and making emotional appeals to the readers to shed their prejudices. "Nāṭak" constitutes an illuminating discourse on the status of theatre at the time and the impetus for its reform, and it is to an analysis of this text that we now turn.

Bharatendu's essay is explicitly directed at an elite readership, a group he repeatedly refers to as the *sabhyashishṭagaṇ, sabhya* meaning "civilized," and *shishṭa,* "cultured" or "courteous." Underlying the essay is the assumption of the aversion of this class to the theatre. As Bharatendu notes, "Nowadays people have no enthusiasm for the practice and study of drama, but on the contrary consider it mean and low and flee from it" (Mishra 1974:777). "Nāṭak" is thus an apologia, a defense of drama and the theatre, which seeks to win over the audience and turn its hostility into admiration and support. Bharatendu's initial tactic is to disarm his audience by conceding the justice of their point of view. He begins the essay by defining the work *nāṭak* (drama) as "the action of *naṭ*s," thus associating the art with the debased caste of professional actors, acrobats, jugglers, and popular performers. After further defining drama as *drishyakāvya,* loosely "poetry for the eyes," he proceeds to divide it into three types. The first is *kāvyamishra,* "mixed with poetry," about which nothing further is said. The second is *shuddh kautuk,* "pure entertainment," which is described as "all types of shows, such as puppet and toy shows, mime acts, juggling, dialogues during horse shows, imitation of ghosts and spirits, and other civilized entertainments." This category is clearly ranked above the third, *bhrashṭ,* or "depraved," types of drama. Here the list is extensive and includes almost every type of popular theatre known at the time: "Bhāṇḍ, Indarsabhā, Rās, Yātrā, Līlā, Jhānkī, etc.," as well as "Parsi drama and Maharashtrian plays, etc." The basis of the depravity of these forms is obscure; Bharatendu says only that "there is no theatricality (*nāṭakatva*) left in them," and in the case of Parsi and Maharashtrian plays, he comments that they are "lacking in poetry" (*kāvyahīn*) (Mishra 1974: 749–50).

Thus from the outset Bharatendu dissociates his concept of theatre from the very forms that had popular appeal in his day, confirming the distaste with which the "civilized" class views these arts. He then proceeds to establish the legitimacy of elite drama, in contradistinction to the debased forms that have been dismissed, by linking it with the most prestigious sources of authority: the classical Sanskrit dramatists and theorists, on the one hand (Bharata and Kalidasa in particular), and the European playwrights and men of the theatre, on the other, from the Greeks and Shakespeare down to the Sahebs in the cantonment. He includes a lengthy exposition of the categories and terminology of Sanskrit drama, not so much as a framework for analysis of current plays, I suspect, as proof of the sophistication of the ancient tradition. In a similar vein, the essay closes with a description of Western theatre that is nothing more than a list of playwrights and periods, again serving to demonstrate the historical depth and respectability of the drama. In discussing his own recommendations for the "new" theatre, Bharatendu too attempts to establish legitimacy through shastraic precedent. Thus he traces the use of curtains and scene divisions to Sanskrit dramatic practice, although the popularity of these elements in his day came directly from European and Parsi theatre conventions.[24]

Although Bharatendu originally defined *nāṭak* as the province of *naṭ*s, much of the essay is devoted to disproving that assertion. He repeatedly refers to the fame of drama in ancient times, when it was patronized by royalty and acted in their palaces (Mishra 1974:754). "These dramas were not always performed by professional actors (*naṭ log*). Aryan princes and princesses also learned them." He cites a lengthy example from the *Mahābhārata* which tells of a drama put on by the Yādav princes Pradyumna and Samba (Mishra 1974:776). Later he joins to this the English example. "And if performing dramas were a bad thing, why have the English, those pinnacles of civilized wisdom, made such efforts on its behalf, and why do prominent officers every day put on costumes and perform in their large auditoriums?" (Mishra 1974:778). He regrets that "people adept at acting are considered ordinary drum-beating *naṭ*s and are hated" (Mishra 1974:777). These negative attitudes, to Bharatendu, simply indicate a defective upbringing (*kusamskār*), based on ignorance of the illustrious history of drama in India and the West.

24. Mishra 1974:756–57; Taneja 1976:42. Bharatendu's fondness for painted curtains seems related to the fascination with perspective that characterized the Company school of miniature painting, which was much in vogue with the Banaras gentry (Sukul 1974:60–61). It is curious that Bharatendu found fault with the folk theatres of Rāslīlā and Tamāshā, accusing them of lack of realism, because they did not use backdrops and curtains.

An important element of Bharatendu's revision concerns the aims of drama. Alongside the traditional *rasas, shringār* (eroticism), and *hāsya* (humor), and the conventional motive of *kautuk* (surprise), he joins *samāj samskār* (social reform) and *deshvātsaltā* (love of country) as suitable ends to be aroused by a play (Mishra 1974:754). The latter two aims operate with special force in the present period, when every play must have a moral or an educational purpose. If such a purpose is lacking, the cultured class will not respect the work (Mishra 1974:773). This moral purpose must be especially apparent at the conclusion of a drama; the evil characters must be punished and the good rewarded (Mishra 1974:774). Drama ought properly to be *ras rūpī updesh,* instruction in the form of aesthetic delight. When it is such, it has tremendous power to reform society, because of the irresistible force of the educational message made pleasant through entertainment. Bharatendu predicts a moral renaissance from the propagation of plays:

> Just as men addicted to prostitutes come to hate their behavior by seeing actors dressed as men addicted to prostitutes, . . . so are drunkards made to experience their sorry situation by those impersonating drunkards, and in the same way gamblers, liars, debtors, those who oppose their brothers, misers, spendthrifts, harsh speakers and fools will become conscious simply by the depiction of their sorry plight . . . and, becoming cautious by virtue of this pleasant form of instruction, will avoid these evils. (Mishra 1974:777–78)

The unique facility of drama as an instrument of social reform was a cornerstone of belief shared among the playwrights of Bharatendu's day (Taneja 1976:16). It was the trump card in Bharatendu's case against the opponents of theatre; to obstruct the progress of drama meant to stand in the way of the moral regeneration of the nation.

The emphasis on the didactic purposes of drama led Bharatendu to modify the rules inherited from Sanskrit theory. For example, he restricted the types of heroines in the "new" drama to *svakīya* women only, that is, women who are loyal to their husbands. There was no place on his stage for a *parakīya,* a woman who belongs to another. So too the use of music was circumscribed, and of course the arousing dance displays of the popular theatre were curtailed. Bharatendu also recommended a reduced role for the *vidūshaka,* the clown whose mocking of authority is almost a universal in Indian theatre. Hand in hand with these changes, Bharatendu espoused certain realistic conventions that had previously been absent from the Indian theatre, except for the recent Parsi stage. He emphasized the unities of time and place and advocated the use of painted backdrops and stage props to represent the changing settings of acts and scenes. The Sanskrit and folk dramatic practice of establishing the place or time by verbal reference was scorned. He stressed the literal correspondence of costumes to the state of the characters at the time of the action—for example, rags for King Harishchandra when he is working on the burning ghat. He also allowed for the mixing of moods, or *rasas*, a rigid taboo in classical Indian theatre, especially in the case of plays with tragic endings.

The prescriptions of Bharatendu's treatise, written at the end of his life after the composition of his dramas, are not uniformly followed in his own dramatic works. Elements of various folk theatre traditions are visible in some of his texts, pointing to a still incomplete bifurcation of drama into "popular" and "elite."[25] However, the kind of theatre experience that was in the process of formation was fundamentally different in structure and function from the earlier popular theatre. Bharatendu's theatre was moving in a clear direction: away from the open-ended, improvisational, stylized, multivalent theatre of the Svāng and Parsi stage, and toward a controlled, unambiguous, realistic, morally edifying model of theatre. Not only was the social milieu of theatre now pervaded by values of civility and refinement; the means and ends of theatrical representation were purged to eliminate all that was vulgar. Theatre was henceforth an unabashed arena of instruction, whether its actual locus was the schoolhouse or the parlor.

To students of modern Indian literature, the large dose of didacticism and moral idealism that accompanied Bharatendu's theatre program comes as no great surprise. The same infusion of reformist sentiments, coupled with a rigorous purging of eroticism, fantasy, and humor, accompanied the development of other literary genres, such as poetry and fiction, as they crossed the boundary into modernity. Bharatendu's larger corpus illustrates the split. It contains the sober, message-laden "modern" dramas, as well as volumes of flippant, sensuous lyric poetry that adhere to the traditional type. What was "modern" in literature had less to do with turning one's view toward "real life" (the heroes and heroines of Bharatendu's plays were still the ideal princes and princesses of yore) than toward affixing a conscious purpose to the literary work, making the work subservient to the larger task of the betterment of "society." What writers like Bharatendu

25. Susham Bedi, Krishna Mohan Saksena, Mahesh Anand, and others have made rather inflated claims regarding the folk elements in Bharatendu's plays. To cite one extreme example, *Nīldevī* and *Andher nagarī* have been characterized as written in Nauṭankī style (Bedi 1984:31–36), although the texts of these plays contain none of the standard meters of Nauṭankī and bear no resemblance to the Svāng texts of the same period. More plausible are the identifications of various scenes, characters, and conventions, which are reminiscent of the Parsi stage. Despite the vehement scorn Bharatendu expressed for the Parsi companies, he was unable to free himself completely from its dominance in the theatre world in which he lived and worked. See Taneja 1976:26–32; Anand 1978:59–60; Saksena 1977:133–38.

meant by "society" is another topic; it still referred primarily to the *sabhyashishṭagaṇ*, the elite.

The reformist spirit that permeated Bharatendu's theatre in Banaras and spread from there may have been a result of growing Arya Samāj influence. Dayanand Saraswati first visited Banaras in 1869, and as early as 1870 his addresses stirred Bharatendu to compose pamphlets deriding "the naked Dayanand of unknown caste" (Gopal 1972:32). Bharatendu initially rejected Dayanand's claims to religious authority and, as a Vallabhite, refuted his denunciation of idol worship and *sanātana* practices. However, Dayanand later became a contributor to *Harishchandra's Magazine,* and the edge of their quarrel seems to have worn off. Many of Dayanand's positions on child marriage, widows, temperance, and education were probably acceptable to Bharatendu. Even though Dayanand made few converts at the time, the impetus to self-purification in Hindu society permeated educated circles in Banaras in consequence of his continued preaching. The same species of influence emanated from Bengal in the form of the Brahmo Samāj; Bharatendu may have come into contact with it indirectly through Bengali authors who had imbibed its teachings.

The reform of the more exuberant and potentially licentious aspects of popular culture was a certain component of Arya Samāj philosophy. The Aryas condemned the singing of "indecent songs" on ceremonial and festival occasions, and they introduced a purified form of the Holi festival which excluded all spontaneous merriment and focused upon the Vedic *havan* ritual. They also abolished the performances of dancing girls at Arya Samāj marriage ceremonies (Jones 1976:95, 99). According to the Vatuks, "The movement's founder, Dayanand, was quite explicit in his writings about the evils of dramatic performances" (Vatuk and Vatuk 1967:48). Proselytizing efforts by the Arya Samāj in Haryana in recent years have included denunciation of the local folk drama form Sāng (another descendant of ninteenth-century Svāng) and concerted efforts to replace it with the more salutary songs of Arya Samāj *bhajan maṇḍalī*s.

By way of comparison, we may refer briefly to the tremendous opposition toward the popular theatre voiced by Plato, the Christian Fathers, the Puritans, and any number of other reformist movements throughout Western history. The "antitheatrical prejudice," as Jonas Barish puts it, is a universal phenomenon, singularly oblivious to transformations of culture, time, and place (Barish 1981:4). As Barish shows, the most vehement attacks against the corrupting influence of theatre have tended to occur when the theatre was at a height of popularity. From this it is reasonable to infer that Bharatendu's denunciation of the Indarsabhā, Līlā, Tamāshā, and so forth, as *bhrashṭ* occurred not because they were almost extinct, as has been generally thought, but precisely because there was an intense degree of public devotion to these spectacles. Swept along by the puritanical fervor of the Arya Samāj, Bharatendu fortunately did not call for a complete ban on play-acting, as the English Puritans did. However, he embarked on a course that served to disengage the modern Hindi theatre from its very roots in the traditions of the people.

CONCLUSION

By establishing far from the disorderly crowd a theatre that voiced the refined tastes and reformist ideology of the elite, Bharatendu in fact did little except widen the divide between popular and elite culture. The effect on the popular stage was negligible. The Parsi theatre was the dominant form of urban entertainment across north India until the advent of talking cinema, while the folk theatre of Svāng developed into two prominent styles in Hathras and Kanpur and gradually absorbed the salient features of both Parsi theatre and popular films. But for modern Hindi drama the results were crippling. Divorced from contact with the living theatre of north India, the Hindi stage shriveled to inconsequence after Bharatendu's death. The dramatic societies became inactive, and no playwright of talent appeared on the scene until Jaishankar Prasad, whose plays, though considered the height of Hindi dramatic literature, were never performed on stage. "Closet drama" remained the norm, and the modern stage in this region, unlike that in Bengal and Maharashtra, failed to gain any sort of credibility until after Independence. The disengagement from popular theatre, which began with Bharatendu at the "birth of Hindi drama," was not reversed until the 1960s, when playwrights began experimenting with indigenous forms and drawing closer to the conventions of folk theatre once again.[26]

BANARAS SĀNGĪT TEXTS (1868–1885) IN THE INDIA OFFICE LIBRARY AND THE BRITISH MUSEUM

Dhurū Līlā. Author unknown. Munshi Ambe Prasad, 1875. 12 pp.

Sāngīt Dhurū jī kā. Author unknown. Lala Ghasiram, 1880. 36 pp. Other editions: Delhi, 1876.

26. A conscious effort to reintroduce elements of indigenous theatre practice and style was made by playwrights like Habib Tanvir, Sarveshwar Dayal Saksena, Mudrarakshas, and others in the 1960s. This phenomenon also became widespread in other regional theatres, and received and still receives the support of government cultural agencies such as the Sangeet Natak Akademi. See Hansen 1983.

Sāngīt Gopīchand Bharthari. Lakshman Singh [Lachhman Das]. Munshi Ambe Prasad, 1883. 32 pp. Other editions: Agra, 1867; Delhi, 1867; Agra, 1868; Delhi, 1868; Delhi, 1869; Agra, 1870; Delhi, 1870; Agra, 1871; Meerut, 1871; Delhi, 1873; Delhi, 1874; Lucknow, 1874; Delhi, 1875; Delhi, 1875 (Urdu); Lucknow, 1875 (Urdu); Delhi, 1876; Delhi, 1877; Calcutta, 1878; Delhi, 1878; Meerut, 1878; Delhi, 1879; Delhi, 1879 (Urdu).

Sāngīt Prahlād. Lakshman Singh [Lachhman Das]. Munshi Ambe Prasad, 1882. 48 pp. Other editions: Delhi, 1866; Delhi, 1868; Agra, 1869; Delhi, 1869; Delhi, 1869 (Urdu); Delhi, 1870; Delhi, 1874; Delhi, 1875; Delhi, 1876; Delhi, 1877; Delhi, 1877 (Urdu); Delhi, 1878; Meerut, 1878; Delhi, 1879; Meerut, 1880.

Sāngīt Raghuvīr Singh. Hardev Sahay. Munshi Shadi Lal, 1882. 16 pp. Other editions: Meerut, 1876; Meerut, 1877.

Sāngīt Rājā Harichandra kā. Jiya Lal. Munshi Ambe Prasad, 1877. 52 pp. Other editions: Delhi, 1877; Delhi, 1879; Delhi, 1881 (Urdu).

Sāngīt Rājā Kārak kā. Author unknown. Munshi Shadi Lal, 1882. 32 pp. Other editions: Meerut, 1878.

Sāngīt Rānī Nauṭankī kā. Khushi Ram. Munshi Shadi Lal, 1882. 36 pp.

THREE

The Rise of a Folk Music Genre: *Birahā*

Scott L. Marcus

Birahā is a folk music genre of the Bhojpuri region, a cultural and geographical entity comprising eastern Uttar Pradesh and western Bihar.[1] From the writings of G. A. Grierson in the 1880s we know that *birahā* existed as an isolated village genre in the nineteenth century (Grierson 1886). By the 1960s and 1970s, however, it had developed into the single most popular folk music genre of the region, thriving not only in village areas, but also in the cities of the region and, most prominently, in the city of Banaras.

Birahā's development from relative obscurity to its present position of popularity has been accompanied by changes in virtually every aspect of the genre: song structure, performance context, the concept of ensemble, the use of musical instruments, economic circumstances, and so forth. In this chapter these and other points will be discussed in turn. Special attention will be given to those developments which facilitated the genre's success in the urban environment.

Birahā is an entertainment genre of the lower castes of the region, the common folk. As it exists today, the performing ensemble, consisting of a lead singer accompanied by musical instruments and a small chorus, performs narrative songs, each lasting about forty minutes.

Research in India (1983–84) was funded by a Fulbright-Hays fellowship. Copies of recordings made during this period are housed at the UCLA Ethnomusicology Archive and at the Archive and Research Center for Ethnomusicology in New Delhi. The collection includes over seventy-five hours of recordings of live *birahā* performances and over thirty-six hours of recorded interviews. Later references to this collection will be to the "Marcus Collection."

1. The indigenous language of this region is Bhojpuri, a dialect of Hindi. For this study the main areas involved are the districts of Varanasi, Mirzapur, Ghazipur, Azamgarh, and Jaunpur. Banaras is in the center of this immediate area.

Performances usually feature two or more ensembles and include five to ten hours of continuous music. Each ensemble, of five to six people, positions itself on a raised platform; the main singer stands while the other members of the ensemble sit below him.

Birahā is, for the most part, performed in two distinct contexts: in the villages, and in the city. Village performances occur during the wedding season (March to May); city performances occur during the temple festival season (September to early December). In both contexts the performances are free and open to anyone wishing to attend. Audiences range from 150 to 1,200 people. These performances are thus important examples of lower-class culture occurring in public arenas.

Song texts focus on a variety of topics. Songs not only continue a tradition of retelling and reinterpreting stories from the religious heritage, they also keep audiences up to date on significant current events. Songs telling stories of the heroes of the pre-1947 struggle for independence also play a major role.

Birahā's popularity has resulted in a swelling of the numbers of performers. Today there are thousands of *birahā* performers: dozens in Banaras proper and one or more ensembles in virtually every village. The most popular singers have achieved virtual "superstar" status, becoming "household names" throughout the region and acquiring substantial wealth.

DEVELOPMENT OF THE GENRE

In 1886 Grierson published forty-two examples of *birahā* song texts. At that time a song consisted of just two rhymed lines of text and lasted less than a minute in performance. No musical instruments were used. This genre existed solely as a village form and was prevalent among the Ahir (cowherds and milkmen) caste, who now prefer the term Yādav. This genre still exists today with the same village and caste associations but is called *khaṛī birahā,* probably to distinguish it from the new genre that developed over the last hundred years.

This is an example of a *khaṛī birahā:*[2]

Ram kī laṛaiyā ke na pāibe Ravanwa, jekarī bagal mẽ Hanuman
Sonā kai Lanka toharī māṭī mẽ milāi hai, tor dīhai toharo gumān

2. This version was provided by Ram Sevak Singh (2/VI/83 Marcus Collection: RSS interview no. 1). A slightly different version of the same was provided by Lakshmi Narayan Yadav (1975:1) and Nakharu Yadav (Marcus Collection: XXIII:8, 14/III/84). Besides Grierson's forty-two examples (1886), which are in Devanagari script with English translations and commentary, see also Henry (1988; chap. 5, pp. 6 ff.) for seven examples transcribed into Latin script and translated with commentary. For recordings, see Columbia 9102021, *The Columbia World Library of Folk Primitive Music,* vol. 13: *Indian Folk Music* (as listed in Henry 1988, chap. 5:5). A single example is provided. Rounder Records: Chant the Names of God. Marcus Collection (VII:30 and VIII:11) includes eight examples.

Fig. 8. Bihari (center), said to be the creator of *birahā,* and two of his main disciples. On his right is Ramman, the namesake of the Ramman *akhāṛā*. All three are holding *kartāl*s. With the exception of the chairs, this group typifies the early *birahā* ensemble (photograph from the 1920s).

[Ravana cannot succeed in fighting Ram, who has Hanuman at his side, / (to Ravana:) Your golden Lanka will be mixed with the soil (i.e., destroyed), your pride will be broken.]

Oral history holds that the earliest stages of the "modern" *birahā* (as distinct from *khaṛī birahā*) were the creation of one man, Bihari Lal Yadav, who lived from 1857 to 1926 (see fig. 8). Generally referred to as

Guru Bihari, he is universally recognized as the founder of *birahā*. (Thus, we have the remarkable occurrence of a folk music genre with an acknowledged founding figure.)

The form that Bihari used for his own compositions included an unlimited number of rhymed lines: the genre had grown to allow for more content. Among the changes which Bihari is said to have effected were the invention of a new instrument and its introduction into *birahā* performance. This instrument, the *kartāl,* consists of two pairs of tapered metal rods, each approximately nine inches in length. The singer holds a pair in each hand, creating a high-pitched ringing sound by rhythmically hitting the two rods against each other (see fig. 8). This instrument is unique to *birahā* and is thus one of the more obvious identifying elements of the genre.[3]

Bihari introduced his new genre into the urban environment when he moved to the city of Banaras[4] and began performing at city temple festivals, called *shringār*s. At the time, the most prominent forms of entertainment at these festivals were *kajalī* (another regional folk genre), Indian classical music, and performances of courtesans, which included music and dance. Bihari began performing *birahā* at *kajalī* functions. He came away from a number of these the acknowledged "winner" of the event: in *kajalī* performances, two or more ensembles would perform at the same event, and there would be an element of competition between the ensembles. This element of competition was later incorporated into city performances of *birahā*. Thus *birahā* had its first successes in the urban environment.

As Bihari's fame spread (he gained renown as both singer and poet) he acquired a number of disciples (*shishya*s or *chela*s). When his disciples later attracted students of their own, separate lineages developed. These lineages are called *akhāṛā*s or, less commonly, *gharānā*s. Bihari had four main disciples and these in turn have their own students (see table 3.1). The various *akhāṛā*s do not keep records of their members. The system relies on the social contact of the guru-*chela* relationship for its maintenance (generally, poets are the gurus, singers are the *chela*s). All acknowledge that the *akhāṛā* system in *birahā* began with Bihari.[5]

3. The word *kartāl* is used across northern India to name various other idiophones ("a musical instrument—as a gong—that sounds by the vibration of its constituent material" [Webster's Seventh New Collegiate Dictionary]). This version of the *kartāl* is unique to *birahā*.

4. Bihari was born in a village named Patna near the Aurihar station, Saidpur tahsil, in Ghazipur district. He moved to Banaras at an early age in search of employment and eventually took up permanent residence in Ahiriyana, a section of the city adjacent to Nichi Bag (L. N. Yadav, 1975:3; Ram Sakal Yadav, n.d., 3).

5. Some *birahā* singers come from non-Bihari lineages. Most of *these* lineages have their roots in the *kajalī* tradition. *Kajalī* (or *shāyarī kajalī*) is a folk musical genre of eastern

TABLE 3.1 Significant Names in the Main Bihari *Akhāṛā* Lineages

- Swami Sivanand (or Dayanand) (Bihari's spiritual guru)
  - Bihari (1857–1926)
    - Ramman Yadav (d. 1945)
      - Hori Lal (Ramman's younger bro.) (d. 1975)
        - Hira Lal (b. c. 1928)
          - Mangal Yadav (b. c. 1957)
    - Ganes Yadav (c. 1886–c. 1947)
      - Sahadev Yadav (b. c. 1901)
        - Ram Dev Yadav (Sahadev's son) (b. c. 1947)
    - Pattu Yadav (1881–1969)
      - Achevar Yadav (d. 1982)
        - Paras Yadav (b. c. 1935)
        - Bullu Yadav (b. c. 1943)
          - Ram Vilas Pandey (b. c. 1961)
    - Sarju Rajbhar (c. 1880–1984)

These *akhāṛās* play a major role in organizing the social and performance aspects of the tradition. For example, membership in one or another of the *akhāṛās* is mandatory for anyone wanting to become a professional *birahā* singer. One reason for this is that *birahā* singers do not improvise their song texts; rather they obtain and memorize texts from poets who belong to one specific *akhāṛā*. The song texts are the property of that *akhāṛā*. Thus it is only through membership in an *akhāṛā* that a singer can obtain songs to sing.

The *akhāṛā* phenomenon also plays a major role in determining who will perform when the performance is of the competitive, or *dangal,* variety. In *dangal*s the two competing *birahā* ensembles must be from different *akhāṛās*. Thus, it is not only the two singers who are competing but also the two *akhāṛās*. One's membership in an *akhāṛā* is not an obscure piece of information; rather it is announced at the end of every song. All songs end with a section called the *chāp* (literally "stamp") in which the poet has composed lines that list the major figures in his specific *akhāṛā*'s lineage. Thus the audience is constantly being reminded of the singer's *akhāṛā* affiliation. This is a sample *chāp,* written by Mangal Yadav, a poet and singer of the Ramman *akhāṛā:*

> Swami, Guru Bihari, Ramman Hori, dharm anuyāyī,
> Hira, Lakshmi, kavi Mangal sevai mandir nit bhāī . . .

U.P. and western Bihar, which flourished for a hundred years or more, but which met almost total eclipse with the rise of *birahā*. Many *kajalī* performers, wanting to continue their musical careers, came into *birahā*. Thus *kajalī* lineages became *birahā* lineages. Interestingly, the presence of a *gharānā* system within folk music has been little noticed.

[Swami (Bihari's guru), Bihari, Ramman, and Hori are followers of the dharma (i.e., are religious) / Hira Lal, Lakshmi, and the poet Mangal serve the temple daily . . .] ("Lakshmi" is Lakshmi Narayan, b. c. 1941, who, as the grandson of Ramman, is considered the present-day titular head, or *ḳhalīfā,* of the Ramman *akhāṛā.*) Bihari's disciples and others who constitute the next generation of poets composed in a new structure, which included the addition of a periodic refrain called the *ṭerī* (the creation of which is attributed to Bihari himself). In time, the *ṭerī* came to be considered the very essence of the *birahā* form. Recognizable by its distinct poetic structure and melodic line, the *ṭerī,* in content, is said to encapsulate the song's dominant statement and *rasa* (aesthetic quality).

Over a period of some thirty years (c. 1920–1950) three distinct formal structures evolved, all centering around the use of the *ṭerī* line. All three can be said to be variants of the "traditional *birahā* structure," "*birahā* in its maturity." Once evolved, all three continued to exist side by side.[6] Besides the *ṭerī,* two other compositional features characterized the traditional *birahā* form in its maturity. These are the *antarā* (*dophūliyā* and *caukaṛā* varieties) and the *uṛān.*

EXPERIMENTATION LEADING TO THE MODERN *BIRAHĀ* STRUCTURE

The three varieties of the "traditional *birahā* structure" consisted solely of *ṭerī, antarā,* and *uṛān,* and as such were pure "100 percent *birahā*" structures. In time, however, this purity of melodic and poetic structure became undesirable: poets and performers began to feel the need for greater variety. This variety was achieved when, from the later 1940s (and possibly earlier), poets began to substitute new forms and melodies for one or two of the units within the traditional *birahā* structure. Sometimes the *antarā*s were replaced by poetic forms such as *chand,* or *sawaiyā.* However, strict adherence to poetic forms was never a major aspect of *birahā* composition. Rather, poets would apply the art of parody to already existing melodies. (This is a process whereby the poet selects an existing song as a source for a new melody; he composes a new text on the chosen melody, using the song's original text to guide the phrasing.)[7] The common term for these borrowed melodies is *tarz* (singular and plural). Occasionally the terms *dhun* and *lay* are also used.

6. These three structures still exist today but are relegated to use in short songs (the kind that are needed for All India Radio/Akashvani and commercial recordings).

7. This definition of "parody" is common in Western classical music studies; see Grout 1973:142. This use of parody is an extension of a long-standing tradition in Bhojpuri musical culture. Grierson wrote, "In the country districts, I never heard of a new tune being invented. There seems to be a certain stock of melodies ready made, to which the

For *birahā* this new technique of parody had major consequences for the success of the genre. The singer could now keep the interest of his audience not only with the story line, but also by the use of various popular melodies. The technique came to be used in two ways. It was the perfect strategy for keeping up with the trend-oriented aspect of modern popular culture: if a new song were sweeping the city (from a film or on the radio or records), within a week or two *birahā* singers would be incorporating that song into their own. But parody could also be applied using traditional songs. Thus, the singer now had the ability to play up to the conflicting trends of "modernization" and rural and Bhojpuri pride. This could even be done within the same song by first quoting the latest Bombay film song and then introducing a village melody. This technique proved highly successful.

There is a large body of *tarz* available to the poet for use through the process of parody. Bombay is forever providing new film songs. (Films in India usually have five songs each. These songs are the object of a "Top 40" type of popularity.) There are also the melodies used by non-Bhojpuri music ensembles: *qawwālī, ālhā,* and Nauṭankī.[8] And there are the melodies of Bhojpuri folk music. Poets are proud to point out that Bhojpuri musical culture alone offers an unlimited source for melodies ("anant bhandar"). Bhojpuri musical culture has some twenty or more genres that are more or less melody-specific.[9] Among these are songs associated with specific castes (for example: *mallāh gīt,* boatmen songs; *dhobi gīt,* washermen songs, etc.), songs associated with specific rites of passage (*sohar,* birth songs; *vivāh gīt,* wedding songs, etc.), songs associated with specific seasons (*kajalī,* songs of the rainy season; *phaguwā* or *holī,* springtime songs) and a large number of other miscellaneous folk song genres (*khemtā, kaharawā, chaparahiyā, jhūmar, pūrvī, lācārī, bideshiyā,* and others).

To increase the entertainment value of their performances, singers even began to sing a few lines of the borrowed melodies' original text before proceeding to sing the parodied lines. As far as the story of the *birahā* song was concerned, this was a complete digression, but the en-

---

words of every new song must be fitted" (1886:210). Grierson commented further that the songs "by no means follow the strict and complicated metric laws. . . . Any number of syllables, long or short, can be crowded into a line, so long as the need of a musical ictus is satisfied" (1884:198–99). He added, "In these . . . songs the melody to which they are sung is the only guide, and so long as the accent or musical ictus is provided for, the author cared little whether his syllables were long or short" (1886:209).

8. *Ālhā* and Nauṭankī both exist as Bhojpuri genres, but their roots are to the west of the Bhojpuri region (see chapter 2 for a discussion of Nauṭankī).

9. For example, Grierson wrote that his forty-two examples of *kharī birahā* were "all sung to the same melody" (1886:211). He adds that "every mill-song must be sung to the melody called 'jatsār'" (1886:210).

tertainment value could not be denied; audiences loved it then and continue to do so now.

Beginning in the late 1940s, there followed a long period of experimentation. Poets tried all varieties of *tarz* in differing orders. By the late 1960s a new structure began to emerge. By about 1970 this new structure became standard for virtually all full-length *birahā* songs. This is still the case today. The most surprising aspect of this structure is that the formal elements of the traditional *birahā* (the *ṭerī, caukaṛā* and *uṛān*) have been reduced to minimal representation. Non-*birahā* melodies now outnumber the traditional *birahā* melodies! This has given rise to frequent statements that *birahā* no longer exists; it is now a composite genre best called simply *lok gīt,* a "folk music." It is now common to hear someone say, "Yes, *lok gīt* is happening up the street," referring to a *birahā* performance. However, despite their own statements to this effect, the *birahā* community continues to call their genre *birahā.*

Poets and singers emphasize that the new structure is flexible; the requirements of a particular story line might necessitate a change in the structure. But there is an inviolable aspect of the above progression: the song as a whole must progress from *naram* to *garam* (literally "soft to hot"), that is, the level of excitement must build. There can be no slackening of the energy level in the middle of the song. The climax should come at the end (before the final *uṛān*). Accordingly, *tarz* are judged for the quality of energy that they evoke. The beginning and ending progression are stable features of virtually every full-length song because of the "naram to garam" effect that they help create.

THE ENSEMBLE: *BIRAHĀ* AS A PROFESSION

During the period when the above changes in song structure were taking place, there were also major developments in the performing ensemble. During Bihari's time, there was no concept of a fixed ensemble. A singer would bring one or two companions to serve as a chorus, or he might ask one or two people from the audience to sing with him. All three people would play the *kartāl* (see fig. 8).

When *birahā* poets began to experiment with the traditional structure of the *birahā* song, the resulting complexity necessitated that the chorus members be specialists. Uninitiated singers were no longer able to sit in casually as chorus members. Thus, a new entity emerged, the *parṭī* (the English word "party"), consisting of a lead singer and usually two steady chorus singers (*ṭerī bharnewāle* or *ṭerī kahnewāle*).

At about the same time, changes in the genre's instrumentarium expanded the ensemble's size. In the late 1940s a few singers experimented with adding a *ḍholak* player to the ensemble (a *ḍholak* is a barrel drum with skin heads stretched over the two open ends of the barrel).

Shortly thereafter, the harmonium was added (a portable keyboard instrument; the sound is produced by air from hand-pumped bellows passing through reeds). In time, both the *ḍholak* and the harmonium gained wide acceptance. While it was still common in the 1970s to find village parties that did not include a harmonium player, by the 1980s the *ḍholak* and harmonium had become standard features of all *birahā* ensembles. The standard *birahā* party today is a five- to six-man ensemble: a lead singer, a *ḍholak* player, a harmonium player, and two or three chorus singers. The latter provide rhythmic accompaniment by playing the *kartāl* and another idiophone called the *jhāñjh.* Recently a few parties have experimented by adding a flute player in some of their city performances. However, this is as yet an isolated phenomenon.

An important aspect of the modern-day party is an explicit hierarchy among the party members. While many comment that in Bihari's time the ensemble was an informal group of equals, today the lead singer is clearly the head of the ensemble. A party is known by the name of its lead singer alone (e.g., Hira Lal and Party). It is the lead singer who is hired to give a performance and it is he who is paid. He in turn pays his party members. The pay scale for the different members reflects their relative status. Today, the best-paid parties are paid for each performance: Rs. 40 for the harmonium player; Rs. 35 for the *ḍholak* player; Rs. 30 for the two chorus members. After paying out these fees and any travel expenses the lead singer keeps all remaining money.[10] This often amounts to from five to ten times what he has paid his individual party members. Thus, it is only the lead singer who achieves substantial wealth and fame. It is not uncommon for the party members to comment on their second-class status.

The addition of musical instruments to the ensemble has been credited with instigating the change in the genre from avocation to vocation. Before the introduction of the *ḍholak* and harmonium, singers were invited only informally to sing at a given function. Remuneration, only in the form of *inām,* was minimal. Older singers all point out that singing was then an avocation, an act of love ("Log shauk se gāte the.") With the introduction of the *ḍholak* and harmonium players, the situation had to change. The *ḍholak* and harmonium players were not members of the *birahā* community. Their skills were in demand among a number of other performance genres that coexisted in the area (especially *qawwālī* and *kajalī*). Thus, they had to be paid to assure their steady attendance and loyalty. This meant that the *birahā* party could

10. Besides a preset fee that a singer receives, a large part of the renumeration for a performance comes in the form of *inām,* gifts of money and other miscellaneous items that members of the audience bring up to the lead singer during the performance. The lead singer keeps all *inām* for himself. During weddings, members of the groom's family are usually quite generous with *inām.*

no longer be invited informally, but rather had to be hired for the occasion. The lead singer was now obliged to ask for preset fees. Initially these fees were small, but as the genre grew in popularity, so the fees increased accordingly. Today there are a number of lead singers who have become very wealthy from their performances, earning over Rs. 50,000 a year.

THE LARGER SOCIAL CONTEXT

Birahā has traditionally been a genre of the Ahir and neighboring castes (Rājbhar, Kurmi, Mallāh, etc.). These groups are from the lower end of the caste system. Common ranking (by members of the upper castes) places these groups at the top of the fourth (Shudra) *varna* (the fourfold ranking of the various castes: Brahmin, Kshatriya, Vaishya, and Shudra).

Performers and members of the *birahā* audiences are usually from the lower castes. People from the upper castes consider it beneath their dignity to attend *birahā* performances; they do not consider *birahā* to be worthy of their attention. Recently, however, the lucrative aspect of *birahā* has attracted singers from all castes. Today some 20 percent of *birahā* singers are from outside the traditional group of castes. Everyone associated with the genre is proud to state that today there are singers from *every* caste. (One of the great figures in the history of the genre, Ram Sevak Singh, is a Thakur, i.e., of the Kshatriya *varna.* Among the top performers today are a Brahmin, a Thakur, a Harijan, and a Muslim.)

As was mentioned, *birahā* is performed in separate village and city contexts. In the rural areas, weddings occur during the spring months; it is here that *birahā* finds its village context. (The length and dates of the wedding season vary each year according to astrological considerations. In 1983 it lasted three months, from April to June. However, in 1984 it lasted only one month, from April 14 to May 14.) Marriages in this part of India are village exogamous. Weddings take place in the bride's village, at the bride's house. The groom, his male relatives, and a large number of their male guests all travel to the bride's village in a procession called the *barāt.* The *barāt* arrives in the evening (6:00 to 9:00 P.M.) and leaves around 4:00 or 5:00 P.M. the following afternoon. The members of the *barāt* set up camp in a field near the bride's house. Large tarps are spread out; a colorful tent is often erected for the occasion.[11] *Birahā* performers are hired to entertain the groom's marriage-party members during their stay in the bride's village. There are two time periods when entertainment is considered necessary: two to three

11. By late March or early April most crops have been harvested and the fields are empty. Thus there is ample room to accommodate large wedding parties.

hours (from 9 or 10:00 P.M.) on the first night, and some five to six hours (usually beginning around 10:00 A.M.) during the following day.

When *birahā* existed only as *khaṛi birahā* and then later as the early stages of the modern *birahā,* the genre was performed at weddings in an informal manner only. (*Khaṛi birahā* is still performed in this fashion.) But as the expanded party came into being, *birahā* became part of the formal entertainment. Today, *birahā* is the featured entertainment at weddings of the Ahir and neighboring castes, that is, *birahā*'s constituent castes.[12] (*Birahā* singers from other castes perform regularly for their own castes' weddings.)

When *birahā* is performed at weddings, the person in charge of the entertainment is the groom's father (called the *barāt mālik,* the lord or master of the *barāt*). He or one of his sons, brothers, or helpers travels to the *birahā* singer's house and hires the latter to perform at the upcoming wedding. The *barāt mālik* can hire as many parties as he wants. If there is more than one *birahā* party (occasionally there are three, four, five, or more), the parties will take turns, each performing one song at a time.

The second major context for *birahā* performances is the city temple festival season. The festivals, called *shringārs*, are held annually for each functioning Hindu temple and serve as festivals of rededication and redecoration. Residents of a temple's immediate neighborhood form a committee to organize the festivities. Besides arranging for fresh coats of paint and occasionally major and minor building renovations, the *shringār* committee also organizes one, two, or three nights of religious and social functions. Many temples have a regular date for their *shringār* (reckoned by the Hindu calendar). The *shringār* season as a whole is said to start with Krishna *Janmāshtmī* (late August to early September) and run until early December.

Religious functions include a *hawan pūjan* (a ritual performed by Brahmin priests which centers around a sacrificial fire) and possibly a reading of the Rāmāyan in its entirety (called *Rāmāyaṇa pāṭh*), or a communal session of *bhajan* singing led by a local *kīrtan maṇḍalī* (an informal group of men who gather, usually weekly, to sing devotional songs), or both. For the social functions the *shringār* committee arranges one or more of the following forms of entertainment:

1. *birahā;*
2. *qawwālī* (a Muslim musical genre, which is often adapted with Hindu themes for these occasions);

12. The top singers are in great demand during this period. It is not uncommon for them to be booked daily for the length of the wedding season. After finishing a performance at about 5:00 P.M., the party members eat and then set off for their next performance, usually later in the same day at some other village.

3. *orchestra* (a recent phenomenon in which a band performs imitations of hit film songs; these bands appeared in Banaras in c. 1978);
4. the showing of a film;
5. Indian classical music (chosen only rarely).

If the *shringār* is to last more than one day, it is common to have two or more of the above, that is, one performance each evening.

As was mentioned above, when *birahā* first entered the *shringār* circuit, *kajalī* was the most common form of folk music to be performed at these functions. Initially, *birahā* singers sang on the same programs with *kajalī* singers. A number of *birahā* singers fared very well in these events. In time, some committees decided to hire only *birahā* parties. Armed in the 1950s with new instruments and the newly developing formal structure, which put a premium on the entertainments and sentimental values of its melodies, *birahā* began to take over performance opportunities from *kajalī*.[13] By the mid-1960s this had become a major trend, so that by the 1970s *kajalī* (the *shayarī kajalī* that was performed at *shringārs*) had virtually disappeared. The expression on everyone's lips today is "kajalī ṭūṭī," *kajalī* broke. *Birahā* (and, to a lesser extent, the other forms listed above) has taken its place. Today, *birahā* is the dominant form of entertainment at Banarsi *shringārs*.

Once a *shringār* committee has decided on the type of entertainment it wants, one or more of the committee members will approach the performers of their choice and hire them for their *shringār*. The money needed for these functions is collected by door-to-door solicitation from the homes and businesses in the immediate neighborhood. Contributions (called *candā*) are usually Rs. 2, though some people and the larger neighborhood businesses might give Rs. 11, 21, or more.[14]

The entertainment functions take place on the city street nearest the temple. They begin at 10:00 or 11:00 P.M. when normal city activities have come to a halt. Most functions are of sufficient size to warrant the closing of the street. The entertainment continues until after sunrise. In fact, the hustle and bustle of the morning activities (especially the street traffic) play a major role in bringing these functions to a close.

These events are free and open to everyone. Most of the people in the audience are residents and shopkeepers of the neighborhood.

13. *Birahā* was further aided in its overtaking of *kajalī* by its flexibility of content. *Kajalī* was restricted in content, as it had been inexorably linked to songs depicting aspects of the rainy season. As such, *kajalī* was also restricted to only a certain segment of the year (end of June to September, the Indian rainy season), whereas *birahā* could be performed all year round.

14. N. Kumar (1984:201) reports that this door-to-door collection of donations is a recent phenomenon. "Previously, only those temples which had wealthy donors had grand *shringārs*," i.e., *shringārs* that include one or more evenings of entertainment.

Women, however, attend only in the morning as the events are coming to a close. A significant percentage of the audience are people who just happened upon the function while traveling to or from other engagements. There are also devoted fans who will travel across the city to hear their favorite singers. Audiences range from 150 people at some poorly attended functions to over 1,200. Attendance depends largely on the fame of the two lead singers.[15]

These functions are advertised in three ways. Sign boards called *liṣts* are hung by the sides of the road or are painted on any available wall space. Announcements of upcoming events are often published in the local Hindi newspaper, *Āj,* on its third page. But the most effective source of advertisement is the loudspeakers that are placed up and down the street for one to two hundred yards on the morning of the first day of the *shringār.* All of the *shringār*'s activities are broadcast over these loudspeakers, bringing the occasion to the attention of thousands (often tens of thousands) of people.

When *birahā* is to be performed at these functions, two ensembles are hired. These performances are called *dangal*s, a word which emphasizes that the program is viewed as a competition between the two parties. Two stages are set up approximately a hundred feet apart. The audience sits between the stages either on large tarps that are spread on the street or (more rarely) on chairs that are provided. The audience first faces one party, which will sing two songs. Then the audience turns around and hears two songs from the other party. The two parties alternate in this fashion throughout the night. Each set of two songs usually lasts from one to one and a half hours.

The success of the entertainment functions within *shringār*s can be attributed to a number of factors. Since the events are held in the name of religion, the committees usually have no trouble collecting the necessary funds. The functions themselves fit into the general mold of Banarsi festivals by incorporating the standard repertoire of lights, decorations, music, an open-air setting, and all-night activities (N. Kumar 1984:289, 291). The lights include long strings of mini-bulbs

15. There is a markedly different ambience in the wedding and *shringār* performances. At weddings, the members of the audience are all considered to be guests of the bride's family. One's every need is attended to. Water, snacks, and food are all provided. Attention is given to assure that everyone has sufficient room to sit. These points are in contrast to the circumstances at the city *shringār*s. One can buy refreshments from nearby food stands or tea shops; however, nothing is provided free or brought to the members of the audience. Seating is generally first come, first served. There is seldom any feeling that one is a guest, although the members of the *shringār* committee are supposed to ensure everyone's comfort. (The exception to this comment are the large contributors in the *candā* collection drive. These people are treated as guests of honor with special seating being provided for them.)

("Christmas lights" in the United States). These are hung from poles along the side of the road. The resulting effect is that of curtains or a lengthy canopy, which helps to define and ornament the site for the event. Further decorations are provided by folk painters who are hired to paint on any available wall space in the immediate *shringār* area.

The element of competition has also contributed to the success of these events. When performed at *shringārs*, *birahā* (and *qawwālī*) features an aspect of competition between two lead singers (and their ensembles). A few *shringārs* have also sponsored programs of wrestling and forms of weight lifting (using *joṛī,* a pair of long, cone-shaped weights, and *gadā,* a club with a spherical mass at one end), with trophies being given to the winners of the various events. Members of the audience often comment that the aspect of competition is one of the major attractions of these musical and athletic events.

There is also an implicit sense of competition among the various neighborhoods as to which area has the best *shringār*. This has resulted in numerous two- and three-day *shringārs* and in the committees vying for the most famous performers. A few committees have recently sponsored two or three consecutive nights of *birahā* as a way of distinguishing their *shringār* from others in their vicinity.[16]

Birahā's position of prominence at these festivals reflects, in part, the major change in the nature of *shringārs* that has occurred over the last fifty years. Nita Kumar (1984) reports the withdrawal of members of the upper classes from these and other public festivities. A new "morality" caused the upper classes to frown on culture in public forums. Classical music and the music and dance of courtesans, prominent on the streets of Banaras some forty to fifty years ago, both retreated to indoor, usually private settings. Banaras's classical musicians began following "a different set of expectations of the constitution of a 'proper' audience, of audience appreciation, and of the value of a professional artist. The 'public,' crowds, and open gatherings have become negative concepts now" (N. Kumar 1984:193). *Shringārs*, with but a few exceptions, have been left to the domain of the lower classes.

With the withdrawal of the upper classes from the audiences, if not the financial support, of *shringārs*, these festivities became an important symbol of lower-class identity and a major forum for lower-class cul-

16. Competition exists in many other aspects of Banarsi culture: within the wrestling and weight-lifting clubs (called *akhāṛās*), which are common throughout the city; in the singing of *nāt* by different Muslim groups on the occasion of the birth anniversary of the Prophet; and informally in the desire to have the best images (religious statues) for Durgā Pūjā or Vishwakarma Pūjā, the best tazias for Muharram, and the best martial arts groups (groups that use swords and sticks) for Rāmlīlā processions, etc. (see Kumar 1984).

ture.[17] "*Shringārs* . . . are indicative of a 'lower class' identity, in that they serve to separate and define their participants. . . . The event is considered to be one belonging to the low classes, of the poor and uneducated" (see chapter 5 in this volume). *Birahā,* a music of the lower classes, was embraced as the appropriate form of entertainment for these events.

BIRAHĀ, THE MASS MEDIA, AND STARDOM

Besides offering the potential for asserting lower-class identity, *shringārs* were also vehicles for developing neighborhood pride. Today each neighborhood wants its own *shringār.* This trend has been supported by major increases in the size and population of Banaras: surrounding rural areas are becoming urbanized; thus the number of neighborhoods is increasing. Also neighborhoods within the city are becoming subdivided, with each smaller division wanting its own festivals.

It is clear from the above that there are a number of performance contexts available to the performer. Fame and fortune are real possibilities. Besides the separate city and village seasons described above,[18] there has also been, for the top singers, a third season. Since the early days of the modern-day *birahā,* the top performers have been called to Calcutta, Bombay, cities in Gujarat, and the like to give performances for laborers who are originally from U.P. and Bihar. These performances take place from December to February when winter's cold puts an end to all performances in eastern U.P. and Bihar. These programs are unusual for two reasons. First, many are "ticket programs," that is, one must buy a ticket in order to gain admission. Second, the performers are often paid as much as ten times what they earn for performances in the Banaras area (this being above travel expenses, which are provided separately). Thus, except for the monsoon season, the top *birahā* parties have performances throughout the year.

When the initially skeptical producers of commercial records became convinced of the lucrative aspect of producing regional folk musics, *birahā* and other Bhojpuri genres began to appear on records. For *birahā* this first happened in 1955. Since then a number of recording companies have produced records of *birahā,* initially on 78-rpm and now on

17. As Sarma (quoted in Kumar 1984:321) states for Durgā Pūjā associations, the *shringār* committees have also played an important role by offering "chances for the young men to organize and show their organizational and artistic talents on a mass scale."

18. There are exceptions: some city families call for *birahā* at their weddings; temple *shringārs* also take place in the villages. *Birahā* is also commonly performed at the *griha pravesh* ceremonies of *birahā*'s constituent castes (the formal ceremony before a new house is officially occupied).

45-rpm. These recorded songs have been either three or six minutes in length.

Birahā was first broadcast over the radio from All India Radio's Allahabad station in about 1960. Later the government built AIR Sarnath, the Banaras station. There are presently some eighty-five groups that perform folk music on AIR Sarnath's folk music show. Each day a different group's music is broadcast: six songs spread out over three different shows, at 1:50 P.M., 5:15 P.M., and 6:40 P.M. The songs, five minutes in length, are in any of some fifteen different folk genres. *Birahā* is one of these genres. A given group's music is usually broadcast four times a year. Musicians and poets refer to the short songs that they must prepare for radio or records as *chote* (small) *lok gīt* or simply *lok gīt* to distinguish them from the longer songs that make up the bulk of their repertoire.

In the last eight years audio cassettes of *birahā* have also appeared. With audio cassettes, recording of full-length songs is now possible, as the time limitations imposed by records and the radio are no longer a factor. Today cassette stores in Banaras offer dozens of cassettes of live *birahā* performances. (The *lok gīt* of radio and records are all studio recordings.) However, 99 percent of these cassettes are illegally produced. Microphones are set up, often near the loudspeakers that are a part of every live performance, without the knowledge or consent of the performers involved. The people who produce cassettes from these recordings establish no contact whatsoever with the performers themselves. Needless to say, performers are not paid for these recordings.

The relative ease and low cost with which cassette recordings can be made and duplicated has resulted in a major pirated-cassette industry. Within days after a legitimate cassette or record appears in the market, there are two, three, or four pirated copies of the new release available on various spurious labels. The duplicate cassettes all have different covers and designs, but they are identical to the original in content. Because of this pirated industry, all but two legitimate companies have been forced to stop producing commercial recordings of *birahā*.

In the last few years, a few *birahā* ensembles have performed on television. The shows are taped in Lucknow. In 1984 *birahā* appeared for the first time in a film ("Sonawā ka Pinjarā"). Two ensembles performed, each presenting one short song. Television and film will undoubtedly play significant roles in the future of the genre. (In late 1984, Banaras received its own TV relay station; however, shows are not as yet produced locally.)

This variety of performance contexts has made *birahā* a compelling profession to which performers are attracted from a very young age. A child first enters the active *birahā* community of performers by casually sitting in with the chorus members. This is allowed on an informal level: there is always room on the performers' *chaukī* (the platform on which the performers sit or stand) for such an individual. After a while the child will learn the format structure of the songs and the melodies that are used. Next he must memorize a few short songs. Children who show the desire and ability to master a few songs are occasionally given a chance to perform at the end of a *birahā* program. (During the *shringār* season, this would be at about 7:00 A.M. following a night of continuous music.) These children would use the party of one of the professional singers.

Over the past fifteen to twenty years, singing in school competitions has played a role in the training of new artists. Yearly competitions are held in October/November. The singing of folk songs is just one of the activities in competitions that also include marching and wrestling. Winners in each category progress from school-wide competitions to *manḍal*-wide, district-wide, regional, and then state and national competitions. One of the younger *birahā* singers who has gained considerable popularity recently had his training and gained recognition in these competitions.

When a singer wants to become a lead singer in his own right, he must do two things: he must organize his own party and he must decide which *akhāṛā* he wants to join. Once he has decided on a particular *akhāṛā*, he arranges for a public ceremony to be performed (called *sinnī*), during which he officially pledges his allegience to that *akhāṛā* (he "sinnī caṛhāte hai," raises up *sinnī*). At the same time, a member of that *akhāṛā* (either the titular head of the *akhaṛā*, called the *ḳhalīfā*, or one of the *akhāṛā*'s poets) publicly and officially accepts the singer into the *akhāṛā*. Having performed this ritual, the new member is then given access to all the songs of this *akhāṛā*.[19]

One of the earlier stages on the road to fame is becoming a "radio artist." A singer and his party must sit for an audition, called a "voice test," before a panel of judges appointed by the radio station. These auditions happen four times a years. A group must pass this test for their music to be broadcast over the radio four times a year.

At a given function, singers and their parties usually perform only with other singers of equal age and status. As a young singer becomes popular and gains a following, his big break will come when one of the superstars agrees to sing "against" him (i.e., in the same program). This

19. The territorial aspect of song ownership is taken very seriously. A singer may not sing a song that belongs to another *akhāṛā*. If a singer changes his *akhāṛā*, he can no longer sing any songs of his former *akhāṛā*. If he were to go ahead and sing such a song, any member of the *birahā* community who is in the audience and realizes what is happening can speak up and demand that the performance be stopped.

becomes the young singer's "ticket to fame." Word spreads that he has sung against the famous "so and so." If he fared respectably in that performance, other singers of fame will soon agree to perform "against" him. Once the young singer has performed with the most popular singers, he has officially "arrived." The frequency with which he is asked to give performances will increase dramatically. He will enter a very substantial income bracket, leaving behind the poorer economic circumstances of the majority of his audience.

In the past, the most popular singers lived either in village areas or in the city. Recently, however, with the rise in the popularity of the genre and the development of "superstar" status for the top performers, there is a new prerequisite for becoming a full-time professional singer: the singer must take up lodging in the city of Banaras, so that he is easily available for those wanting to hire the top artists. The result of this newly felt need is that all the main performers are now residents of the city of Banaras. Banaras has thus become *the* center for the genre.[20]

CONCLUSION

Members of the *birahā* community are unanimous in emphasizing that *birahā* is a product of Bhojpuri culture. It is village life that typifies this culture. Significantly, the genre had its roots in the villages: its earliest stage, *khaṛī birahā,* has existed solely as a rural genre. When poets began to introduce non-*birahā* melodies into the *birahā* form, they continued to rely heavily on traditional Bhojpuri songs. In interviews and even within the notes inserted into performances, poets and singers have stressed the traditional roots of many of the *tarz:* "There is an endless store of Bhojpuri *tarz, tarz* which our people have been singing for ages." Singers have introduced these melodies with pride: "This is a Bhojpuri *tarz,* a completely traditional *tarz.*" Furthermore, the *kartāl,* the instrument that most typifies the genre, is a product of village life: it closely resembles the iron rod that is the major functional element in the ploughs of the region. Members of the *birahā* community take pride in stressing the grass-roots elements of the genre. At the same time, many aspects of *birahā*'s development are the result of urban influences, such as the emphasis on film tunes as a source for new melodies and the introduction of the harmonium into the ensemble. (The harmonium is not traditionally found in the villages.)

20. While villages continue to have *birahā* ensembles (informants tell me—and my own observations support the claim—that every village has one or more *birahā* ensembles), these ensembles are nonprofessional or semiprofessional. Many of the younger singers who move to the city do not abandon their villages; rather, they maintain dual residence.

Birahā, increasingly, is an urban genre that can thus be seen as being informed by two opposing urges: the desire to stress the genre's rural and vernacular (Bhojpuri) roots; and the desire to adopt new features and new developments (new instruments, the latest film songs, or the latest developments in structure). In order to reconcile these two urges a song structure has developed which uses a number of different melodies, all within the same song. A single song can thus respond to both urges simultaneously: after presenting one or two traditional folk melodies, the singer can move on and introduce the latest film song.

The two opposing urges are further reconciled by the new Bhojpuri film industry: the latest film songs can now be Bhojpuri songs. Until recently, Bhojpuri films were a rarity; now they are quite common: in 1983 there were five or six newly released Bhojpuri films. Poets have remarked that they now seldom include the new Hindi film songs; new songs from the latest Bhojpuri films provide an ample supply of new melodies.

The urban influence can be seen as having affected more than just the content and structure of the songs: it can be argued that it was Banaras's urban environment which helped to break down the genre's social isolation. In the villages, it might well have remained restricted to the Ahir and neighboring castes. Performed on the streets of Banaras, the genre came to have a wider following. It became not so much a genre of a certain group of lower castes as the property of the lower classes in general. As such, *birahā*'s fortune came to be linked with the rise of lower-class culture and the growth of the *shringār* phenomenon that has taken place in Banaras over the last fifty years.

The success that *birahā* has experienced has been aided by forces both external and internal to the genre itself. For one, *birahā* appeared in Banaras at an advantageous point in time, when lower-class culture and its temple festivals were expanding. Equally important, singers and poets proved remarkably flexible in their understanding of what constituted the genre. Change was never shunned. Rather, the genre was shaped and reshaped over the years to keep it responsive to the interests of its audiences.

AN EXAMPLE OF A MODERN-DAY *BIRAHĀ*

[This is an excerpt from a live performance. The song tells the story of a theft that occurred at the Vishwanāth temple in Banaras in January 1983. The lines in italic were sung; the rest were spoken (*not*s or the accepting of *inām*). The excerpt begins when the singer, having just finished singing the *gazal,* is accepting an *inām*]:

O.K. my dear brothers, I've received a *puraskār* of Rs. 6 and a garland of flowers from my brother, Debi Lal.

But the *tarz* has changed, my dear friends. This is a Bhojpuri *tarz*:

My Rs. 125,000 nose-ring fell in the middle of the bazaar.
O king, I've lost a lot in my young age.

Yes, this is the *tarz,* my dear friends, but the words of the song [the new text superimposed on this melody]:

The thief took Rs. 1,600,000 in gold in the dark of night.
The sinner desolated the Shiva temple in Kashi [Banaras].

Four thefts had taken place, little was taken.
On the fourth of January in the early morning the thieves entered the temple.

The thieves got gold in the fifth theft.

The sinner desolated the Shiva temple in Kashi.

O.K., brothers, I've received a Rs. 2 *puraskār* from the honorable Lal-ji Yadav. Thank you.

Pay attention, my dear friends. This was not the first theft. Before this there had already been four thefts at the Vishwanath temple [the most important temple in Banaras]. But in the previous four thefts, the thieves couldn't get their hands on a significant amount [of money]. If you'll remember this winter's weather, from the first of January [1983] till the fifteenth, the weather was so bad that, forget about the night time, in the *daytime* darkness remained spread [over the city]. All day long it remained foggy. So what can be said about the night time? During that fiercely cold night, on the early morning of January fourth, the thieves entered the temple. When they tried to pull up the gold at the base of the Shiva *lingam,* they weren't able to do so. So the thieves began to hit their heads on the *lingam;* calling out in appeal, they said, "O Bhole Nath [an epithet of Shiva], you are very merciful. It was with great difficulty that we've come here. Bhole Nath, please give us the gold." Shiva is *so* merciful that he closes his eyes and gives the thieves the gold! But the next day, the police officials [realize the situation and] become troubled. They go into the Shiva temple and begin to hit *their* foreheads [against the *lingam*]. Appealing to Shiva, they say, "You are so merciful, O Bhole Nath, please help us catch the thieves." He gave the gold to the thieves, and now, it might take some time, but surely He'll turn over the thieves to the police.

Now comes a *tarz* from the Balliya-Chapara border [an area 170 km. northeast of Banaras on the U.P.–Bihar border, very much in the heartland of the Bhojpuri region]. Which *tarz* is this? A completely traditional *tarz.* This is a Bhojpuri *tarz* that people have been singing for ages. Which *tarz* is this?

O Ma, I went to wash my hair at Father's pond, when a sparrow took away my nose-ring and a crow took my necklace.

In this *tarz* the words of the song:

The gold wasn't coming into their hands so the sinners starting praying,
the thieves asked "O Lord of the World [an epithet of Shiva]
give us the gold."

The merciful Shiva closed his eyes.
The thieves took the gold; the news spread.
Trying to get a lead they ran around; then the police officials asked,
hitting their heads, "O Bhole Baba, give us the thieves."

Not only in India, but throughout the whole world, commotion spread. What commotion spread? This is set in the *ṭerī:*

The thieves desecrated Tripurari [an epithet of Shiva],
In every direction commotion spread that a major theft has taken place.

[The song goes on to describe the public outrage, the mass demonstrations that took place on the streets of Banaras, and the events that let up to the capture of the thieves and the recovery of the gold.]

PART TWO

Identity and Constructions of Community in Banaras

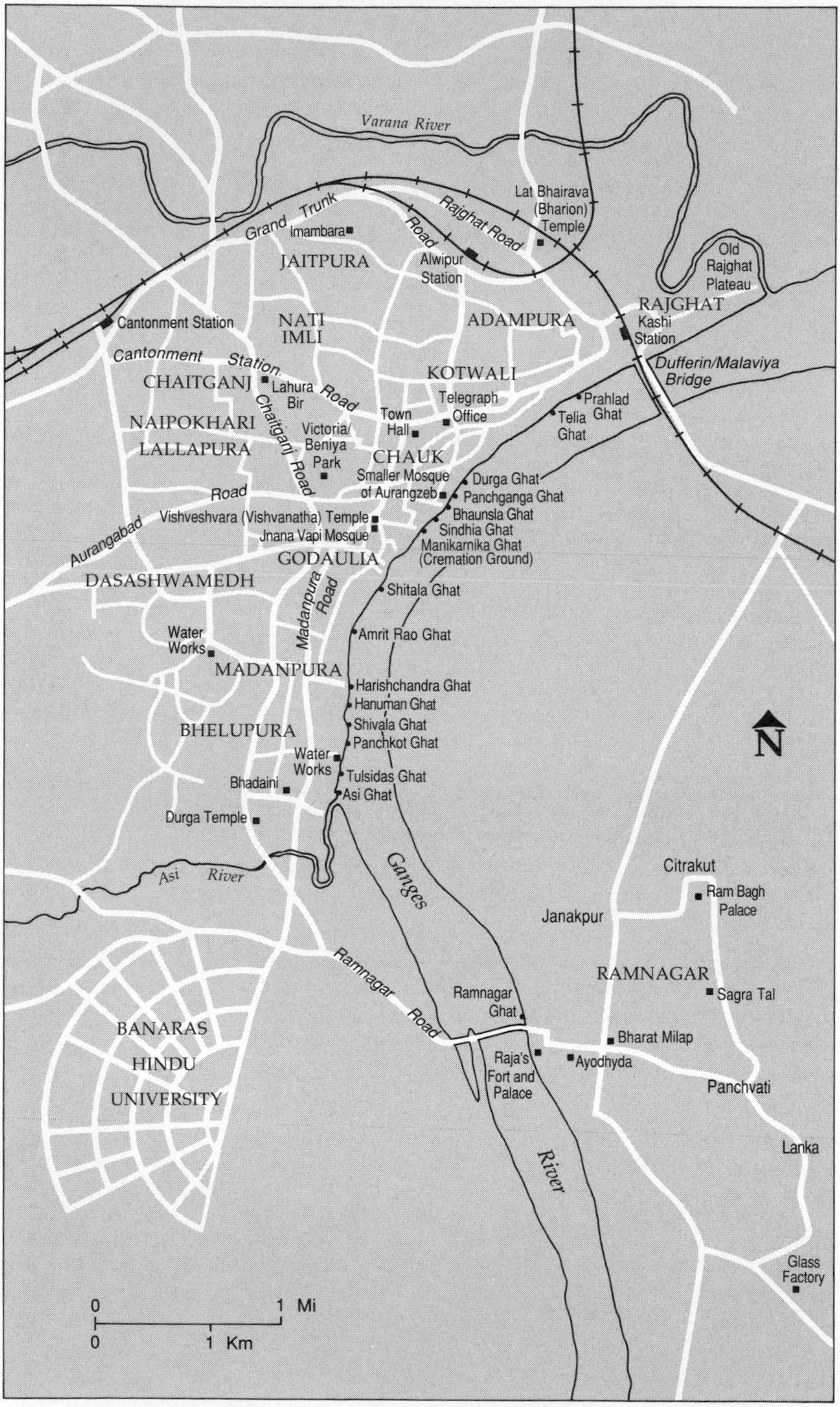

Map 5. City of Banaras. Places marked on this map are sites important in the 1890s and after. Where necessary, they have been identified by the names used in both the British and post-independence periods.

Introduction to Part 2
Identity and Constructions of Community in Banaras

The following two chapters focus on local communities in Banaras. Although approaching the subject from different vantage points, they both address a process central to South Asian social history: the formation of collectivities, through the various affiliations by which Banarsis identified themselves, and the potential inherent in such formation for popular support of political, religious, and social movements. The constituent elements of this process were a series of interrelated choices made by individuals: on place of residence, means of livelihood, forms of leisure, and participation in ceremonial, ritual, and other collective activities (see map 5).

Through such choices individuals defined their own identities. Taken together, these individual actions also constituted what we may call constructions of community ("construction" emphasizes the active and largely self-conscious involvement of participants in the process). That is, in the aggregate, such actions delineated the outlines of a community by underscoring the particular affinities shared by members of the group. Given the wide variety of affinities from which urban residents might choose, such constructions could vary from moment to moment or context to context, depending on circumstances that changed often and regularly: community identity was neither static nor marked by a lineal development. Moreover, particularly in moments of conflict, residents chose to identify with particular groups often in contradistinction to an "other"; this, too, could change over time.

Conceptualization of the north Indian city as a congeries of communities whose interaction constituted the basic line of historical narrative not only is the underlying premise of this volume but also suggests the way residents of Banaras often perceived themselves. A recent *birahā* song text collected by Marcus, for instance, chronicles the events relating to a temple theft in Banaras. Public outrage, the lyrics tell us, was expressed symbolically through a series of parades, each one representing a particular "community" in Banaras (and we might note the differing bases for identity implied by this list):

> Seven big parades went and demonstrated at the chauk police station.
> One day the parade consisted only of women, only of women, only of women. . . .
> The deaf and dumb, lepers and beggars took out a parade; political leaders organized their parade;
> Astrologers, students, and sadhus went ahead, and demonstrated at the chauk police station.[1]

The conscious choices of community affiliation made by participants thus provide points of entrée for scholars interested in the shared values and organizing principles embraced by constructed communities. These essays use as entrée variations of local identity, examining the process at its most basic units, in the small communities of occupation, neighborhood, and local belief system. There were other ways of constructing communities as well—identities that reached beyond these most localized forms. Several of these have been touched on in other chapters in this volume. Most notable, perhaps, were those of gender and that intriguingly prevalent form of association, the *akhāṛā.* In part to encourage further research on such subjects, we summarize briefly here what we know of these topics, before turning to neighborhood, work, and leisure—the vantage points used to view community delineation in this part.

ORGANIZING EXPRESSIONS OF IDENTITY

Generally speaking, the literature has discussed women in South Asia from a variety of viewpoints, but has not yet dealt adequately with the special place for women in Indian popular culture activities.[2] Indeed, we may suspect that, once sufficient research has been done, the "popular culture" of women may well constitute a rather different world from that presented in this volume. As Narayana Rao recently argued, this separation seems to result, in part at least, from the different emphases and worldviews of women (N. Rao 1988). Discussing the "domestic" versions of stories from the Ramayana presented in the women's quarters in South India, Rao noted that both the sections of

1. Translation provided by Scott Marcus. [See chapter 3 for narrative "notes" interspersed by various singers in this folk song.]

2. This may emerge as especially significant in Banaras, since the number of women there was unusually high, swelled by the widows who migrated to spend their final years in Banaras.

the narrative that are selected out for retelling, and the interpretations of behavior implicitly conveyed through these oral presentations, differ strikingly from the public (male?) versions discussed in this volume. In the women's version the heroes are not larger than life: all demonstrate typically human character flaws (illustrated by Rao in a particularly revealing scenario in which Varuna's laughter is taken by each listener as a judgment on his personal shortcomings). And in contrast to the public presentations of the epic where the action ranges across the subcontinent, the women's Ramayana, not surprisingly, presents an enclosed world both loving and tension-filled, much resembling the domestic structures of an extended family.

Another important contributor to the separation of women's popular culture from that studied here will be the fact that, in many cases, the activities occurring in public spaces, and at late-night hours, were considered inappropriate venues for women. Women did not attend the performances of street theatre described in chapter 2. They seldom constituted more than a small part of the audience for *birahā* performances, and then only appeared in the early-morning period, when they could stop to listen on the way back from their walks to the open areas of the city for defecating. Devotion, however, lent a legitimacy to public activities, serving as a rationale for women's participation. They figured largely in temple *shringār*s and among Bīr worshippers. Lutgendorf notes, too, that they not only swelled the audiences for *kathā* (in any case, a safer venue because staged "indoors"), but even figured occasionally among the exegetes.

As the *birahā* lyric suggests, however, women did, sometimes, even publicly mobilize to present their opinions. After marching to the chauk police station, this song goes on, they symbolically enacted their displeasure with police inaction, by presenting to the police a tray with women's "petticoats" and jewelry, thus suggesting that—since they were so ineffectual in the public world—the police might as well take on women's roles and dress.

The implications in Hess's work on Rāmlīlā, too, suggests that women did have certain, albeit specialized, places in public activity. "A large majority of the audience [is made up of] men, but many women come in the course of the month. Usually an informal 'women's section' takes shape. Women are not strictly required to stay there, but most of them do, along with the children they often have in tow" (Hess 1987:3). Most striking, many of the women observing the Ramnagar Rāmlīlā do so at the side of the actor representing Sītā. During her exile, they remain with her in a remote part of the city, removed from the main drama being enacted elsewhere, for days on end (Schechner and Hess 1977:55). Clearly this reformulation for women of the very nature of public spaces, and of the nature of participation in collective activities, will require much more work before we can understand the meaning of this specialized world of women within the urban environment.

Similarly, no systematic discussion and analysis of the structure or functioning of *akhāṛās* has yet been made, although analyses specific to music and medicine point the way (see Neuman 1980; B. Metcalf 1986), buttressed by the implications of work on sannyasis and courtesans.[3] The essays in this volume suggest an outline that, while still shadowy, conveys some of the significance of this organizational form. Based on a recruitment of members who joined voluntarily, *akhāṛās* nevertheless expressed connections between members in fictive kinship and familial terms. They relied as well on variations of the guru-*chela* relationship to connect teachers/leaders to members/followers.

The *akhāṛā* form emerges as the basic unit for a number of very different activities, including "physical culture" clubs, medicine, and even the organizational structure used by mendicants, but preeminently for the organization of cultural performances—particularly in music (both classical and folk), theatre, and the mastery of courtesans over poetry, musical instruments, singing, and dancing. (For a discussion of the timing of the elaboration of this organizational form, see the introduction to Part 1.) Of these, we are most familiar with *akhāṛās* in the form of physical culture clubs, which encouraged athletic prowess in wrestling, sword and stick performances, and the like (e.g., Chandavarkar 1981; and examples cited in Chaudhuri 1951).[4] These clubs often performed during ceremonies and processions; they also could form the basis of marauding gangs during communal clashes.[5]

Akhāṛās fulfilled other significant functions as well. The discipline of of the guru-*chela* relationship proved important, as chapter 3 suggests, as a method not only for perpetuating but also for controlling quality as well as the dissemination of material. It is not irrelevant that *birahā* performers could not sing materials created by a rival *akhāṛā*, or have their materials printed. Beyond neighborhood, *akhāṛās* provided a basic unit for mobilizing for collective action of various kinds; depending

3. See especially Veena Talwar Oldenberg's essay on the forms of resistance practiced by Lucknow's courtesans, organized through a *gharānā* structure that enables them to train the next generation as well as pass property to their daughters (V. Oldenberg, 1987). Significantly, Oldenberg draws parallels between this organization and that of sannyasis discussed by Romila Thapar 1978:63–104.

4. It is in connection with this function that *gundās* (urban hoods) most often became affiliated; in the workshop discussion, volume contributors suggested that the British preoccupation with this *gundā* connection gave *akhāṛās* and their members a bad name; yet contemporary informants assured Kumar that they regarded such skilled athlete members as "heroes," not petty criminals.

5. Evidence is particularly strong for this role in cities with large *gundā* populations, such as Calcutta and Kanpur (see Basu undated; Freitag 1989).

on the eclecticism of the membership (some *akhāṛās* were more heterogeneous than others, drawing members from a broader social base and geographic area), *akhāṛās* represented a potentially diverse and distinctly voluntary form of social organization. They may even, as one scholar has recently suggested, have proved particularly important as an alternative form of society for groups like women and sadhus, thus providing structures to control and use resources, as well as refuge from the world dominated by traditional social structures (Oldenberg 1987). In any case, local perceptions of such *akhāṛās* awarded them great significance. A recent essay discussing the "histories" written by its residents of an eastern U.P. *qaṣba,* for instance, shows us that two of the thirteen events deemed "important" by one author involved disputes between teams of wrestlers (G. Pandey 1984:244).

If *akhāṛās* provide an important point of entrée for discussing the nexus of various cultural activities and local social organization, neighborhood provides another important avenue of analysis. Approaching the subject from one vantage point within the neighborhood, Coccari examines the *muḥalla* as a base for forming and expressing identity through worship of particular neighborhood Bīrs. Her discussion of local deities also suggests the process, discussed by Marcus as well, by which activities originating with one caste or subcaste (in this case, Ahirs or Yādavs) become generalized to lower-class culture, thus incorporating ever-larger numbers of people. Coccari and Kumar note two important characteristics of this expansion: first, the sheer number of activities and occasions have been expanding significantly in the last decade or two. Implied by this increased activity is an elaborated and inclusive lower-class culture that gradually is laying claim to the public spaces of north Indian cities. Second, expansion of such activities has tended to take forms, such as the worship of neighborhood deities, that elicit little orthodox or upper-caste opposition. Thus it appears that a discrete world may be in the process of being fashioned, one that underscores by its very separateness the differences now perceived between upper- and lower-caste urban culture. A third point might be noted as well: the dispersion of this lower-caste urban culture through the movement to industrial centers of up-country workers, particularly weavers. Indeed, one of the more striking aspects of the work of Chandavakar (1981) on Bombay millworkers' neighborhoods, and Chakrabarty (1976) on the popular culture of Calcutta *bastīs,* is the extent to which collective ceremonial activities resemble those the millworkers left behind them in U.P.

This would present a very different pattern from that prevalent in Banaras throughout the nineteenth and into the early twentieth century, a phenomenon examined in greater detail in Part 3. Yet there are still, at present, some indicators of ties to upper-caste values (or, perhaps more accurately, to values shared by upper and lower castes), for these local forms of worship focus on *bīr* figures that combine warrior and saintly paradigms—a combination historically important in Banaras through the dominance of the Gosains, the group of soldier-trader mendicants discussed in the introductory essay on political economy. The meaning inherent in such symbolic public activity is, however, quite complex. Popular support, for instance, may be inferred from the wholesale audience participation by the lower castes in the Ramnagar Rāmlīlā. We noted earlier Hess's point that the messages of the *Rāmcharitmānas* are multistranded, with inherent tensions between egalitarian and hierarchical values. Such complexities doubtless enable its participants to pick and choose those they support. How this works is suggested by a conversation Hess reported with Mahesh Prasad Yadav, "one of the most deeply committed, long-time devotées at the Ramnagar Ramlila, and a member of the Yādav or milkman caste (associated with the Shudra *varna,* though he was prosperous and highly respected)." She asked him what he thought of the *Mānas* line, "A drum, a peasant, a Shudra, an animal, a woman—all these are fit to be beaten." He replied:

> I don't believe that. I am a Yadav. When people say [using an honorific], "Panditji, Panditji" to me, I say, "Listen brother, don't call me Panditji. I am a Yadav.". . . Look: *karama pradhāna vishva kari rākhā* [the world is based on the law of actions]—this is in the *Ramayana.* It is not written *jāti pradhāna vishva kari rākhā* [the world is based on the law of caste]. Write it down, in this one verse is all meaning. Not *jāti pradhāna.* (Hess 1987:25)

This devotée, then, simply chose from the larger whole which verses he would credit as authentic. We may assume that other participants do much the same, basing their selections on the insights they have gained by their experiences as members of particular groups with certain kinds of identities.

Hess's Yādav informant makes it clear that, in this context, his caste (*jāti*) identity as Yādav was important (and thus that he should not be given titles inappropriate to his station in life). So too, however, were his actions. Many of these actions would have been organized through the devotional, recreational, occupational, and residential structures of urban life. Residence—neighborhood—meant many things. In the Banaras of these essays, residence patterns in many *muḥallas* (particularly of artisan and service castes) tended to be coterminous with occupation; similarly, caste or class affinities may have substituted as a shared basis for residence for those among the elite. Primarily because of migration patterns into a city, *muḥalla* residence patterns also often, but not entirely, coincided with extended kinship patterns, regional and linguistic affinities, and even natal village origins. Shared religious beliefs often followed from these other affinities.

Although in the eighteenth century the boundaries of a *muḥalla* could be traced by the actual construction pattern—that is, a *muḥalla* coincided with a single, coterminous building (Blake 1974)—the concept evolved so that even this basic attribute could not define the functional boundaries of a *muḥalla* later on. Instead, the boundaries of a *muḥalla* were often perceptual, unofficial: the neighborhood did not correspond to any official unit such as "ward." At the same time, however, *muḥalla*s did have a formal role in self-government, with spokesmen pronouncing their decisions affecting taxation and organizing themselves for collective activities such as processions and neighborhood-based religious observances. *Muḥalla*s had unofficial roles as well, often channeling competition and conflict along these lines of identity. One Muslim weaver *muḥalla* in Banaras, for instance, generally saw itself in opposition to another located elsewhere in the city: in this case, their shared occupation functioned as an avenue to channel competition—a competition in which specific neighborhood identity, instead, provided the basis for fellow-feeling (see chapter 5).

Expression of a coherent and self-conscious identity at the neighborhood level emerged particularly in leisure-time activities and in collective religious observances, as chapter 4 suggests.[6] Much associational activity featured neighborhood residents as "audience," and in connection with this role, the public space of the *muḥalla* figured prominently. As is noted by Chandavakar, "Street life imparted its momentum to leisure and politics as well; the working classes actively organized on the street. . . . Thus, street entertainers or the more 'organized' tamasha players constituted the working man's theatre. The street corner offered a meeting place. Liquor shops frequently drew their customers[,] and gymnasiums [i.e., *akhāṛās*] their members[,] from particular neighborhoods."[7] Indeed, both Chandavakar and N. Kumar (1984) have documented the extent to which recreation for lower-class males frequently consisted simply of "roaming" the streets of the *muḥalla* (see fig. 9).

Ritual and neighborhood identity were closely connected as well.

6. Perhaps the most important form of identity was gender, which dictated that women's activities would be very different from those described here, since most associational activities occurred in public spaces (see chapters 2 and 3 in this volume).

7. While the physical reality of the Bombay *bastīs* of millworkers differed greatly from the urban neighborhoods of weaver artisans in U.P., the workers in Bombay brought with them from north India certain notions about association; thus their leisure-time activities, even transplanted and characteristic of males away from their extended families, tell us something about the process by which neighborhood served as a focus for identity and collective activity. (Chandavakar 1981:606–7.)

Fig. 9. A neighborhood street in Banaras in about 1910. C. Phillips Cape, *Benares, the Stronghold of Hinduism* (Boston: Gorham Press).

While some activities remained confined within the *muḥallas* and made important statements for their occupants, many were extra-*muḥalla* in nature. These larger collective activities depended on *muḥalla* contributions in money and manpower; examples of both types of ritual activities are examined in chapters 4 and 5.

THE WORLD OF WORK

Nita Kumar, too, uses a local focus to trace the overlapping identities invoked, in varying circumstances, by Banarsi weavers who are also Muslims: at what moments, she asks, do they perceive their preeminent community to be (respectively) that of weavers? that of Muslims? that of Banarsis? While Kumar and Freitag (see Introduction and Part 3) may not agree completely on the nature or context of this process of identity formation, they both recognize the centrality of the process for the social history of Banaras. From their work, in any case, it is possible to trace in outline, at least, the relationship of a particular lower-class group to an urban place and its culture, and to begin to delineate the process of identity formation and construction of community within this central-place idiom.

In a very illuminating contribution that could not be included here, American artist Emily DuBois detailed for the contributors the material world of the weavers that she encountered when she researched brocade weaving in Banaras in 1981.[8] Beginning with a historical summary of the changing patterns of courtly consumption, she showed us the implications of this form of patronage for the survival and relative security of Banarsi artisans. In particular, her discussion of changing styles (influenced primarily by courtly culture), and of the vicissitudes of the changing economy of weaving (affected by larger technical and economic trends) demonstrates the connections between the everyday lives of weavers and the imperial order. Indeed, the extraordinary longevity of the appeal of Banarsi brocade may go far to explain the social stability and integration of Banaras's weavers in the city's political economy. Further, we may see certain parallels in her discussion of changing patronage with the history traced in Part 1 of patronage for performance artists. That is, there is a very similar movement from the central role played by the Mughals to the importance of the successor-

8. Emily DuBois (B.F.A. from School for American Craftsmen, M.F.A. from California College of Arts and Crafts) is a studio artist and teacher of weaving and related arts, whose honors include a 1984 National Endowment for the Arts Individual Artist Fellowship. Her research of brocade weaving in Banaras was sponsored by the Berkeley Professional Studies Program in India, 1980–81, and resulted in a description of the technical aspects of the weaving published in DuBois 1986.

state courtly culture for survival of the handloom industry; from the consistent consumption patterns of Indian brides over several centuries to the new, self-conscious efforts of the independent Indian government to preserve and extend the art and skills of handloom weavers: patronage has provided the key element in the survival of the Banarsi style of weaving. Even for vast numbers of weavers who remain unaware of the role played now by the Weavers' Service Centers (N. Kumar 1984), the impact of the government on their livelihood has been far-reaching, as it has expanded foreign and domestic markets and trained personnel to manage the marketing of handloomed cloth.

Equally important has been the Banarsi context in which handloomed cloth is produced. The independence enjoyed by the Muslim weavers of Banaras has fostered a very special and individual sense of self among these weavers, who take great pride in their "freedom" and control over their work conditions, particularly, in the fact that they have been able to continue to work in their homes or in the relatively small *kārkhānā*s that characterize the workplace. The description of the nature of the work provided by DuBois conveyed the degree to which weavers do control their work time and rhythm; but it also suggests the interdependent relationships they have with zari (gold-wrapped thread) producers, their women who wind the silk thread, and especially the merchants and middlemen who supply them with credit, yarn, some of the marketing outlets, and even many of the designs they use. Only by understanding this complex of working conditions can we fully appreciate the world of Banaras weavers.

DuBois's detailed discussion of the physical world and procedures of weaving provides us with a richer understanding of what identification as "weaver" meant: it enables us to connect elements of identity to the material processes in which weavers are involved daily. For that reason, we have included here the section of her essay describing that world as she was permitted to enter it (which nicely complements the description provided by Kumar in Chapter 5):

> There are several areas in Banaras where brocade weavers traditionally live and work. On the northern edge of the city is a neighborhood called Rasulpura, not far from the Weavers' Service Centre in Chowkaghat. Quite different in character from the central city, Rasulpura has the character of a small Muslim village. The area lies a little apart. A dry road leads past a mosque, an expanse of open ground where men prepare the warps for their looms, then into the narrow streets and closely walled houses. In a courtyard one man sets the hooks on a jacquard box while in the balcony above several women are winding silk threads onto reels. An open window reveals a cool dark room filled completely with looms. It appears that in almost every home people are making the brocades for which this city is famous.

The loom traditional to Banaras brocade weaving is the pitloom, which is still used today. A hollow is dug into the dirt floor underneath the front of the loom. The weaver sits on a bench at floor level with his feet in the pit containing the treadles. The harnesses and other hanging parts are suspended from the ceiling, while the horizontally stretched parts are attached either to the walls or to posts built into the floor. Thus the entire room becomes the loom. In brocade weaving, two men work together, the weaver at the front of the loom and the helper or drawboy on a plank placed above the warp at the back of the loom. The jacquard and *jālā* mechanisms are attached behind the two or more standard harnesses used to weave the ground cloth.

While brocade may be woven on looms of various types, it is the *jālā* drawloom system that makes Banaras brocade unique. The character of the design elements and their layout within the boundaries of the fabric which so readily define a sari as Banarsi, are in great part a function of the capabilities of the *jālā*. Even when used in conjunction with the jacquard, *jālā* is preferable for smaller motifs with 2 repeats. It is easier to design a *naqshā* than to punch jacquard cards, easier to set up the *jālā* and to store it, and in some ways it allows for more flexibility of design. The weaver can select the sequence (forward or reverse) and therefore the direction of the motif, and can choose to weave some or all of the repeats of the motif on the fabric. (For details on the weaving processes, see DuBois 1986.)

One home-based workshop in Rasulpura is operated by some eighty-five members of an extended family, supervised by the master weaver Anwar Ahmed Ansari, a man in his fifties who learned weaving within the family. What makes him different from most master weavers is that he received advanced training at the Weavers' Service Centre and continues to maintain business connections there.[9] As in all the weavers' homes, the weaving, dyeing and other tasks done by the men are all carried out in several loom rooms and open courtyards at ground level, while upstairs the women work at silk reeling and fabric finishing as part of their daily housework. There are eleven children from the family presently learning weaving as well as more than twenty related operations. The *kārkhānā* also hires weavers from outside the family, some Muslim and some Hindu, and sometimes employs a designer/weaver who was trained at the Weavers' Service Centre. The master weaver owns a collection of brocade designs from outside sources. In addition to weaving brocade saris and yardage, this workshop occasionally takes on projects such as weaving jute and wool wall hangings developed through the Weavers' Service Centre with contemporary designs intended for export. Orders for brocades may also come through the Weavers' Service Centre as well as from private commercial sources.

According to Anwar Ahmed Ansari, two workers can produce a sari in about a week. The work is somewhat seasonal, particularly for wedding

9. This is also, of course, a much larger operation than that engaged in by most of the weavers in Banaras. See chapter 5.

saris, but generally steady. Weaving may be done to fill specific orders or on speculation. After the sari is removed from the loom it may be given to other workers who press, size and polish it by machine rolling. Often the shopkeepers prefer to keep unfinished saris in stock, which are only polished after being purchased by the customer.

We might note that the weavers' connections to the larger world through their weaving includes more than these merchants and the producers of the materials they use. In Banaras today, designs, too, come from various sources. Master weavers may have collections of old designs or may purchase new designs from traditionally trained designers or from merchants or middlemen. The government-sponsored Weavers' Service Centre in Banaras is another important source.

Since 1952 with the constitution of the All India Handloom Board, the central government of independent India has taken an active role in revitalizing the handloom industry in India, building on the colonial government's experiments of the 1930s and 1940s. Members of the Handloom Board represent various interests including handloom weavers, exporters, cooperative banks, mill industry and central and state governments, with programs administered by the Office of the Development Commissioner under the Ministry of Industry. The programs are geared primarily toward weaving of simple cotton cloth by rural, relatively unskilled workers, the largest cottage industry in India second only to agriculture in the village economy. By contrast, Banaras brocades have always been woven by highly skilled artisans and served by specialized markets, and so were not as affected by the competition from industrialized Britain nor targeted for development by the Indian government.

While supportive schemes of the All India Handloom Board—as weavers' cooperatives, direct subsidies on production and sales, and setting up of pre- and post-loom facilities—did not directly affect brocade weaving, the establishment of the Weavers' Service Centre in Banaras has made a profound and subtle difference. Set up in 1956 by the All India Handloom Board, there are presently twenty-one Weavers' Service Centres throughout India, including the one in Banaras. The Weavers' Service Centres contain three sections: artist studio, dye lab, and weaving section; the work done in each has made technical differences in the physical processes and end results of the weaving. Once again, it reflects the impact on weavers of governmental patronage, this time suggesting an interplay between a "national" culture, and the long-lived local one of brocade production.

These discussions of neighborhood, leisure, and work patterns, then, enable us to begin sorting out upper and lower caste/class values, belief systems, and behavior in a north Indian urban setting. Within the range of approaches and subject matter presented in this part are embedded a number of important issues discussed throughout the volume. Taken together, the essays are richly suggestive of the ways in which Banarsis use identity to mobilize for work and leisure.[10] Such mobilization, in particular, is an important subject for this volume as it demonstrates most directly the connections between popular culture and the power relationships that affected larger events in the history of Banaras and colonial South Asia. The processes and value systems expressed in the culture shared at this local level constitute building blocks contributing to the events we think of as "history," including popular values and assumptions; ways of expressing as well as solidifying constructions of community; the role of the neighborhood and other voluntary associational activity in mobilizing Banarsis for action. These building blocks will recur in Part 3, where their connections are traced to broader issues and contexts.

10. See Preface to this volume and Eileen and Stephen Yeo (1981) for more discussion of this issue.

FOUR

Protection and Identity: Banaras's Bīr Babas as Neighborhood Guardian Deities

Diane M. Coccari

One can hardly walk the streets, narrow alleyways, and suburban lanes of Banaras without noticing the many small shrines that are the objects of ongoing ritual attention. Iconic and aniconic images rest on raised platforms, nestle in the roots of large holy trees, are set into the niches of boundary walls, or are housed in simple temple structures. Many of these images are familiar: the ubiquitous lingas of Shiva, representations of Ganesha, Hanuman, Bhairava, Durga, Kālī, Sitala Mata, the recently popular Santoshi Ma. There are goddesses with unfamiliar names (Sambho Mai, Saiyari Mai), memorials to ascetics ("Babas"), and other shrines dedicated to the memory or power of the human dead: the satis, *bīrs* and *brahms*.

The Bīrs—also called Bīr Babas[1]—appear to be the most numerous among these. The city of Banaras contains hundreds of Bīr Baba temples and shrines, many showing signs of recent construction or repair (see fig. 10). Once alerted to the existence of these shrines and the range of their iconography, one suddenly sees them everywhere. Extending the search to rural areas around the city, one discovers few villages that do not contain a Bīr shrine that is focal for a significant part

Research for this article was conducted between September 1980 and May 1982 under the auspices of the American Institute of Indian Studies. See also Diane Marjorie Coccari, 1986. Thanks to Sandria Freitag and Philip Lutgendorf for their comments and suggestions.

1. *Bīr:* Sanskrit *vīra,* a "brave, eminent man, hero or chief" (Monier-Williams 1899:1006). *Bābā* is a term of endearment or respect for a male family member—a son, husband, father, paternal grandfather—or of deference for an ascetic or very old man (R. C. Varma 1966:114).

Fig. 10. Lahura Bīr's annual decoration ceremony; wife of the *pujārī* (officiant) fills in. Photograph by Diane Coccari.

of the population. Who are the Bīr Babas, what do they mean to the Banaras people, and what is their place in the profuse and multifaceted pantheon of Banaras's deities?

Frequently dismissed by the scholarly and the lay community alike as subjects of minor importance, the Bīr Babas offer a unique glimpse into the religious and social lives of a sizable portion of Banaras's Hindu population. The following will introduce the reader to the identity, iconography, and worship of the Bīr Babas, and suggest what might be learned from the interdisciplinary study of these local deities.

THE BĪR IMAGE AND SHRINE

The Bīr Baba images of Banaras and surrounding villages fall into four general categories: (1) aniconic mounds, cones, or posts, (2) imageless enclosures, (3) small, carved figures in bas-relief, and (4) images reconstituted from recovered, broken sculptural fragments. Among these, the aniconic mound-shapes and imageless shrines are most frequently encountered in rural settings, and the carved figures and sculptural fragments in the denser sections of the city. The ongoing process of urban expansion, however, has resulted in the incorporation of many rural-type shrines into the life of growing city neighborhoods.

The low mound or the taller, rounded cone is the fundamental form in this area of the propitiatory *sthān*[2] of the "untimely" or powerful dead, including *brahm*s (the ghosts of Brahmins), satis (virtuous wives who die on their husbands' funeral pyres), *marī*s or *bhavānī*s (ghosts of females who die unnatural or untimely deaths), and the tombs or memorials (samadhis) of certain sects of ascetics. When questioned, informants invariably report the original form to be a low mound of packed clay, later remodeled by devotees with brick, clay and whitewash, metal, tile, cement, or stone. A bronze or silver mask may be attached to the aniconic form, effecting its transformation to iconic image. The Bīr masks are similar in type to the city's main Kal Bhairava image (another composite of mask and rough stone), sporting royal headdresses and large moustaches typical of the South Asian warrior-hero. Examples of this treatment are Lahura Bīr—the namesake of a major city intersection—and Daitra Bīr in Chait Ganj, said to be the younger brother of Lahura Bīr. It is interesting that the mound or postlike images, even without anthropomorphic characteristics, are approached in worship as though they were a human frame: they are garlanded and the "feet" are pressed.

The small, imageless enclosures are understood to house the spirit of the Bīr and provide a platform for offerings. These miniature templelike structures are often associated with large old trees (many the sacred pipal, *bel,* or *nīm*) which may lend the figure its name, as Pipala Bīr in Bari Gaivi, or Belawa Bīr in Shankudhara. The proliferation of small shrines and images among the roots of sacred trees can be viewed as an expression of the underlying cultural conviction that trees themselves are venerable or are the proper abodes of godlings or spirits (*yakṣa*s, *yakṣī*s, *daitya*s, etc.) to whom the shrines are built to honor and placate. Many of these shrines house a Daitra Bīr (from the Sanskrit *daitya*), wit-

2. Hindi *sthān* and Bhojpuri *asthān* derive from the Sanskrit *sthāna,* a "place, spot, locality, abode, dwelling, house, site" (Monier-Williams 1899:1263). These may also be called *devasthān, bhūtasthān,* or *bīrasthān,* depending on the nature of the being believed to reside there.

ness to the continuity of this older tradition. Popular explanation of the association of shrine and tree often points to the accidental death of a climber. Tar Bīr on Lanka Road (*tāṛ*, a palmyra palm) is said to be a toddy-tapper (Pasi) who died in such a fall.

The majority of the carved Bīr images are small bas-relief plaques depicting standing figures with an axe or a club in the right hand and a water pot (*loṭā*) in the left. Newly carved or painted images reveal details obscured in the older images, such as beard and topknot, loin cloth, sectarian markings, and beads. Daitra Bīr near the Women's College of Banaras Hindu University campus, the newly established Daitra Bīr in Nawab Ganj, Sahodar Bīr near the Assi Nala, Anjan Bīr in Assi, Panaru Bīr near Laksmi Kund, and Kankara Bīr in Shankodhara are among the many examples of this type. Some, like Naukare Bīr, next to the city's main Durga Temple, or Akela Baba on Banaras Hindu University campus, are seated in the lotus posture with weapons in hand. These Bīr images, of a "martial ascetic" type, are nearly identical to those associated with small neighborhood samadhis (tombs) of ascetics throughout the city. The images of Macchodara Nath Baba in Macchodara Bag and of Mishra Baba on Luxa Road—both described by devotees as accomplished yogis—invite this comparison. While a number of Banarsi *mūrti* sellers admit to offering this generalized type of image to patrons wishing to establish an ascetic's samadhi or the *sthān* of a Bīr or a Brahm, the conflation of elements of heroic and ascetic traditions is clearly at the root of these imaging practices. There is a great deal of similarity in the role these small shrines play in the lives of city neighborhood dwellers.

The broken images, often discovered during construction projects or fished out of the Ganges, are another kind of solution to the representation of a Bīr's human form. The appearance of the fragment determines the iconography and occasionally the figure's name as well. Nangan Bīr ("Naked Hero") of Bhadaini has the body of a Jain Tirthankara, and the well-known Mur Kata Baba ("Head-Cut Baba") on Durga Kund Road is a decapitated sculpture of, many think, the Buddha. These found images are said to be ancient deities who "reveal" their location to favored individuals in a vision or a dream, or emerge into the light of day under their own power (*mūrti apne āp niklī* or *apne āp prakat huī*). This revelation is evidence of the deity's renewed vigor and is itself the legitimation of the image's establishment and worship. The original identity of the piece is unknown and unimportant, as is the *shāstrik* convention that prohibits the use of a badly mutilated *mūrti*.[3] What is authoritative is the revelation of the image and the

3. "If an image is broken in parts or reduced to particulars it should be removed according to *shāstrik* rules and another should be installed in its place" (Kane 1973, 4:904).

subsequent proofs of power and efficacy the deity is believed to exhibit. Some Banaras Bīr images are said to have been established by Brahmin priests with the proper *pratiṣṭhā* ceremony, but most are set up by non-Brahmin priests or their finders with a simpler ritual dedication.

Several processes are at work, then, in the creation of Bīr Baba shrines: a propitiatory *sthān* is established and worshipped in order to quiet the "untimely" dead, or a preexisting shrine is incorporated into the religious life of a new neighborhood; an older presence—often associated with a large, sacred tree—is given new life as a Bīr Baba, or broken images from a former era are found ("revealed") and established by their finders.

THE IDENTITY OF THE BĪRS

The most critical distinction in the Bīrs' ontological status involves their classification as "ghosts-spirits" (*bhūt-pret*) or "deities" (*devatā*). Some Banarsis maintain that the Bīrs are beings of the *pret yoni,* the "birth as a ghost," a painfully liminal condition which is neither of the gods, ancestors, or humanity. These ghosts or spirits suffered violent, unnatural, premature, or "untimely deaths" (*akāl mrityu*), which rendered them unqualified for the normal rites of death, or incapable of being advanced to the world of the ancestors (*pitri lok*) and beyond. Angry, jealous, and seething with unfulfilled desires, the ghost has no recourse but to harass or otherwise persuade the living to offer the desired attention. A ghost may appear to an individual in a vision or a dream, cause illness and other misfortune, or take active possession. People bothered in this way may seek the help of a professional exorcist (*ojhā*) to remove or transfer the spirit to another individual or location, or perform rituals of appeasement, including the creation of a shrine to "quiet" (*shānti karnā*) the spirit.

Although the stories of most Banaras Bīrs are of untimely and violent death, the people who worship the bīrs consider them "gods" or "deities" and not mere ghosts (*ham devatā mānte haĩ*—"We believe they are deities"). A bīr's power is generated by a violent and tragic death, channeled and transformed by the ritual establishment of a shrine, and further enhanced by worship. The bīr is distinguished from lesser spirits because he is the powerful "master" (*mālik*) who controls the supernatural activity within a particular domain. Bīrs are believed to be especially "awake" (*jāgta hai*) among the local gods, and active in the fulfillment of human desires.

In addition, Bīr worshippers take the *vīra* ("hero") part of the deity's description quite literally: most reported the Bīrs to be heroic "martyrs" (*shahīd*) who sacrificed their lives in defense of family, friends, caste group, village, or religion. "Anyone who dies on the battlefield is a Bīr" is a repeated refrain. Many of the Banaras Bīrs are said to have died at the time of the Mahābhārata war, in battles among regional, historical chieftains, fighting the Muslim armies of Aurangzeb, the English army of the Raj, or in more recent altercations with local enemies. While most of the Bīr stories continue to be flavored by the *bhūt-pret* complex or a more archaic and local brand of heroism, an attempt is made to relate these events to wider and more universal values. Even if the circumstances surrounding the death of a Bīr do not at first glance appear particularly heroic, the teller will expand upon the exceptional qualities of the individual or emphasize that the hero was tricked, outnumbered, or otherwise overcome by fate in order to be killed. The Bīr's physical strength and size, leadership ability, bravery, fighting and wrestling prowess, loyalty, self-sacrifice, and devotion to God are extolled.

One example of righteous conflict and untimely death is the story of Bachau Bīr, whose temple lies in the village of Sir Karhiya just outside Banaras Hindu University campus. Bachau's story is widely circulated in the Banaras area, assisted no doubt by the existence of a *birahā* song detailing the climactic events that resulted in Bachau's violent death. Bachau, an Ahir by caste, was a historical individual who lived in the early part of this century. Legend has it that his extraordinary strength and bravery were matched by honor and compassion. He was famous for saving the life of a village headman by killing a jungle tiger with his bare hands. Yet Bachau had many enemies, especially among the local Thakur caste. A dispute over land rights ignited this long-standing rivalry, and Bachau, who refused to bring a weapon to a confrontation with his enemies, was outnumbered and beaten mercilessly to death. The *birahā* song, written by an Ahir songwriter, concludes with the hero's ascension to Heroes' Heaven (*bīr gati*) immediately upon his death (Coccari 1986:185–89, 249–52).

As was indicated above, the figure of the Bīr is easily conflated with that of the entombed ascetic. The association of virility and asceticism is ancient on the subcontinent, and we are offered many examples—both mythic and historical—of warrior ascetics, yogis who become physically powerful as a result of ascetic observances, and heroes whose physical might implies disciplined spiritual attainment or "saintly" characters. There are Bīr Babas in the Banaras area—such as Jog or Jogi Bīr of Narayanpur village—who are described as yogis who met with violent ends, and others who achieved perfection as a result of the Tantric *vīra-sādhanā,* the dangerous and empowering "Hero's Path." Both Bīr and memorialized yogi are addressed as "Baba," their shrines—containing a mound or "martial ascetic" image—are nearly identical, and both are thought to be present and available to worshippers at the tomb or temple location. The nature of the presence of a Bīr and an entombed ascetic are theoretically distinct—the Bīr a deified ghost and the yogi in an immortal body or a disembodied consciousness—but this makes little difference in the outcome of worship of either figure. Both are petitioned by worshippers for the fulfillment of desires and relief from illness, misfortune, and infertility. The shrines are identified with particular neighborhoods or social groups and are publicly celebrated by these patrons in similar ways.

The Bīrs are said to derive from any (especially low) caste, such as Teli, Pasi, Naṭ, Bhar, Khāṭik. Yet it is the Ahir caste, whose traditional occupation is keeping and breeding cows and buffalos and marketing their milk, who are most consistently identified with the Bīr phenomenon. Typical of pastoral groups (see Sontheimer 1976) and because of the profession of cattle keeping and herding and the related activities of cattle raiding and protection, the Ahir possess an authentic heroic tradition in which they cherish a view of themselves as brave and mighty warriors and leaders among a collection of allied castes with whom they are found in village settings. This self-image is vividly portrayed in regional versions of the centuries-old Ahir oral epic *Lorikī* (see Pandey 1979, 1982; Kesari 1980; Elwin 1946:338–70; Grierson 1929:243–54) and in more recent evidence in the pronouncements and programs of the Yādav movement.

The epic world of the *Lorikī* is one of many small kingdoms—Ahir, Rajput, and Aboriginal—vying for cattle, land, women, and power. It is a world in which the Ahir stand as equals to the "twice-born" warrior castes, where marriage by capture is the norm, and expressions of strength, bravery, loyalty, nobility, and honor are valued. Like many other epic traditions, it is a story of a flawed hero (Lorik) who meets with a tragic fate. Episodes of the *Lorikī* are localized in the various regions that know the epic, and it is viewed—especially by rural Ahir—as a caste history to which many of their distinctive customs can be traced. The hero Lorik himself is seen as a historical hero of great stature and the Ahirs' most illustrious ancestor.

More sophisticated and urbanized Ahir eschew any connection with the *Lorikī* and other rustic caste traditions, including wrestling (popular among the Ahir) and the singing of *birahā*. These Ahir elites, many of whom support the Yādav movement, are anxious to distance themselves from the more archaic expressions of caste heroism in favor of Brahminical symbols and genealogical "histories" proving descent from the Yadu dynasty of Krishna. The Yādav movement has sought, among other things, to establish the Ahir as a bona fide martial race. The movement was launched during the turn of the century by the rulers of the royal state of Rewari, members of the Yaduvamsī subcaste of Ahirs. The teachings of the Arya Samāj were impetus to the growth of the movement, which adapted these to its own agenda of caste uplift and political organization. In particular, many Ahirs adopted the "twice-born" symbol of the sacred thread in support of their claim to Kshatriya status. The Janeū (sacred thread) movement was strong in the states of Uttar Pradesh and Bihar in the 1910s and 1920s, and encountered opposition from powerful Thakurs and Bhumihar Brahmins (Rao 1979:134). Many Ahirs adopted Yādav as a last name, and it soon became a reference category that served to associate many diverse regional cow- and buffalo-herding castes throughout the subcontinent. More recently Yādav organizations have agitated for a separate regiment in the Indian army, as have the other "martial races" of India (Rao 1964). Yādavs have played leading roles in recent decades in "backward class" associations (Rao 1979:157–58).

In both the *Lorikī* and the Yādav movement we find expression of an Ahir heroic tradition, reflected also in the large number of shrines to deified Ahir heroes and their reputations as powerful guardians. The relatively high percentage of Ahirs in Banaras and surrounding districts may also help to explain the predominance of these shrines.[4] Unlike many caste groups in other regions of India (see, for instance, Blackburn 1981), the Ahir from the Banaras area—primarily worshippers of the Goddess and Krishna—do not center their religious life entirely around these deified caste figures. The Ahir Bīrs do not necessarily become the foci of elaborate and organized cultic activity that reifies caste or clan identity or that represents a system of ancestor worship. It is possible that caste heroes played a more central role in the religious life of the Ahir in the past, and that the upwardly mobile aspirations of this caste and the Yādav movement's opposition to "local deities" have taken their toll. Yet the Ahir deities retain a certain stature among other low- to middle-ranked castes of the locality, and will often be adopted by them. A neglected image will be taken over by another caretaker, a revelation of special power will rekindle worship, an older shrine will be incorporated into a newly formed neighborhood. In this way the Ahir Bīr shrines of the Banaras area may move out of Ahir control to become the gods of all (especially lower) castes who possess great faith in the vigor and attentiveness of these beings.

BĪRS AS VILLAGE GUARDIAN DEITIES

In the countryside around Banaras (see fig. 11) the word for the village guardian deity is *ḍīh,* used interchangeably with variants *ḍīhā* and *ḍīhwār*. These are generic terms that signify the guardians or protectors of the entire village unit and do not refer to village deities in general,

4. In 1931 the Ahir made up 12.5 to 25 percent of the total population of Ballia, Ghazipur, and Jaunpur districts, U.P., and Shahabad district, Bihar (Schwartzberg 1978:106).

Fig. 11. Karman Bīr (one of two), Banaras Hindu University campus. Photograph by Diane Coccari.

many of which are perceived as guardians of more specific functions or smaller social entities. A *ḍīh* will often have a proper name, in which case a villager might say, "This is Karman Bir. He is the Dih Baba of our village." It appears that the term *ḍīh* derives from the Persian *deh* or *dih,* meaning a town or village (Johnson 1852:585), but in the Indian context the word took on the semantic dimension of "haunt, the site or ruins of a deserted village, the dwelling place of the ancestors, a heap of earth or mound, the place where worship of the village gods takes place," and simply "village gods (*grām devatā*)."[5]

The designation Ḍīh (Ḍīhā or Ḍīhwār) is most frequently used for the male guardian, or Ḍīh Baba, but it may also refer to the female guardian or to the guardian pair, understood either as husband and wife or as two separate deities associated only in their role as protectors of village boundaries. Occasionally the female guardian will be referred to as Ḍīhwārin, a feminized form of Ḍīhwār. This is true of the city's

5. "*dīh*- Haunt, place, dwelling, village, site of a deserted village. *dīhā*- Heap of earth, mound, bank" (Platts 1960:576). "*dīh* m. [Hindi] 1. habitation, settlement 2. small village 3. the ruins of a deserted village 4. mound 5. the place [*sthān*] where worship to the village gods takes place 6. the dwelling place of ancestors" (Sundardas 1965, 2:472 [my translation]); "3. village gods [*grām devatā*]" (Sundardas 1965, 4:1954–55).

Lahura Bīr Baba and his partner, Sitala Mata. A division of labor exists between them in which the Devi checks or manifests her afflictions (if she is a disease goddess) and the Ḍīh Baba controls other, more vaguely defined supernatural forces that influence the health and well-being of villagers. The Ḍīh's partner may also be a more benevolent village goddess—a Sati or a related figure—sometimes said to be his wife. With either type of goddess, however, the Ḍīh Baba appears to retain ultimate control; even Sitala must have permission before her anger (*devī kā kop*) may be loosed upon errant villagers.

Thus "Ḍīh Baba" nicely expresses the guardian's identity with its village, as well as with its origin as mound deity—the enshrined remains of an ancestor, defender, or even human sacrifice ritually compelled to protect the village and thereby actualizing its existence as a sacred entity. What is suggested by the dictionary meanings of *ḍīh* corresponds perfectly with the statements made by residents about their village guardians: these deities were once living members of their community, now valorized as ancient heroes associated with a village's dim beginnings. The village Ḍīh is said to be an "ancient" (*prācīn*) deity whose shrine was established when the village itself was founded. What helps define a village as such is the existence of its guardian deity or deities, who control the ingress and egress of all supernatural forces and influences across village boundaries. Village people use the following expressions to describe the Ḍīh Baba's function as guardian: he is the "village protector" (*gaon kā rakṣā kārne wālā, rakṣak* or *rakwārī*), the "head" of the village (*mālik, mukhiyā*), the village "police chief" (kotwal), or—by those familiar with the Sanskrit term—the "area or regional guardian" (*kṣetrapāl*). The Ḍīh, as "head" of a village, performs similar functions to those of the human official, except that his realm of authority extends to minor village deities, ghosts, other more vaguely defined magical energies, and—by extension—those humans who would wish to manipulate these beings and forces. Any human act that attempts to propitiate, exorcise, or otherwise control the supernatural must begin with the Ḍīh's permission and blessing, or the "work" cannot succeed.

Yet because the deity is ambivalent in character, one is not always assured of the desired results. One individual explained the Ḍīh's authority in the following way:

> Before any work begins, one must worship the village Dih. Every village has one Dih. The Dih must first give permission. A ghost must also ask the Dih's permission to enter the village. If the Dih is happy with you, he will not allow the ghost to enter the village. But sometimes the Dih will "eat" the offerings and still allow the ghost to enter the village.[6]

6. Personal interview with Bhagat Channu, Adityanagar, Dec. 11, 1980.

Likewise, when the installation of another deity is to take place in the village or the home, it must be accomplished with permission from the Ḍīh Baba. At the time of a village wedding, part of the worship of all important family and village deities by the couple includes offering the ceremonial thread (*kangan*) or the groom's headdress (*maur*) at the shrine of the Ḍīh. At the birth of a child—especially a son—offerings will be made at the shrine. Similar rituals are performed when a special desire has been fulfilled by the guardian deity (see also Planalp 1956:190–91). The Ḍīh is ideally worshipped by the entire village once or twice a year, but human nature and village politics may make this difficult to accomplish. If this neglect results in misfortune, disease, or disaster for all or part of the village, special ceremonies must be conducted to correct this lapse in ritual responsibility. In 1982 the village of Kojawa, immediately flanking Banaras, collectively worshipped its Ḍīh when great hardship was caused by monsoon floods.

In India it is not uncommon for *vīra* types of deities, including pan-Indian mythological figures and deified local or quasi-historical martial heroes, to function as village guardians. Local manifestations of the "Monkey God" Hanuman, Bhairava, or the powerful Pandava Bhima or Bhimsen are examples of the first; martyred Muslim generals, warriors of a bona fide Hindu martial caste, tribal chieftains, or other local figures who attained the status of "hero" before or after their deaths are examples of the latter. As deities, the once-living *vīra*s continue their rightful occupation after death; those who ruled and protected while living are expected to continue this service in exchange for the honor and worship of the local population. The hero is empowered as a deity through martyrdom and sacrifice; this abundance of power is then channeled by worship to serve the living.

Consistent with this, in many of the villages immediately surrounding the city of Banaras, a Bīr fulfills the function of male guardian deity, or Ḍīh Baba. These Bīrs are valorized by believers as courageous leaders and fighters, as individuals who championed the powerless. But even without these overtly martial overtones, the Bīrs clearly fall within the tradition of the "mound deity" described earlier, the original ancestor or martyr ritually enjoined to the protection of the living. There are also rural Bīrs that do not function as Ḍīhs but remain family, lineage, clan, or caste deities, still identified with those groups who originally established the shrines. Others are village deities of more specialized function, such as protectors of fields and livestock. By contrast, in the *city* of Banaras, the identification of Ḍīh and Bīr is almost complete: every Ḍīh this writer surveyed was a Bīr, and almost every Bīr was reported to be a Ḍīh of some area, however small.

THE BANARAS CITY NEIGHBORHOOD GUARDIAN

The urban counterpart of the village guardian is the Banaras neighborhood Bīr/Ḍīh. This urban Ḍīh, often but not necessarily paired with a goddess, is conceived in almost identical terms as the village guardian except that its territory is the considerably smaller and more intimate unit of the city neighborhood. This deity is described as "the god" or "protector of the neighborhood" (*mahal kā devatā, muḥallā kā rakwārī*) rather than of the village. There are hundreds of Bīr/Ḍīh shrines in the city of Banaras. Every section or minutely divided subsection of the city seems to boast its own "Bīr/Ḍīh Baba" or Ḍīh pair, integral to that neighborhood's conception of itself as a discrete and bounded unit within the larger and sometimes intersecting official and historical divisions of the city.

Like the village deities, the urban Bīr/Ḍīhs control the boundaries of their domains, especially with regard to the exit and entry of the intangible agents of illness, misfortune, and disease. They are approached for blessings as part of any major undertaking—ritual or otherwise—and are propitiated when trouble occurs. The Bīrs are the appropriate deities to seek out if one feels harmed by the "evil eye" (*burā tāke*), they are plied with the "heart's desires" (*manokāmanā, manautī*) of local people, and they are important to the work of *ojhāī:* exorcism and divination. People will boast of their own Bīr as the most powerful among the neighboring Bīrs with whom they are familiar. Some of the neighborhood Bīrs are known to all of the city residents or are seen to specialize in certain kinds of rituals or cures. Both Tar Bīr of Lanka and Daitra Bīr of Chait Ganj are said to cure a disease that causes the hands to shake, and the Siha Bīr shrine—across the river in Ramnagar—is famous among the villages and neighborhoods on the south side of Banaras as a place where *ojhā*s perform tantric ritual.

These guardians are often conceived in very personal terms. The neighbors of Nangan Bīr in Bhadaini refer to the deity as their "son-in-law" (*damād*). Many Bīrs are said to have a special fondness for children. Neighbors talk of their guardian's love of children, and the shrines are often a place where children as well as adults congregate. An elderly neighbor of the Anjan Bīr shrine in Assi related how he, as a frightened child, was guided home safely by the Bīr Baba. If one merely invokes the name of the guardian deity, it is said, he will dispel all fear and see to the safety of the traveler. It is told how a neighborhood Bīr would help laborers carry their heavy loads when they stopped to rest near the shrine. The Bīr is especially active at night. He patrols the boundaries of his district, wrapped in a black blanket, visiting and smoking ganja with neighboring Bīr friends and brothers. If one listens carefully, one may hear the hollow sound of his wooden sandals (*kharāū̃*) on the cobbled alleyways of the city. The Bīr shrines of the city are often associated with a large shade tree under which people may congregate. Many shrines in open areas of the city have a water tap and a small wrestling or exercise ground.

WORSHIP OF THE BĪRS

The lower end of the caste spectrum makes up the largest portion of Bīr worshippers, from middle-ranked herdsmen, agriculturalists and artisans, and groups of aboriginal ancestry, to those considered "untouchable" or Harijan. These include Ahir, Gaḍeriyā, Kunbī, Kurmi, Kumhār, Mali, Pasi, Bhar, Rājbhar, Kol, Gond, Manjhī, Mallāh, Khāṭik, Teli, Dhobi, Ḍom, Chamar, Raī Dās, and so forth. A small percentage of middle- and high-caste members, including Brahmins, are devotees of particular Bīr Babas as well. This is especially true of older community shrines that house venerable local deities viewed as protectors of all rather than identified with particular castes or occupational groups. The uneducated are most numerous among Bīr worshippers, but the reputation of certain shrines may draw considerable attendance from the ranks of the educated, including the more Westernized middle class.

Women are equal in number to men among the devotees, although they are less likely to hold priestly roles. The faith of women in Bīr Babas is displayed most dramatically during the large religious fairs (melas) of regionally famous Bīrs, when female pilgrims attend in the tens of thousands and far outnumber the men present. This may be witnessed at the annual melas of both Bechu Bīr (near Aharaura, Mirzapur) and Kedariya Bīr (outside the city of Jaunpur). Fertility ranks high among female concerns, but many come also to work through or be relieved of ghost affliction.

Worshipped chiefly by the neighbors of a shrine, the urban Bīrs are attended most frequently on Tuesdays and Sundays and during seasons of festival activity. Individual petitioners approach the Bīrs privately with their special needs or desires (*manautī*) with an initial offering when the deity is confronted with a request, and a vow (*manautī mānanā*) to perform further services or ritual offerings if a wish is fulfilled (*manautī pūrī ho jānā*). The requests are familiar: the cure and prevention of illness, help with family problems and disputes, aid in finding a lost object, removal of the obstacles to fertility, the finding of a job, success in a court case or in the outcome of an exam. A supplicant will salute with folded hands (*praṇām*) or prostrate before the image, and offer sweets, flowers, incense, and *dhār:* a "cooling" mixture of five dried and powdered fruits mixed with Ganges water and poured from a *loṭa* before the image. Substances of a more *tamāsik* quality are also acceptable to the deity: camphor, cannabis, liquor, cut nutmegs or lemons (the simulacrum of blood sacrifice), and the slaughter of cock, pig, or goat. These latter substances are considered more potent and dangerous, and are offered by those who subscribe to "tantric methods" (*tantrik paddhati se*) of pleasing and coercing the deity. The Bīr Babas are said to accept these offerings (literally to "eat" them), and are especially fond of ganja, which is smoked frequently by men in the vicinity of some shrines. Numerous among the private petitioners are the healers and exorcists (*ojhā, sokhā, guṇī*) who depend upon the cooperation of the Bīr Babas in their dealings with the spirit world.

It has become very popular of late to organize a *vārṣik shringār,* an "annual decoration" ceremony in imitation of the annual festivals of the city's major temples. The small shrines are whitewashed, painted, and elaborately decorated with flowers and strings of electric lights; *āratī pūja,* all-night performances of folk and devotional music, and even martial competitions among some of the city's wrestling *akhāṛās* are financed by neighborhood donations. Kumar notes an upsurge in the number of *shringār*s of small neighborhood shrines in recent years, evidence of the increasingly popular nature of public celebration (N. Kumar 1984:200–210). The annual *shringār*s of Bīr temples are foremost among the occasions to celebrate neighborhood identity.

PROTECTION AND IDENTITY

The Bīr shrines of the city of Banaras are in one sense a transposition of a rural deity onto the urban environment; in the role of Ḍīh Baba the Bīrs are a projection of the idea of the bounded, guarded microcosm of the village onto the city neighborhood. This is not to say that Kashi—the ancient name of Banaras—is lacking in guardian deities, but that the Bīr Babas are an additional set of these. Diana Eck has ably described the classical *mandala* of protective deities of the city of Banaras—the Ganeshas, Bhairavas, Devis, Yakshas, and so forth, which guard the borders and regions of the sacred city (1982:146 ff.). The Bīrs complete this complex *mandala* of guardianship; they are the protectors of even more minutely divided and subdivided bits of inhabited territory—the most personal, immediate, and responsive among the guardians of the microcosm. The establishment, worship, and celebration of Bīr shrines is eloquently expressive of the need of people in the growing and ever more densely crowded city environment to continue to remap and redefine the boundaries of where they live, carve an ordered space out of the city's chaos, and protect that intimate space through the worship of a boundary deity.

Some of the urban shrines are clearly the foci of identity for specific social groups, if not of attempts to establish an alternate power base or resistance to traditional authority. When a neighborhood Bīr shrine is relatively old, it is more likely to be viewed with fondness and respect by all of the local residents, regardless of caste. These deities might be viewed by the upper castes as legitimate, albeit minor gods: the "watchmen" or "servants" (chaukidar, *chaprāsī*) of the major deities. Yet a large portion of the shrines surveyed in Banarsi neighborhoods in 1980–1982 were established or reclaimed within the last twenty to thirty years. These relatively recent shrines are more likely to be identified with narrower segments of the population; this is especially true in the new neighborhoods that are forming on the outskirts of the city.

As has been suggested, this vision of the neighborhood Bīr/Ḍīh Babas and their consecutive domains is strongest and clearest among the lower classes. Many of these new shrines are found in low-caste neighborhoods or by low-caste people in mixed neighborhoods. Some of the shrines are the only sanctified areas in the entire neighborhood, places of worship and congregation for groups of people who may have no such location to call their own. Not infrequently a Bīr temple is championed as the patron deity of a coalition of low castes, hoping to exercise their collective power to save or develop a cherished bit of ground. The Daitra Bīr shrine in a small Harijan neighborhood near Nawab Ganj is one example of this process. In 1981 the Raidas caretaker told how he and other neighbors cleared the area and established the small shrine of the Bīr in an effort to improve their neighborhood and resist the ownership claims of a local landlord. In a similar way a local group may attempt to enhance its prestige or foster its political interests by sponsoring the building of a new neighborhood Bīr temple, or an occupational group will patronize a temple near the workplace. Many of these newer shrines are the objects of ongoing litigation by way of determining land rights and ownership. These sorts of tensions are typical of the politics of newly constructed or activated shrines, a frequent occurrence in this rapidly growing city. The Bīrs are not the only personalized neighborhood deities around which a sense of neighborhood solidarity may be built, yet the Bīr Babas as territorial guardians are the natural candidates for this role.

Because they originate as the honored or powerful dead of particular communities, Bīrs are easily enshrined without help from the orthodoxy. Individual shrines have been ritually installed and worshipped by Brahmin priests, but this is clearly not the norm. The Bīrs are discovered by or revealed to "small people" (*chote log*) in a vision or a dream and may be enshrined by them with the simplest of ceremony. The stories of the Bīrs themselves are of low-caste heroes and martyrs: champions of the castes from which they spring and to whom they belong. The stories of some Bīrs reveal the tensions between these castes and the orthodox and powerful. The Bīr cult displays in many respects a self-consciousness and even rebelliousness vis-à-vis Brahminical modes of worship and ritual. The participants in this tradition are proud of the fact that anyone may directly worship the Bīrs—even an untouchable—without the necessity of a priest or other intermediary.

The political use of these temples, as well as the challenge they represent to traditional authority, does not go unnoticed. Some point to the recent increase in wealth and political clout of members of the Ahir caste as reason for the growth of many shrines. One Brahmin pandit spoke about the proliferation of city Bīr shrines as a degeneration of Dharma. He said that it was the traditional responsibility of the Raja (and now the "government," *sarkār*), to use his authority (*daṇḍā,* lit., "staff") to protect Dharma. But this is no longer done. He explained that any "hoodlum" (*gunḍā*) can now establish a temple for his own purposes.[7] One need only witness the annual procession through the city of the devotees of Ravi Das—the patron saint of the untouchables—to know that there is reason for anxiety over the potential power of the organized lower classes (see Juergensmeyer 1982). Yet formal opposition to the building of a temple—a sanctified and holy place and the seat of a deity—is not offered lightly. Disputes over these small temples and shrines tend to be carried on as ostentatiously as possible in the public eye, and it is not easy for a Hindu to put himself on record in opposition to a place of worship, whether or not he concedes the stature of the resident deity. Yet in another sense, the Bīr cult—associated as it is with the lower classes—may possess inherent limitations to upward mobility, something perhaps more easily accomplished outside the orthodox stronghold of Banaras. I saw no evidence of Bīr Baba shrines in the process of identification with a "Sanskritic" and pan-Indian deity such as Shiva—a reasonable option considering the aniconic representations of both deities and the "vīra" aspect of Bhairava in the Shaivite pantheon.

CONCLUSION

The Bīrs in the city of Banaras are almost always said to be the Ḍīh Babas, or guardian deities, of specific neighborhoods, a formal expression of their identity with and patronage of a group or area. Moreover, this

7. Personal interview with Pandit Ram Puri Divedi, Sept. 25, 1981.

urban Ḍīh Baba appears to be a projection of rural patterns of sacred geography, another example of the penetration of a rural world view with its *grāmadevatā* into the urban environment in the minds of lower-caste people, and witness to the connectedness of rural and urban areas.

The appeal of the Bīr Babas to their worshippers has many facets: issuing forth as the deified dead of the lower classes, the Bīrs are directly identified with those whom they champion. They are among the immanent and "awake" deities in whom people hold their faith in the degenerate age of the Kālī Yuga. The establishment, worship, and celebration of the shrines require no orthodox mediation; at the same time these activities are difficult to oppose overtly. The increasingly conspicuous celebration of Bīr Baba shrines and the growth in the actual number of shrines is no doubt part of the trend toward lower-class patronage of public events and celebrations noted by Nita Kumar (1984), with the Bīrs providing a religious and organizational focus for social groups who lack other appropriate objects of patronage.

FIVE

Work and Leisure in the Formation of Identity: Muslim Weavers in a Hindu City

Nita Kumar

The most renowned and commercially important product of Banaras is the "Banarsi" sari, with a history of many millennia behind it and a working force that includes almost 25 percent of the city's population. These weavers are proud craftsmen who trace their presence in the city to anywhere between three hundred and a thousand years. They are Sunni Muslims, articulate about their beliefs, rituals, and religiosity. They refer to themselves as "Ansari" rather than by their old "caste" name, Julāhā, and consider the new name replete with suggestions about their character and behavior. They have no economic or social ties in the countryside or other cities, and call themselves unequivocally "Banarsi" ("of Banaras").

The characterization of their identity is not a simple task. If we begin with a consideration of them as an occupational group, that is what they primarily seem to be. If we discuss them first as "Muslims," we will find ample data to support a case for their religious or "communal" identity. They may further be labeled "urban," "lower class," the "poor," and perhaps a "closed social community." This chapter looks at different manifestations of identity, using the methods of both history and anthropology. The routine of work reveals the common elements of poverty, insecurity, and illiteracy, as well as the more positive aspects of a high level of skill and a lack of regimen in the workday, which are common to all artisans. The patterns of leisure demonstrate the common attachment to place and tradition, the practical demonstration of freedom, and the priority given to individual preference, taste, mood, and occasion in deciding the use of time. A consideration of the two—work and leisure activities—together, enables us to construct a suitably complex picture of what it means to be a Muslim weaver in the Hindu pilgrimage center of Banaras.

THE WEAVER AS ARTISAN

The first thing that defines a weaver is his work. The technological dimensions of the work consist of the difficulty of operating the pit loom, of weaving jacquard designs, and of maintaining unfaltering originality in every piece woven (see fig. 12). The stories and legends about the incomparability of the Banarsi sari and its attractiveness for all people in all times are part of the weaver's way of conceptualizing himself. The first reaction of the weaver to a question about his place in society is to bring down the three-by-one-foot cardboard boxes that house the Banarsi sari, if he is a prosperous or master weaver, or to open up the weaving side of the loom to reveal the precious product being created there, if he is too poor to have anything in store.

The weaving technology of Banarsi silk has not undergone major changes over the last century; in fact, in contrast to the fate of many other craftsmen and domestic industries, the lack of mechanization has been a powerful aid in its survival. The two simplifications introduced were the use of the jacquard machine in place of the intricate cotton-thread designs strung over the loom, and the adoption of the Hattersley domestic loom, both in about 1928 (for the technology, see DuBois 1986). While traders consider these changes to indicate a decline in traditional skill, weavers themselves consider them only labor-saving devices that leave the skill untouched.

Ironically, the corollary to their skill and excellence is poverty and insecurity. All artisans are poor, their lives characterized by the seemingly essential features of cottage industries: low capital investment, the control of the market by middlemen, the uncertain supply of raw materials, and the impossibility of achieving economies of scale beyond a point. All artisans are accustomed to insecurity as well, insecurity at the daily and weekly level attendant on earning by the piece, implying earning exactly as much as health and "mood" permits; and to larger-scale periodic slumps dictated by the market, any of which may signal long-term decline. Their products are culturally valued ones, dependent on the vagaries of "fashion," and alternative products may outmatch them in dazzle at any time.

There have been two major periods of decline in the silk industry over the last hundred years, in the 1880s and the 1950s. In 1884 ten to twelve thousand Muslims of Banaras were reported to have gathered for special prayers, as their work was at a standstill (*Bharat Jiwan,* 15 Dec. 1884, 3). In December 1891 one thousand to twelve thousand weavers went to the house of the District Magistrate, Banaras, with a petition asking for lower grain prices and complaining of no work. The industry was so depressed that the government considered diverting all

Fig. 12. Brocade weaver in Banaras working at pit loom with *jālā* and jacquard attachments. Photograph by Carley Fonville; thanks to Emily DuBois.

the weavers to a new industry of weaving carpets (GAD 155B 1891, Ind 110 1910, Ind 253 1911). Weavers in this period were supposed to be full of discontent: "The Julahas are a disaffected class of people as the weaving industry has given place to the piece-goods of British manufacture" (GAD 255B 1891 no. 30). In April 1891 they successfully persuaded Hindus not to hold their "river carnival," the Burhwa Mangal, in sympathy with their problems. Later in the year they were suspects in the riots related to the destruction of the Rama temple: they were supposed to have joined the Hindu "rascals" to create trouble for the government (GAD 255B 1891 no. 30 and see chapter 7). At this time, too, the leading weekly of the city and province made its only passing allusion to the decline in exports of silk from the U.P. (*Bharat Jiwan,* 26 Dec. 1892, 5). By 1900 there is no more mention of any trouble in the silk industry (Ali 1900). Banaras weavers were preparing to demonstrate their techniques and display their brocades at the Delhi Exhibition, and were referred to as "a prosperous community" (*Bharat Jiwan,* 5 May 1902, 7; Adampura TR 8-IV).

These periodic slumps are part of a cyclical process and do not detract from the overall expansion experienced by the silk industry in the last century. They do contribute to a feeling of insecurity, however, that is characteristic of all artisans. The consciousness of the weavers is colored moreover by smaller, more frequent ups and downs, and every weaving family uses an idiom of flux and change to describe its fate (see Bismillah 1986). Yet the weaver's world is an expanding one, and the overall progress in the industry—in the number of workers (see table 5.1), the volume of sales, the variety of markets (N. Kumar 1984)—does affect the weaver positively. As contrasted with the metalworker, the woodworker, the potter, and the painter, the weaver continues on top of the swift currents of change and has a positive outlook on the world, based on the recent history of his industry.

A small part of this is also composed of positive expectations from the government. A weaving school was opened in 1915, and agencies such as the All India Handloom Board were set up to tide over the crisis in the 1950s (UP Admin Rpt 1916, Ind 820 1922). Although most of the schemes for rationing of silk yarn, registration of looms, and loans to weavers have remained confined to paper, there is a sense of optimism about the government's role, which contrasts with the sense of other artisans, particularly metalworkers and woodworkers.

The positive outlook of weavers is further compounded by the progressive possibility of mobility in the industry. In about 1900 there were three main silk products in Banaras: *kamkhwāb* (brocade), material for specific apparel purposes, and plain silk yardage. Corresponding to

TABLE 5.1 The Numbers of Weavers in Banaras

Year	*Numbers*	*How described*
1872	245	kincob makers
	1,185	silk weavers
	3,670	weavers
1881	1,000	silk weavers
	137	gold-cloth weavers, sellers
	62	silk dealers
	4,239	cotton weavers
	2,115	silk weavers
1891	12,871	silk weavers & dependents
1901	12,269	silk weavers & dependents
	5,923	actual workers
1911	6,820	silk spinners & weavers
	2,122	workers in "insufficiently described textile industries"
1921	15,504	total workers in textiles
	1,431	silk spinners & weavers
	4,648	workers in "insufficiently described textile industries"
1931	5,680	silk spinners & weavers
1951	6,505	workers in "textile industries otherwise unclassified"
	10,915	manufacturers of wearing apparel & made up textile goods
1961	35,000	"karghe" (looms)
1981	1,50,000	silk weavers
	5,00,000	"people . . . engaged in the silk industry directly & indirectly"

NOTE: Unless otherwise mentioned, the numbers are all of actual workers, whether given by the source or calculated by me. The 1981 figures are for Banaras district and the rest for Banaras city. Large discrepancies are due mostly to inconsistent classification of these artisans and frequent inclusion of them in "labourers" or "traders."

SOURCES: For the years 1872, 1881, 1901, 1911, 1921, 1931, 1951, the Census for each of those years; for silk weavers in 1881, Adm. Report NWP 1982; for 1891, Chatterji 1908:40; for 1961 Kamala Prasad Mishra 1975: 125; for 1981, B. P. Pandey 1981:21.

these were three levels of production: the dependent laborer working for the *kārkhānēdār,* or firm owner, the dependent laborer working for himself at home, and the independent weaver or master weaver (Ali 1900; UP Admin Rpt 1882). Today there is relative homogenization of products, and almost every weaver is a weaver of Banarsi saris. The three levels of production continue to exist, constituting a hierarchy in relative well-being for the weavers: from the bottom up, laborer working under another's roof, weaver working at home for others, weaver working at home for himself. The difference between the earlier hierarchy and the present one is that now there is more mobility among the different levels, and today a laborer can conceivably move up the ladder in a decade or two to an independent weaver's status.

Poverty is one corollary of the nature of handicraft industry; control over space and time is the other. The home is the workshop, and work time is always time set by the artisan himself. Even when men work in another's place as laborers, the location still remains a domestic one. Even in the largest workplaces the total number of workers is never more than ten or twelve; there is direct interaction between them and the employer, and time remains the worker's, for payment is always by the piece. These conditions have not changed over the last century in that there has been no tendency for larger production units or a new ethic of production relations to emerge. When the Royal Commission on Labour gathered oral evidence on working hours, it found that in the Banaras silk and brocade industry hours were normally seven per day but could be as many as fourteen per day in the wedding season. But there were important features of the work which alleviated this problem. "A good deal of the work is done in the open—in the courtyard of the worker's house or even in the public street or lane . . . there is no discipline to observe. Rest and recreation is taken whenever the need is felt. Contact with the home and familiar surroundings is seldom interrupted. The usual amenities of social life are not disturbed" (Royal Commission of Labour 1931:154). This familiarity with "freedom" has become an integral part of the weaver's identity, as discussed further below.

On all these counts—the perceived level of skill needed for their unique work, the liberties with space and time possible within the dimensions of domestic handicrafts production, and the near guarantee of poverty—the world of the weaver is no different from that of the other artisans of Banaras, including the metalworker, wooden-toy maker, goldsmith, potter, painter, copper-wire drawer, embroiderer, and garland maker. Where he is at all different is in being the best off of the lot, a factor that contributes substantially to his construction of identity.

THE WEAVER AS ANSARI

All the different kinds of Muslim weavers—dependent, independent, and master, as also the owners of firms—call themselves Ansari. The exceptions are so few as to be negligible: a Muslim of a Pathan "lineage" or a barber "caste,"[1] who has wandered into the weaving profession through a series of unusual circumstances. The term "Ansari" is used in a number of ways. Trading or manufacturing firms and weavers who are expanding their production use "Ansari" as a "title" in their or their firm's name, such as Swaleh Ansari and Company. Many master weavers treat "Ansari" as part of their full name, such as Matiullah Ansari or Hafizullah Ansari. Poorer master weavers and all ordinary weavers, like all poor and uneducated Hindus, particularly of the lower castes, call themselves simply by their first names, such as Alimuddin or Jameel Ahmad. They may acquire an epithet ("Sahab," "Banarsi") if they achieve any distinction, but if required to give their "last name" for an official purpose such as in a school, bank, or hospital, they use "Ansari." All of them, if asked "what" they are, will reply not "Julāhā," the term used for them by others, but "Ansari." The term is explained by them as referring to a *birādarī* or *qaum,* comparable to a Hindu endogamous caste in its traditional occupation, with implications of honesty and sincerity, thus infinitely preferable to "Julāhā" with its allusions of poverty, stupidity, and backwardness (see Sherring 1872:345–46, Nesfield 1885:26, 131, J. Brij Bhushan 1958:73–74, Naqvi 1968:165, Ansari 1960:44).

This preference was largely responsible for the adoption of the new name as part of a larger movement for social uplift and higher status among both Hindus and Muslims around the turn of the century. The movement was formalized in the 1930s in the All India Jamat-ul-Ansar, a fact unknown to the great majority of Banaras weavers, who consider Ansari to be a broad definition of a lineage or descent group, or at least of an occupational community whose work was first inspired and sanctified by Hazrat Sees Paigambar alah-e-salam.

Such a "creation" of identity is a feature that may be witnessed from approximately the first quarter of this century in other artisan communities in Banaras as well. The metalworkers, Kasera by caste, call themselves Haihayavamshi Chhatri, although no one else calls them that. Goldsmiths, ironsmiths, and woodworkers are called Sonār, Lohār, and Baṛhaī by others, but refer to themselves as Vishvakarmas. Compared

1. The four high Muslim "lineages" recognized in most of India are the Mughals, Sheikhs, Sayyads, and Pathans; the weavers, as Ansaris, now claim Sheikh lineage. These, and all occupations, such as butcher, sweeper, barber, and of course weaver (whether called Julāhā or Ansari), are also regarded as castes.

with other artisans, the weavers have been the most successful in perpetrating their new identity.

The new identity that is put forward is based on occupation in each case, but goes beyond that to make a case for a certain kind of personality. The components of this differ considerably in the versions offered by the outside observer and by the member of the community. Ansaris maintain themselves to be a united people: all feel equal, as members of one family; anyone may marry another, in spite of income differences; and anyone may sit down and eat with another, in spite of status inequalities. These are sentiments voiced frequently by more prosperous Ansaris, although lower-class weavers do not contradict them if pressed to give an opinion. In actuality, marriages are preferably made between families of equal economic standing, and food is shared at festivals, but the occasion of *sitting down* together rarely occurs. What is in fact common to rich and poor Ansaris is not noted by them: certain aspects of lifestyle, such as house design and clothes.

The houses of all Ansaris have a similar pattern: a dark entrance, with very likely a latrine on one side, leading to an enclosed courtyard, with tap or hand pump. The *kārkhānā* (loom or weaving room) is located on one side, or two, depending on prosperity, and stairs go up on the third. Above are the family rooms all around the central opening. The kitchen is on a separate mezzanine off the stairs, or on the roof itself. No furniture is kept except some string cots standing up during the day, and trunks and canisters of stores. There is a total separation of working and living areas, and the *kārkhānā* never doubles as sleeping or playing space for the family, though it does as sitting room for the weavers and their guests. Even the newest, most expensive homes of Ansari businessmen have this basic design, which may become elaborated with the multiplication of floors, rooms, and even courtyards, and the addition of rugs, television, and refrigerator.

The houses of metalworkers and other artisans of Banaras have the same design as well, leading to the conclusion that the decisive factors are occupation—the need for a *kārkhānā* at home—and culture, such as the understanding of convenience, as in the case of bathroom and kitchen. In other words, there is a Banarsi artisan house design, not a peculiarly Ansari one. When the pattern does not immediately seem obvious, it is always due to fraternal partitions that split the house in the center, resulting in disproportionately tall and narrow houses with only half a courtyard, rooms on only one side, and an even narrower, tunnel-like entrance.

Ansaris almost always wear a lungi, topped with a shirt or vest, and a *gamchhā* strewn over the shoulder. Muslims in other professions often dress this way, but not with any consistency. The choice of dress is an interesting combination of the practical and the culturally preferred. A lungi suits the postures demanded by the pit loom, which does not explain why prosperous Ansaris who do not themselves weave habitually wear the lungi at home. It is perhaps a carryover from their weaving days, but more, it is closely associated with the Ansari identity. All other artisans dress also in lungi and *gamchhā,* though in knee-length lungis as opposed to the Ansari ankle-length version. The preference for this choice of clothes is articulated not in Ansari but in Banarsi consciousness. Clothes are supposed to emphasize your simplicity, your inner wealth, and the absence of need to make any kind of external show. Material display is vulgar and indicative of little but poverty, weakness, and shallowness of character (see also N. Kumar 1986). Ansaris and all other artisans dress the way they do, not simply because they are poor or because it is convenient, but because it is an idealized way of dressing.

After skill and poverty, what Ansaris cite as the most telling indicator of their community character is their illiteracy. This is mentioned matter-of-factly as a problem that undoubtedly leads to their proverbial "backwardness" in that it makes them easy victims at the hands of the middlemen, but a problem of such dimensions that it is completely outside their ability to tackle. The some thirty *madrasās* (Muslim schools) of the city have hardly 10 percent of the Muslim children of school age attending them, and an even smaller percentage attends the public and private secular schools of the city. The *sardar*s, the social leaders of the Ansaris, do not recognize education as one of the urgent goals before them. The reformist sects of Wahabis and Deobandis are somewhat more concerned,[2] but their numbers are small (5 to 10 percent of the population) and their influence is limited. The largest madrasa of the city, Islamia, as well as a new college, the Salfia Dar-ul-ulum, is Wahabi, but the ordinary weaver identifies with neither. Although the subject needs much further research, my estimate is that the fact of illiteracy, or at least the relative lack of education, contributes strongly toward the particular complexion of weavers' identity that I am describing in this chapter.[3]

The most interesting characteristic claimed to be shared by the Ansaris is their "simplicity" and "tenderheartedness" ("we are *narmdil, dilraham*"). While simplicity may be understood in terms of lifestyle and lack of material ambition, both of which are easily observed and sup-

2. An excellent background and discussion of the Wahabis (Ahl-i-Hadith) and Deobandis is given in Metcalf 1982.

3. In research conducted recently, I have looked at the differences in popular perceptions that result with school education. This work is being written up, and the conclusions are not yet quite clear.

ported by our data, the idea of "tenderheartedness" is a more puzzling one. It seems to be the absolute counterpoint to the version of those who have a relationship of dominance over them: the government, especially in British days, in its regard of them as "bigoted" (GAD 210B 1892; see also G. Pandey 1983b: 19–28), and the middlemen and master weavers, who complain unceasingly of their love of idleness. The weaver's tenderheartedness is an aspect of his self-image, as someone urbane and cultured, who has perfected an unerring philosophy of contentment. He will work himself to the bone, but will cherish his freedom. "Ansaris are not afraid to work. They will work twelve hours a day, but they cannot do *naukrī* (service) because then we will become slaves."

Curiously, all nonweavers consider that weaving is easy, leisurely work, and that weavers are easygoing people. In the opinion of upper classes, "These weavers are too fond of *mauj* and *mastī* (carefreeness, fun). Whenever they feel like it, they will close up their *kārkhānā*s and go for a stroll." To support this, half a dozen festivals are cited when work is suspended for days at a stretch and the fact that the end of one length of warp marks the appropriate time to take a few days as holiday. Most of these negative judgments are identical to those made of other artisans by their suppliers and buyers. Like other artisans, Ansaris never feel obliged to defend themselves on these counts. Leisure is considered as fundamental as work. What is described derisively as "love of idleness" by outsiders is regarded very positively by Ansaris as part of their identity.

THE WEAVER AS MUSLIM

Ansaris regard their religiosity as an inalienable part of their identity: the complement to being poor, illiterate, simple, and sincere is a purity and directness of faith. Regarded as fervent, passionate, and bigoted by others, particularly by British administrators in the last century of their rule, they consider themselves very positively as "strong of faith" (*dharm ke pakkē*) and "firm to their tradition" (*usūl kē pakkē*). Their work itself is considered, as with every Hindu caste in its hereditary occupation, a sanctified task. *Nyāz* (a food offering to be later distributed to the attending company) is given to the Paigambar with whom the craft originated, at the very beginning of one's career. Other Muslims in other professions similarly have a patron saint to whom they offer up, as it were, their efforts. For instance, *zardozī* workers (embroiderers in gold and silver thread) consider their craft to have been started by Hazrat Yusuf alah-e-salam, in whose name are offered food and prayers, and whose anniversary is celebrated as a minor festival, Huzur ki miraj.

The religiosity of the Ansaris finds expression in their self-description, in which faith always finds a place. It is equally evident in what they do, that is, in their enthusiastic celebration of religious festivals, their visits to shrines, and their belief in pirs. Their religiosity is problematic, however, for their community leaders. Most of these leaders belong to the reformist sects of Wahabis and Deobandis, known for criticizing the very activities that the Ansaris prize most: their dependence on pirs, their visits to shrines, and the fairs and festivity they enjoy during a dozen celebrations during the year.

The chief festivals of the Muslims are ᶜĪd (ᶜĪd ul Fiṭr) and Baqr ᶜĪd (ᶜĪd ul Zuha), when special foods and new clothes are ideally required by every member of the family. On both occasions, the *namāz* (prayers) is mentioned as the main event and as the marker of the specialness of the day. The poorer weavers find it impossible to live up to the ideal image of the festivals in terms of feasting and celebration. For them, these are the major holidays of the year when they may close their *kārkhānā*s for a week to ten days. Depending partly on the time of year in which these festivals fall, the holidays are occupied with outings, pleasure trips, visits to relatives, and picnics. The ideal of ᶜĪd as the reassertion of solidarity for Muslims is very strong, so that even while households vary drastically in their ability to afford festival food and clothes, the perception of most participants is that of unity and mutual sharing. ᶜĪd can also, on occasion, stand for a more pragmatic assertion of solidarity, as at the time of the special *namāz* at Banaras's Idgahs. Two of these particularly, Lāṭ and Gyān Vāpī *masjid,* are sacred spaces in historical dispute between Hindus and Muslims. While no communal outbreak has actually occurred at ᶜĪd in Banaras, the situation has often become a "sensitive" one at these places (*Bharat Jiwan,* 11 May 1891, 8; UP Admin Rpt, 1924–25; Chauk and Adampura TFR). In everyday life, Hindus and Muslims conduct their respective worship without getting in each other's way, nor is there the memory of any actual violence associated with the places. But at ᶜĪd and Baqr ᶜĪd, the very presence of scores of armed policemen and elaborate preparations by the administration make the places seem like the settings for familiar, prerehearsed scenarios.

Baqr ᶜĪd also includes the ritual of the sacrifice of a goat (in the past a cow or a buffalo) or even a camel, followed by sharing of the meat among family, neighbors, and the poor. The less prosperous weavers can afford neither a goat, nor, as at ᶜĪd, new suits of clothes for everyone. Nor do they "feast" unless invited to do so by patrons, employers, and wealthier acquaintances. As at ᶜĪd ul Fiṭr, some presents of food, clothes, and cash pass from rich to poor, but solidarity is more an ideal than a reality. Except at the time of *namāz,* the festivals do not become intense as occasions of identity. The absence of public processions and meetings serves further to diffuse the unity of the occasion. While the symbolism of Baqr ᶜĪd, with its slaughter, blood, and feasting on meat, remains the most foreign of all Muslim festivals for Hindus, there is again no communal quarrel on record on Baqr ᶜĪd in Banaras, a fact that contrasts with the experience of the rest of the province (*Bharat Jiwan*, 7 Aug. 1893, 6; 19 Dec. 1912; *Aj*, 10 March 1938, 3; UP Admin Rpt, 1917, 1919, 1924, 1926, 1929; Pandey 1983a; Freitag 1980; Yang 1980). Even the cow, for all its potency as a symbol in a place like Banaras, has never been a political problem in the city. Cow slaughter has been banned since the 1950s, and its memory does not serve to arouse anyone.

The other major festivals of the Muslims, Muharram and Barawafat, seem to provide a more explicit context for an assertion of a "Muslim" identity. They have both been expanding in recent years and bear strong outward resemblance to Hindu celebrations that are likewise expanding, such as Durga, Saraswati, Govardhan, and Vishvakarma Puja. Muharram is the better known and is celebrated in Banaras with great pomp (*shān*) by both Shias (a microscopic minority) and Sunnis (all the weavers). The observation of Muharram may be analyzed in two parts: (1) the establishment of the tazia (the replica of the martyr Husain's tomb) on the *chauk* (platform) of the *muḥalla* (neighborhood); and (2) the processions on the tenth day of the month, each carrying a tazia for immersion or burial, and all other processions in the next fifty days, featuring battle symbols (ᶜ*alam*), marriage symbols (*mehndī, dulhā*), and symbols of martyrdom (Duldul, the horse of Husain). Each of these two parts may in turn be interpreted as reflecting both Islamic identity and the identity of otherwise defined populations, and it is necessary to sift the different aspects.

The majority of tazias are constructed out of paper, cloth, wood, and other materials by professional *ātishbāz* (manufacturers of fireworks), and financed by the contributions of the *muḥalla*. Thus the *muḥalla* is the taziadar for the most part and not, as elsewhere in India, an individual (see Bayly 1975). The tazias become a focus of inter-*muḥalla* competitiveness, particularly for children and young men. Around the tazia take place wrestling, lathi- and sword-wielding demonstrations, and the singing of the special poetic form called *marsiyāh* (see Sadiq 1984:20). All of these are specimens of the skill, talent, and excellence of the *muḥalla* in implied competition with others. The larger symbolism of the tazia-on-the-chauk is that of Islam, and in Banaras not Shia or Sunni, but nonsectarian Islam. There are two spaces in Banaras each shared by a tazia chauk and a Hindu shrine, and, as with the major mosques, the places become annually vulnerable to violation by one community of the perceived rights of the other.

The processions (*julūs*) are similarly complex phenomena. The tazia *julū* is very old in Banaras, having supposedly been introduced in 1753 (Siddiqi n.d.). In its popular form, it consists of a shoulder-borne tazia surrounded by crowds of mourners who chant, cheer, lament, and simply crowd along. There are one or more *anjuman* ("clubs"), singing *marsiyāh;* there are one or more *akhāṛā* (also "clubs"), demonstrating their skill with the lathi, the sword, and dozens of other lesser-known instruments. Each procession is identified with a *muḥalla,* sometimes with a group of *muḥalla*s called after the dominating one. Together with this taken-for-granted *muḥalla* competitiveness occurs the presentation of Islam to non-Muslims. Many of the tazia processions pass through crowded localities in the center of the city where lanes are only a few yards wide. Common threats to the sacredness of the occasion arise from possible collision between relatively oversized tazias or absolutely oversized *ᶜalam,* and low tree branches or telephone wires. A collision portends Hindu-Muslim conflict: the locality, the surrounding houses and porches, and the public spaces being Hindu, the "victimized" processionists Muslim, and the offending tree probably the sacred pipal. Such potentially explosive situations have occurred throughout the last hundred years (Chauk and Dasashwamedh TFR) but have been saved by the timely intervention of authorities and volunteers. In Adampura, a tazia is taken through Gola Hanuman Phatak, which has a temple to Hanuman at the crossroads in the center (see fig. 13; compare with fig. 15). The main business of the day is to keep the temple and the oversize tazia from touching each other. The task is performed by dozens of policemen, officers, and community leaders, some of whom physically hoist it over a threatening bend of the street. The provocateurs from whom a breach of peace is feared may be Hindus or Muslims (according to which side is reporting), but are clearly professional troublemakers (budmash, *khurāfātī*), according to both. It does not occur to either side to redefine the boundaries of rights, to make it possible, for example, for the tazia to avoid that lane altogether, or to refashion the temple walls to change their angle slightly. The event has taken on the character of a local drama, and as such, its tension, intensity, and accompanying fun are very localized. Hindus and Muslims in other parts of the city, even in other parts of the same ward, are neither knowledgeable about the excitement nor impressed by it. It was described to me with many dramatic flourishes by the chief officer of the local police station, Adampura, who functions as the master of ceremonies on the occasion, before I had a chance to witness it. As I suspected and was able to confirm later, other police officers in the city were not aware of the proceedings at Gola Hanuman Phatak.

If what makes Muharram interesting is its proliferation in terms of processions, what is fascinating about Barawafat is its very invention:

Fig. 13. Tazia being paraded at Muslim observance of Muharram. Procession took place in 1987 at Gola Hanuman Phatak (the temple of Hanuman), in Adampura ward. All the houses are Hindu; the temple's platform is visible on the right, protected by a row of policemen. Photograph by Nita Kumar. (Compare with fig. 15.)

the day of both the birth and the death of the Prophet, in Banaras it is celebrated most loudly by the Sunnis as the former, and takes the shape of a rejoicing (*jashn* ᶜĪd Milāud-ul-Nabī). At the core of it lies competitive performance by *anjumans* of the poetical form called *nāt,* around which is constantly growing and becoming elaborated the accompanying paraphernalia of lights, paper decorations, flags, loudspeakers, stages, trophies, and all-night mela activity, including stalls of edibles, balloons, and toys. None of this was known two or three decades ago (Chauk TFR). Barawafat was an important festival, but observed only in the mosques and the home, with the recitation of *milaud sharif,* without a hint of competition, amplification, mela-like decoration and all-night festivity. The young do not remember a past when Barawafat in its present form was totally unthought of. The festival is also expanding in the equally interesting direction of the multiplication of locales. Dalmandi *muḥalla* in Chauk ward was the only center for Barawafat celebrations until about two decades ago. Now it is Dalmandi on the eleventh day of the month, Alaipura on the twelfth day, Madanpura on the thirteenth, Kotwa and Baribazar on the fifteenth, Ramnagar and Gauriganj on the sixteenth, and Shivala on the seventeenth.

While Muharram partially represents Islam to outsiders, we have seen how it also renews and furthers *muḥalla* differences. The very residential patterns of the city work in both an organizational and an ideological way to weaken any potential alignment of "Muslims" as one unit. Weavers are distributed over most of the wards of the city and are concentrated in two, known as Alwipura (or Alaipura, the two wards of Adampura and Jaitpura) and Madanpura (all the *muḥalla*s of Dasashwamedh ward around the *muḥalla* Madanpura). The latter sees itself as extant for almost a millennium, from the first Muslim invaders to the city, and to be the oldest center of the silk-weaving craft. The northern localities of Alaipura, though older in terms of absolute settlement, became important for weaving much later, and were accepted as integral parts of the city only in the eighteenth century (Nomani 1963; Siddiqi, n.d.). The weavers of Madanpura emphasize their absolute superiority over those of all other wards, characterized as "rural" (*dehātī, gāwār*), backward, crude, and uncultured. The weavers of these other wards, equally self-sufficient, progressively prosperous, and more numerous than the Madanpura weavers, do not react with actual hostility to the opinion of their backwardness. In reply, they stress their simplicity, honesty, and unspoilt nature, and prefer not to intermarry with Madanpura. Indeed, it is the boast of both parts of the city that one will never find in either part a wife who is from the other part. This ideological distancing is constant, and overcoming it would require a very powerful force that is not provided by any festival: even the ᶜĪd namazes are read by the Alwipurites at the Lāṭ and by the Madanpurites at Gyān Vāpī. Muharram particularly provides a referent limited to *one muḥalla* or a group of *muḥalla*s regarded as one. Each procession is one of many, showing off precisely its superior tazia, its skilled celebrants, its *akhāṛā* competing with all others in talent and training.

Barawafat, even more than Muharram, cannot be understood as reinforcing the social solidarity of the whole Muslim community. The main separation that occurs is between *muḥalla*s. The chief actors at the event are the *anjuman*s, and each *anjuman* consists of young enthusiasts whose social base is the *muḥalla*, or proximity of residence, and who buy or learn poems from a poet of their choice. The very expansion of the celebration to new localities is indicative of the identification made by people with their immediate residential area, and states the friendly rivalry of *muḥalla*s in their attainment of cultural refinement and their passion for a lifestyle of well-measured enjoyment.

There are three other kinds of divisions within Muslims which are well exemplified by Barawafat. Unlike the other two ᶜĪds, it is not a *festival* (*tyohār*, ᶜ*Īd*) in the strict sense of one established by Muhammad. It falls in the grey zone between classical, ordained celebrations and local, folk ones, being unequivocally condemned by imams and maulanas while passionately favored by ordinary weavers. The process described as "Islamic revitalization" has met with limited success in Banaras, and is in my view neither as simple nor as unopposed and unidirectional as is made out by certain scholars (Robinson 1983; see Veena Das 1984). The Wahabis and Deobandis, constituting hardly 10 percent of the Muslim population of Banaras, are no doubt preoccupied with it. Among their successful ventures in reform over the last century is the simplification of marriage ceremonies, rejection of music at life-cycle rites, and maintenance of strict dowry and divorce rules (Siddiqi, n.d.). But their intolerance for most of the practices that constitute pleasure and entertainment for ordinary weavers, and undoubtedly their small numbers, make their image among the weaving population a sorry one, and they prefer to follow a policy of withdrawal and criticism rather than anything more active. They condemn the trends visible at Barawafat and ᶜ*urs* (the anniversaries of Muslim shrines, literally the reunion of the soul with God), characterizing it as the tendency of lower-class, illiterate people to go astray. Such criticism is freely voiced in private conversations, for example, but never publicized in the main Urdu newspaper, *Qaumī Morchā*, which happens to be Deobandi, because, in the words of a poor weaver, "it needs readers."

At another level, among those who would celebrate Barawafat, there are crucial differences between Sunnis and Shias. In the Sunni version: "The Shias believe it is wrong to be happy. And Sunnis cannot accept that all you must have is lamenting and self-abnegation." "Victory" for either side lies in a demonstration of their preferred way through a celebratory mode. Sunnis are far more numerous in Banaras than Shias, who are estimated at perhaps five hundred houses, and would have no trouble in having their way, except that Dalmandi, the center of Barawafat celebration, is also the nucleus of Shia residence. So police mediation is required, and according to entries in their Festival Registers, "There should be careful duty at Shias' homes. Anjumans should not be allowed to sing those songs near there which may be considered anti-Shia" (Chauk TFR).

Finally, there is a separation of classes within the Muslims such as has been mentioned in the case of ᶜĪd and Baqr ᶜĪd, which is very explicit at Barawafat. Wahabis and the reform-minded are not restricted to the upper classes, but most of them do seem to belong to the business and trading families. It is difficult to be precise in the absence of statistics on the subject, especially as those who favor a stricter Islam do not always make their views very public, but the opinion of most ordinary weavers, as well as the educated and politically conscious among them, is that the "bigger" people are also those who are very particular about observing only the canonically correct Islamic occasions. The committees formed for fund collection and decoration at Barawafat are all drawn from the ranks of ordinary weavers, dyers, printers, designers, sari embroiderers, and petty shopkeepers. The needs of a particular *muḥalla* range between Rs. 2,000 and Rs. 20,000, satisfied mainly by individual donations of, usually, two to five rupees each. The bigger people in the *muḥalla* are also obliged to contribute, but they neither participate in the activities nor are expected to. The "diases," consisting of judges, honored guests, trophies, and gifts are produced by yet other committees, which generate funds from donations for prizes and decorations.

All this mobilization is the result of *shauk,* intense love for an activity for its own sake. *Shauk* itself was not class-bound in Banaras in the past, but as I have shown at length elsewhere (Kumar 1988), it is progressively becoming a quality that characterizes the poor rather than the rich. With change in the cultural role of upper-class patrons, indeed a withdrawal on the part of the elite from the city's traditional cultural life, *shauk* is not something that the prosperous and educated boast of any longer, with the exception of a few older, clearly old-fashioned, partially eccentric members of the traditional elite. The typically Banarsi pleasures of public organization for poetry, music, inter-*muḥalla* competition, mela decoration, and festivals are significantly characterized as "idleness," "ignorance," and "backwardness" by the rich and sophisticated, and as "shauk" by the poor.

THE WEAVER AS BANARSI

One aspect of Muslim religious practice that I have intentionally excluded from discussion above is the practice of visiting *mazārs*, the tombs of *pirs* (saints) and *shahīds* (martyrs). There are some thirty important *mazārs* in Banaras which most Muslims would recognize and a few dozen more of local importance to *muḥallas*. They each have a special day of the week for visits, and an annual ᶜ*urs* celebration, the death anniversary of the man entombed (popularly believed to be resident) in the shrine. These shrines are a potent force in the minds of devotees, and also the homes of dear and familiar figures. As sources of power they are not given recognition by Muslim religious leaders, and they have found no avenue of assimilation into orthodoxy. This last fact aside—for in Hinduism the distinction between "classical" and "folk" religion is neither clear-cut nor real—the practice of visiting shrines and the celebration of ᶜ*urs* in particular is parallel to the Hindu popular practice of worship at local shrines. The term *mazār* is itself etymologically related to *ziyārat,* "having the vision of," thus making the purpose of shrine visitation comparable to *darshan.* What especially concerns us here is the development of ᶜ*urs.* Like the annual celebrations at Hindu temples, called *shringārs*, ᶜ*urs* have been expanding in recent years in number, multiplicity of locales, sound, dazzle, and effect.

There is an orthodox way of celebrating the ᶜ*urs:* the grave is bathed and sprinkled with rose water and perfume, and old covers are replaced by new ones. *Halqā* (calling out the name of Allah), *qurānkhānī* (reading the Quran), *tabarrukh* (the offering and distribution of food), *fātihā* (praying), *nāt* and *qawwalī* (verses set to music) are accompanying sanctioned activities. The patron of the ᶜ*urs,* as we know from the details in the Festival Registers of each police station (see Kumar 1985), is traditionally one of the devotees willing and able to finance the whole affair. In both *shringārs* and ᶜ*urs,* there is one major pattern of change over the last fifty years: their number seems to be increasing manifold (see chapter 4, this volume, for related discussion). Every deity and shrine must always have its anniversary, thus "increase" means that the annual celebrations are more noticeable now: bigger, brighter, louder, and far more public than before. The new style of celebration that has evolved has taken the following form: a team of professional musicians is invited to perform late at night, usually at midnight. A public stage is set up with lights, frills, flowers, and so on, and the street in front is turned into an auditorium with cotton rugs, tents in some cases, and plenty of loudspeakers. An audience collects for the show, which goes on most of the night. The most popular program consists of *qawwālī* at ᶜ*urs,* and at the comparable *shringār* celebrations, of *qawwālī* and *birahā* (for the latter see chapter 3, this volume).

This form of celebration dates back no more than twenty-five to thirty years. Its evolution may be documented from oral sources of three kinds: the polemics of *maulavī* and *maulānā*; the testimony of older weavers; and, most significant, the accounts of musicians. Sources of accounts are men such as Bismillah Khan, who has performed in every temple and shrine in Banaras; Chand Putli, the most popular *qawwāl* in Banaras today; and Majid Bharati, perhaps the second most popular *qawwāl,* who contrasts his popularity with that of his teacher, Rafiq Anwar, over thirty years ago. These performers can describe in graphic detail how tastes have evolved and the world of popular culture in Banaras has expanded. The religious leaders are critical of *shringār*s and ᶜ*urs,* regarding the latter as imitations of the former, and as evidence of the unfortunate ignorance and backwardness of the weavers and of their tendency toward lower-class behavior. *Shringār*s and ᶜ*urs,* to my mind, *are* indicative of a "lower class" identity, in that they serve to separate and define their participants. Not only are the funds again collected totally by donation within the neighborhood, the event is considered to be one belonging to the *nīch qaum, choṭē log* (lower orders, small people) and *garib* (the poor). There is no educated, well-off person, including those who enjoy *ghazal* and *qawwālī* otherwise, who would acknowledge enjoying the music and all-night festivity of the *shringār* or ᶜ*urs,* or who would consider the celebration to be *his* in any way.

The conflict experienced by *maulānas* and social leaders between an orthodox Islamic practice and local "distortions" is not shared by participants themselves. The weaver of Banaras claims an "Islamic" identity, and considers his veneration of *pir*s, babas, and *shahid*s an important part of his faith. There is no experiential problem of "adjustment," as is spoken of in other parts of South Asia, of an Islamic identity with a territorial-cultural one that is heavily oriented toward local Hinduism (Ellickson 1976, Fruzzetti 1981, Madan 1981). The observer's temptation to claim imitation or adjustment of an ideal to a local version is strong, but not necessarily appropriate.

As with the style of celebrations, the process of identity formation derives from a cultural fund common to both Hindus and Muslims. In the case of celebratory styles, for instance, there is a common response to certain sensory forms: lights, loud sound, crowds, openness, all-night participation. In the case of identity, there is a way of emphasizing the local, the immediate, and the contextual (the "traditional," the "way of the place") that prompts me to make a case for the weaver as "Banarsi."

The emphasis, that is, should be placed on the elements shared by these artisans. The Muslim weaver of Banaras is as *shaukīn* (characterized by *shauk,* passion and taste) a man as the Hindu metalworker and milk seller, and central to his lifestyle is the love of the outside, of *akhāṛā*s for wrestling and body building, for music and poetry, and of the city itself. He has different occasions and locations around which his activities are structured: he will prefer to go to Chunar and to Rajghat, to the *mazārs* of Shah Washil and Chandan Shahid, whereas the metalworker will go to the Devi temple in Vindyachal. Both Hindu and Muslim artisans agree that Chaitra (March–April) is the best "season" for going on outdoor trips. While both share an attitude of passion for the freshness and openness that constitutes the outside, a commitment to the freedom to be able to go when they please, and a sensitivity to seasonal and geographical variations, the difference in their attitudes is that in the Hindu case, the popular version of "the good life" has sanction from religion, while for Muslims it explicitly does not. Those at the top of the Hindu hierarchy—*pandit, sadhu, raja, rais,* politician, businessman, and otherwise important or respected men—will always be thought the better of for being appreciative of *bhang, darshan,* and the outside (see Kumar 1986). In the Muslim case, the *maulānā, maulvī, sardār,* social leader, rich businessman, find the pleasures of the ordinary weaver only something to denigrate. Correspondingly, while Hindus feel that entertainment, religion, natural beauty, God's presence, all do and should coincide, a Muslim does not make explicit connection between a religious mela and the beauty of the season. The largest festivals—ᶜĪd, Baqr ᶜĪd, Holi, and Diwali—are all celebrated with outdoor trips. The ideas of Hindus and Muslims regarding space and time coincide. The ideas of Hindus draw from many different sources, including medical lore and the teaching of the sages. Those of Muslims are thoroughly Banarsi, with no support in Islamic teaching or tradition.

Many other favorite activities may be discussed to support the claim of a common lifestyle and expression of *Banārsipan* (Banaras-ness) for both Hindus and Muslims. Both are articulate about their love for music and poetry, especially as performed and produced by themselves. Artisans of all castes and communal affiliations meet regularly in informal groups to sing and recite. They organize the *shringār*s and ᶜ*urs* already discussed, and music and verse underlie the attractiveness of major festivals such as Barawafat and Holi. Or one could talk at length of the importance of *akhāṛā*s, such as Amba Shah ka Taqiya in Madanpura, where local boys work out every morning and evening, and informal wrestling competitions are held every Sunday, attracting members from *akhāṛā*s all over Banaras. Equally indicative of a common popular culture is the art of sword and lathi wielding, taught in some one hundred Hindu and Muslim *akhāṛā*s all over the city, distinguishable from each other only on the basis of their expertise, not religion. These *akhāṛā*s are informal clubs, organized into two "federations," that of "the fifty-two" and that of "the eighty-two" (*bāvanī* and *bāyasī*), both called panchayats and united under an umbrella organization called the Bhāratīya Shāstra Kalā Parishad (Indian Association for the Art of

Weapons). Each *akhāṛā* has its own flag, ustad, and "office," and the members of these perform under their respective banners at Muharram, Nakkatayya, Durga Puja, and other assorted Hindu and Muslim processions.

A large part of the identification of weavers with Banaras comes from their understanding of the city itself. Both the terms "Banaras" and "Banarsi" have a Hindu ring to them, and in fact the Hindu imagery in the city is quite awesome. Muslims have some techniques to keep themselves from being overawed. While recognizing the centrality of Banaras for Hinduism and the sacredness of the Ganges as an "objective" fact, the Muslims of Banaras treat it as an important Islamic center. The older mosques of Banaras, Aṛhāī Kangūrā, Ganj-ē-Shahīdā, and Abdul Razzāq Shāh, are regarded as evidence of the age of the Muslim presence in the city. The tombs of Lāl Khān, Fakr-ud-dīn, and Ghāzī Miān, among many others, are seen as testimony to the legitimacy of Muslims, having supposedly arrived with the very first waves of conquest and conversion in northern India. Since their craft, in this version, dates from that time, there is no better confirmation of their share in the city's culture than the existence of old mosques and tombs, practically in every *muḥalla* bearing witness to their age and numerical strength. Among later mosques, those that date from Aurangzeb's time, such as the Gyān Vāpī, the Lāṭ, and the Dharharā, are regarded with special pride, and are indeed imposing architectural artifacts (Sen 1912:71–80). From the minarets of Gyān Vāpī, Razzāq Shāh, and Dharharā, the whole city may be swept in one glance, that is, visually controlled. Besides these more formal landscape markers are the myriads of shrines to beloved teachers and respected men, the scenes of weekly visits, seasonal melas, and annual ᶜ*urs,* and the centers of everyday life. All these geographical devices create a sense of a "Muslim" history of Banaras, rendering the place no longer "Hindu" or alien, but open, friendly, and benedictory. Most Hindus, of course, are ignorant or indifferent to the Muslim perspective on the history and geography of the city (as are most scholars, including those in this volume; see Kumar 1987) and do not question why Muslims feel so much at home in Banaras. Muslims regard themselves for most purposes as residents of particular wards and *muḥalla*s, but share this overall perspective on the larger whole of the city without perhaps demonstrating it in a comparable way.

Given the strength of the arguments in favor of a Banarsi identity, the question of Hindu-Muslim conflicts in Banaras becomes a particularly pertinent one. It is far larger than may be resolved with the scope of this chapter. By 1885, the beginning of our period of study, Hindu-Muslim conflict on various occasions was already an accepted phenomenon on the north Indian stage, and for the next four decades, until 1930, there is reporting in Banaras newspapers of riots in the rest of the province. No riots occurred in Banaras during this period, but the reiteration of this very fact began to seem ominous. The first riot in more than a hundred years took place in 1931 and is retained in public memory as the turning point in a stretch of extraordinary social relations. Since 1947, a peaceful year for Banaras by all-Indian standards, there have been perhaps half a dozen incidents necessitating police action (*Aj;* Thana Registers). At none of them, including the last one I witnessed in February 1986, does the situation become "tense" for the whole city. There are well-delineated places, routes, and crossings that are fields of tension, and these relive a drama every year in a local way. The total number of these have not expanded in any proportion to the increase in the number of processions, the increase in the population itself, and the multiplication of amateur "politicians"—local leaders alive to the dynamics of petitioning, agitating, and seeking any possible base for arousing a following. Peace is difficult to measure, and disturbances are not, but by any criteria most of the neighborhoods of Banaras are free of regular, annual, or even rarer tension. And by the common assent of poor weavers, prosperous firm owners, and all Hindu classes, the nature of Hindu-Muslim relations in the city is exceptional—given the fact that "Hindu" and "Muslim" are already politicized identities.

Many scholars (see Freitag, Introduction) consider this to be attributable to the existence of a culturally homogeneous, "Hinduized" style of leadership in the city, with a tradition of political, antigovernment agitation rather than communal strife (see also Bayly 1975, 1978; Freitag 1980). While leadership is certainly a factor, I tend to consider it less important than the complex nature of popular consciousness in the city. This consciousness is well rooted in economic life. What is usually cited in this connection is the fact that Hindus and Muslims are totally interdependent within the silk industry, most obviously in the relationship of purchaser and supplier. The majority of silk merchants are Hindus, and almost all weavers are Muslims. This contributes to harmony, not conflict, although given the exploitation by merchants, it may also be regarded as a desperate kind of harmony. There have been occasions when weavers refused to participate in a communal quarrel of larger provincial dimensions because "our *rozī-roṭī* (livelihood) depends on the Hindus" (*Bharat Jiwan,* 27 May 1907, 8). Weavers have also been known to exercise leverage on the merchants because of the latter's dependence on them, as in the Burhwa Mangal incident mentioned earlier.

This interdependence is of limited influence, it seems clear, in that there are plenty of Muslim merchants and middlemen, and their mutual relations with weavers are different in no respect from those of their Hindu counterparts. Similarly, the other dozen or so artisans who are all Hindus experience no different relations with the traders and shopkeepers in their respective industries. What seems more influential in promoting harmony is the fact of artisan occupation itself. Hindus and Muslims of lower classes share a similar lifestyle and ideology of work, leisure, and public activity. And while that of the upper classes has changed over the last century, that of the lower classes has remained substantially the same. This parallelism in lifestyle and sharing of popular culture, drawing inspiration as it does from separate religious ideologies as well as a common cultural fund, is not coincidental or trivial. It is not self-evident that the actions of Hindus and Muslims should be interpreted more from the perspective of political leadership or religious revivalist and reformist movements than in the light of their own experience based on their culture of everyday life.

CONCLUSION

My analysis of identity has been strictly on the work and leisure patterns of ordinary weavers, and has revealed a cultural system that is not divided primarily into categories of religion or community. Equally defining influences on this cultural system are occupation and urban tradition. The weaver as artisan confronts certain dimensions within which his life necessarily revolves: those of poverty and insecurity and the attendant problem of illiteracy. Yet all poor people are not identical, and the artisan has a peculiar assessment of his skill and worth, and a way of asserting his right over his freedom that is surprising in its aggressiveness. We may feel we have understood the matter, and are also willing to loosen our imaginations to further accept the fact that with a harsh and demanding life go a love of leisure and an elaboration of the festival calendar. A more detailed investigation, however, reveals a richness of practice and a level of articulation that are not too familiar in social science literature. Most striking of all is the discovery of the influence of local tradition and the love of one's place, the importance of the city and the very neighborhood in deciding how one is to view oneself. That all this should be recognized as an integral part of identity is not generally accepted.

My effort has been partly to show the importance of everyday practices of work and leisure, and the close relation of popular culture and identity. The identity of the weaver in Banaras is neither simply "communal," that is to say, religious, nor is it progressively becoming so. It has a vision of Islam, but one that splits up the Muslim population along different lines. Nor is it exclusively occupational, the meaning of which we may prejudge from a knowledge of the work performed, though the most powerful determinants on the weaver remain the economic ones. Finally, the identity is "Banarsi," not in the sense of being imitative of a Hindu Banarsi tradition, but drawing largely from the same roots as do the Hindus, that is, those testifying to the importance of locality and continuity with the past.

PART THREE

Banaras in Wider Arenas

Introduction to Part 3
Banaras in Wider Arenas

Part 3 places Banaras in a variety of contexts that extend beyond its urban boundaries. Focusing on a particular subject, each of these four chapters traces the connections between the city itself and a larger world: of literary and political movements, of regional environment, of such developments as disease. The ultimate goal of this juxtaposition of essays is to illuminate a series of overlapping, broad sketches that suggest a world whose history cannot be summed up simply in the political narrative of elites.

In some respects these contextualizations of a city connect back to themes and central questions posed by the essays in Parts 1 and 2, including the ways in which public performances inform processes of identity formation and constructions of community, as well as the role played by patronage in these processes. The shift in those who fill patronage roles—from an aristocratic, courtly class to merchants and, beyond them in recent decades, to lower-class groups—has great relevance for the larger, imperial political world of which Banaras was a part: examples of this are provided in chapters 6 and 7. Indeed, perhaps the most important contribution to be made by this volume will be its ability to suggest how very localized expressions of such processes link up with larger historical movements; how scholars can look to the most basic building blocks, such as *muḥalla* organization or the role of *akhāṛās*, for explanations of popular support and interpretation of movements previously explicated only through the behavior and interests of elites.

To speak in terms of academic disciplines (and the methodologies used by each), we might say that scholarship on South Asia has reached a point where intellectual interaction can lead us to very fruitful and polished conclusions when history and anthropology, literature and musicology have been brought together. The first essays in this part provide refinements that lead beyond existing literature in this relatively well mined interdisciplinary world of analysis, suggesting as well new ways to deal with familiar source materials and events. Several important historical themes emerge from this interdisciplinary approach, as the essays suggest the extent to which elite and lower-class values have overlapped—as well as pinpointing at what times, over which issues, and in what contexts they separate. This is not to argue for a social stasis, or an integrated, harmonious social structure. It is simply to insist that disharmony can be traced to specific historical causes at particular moments in time, about which scholars must be precise if they are to understand the significance and nuances involved.

This part turns as well, however, to analytical ground less well cultivated. It introduces discussions with few precedents, in which are suggested the potential for a similar combination of social history with the disciplines of economics, demography, and environmental studies.[1] Such an approach would move us in interesting ways beyond the historiographical precedents. From G. R. Trevelyan's "history with the politics left out," social history has become, in recent years, a much more dynamic investigation, particularly of social conflict, consciousness, and change. Now we propose to combine this line of inquiry with a closer scrutiny of the role of physical context and material processes. Such a social history, in David Arnold's words, would be "about human actors against (and within) a landscape only partly of their own making." Such a history "has enormous potential in helping to explain unspoken (or unrecorded) parameters of human existence and struggle, in suggesting *another* set of factors alongside (rather than instead of) the political, the cultural, the conventionally social." Writing such a history, as these beginning attempts suggest, is quite difficult, requiring us "to juxtapose the technical (a knowledge of how a particular disease operates, or a river system functions) with the more familiar cultural and social domain."[2]

Thus, in forging a new interdisciplinary approach to Indian social history, these essays are still quite preliminary, even in the conclusions they suggest for their particular topics. And, although we have tried to use their juxtaposition to delineate the implications when material and cultural analyses are combined, the investigations developed in these essays are still somewhat tentative. As a consequence, it is not possible, yet, to successfully integrate these approaches to present a single, coherent large-scale picture. Nevertheless, taken together, they begin to

1. Thanks to Nita Kumar for suggesting that this point be made.

2. I gratefully acknowledge Arnold's helpful comments on an earlier draft of this introduction. The quotations come from a private communication dated April 28, 1987.

sketch the outline needed for a new Indian history—one that includes changes in material conditions and processes of production, as well as changed social and cultural environments. As Arnold suggests, this new approach may also allow us to refine, within the larger outlines, values and viewpoints particular to certain subgroups within the society whose history we are trying to recover.

To assay a new history, we shift both the subject focus and the level of analysis in this part. Arnold and Varady thus sketch the implications, for the social processes described above, of the economic and environmental developments that occurred during our period. Jim Hagan has suggested a paradigm for the Gangetic world which begins to connect the conclusions of these authors.[3] The Hagan paradigm considers three interrelated subjects: (1) expansion of arable; (2) population density; and (3) trade networks. A steady increase in these three items had characterized the nineteenth century. From about 1880 to 1890, however, the ratio of cultivation and fallow areas plateaued. In the 1920s cultivation was again extended. Similarly, population trends seem to follow a somewhat similar pattern; scholars should begin to explore the relationship between these trends. Hagan suggests that the development of trade systems also matched land use trends, with an elaboration and buildup of transport prompting nineteenth-century expansion, followed by a plateau from the late nineteenth century until the 1920s. Exploring the possible relationship between these three items, he speculates that trade networks must rise to a certain level before the expansion of arable land and population growth would take off again. Since fertility was always high, he noted, the critical issue in the change in population numbers depended on changes in mortality (an important contribution made by the Clark essay written for this panel). Although not enough is yet known to state definitively the relationship of these three variables—arable, population, and trade—to the social and political narrative outlined in the Introduction, the connections to the timing of the shifts traced in patronage and power relationships in nineteenth-century Banaras seem more obvious. Similarly, we could speculate profitably on the ability of the land-based Bhumihar dynasty, the merchant-bankers with rural connections, and the trader-mendicant Gosains to build their power bases in the district and the city, from these three variables.

3. Hagan served as discussant when several of the volume's essays were presented during the Southeastern regional meeting of the AAS, in Raleigh, January 1986. Particularly important in this discussion was an excellent paper by Alice Clark tracking demographic changes in the region. Regrettably, for reasons of space this essay could not be included in the volume. Hagan's insights draw from a much larger project, based at Duke University, for which Hagan has been analyzing census and other environmental data.

The role played by an urban center in this process may, indeed, have been very important. It is likely, at least, that in the later nineteenth and the early twentieth century such developments led to an increased pace of incorporation, in which the ties between hinterland and urban centers were strengthened. Perhaps because of this, or the general ecological decline sketched by Varady, new actors have been pulled into the urban arenas: the studies in this volume document one such example, in the increased visibility of Ahirs (or Yādavs) in Banaras's urban culture (chapters 3 and 4). (This change in the role and fortunes of the Ahirs dates, probably, from World War II.)[4] It has also placed a greater demand on urban resources for supporting a wider net of people; it is likely that the increasingly tenuous connections between upper and lower classes, and the expanding role played by the lower classes as patrons of "their own" public activities, relate to this development.

Scholars of South Asia have become accustomed to looking for evidence of city-hinterland connections in cultural events and caste activities. Chapter 9 suggests other fruitful contexts in which such evidence can be sought. Tracing the movement of disease vectors, for example, also plots the movement of people—in pursuit of employment, on pilgrimage, seeking longer-term migration—and, by implication, of the ideas and values they espouse.

Finally, and perhaps most important, the juxtaposition of essays on ecological developments and disease and its treatment, with discussions of political, social, and literary movements underscores the significance of the colonial impact on this emerging popular history. As Arnold has noted, "to a degree unprecedented in pre-colonial times (though not altogether absent), the British put 'the environment' on the agenda: forests, irrigation, disease control, etc., became affairs of state and matters on which the British presumed an authority they largely denied to the people they ruled—the 'landscape' in a general sense, came to be managed as did the people."[5] In this respect the history of Banaras may provide a more sharply etched picture than would that of other north Indian urban centers. For Banaras experienced a more pronounced shift from community self-rule to increased interference by the imperial state.

As the Introduction and chapter 7 make clear, community self-rule had been protected in Banaras by the special set of circumstances established there in the eighteenth and early nineteenth centuries. Not least of these circumstances was the intermediary role played by the Maharaja of Banaras and the Hindu merchant corporation of the city.

4. See, for instance, U.P. State Archives General Department, File no. 173 of 1921, Keepwiths: Petition from Ahirs of Banaras Division.

5. Private communication of April, 28, 1987.

Thus, when the British imperial state began to reach down into Banarsi society, as it had elsewhere, strong intermediaries existed to mitigate the impact on the constituent communities of the city. While it did not remain completely protected, nevertheless in this respect Banaras proved virtually unique among north Indian urban centers.

Efforts by the state to intrude took many forms. These ranged from substituting British values for Indian social mores by suppressing sati,[6] to enforcing health measures designed not only to implement Western notions of prevention but also to impose the state as final agent of a "healthy" society. The environmental degradation in the construction of the railroads provided one form of intrusion charted by Varady; the resulting expansion of communication networks along the rail lines provided another. Such intrusion could be intellectual as well as physical: imperial decisions about what constituted local "language" had as profound an impact as did efforts to woo certain groups away from the nationalist movement.[7] In turn, this led to an imposition of an alien world view based on "scientific" principles and Western assumptions about exercising control over the environment. The Indian response was complicated and included not just resistance (e.g., to forest laws) but also translations into the culture and consciousness of Maharajas (e.g., Banaras's support of various systems of medicine) and sweepers (e.g., in their new explanations for pollution).[8]

Although many of the results of such intrusion were unanticipated, there is no mistaking the basic intentions that united these various efforts by the imperial state. As Arnold has argued in chapter 9, the attack on what was perceived as dirty and disease-ridden in Indian society was also an attack on Hindu India. It is an attempt, as well, to substitute the authority of the imperial state for the more localized sources of moral authority located within the constituent communities of the city.[9]

In its turn, this assertion of the overriding authority of the British imperial state had important ramifications in a Banaras buffered by in-

6. For a fascinating study of sati and, particularly, evidence of the way the British misrepresented an exercise that frequently provided an honorable way for aged widows to die, see Anand Yang 1987.

7. Both the efforts in 1910 to create a princely state for the Maharaja of Banaras—explicitly defended by the Government of India as a way to retain the conservative support of "orthodox opinion" in Banaras—and the rather bald negotiations with Ahirs in the early 1920s (to trade increased opportunities in the military for the Ahirs in return for a promise by them to eschew all nationalist agitation) provide examples of this kind of intrusion. See the Introduction for more details on the creation of the princely state; see note 4 on file on Ahirs.

8. For a fascinating discussion of the varieties of responses, particularly to Western science, see Jim Masselos 1987.

9. See extended discussion of issues revolving around authority in Freitag 1985.

termediaries. These ramifications began to emerge in the 1920s and 1930s. Whereas in other urban centers in the north the nationalists could lay claim to this single authority on the grounds that they merited it more than a foreign ruler could, such claims became harder to press in a city that, essentially, had enjoyed many of the aspects of self-rule by an indigenous corporation representing a congeries of constituent local communities. Thus nationalists in Banaras had to pose, instead, a new moral authority for that previously exercised by the local community: in this way, reformist influences—although espousing many characteristics marking them as distinctly Hindu in character—entered Banaras in the guise of nationalism.

In asserting their moral authority over local communities, the nationalists were forced to lay claim to the world of collective activities in public spaces. As they attempted to Sanskritize and sanitize these activities, they alienated increasing numbers of lower-class residents in the city, including, particularly, the Muslim weavers and Ahirs who have been studied here. Chapter 7 touches briefly on the results of this alienation in the 1930s; it can be traced as well in the divergence between elite and lower-class urban culture, sketched in most of the essays (and in N. Kumar 1984). The degree of alienation can be measured in the extent to which collective activities in public spaces are currently designed, funded, and attended primarily by the lower classes resident in Banaras.

Thus a critical issue in any discussion of Banaras in its various larger contexts is that of the role of the imperial state. But Part 3 is designed to suggest that no discussion of these contexts can be complete without a careful consideration of the interplay of local culture and imperial concerns: population changes depended not only on state decisions on how to deal with famine, but on local values dictating who ate scarce foods in any given family; changes in medical treatment of disease vectors reflected not only the embrace by the imperial government of the newest European medical theories, but also patronage patterns at the Maharaja's court and the "fashions" in personal medical practices among Banarsi elite. We hope that this part, particularly, will stimulate students of South Asia to ask new questions of the historical documents and to juxtapose different kinds of sources and insights. The result could be a distinctly Indian (as opposed to European-derived) social history of South Asia.

SIX

Forging a New Linguistic Identity: The Hindi Movement in Banaras, 1868–1914

Christopher R. King

INTRODUCTION: INDO-PERSIAN AND HINDU CULTURE

Queen Abode-of-Truth is speaking, testifying before the court of Maharaja Righteous-Rule on behalf of Queen Devanagari:

> Here's where Nagari dwells, here her own dear country,
> Here our queen was born, in sacred, holy Kashi.
>
> (Datta 188?:8)

A little later Begam Urdu speaks on her own behalf before the Maharaja:

> Persian is my mother, Urdu is my name.
> Here my birth took place, and here I will remain.
>
> (Datta 188?:10)

Each woman claims India as her birthplace, and each asserts her right to rule (see fig. 14). As this late-nineteenth-century Hindi drama develops, the reader soon realizes that the verdict will favor Queen Devanagari, and that the author, Pandit Gauri Datta of Meerut, has passed chiefly "moral" rather than technical judgments in presenting the dispute between the two personified languages and scripts.[1]

The entire action of the play, a short one-act work in the folk theatre tradition of *svāng* (see chapter 2 in this volume) takes place in a courtroom over which Maharaja Righteous-Rule presides. Babu Moral Law

1. Datta's play, judging from internal evidence, seems to have been presented several times, and the audience may well have included visitors to local melas (religious fairs). Thus in April 1889, Datta's own newspaper, the *Devanagari Gazette* of Meerut, reported that four dramas, including at least one critical of Urdu, had been performed by Hindi advocates at a recent mela, and printed the first and last acts of this play (NWP&O SVN 1889:284).

हिन्दी–उर्दू।

उर्दू—अरी क्यों री चुड़ैल! तू मर कर भी नहीं मरती?

हिन्दी—बेटी! तू जुग जुग जी, मुझे क्यों मारे डाले है? मैंने तेरा क्या बिगाड़ा है?

उर्दू—तेरे आछते मुझे राजगद्दी जो नहीं मिलती।

हिन्दी—ठीक है बेटी! कलजुग न है। तुझे इसी दिन के लिये बड़े लाड़ से जन्माया था!
अच्छा तेरे जी में आवे सो कह; पर मेरी तो माता की आत्मा ठहरी; मैं तो आसीस ही दूंगी।

श्रीराधाकृष्ण दास।

Fig. 14. "Begam Urdu," in the garb of a courtesan, addresses "Queen Devanagari," attired as a proper Hindu wife. Illustration for a *svāng* text printed in the periodical *Saraswati* (1910). Courtesy of the Allahabad Public Library. Special thanks to Sanjay Sharma for research assistance.

Singh argues for Queen Devanagari, and Mirza Cunning Ali Khan for Begam Urdu. Queen Devanagari complains that Begam Urdu has usurped her former rule over all works of wisdom and virtue, as well as letters, papers, account books, bonds, notes, and official documents. She testifies that she teaches righteousness and removes falsehood, and that under her rule people could make merry, become wealthy, carry on their business, and learn wisdom.[2] Bribery, continues the Queen, would weep at the very sound of her name, and fabrications and fraud would disappear should she rule again. Her witnesses all attest to her good name, sterling character, and indigenous origins. Indeed, as we

2. Datta may be intentionally echoing the Hindu doctrine of the four ends of life.

saw above, her birth takes place in the hallowed location of Kashi—an older name for the largest of the several sacred zones of Banaras (Eck 1982:350). In short, Queen Devanagari embodies many of the moral and religious values of the Hindu merchant class described by Bayly, especially the core value of credit (*sakh*) (Bayly 1983:375–93). "The behaviour and ideals of the merchant family firm were . . . directed to survival first and foremost, but survival here meant above all the continuity of family credit within the wider merchant community" (381). Queen Devanagari, through her righteousness, guarantees the continuing "credit" of business and government records, while Begam Urdu, through her corruptness, threatens the inextricably combined moral and economic well-being of society.

Begam Urdu defends herself by arguing that although her mother, Begam Persian, was foreign, her own birth took place in India, and therefore she has a right to stay. She describes her own work, however, in terms hardly calculated to make a good impression on her judge:

> This is my work—passion I'll teach,
> Tasks of your household we'll leave in the breach.
> We'll be lovers and rakes, living for pleasure,
> Consorting with prostitutes, squandering our treasure.
> Give heed, you officials, batten on graft,
> Deceiving and thieving till riches you've quaffed.
> Lie to your betters and flatter each other.
> Write down one thing and read out another.
>
> (Datta 188?:10)

Her witnesses, too, bear names unlikely to mollify the judge: Begam Twenty-Nine Delights, Prince Passion-Addict Khan, Begam Wanton-Pleasure, and Emperor Ease-Lover. Urdu's witnesses all testify to the licentiousness and depravity of their mistress and the pleasures that follow in her train.

The climax of the play sees Queen Devanagari's lawyer making an impassioned plea for his client. By restoring the former monarch to her rightful place, the age of falsehood would become the age of truth, fraud would vanish, good deeds would multiply, people would feed Brahmins, hatred and strife would disappear, enemies would become friends, everyone would become clever, and every child would study Nagari in school. Begam Urdu's lawyer in his final summation points to the British recognition of Urdu and claims that should Nagari try to perform the work of courts and offices, everything would become topsy-turvy. In an inversion of the actual power structure of society at the time (typical of the *svāng*—see chapter 2) Maharaja Righteous-Rule brings the case to a close with his judgment, made in accordance with the sacred law of the Hindus: let Urdu be cast out and Nagari take her place (Datta 188?:13–14, 16).

LANGUAGE AND THE FORMATION OF COMMUNITY IDENTITY

Many studies of the Hindi movement have focused on the political aspects, especially at the national level, and have dealt primarily with the twentieth century (for example, Brass 1974; Das Gupta 1970; Gopal 1953; Harrison 1960; Kluyev 1981; Lutt 1970; S. Misra 1956; Narula 1955; Nayar 1969; Smith 1963; Tivari 1982; L. Varma 1964). The great majority of these have used chiefly English sources, and few of them have thoroughly surveyed the relevant sources for the nineteenth century. Almost no studies have attempted to trace the detailed history of the voluntary language associations that played such major roles in the development of Hindi. In this essay I examine not only the political but also the social and cultural aspects of the Hindi movement, particularly on the local and provincial levels, and deal chiefly with the nineteenth century. Moreover, I have made extensive use of both Hindi and English sources, including a thorough search of official records, such as education reports, publication statistics, and the like. Finally, I stress the importance of voluntary language associations, which both reflected and intensified the Hindi movement (see also King 1974).

The play described above well illustrates the social, cultural, and political matrix from which the Hindi movement arose, namely, the growing split between Indo-Persian and Hindu merchant culture characteristic of the late nineteenth and the early twentieth century in north India. As Bayly (1983) has shown in his analysis of eighteenth- and nineteenth-century north India, these two "conflicting forms of urban solidarity" served as the foundations of the later-developing nationalism and religious communalism, which so dramatically affected events in the twentieth century. Urdu effectively symbolized the dominant Indo-Persian culture of north India in the eighteenth and nineteenth centuries, for it formed one of the major parts of this blend. The attack on Urdu and the strong support for Nagari (a term that encompassed both language and script) evident in the play became important elements in the process by which a self-conscious Hindu nationalism emerged in north India. Part of this process involved the separation from and rejection of earlier symbols of joint Hindu-Muslim culture, and part entailed the definition and affirmation of newer communal symbols. Moreover, this process also involved the complete disregard or rejection of various forms of written or oral popular culture, such as Hindustani, the regional dialects (e.g., Braj Bhasha and Bhojpuri), and variant scripts (e.g., Kaithi).[3]

3. Braj Bhasha and Kharī Bolī are the major regional dialects in western U.P., Awadhi in central U.P., and Bhojpuri in eastern U.P. and western Bihar. The first three had major written as well as oral traditions during our period, the fourth only oral. Kaithi, Mahajani, and Muria are cursive variants of the Nagari script, associated with certain Hindu merchant castes and famous for their ambiguity.

This process of separation and differentiation between the Indo-Persian and Hindu merchant cultures led to a shift: the overlapping literary cultures came to function separately, following a new identification of "Hindu" with Hindi and of "Muslim" with Urdu. This shift came about through a wide variety of means, many of which lend themselves to some form or other of measurement. Among these are the development of voluntary organizations to promote languages and scripts; the standardization of languages through dictionaries, grammars, and other publications; newspaper campaigns for or against languages and scripts; systematic searches for, and publication of, old manuscripts; the introduction of large numbers of Sanskrit and Arabic and Persian words into Hindi and Urdu respectively; the publication of books and periodicals, especially elementary- and secondary-school texts; and the production of vernacular literature attacking the joint Hindu-Muslim cultural tradition, especially as it was expressed in Urdu. The "Hindu" and "Muslim" of this shift, however, do not include the Hindu and Muslim masses, but rather refer to a "vernacular elite," that is, Indians educated in the vernaculars and in competition for government service. Likewise, "Hindi" and "Urdu" refer not to the regional and local dialects of the bulk of the population, but rather to carefully cultivated literary dialects, strongly linked to the corresponding classical languages of Sanskrit, Persian, and Arabic.

During our period Banaras played the leading role in the process outlined above. Long famed in India as a center of Hindu learning and religious pilgrimage, by the early nineteenth century the city had also become a major center of Hindu literature (Grierson 1889:108–9). Bharatendu Harishchandra and Raja Shiv Prasad were only two of the most eminent literary figures of the second half of the century to live in Banaras. The peak of the city's influence on the gradual process of the emergence of modern Sanskritized Hindi as an important symbol of Hindu nationalism came with the founding of the Nāgarī Prachārinī Sabhā (Society for the Promotion of Nagari) in 1893.

This organization, the majority of whose membership came from the eastern part of the North-Western Provinces and Oudh (NWP&O), remained the single most influential force for Hindi until the eve of World War I, when a gradual decline in membership, and an increasing concern for things literary and a decreasing concern for things political in the Sabha's leadership, allowed the Hindi Sahitya Sammelan (Society for Hindi Literature) of Allahabad to become the premier Hindi institution. This shift from Banaras to Allahabad also roughly coincided with a shift in the scope of the controversy between Hindi and Urdu from the provincial (NWP&O) to the national level. Significantly, one of the ironies of the Hindi movement is that neither of these organizations promoted popular culture in the form of the regional and local dialects that surrounded them, though both spoke for the welfare of the Hindu majority of the population in the "Hindi-speaking" areas of north India. Let us now focus on the process of linguistic and social change in the NWP&O and other parts of north India, and on some of the most important means through which this came about.

OLD IDENTITIES: THE TERMINUS A QUO

In 1847 a noteworthy encounter took place between Dr. J. F. Ballantyne, principal of the English Department of Benares College, and several students of the Sanskrit College (also part of Benares College). After various unsuccessful attempts to "improve" the Hindi style of his students, Ballantyne lost his patience and directed them to write an essay on the question "Why do you despise the culture of the language you speak every day of your lives, of the only language which your mothers and sisters understand?" (NWP Educ Rpt 1846–1847:32). The ensuing dialogue produced several striking statements that clearly indicated that Sanskritized Hindi had not yet become a symbol of Hindu as opposed to Indo-Persian culture. Ironically, this situation existed among students of the very institution which the founders of the Nāgarī Prachārinī Sabhā (NPS) would attend nearly half a century later. An apparently puzzled student spokesman told Ballantyne:

> We do not clearly understand what you Europeans mean by the term Hindi, for there are hundreds of dialects, all in our opinion equally entitled to the name, and there is here no standard as there is in Sanskrit. (NWP Educ Rpt 1846–1847:32)

The same student went on to say:

> If the purity of Hindi is to consist in its exclusion of Mussulman words, we shall require to study Persian and Arabic in order to ascertain which of the words we are in the habit of issuing every day is Arabic or Persian, and which is Hindi. With our present knowledge we can tell that a word is Sanscrit, or not Sanscrit but if not Sanscrit, it may be English or Portuguese instead of Hindi for anything that we can tell. English words are becoming as completely naturalized in the villages as Arabic and Persian words, and that you call the Hindi will eventually merge in some future modification of the Oordoo, nor do we see any great cause of regret in this prospect. (NWP Educ Rpt 1846–1847:32)

If his students did not yet have a national goal for Hindi, then Dr. Ballantyne did. In reply to this perception of Hindi as a cluster of unselfconscious vernaculars rather than a refined literary language, he urged:

> It was the duty of himself and his brother Pundits not to leave the task of formulating the national language in the hands of the villagers, but to endeavour to get rid of the unprofitable diversity of provincial dialects, by creating a standard literature in which one uniform system of grammar and orthography should be followed; the Pundits of Benares, if they valued the fame of their city, ought to strive to make the dialect of the holy city the standard of all India, by writing books which should attract the attention and form the taste of all their fellow countrymen. (NWP Educ Rpt 1846–1847:32)

Ballantyne's uncannily accurate vision of the future of Hindi struck no responsive chord in the thoughts or feelings of his students. The disappearance of Hindi into Urdu aroused no sense of alarm in these Hindi scholars of Sanskrit, nor did they see any necessary connection between being Hindu and speaking Hindi. Moreover, since the very term "Hindi" struck them as vague and ambiguous, no standard having emerged, we may tentatively conclude that these students would have included the regional and local dialects, the vehicles of popular culture, under this rubric. Ballantyne, on the other hand, clearly intended to separate Hindi from the confused mass of popular dialects, to reject any conceivable influence of villagers on "the national language," and to define and affirm Hindi in terms of a standardized and Sanskritized language created by a vernacular elite.

A decade before Ballantyne's encounter with his students, English and various local vernaculars had replaced Persian in British India. In north India, with one or two exceptions,[4] this meant that Urdu in modified form of the Persian script became the official vernacular. The original purpose of replacing Persian had been to make the official proceedings of courts and offices intelligible to the people at large; thus in 1830 the Court of Directors of the East India Company had intoned that "it is easier for the judge to acquire the language of the people than for the people to acquire the language of the judge" (Malaviya 1897:497), overlooking or ignoring the fact that the great bulk of the population had no acquaintance with either spoken or written Urdu.

Very soon, however, the excessive Persianization of the new court-language of north India made a mockery of the supposed reason for which the change had been made. As early as 1836, for example, the Sadar Board of Revenue of the North-Western Provinces (N.W.P.) had warned division Commissioners that the replacement of Persian by Urdu did not mean "the mere substitution of Hindee verbs and affixes, while the words and idiom remain exclusively Persian" (NWP Lt-Gov

4. Among the exceptions were the Saugor and Nerbudda Territories in the mid-1830s—see King 1974:66–70, 149–54—and the Kumaun division of the NWP&O throughout our period.

Prgs SBRD 19 July to 2 August 1836:Range 221, Volume 77, Number 52). Yet nearly two decades later, exactly this had happened, for the then lieutenant-governor of the N.W.P. felt obliged to inveigh against the style of official Urdu, "little distinguished from Persian, excepting the use of Hindee verbs, particles, and inflections" (Malaviya 1897, Appendix:52). Official protests and notifications did little to change this state of affairs, however, and complaints about the excessive Persianization of court Urdu appeared regularly, well into the twentieth century. In general, British support for Urdu did much to assure the continued dominance of this symbol of Indo-Persian culture. In the province, the heartland of the Hindi movement, most gains for Hindi and the Nagari script in courts and offices came in the face of government neglect or opposition.

At this point, let us posit a spectrum of linguistic popular usage for north India during our period: the term "popular" should be understood in a relative rather than an absolute sense. At one end of this spectrum comes English and at the other, local dialects. In between we have, first, the classical languages Sanskrit, Arabic, and Persian; then, Urdu followed by Hindi; next, Hindustani (in the sense of a language style less Persianized than Urdu, and less Sanskritized than Hindi); and finally, the regional dialects such as Bhojpuri and Awadhi. From this viewpoint Hindi ranks as more "popular" than English or Urdu, but less so than Bhojpuri. The bulk of the supporters of the Hindi movement in Banaras and elsewhere in the province came from the ranks of the vernacular elite, those educated in the more standardized vernaculars of Hindi and Urdu, not from the English-speaking elite on the one hand, nor from the regional- or local-dialect-speaking masses on the other.[5]

The potential for differentiation and separation between the two different sections of the vernacular elite existed long before the 1860s, when controversy between supporters of the more "popular" Hindi and the less "popular" Urdu first began. Bayly concludes that "some of the conditions which fractured the life of modern north India into Hindu and Muslim camps must be dated much earlier than is commonly supposed" (Bayly 1983:455). Similarly, as we shall see, considerable evidence indicates that the potential for linguistic controversy stretched back to the early nineteenth century and before. We must ask, then, what influences kindled underlying differences into open conflict in the 1860s. In general, the pace of economic and social development in the province quickened after the Rebellion of 1857 in a wide variety of ways (see Bayly 1983:427–40). Most important for our

5. This picture may be too starkly drawn, however, since many Hindi speakers knew some English, and most or all of them undoubtedly knew regional or local dialects.

purposes, however, was the rapid post-Rebellion expansion of the three closely related areas of government service, education, and publication (all discussed below). Each of these institutionalized the most refractory difference between Hindi and Urdu—script—and each became an arena of competition in a mutually reinforcing and ever-expanding spiral.

DEFINITION AGAINST EXTERNAL RIVALS: THE HINDI-URDU CONTROVERSY

The Hindi-Urdu controversy, as the long and heated exchange of opinions between opposing supporters of Hindi and Urdu came to be known, began in the 1860s and continued right up to Independence. Confined largely to U.P. in the nineteenth century, the controversy gradually assumed national proportions in the twentieth. On both the provincial and the national level, a major portion of the debate focused on the question of the proper language and script for government courts and offices. The center of the Hindi side of the controversy lay in the eastern districts of the province and especially in the cities of Banaras and Allahabad.

The themes announced early in the controversy appeared again and again with wearying consistency. The protagonists of Hindi argued: the bulk of the population used Hindi; the Urdu script had a foreign origin, and also made court documents illegible, encouraged forgery, and fostered the use of difficult Arabic and Persian words; the introduction of the Nagari script into government courts and offices would give considerable impetus to the spread of education by enhancing the prospects for public service; and experienced Hindi scribes could write just as fast as their Urdu counterparts. The supporters of Urdu maintained: even the inhabitants of remote villages spoke Urdu fluently; the Urdu language had originated in India even though its script may have come from outside; any script could lend itself to forgery; the numerous dialects of Hindi lacked standardization; and Hindi had an impoverished vocabulary, especially in scientific and technical terms. One of the most often repeated arguments for Hindi appeared in blunt numerical terms, where speakers were identified by religious community. An 1873 issue of the *Kavi Vachan Suchā*, a Hindi newspaper of Banaras, argued that the government's duty lay in yielding to the demand of the general public for the introduction of Hindi. Although the Muslims might suffer from the change, they constituted only a minority of the population, and the interests of the few always had to yield to those of the many (NWP&O SVN 1873:528). Such arguments, of course, ignored the fact that the great bulk of the population used nonliterary regional and local dialects, and not the Sanskritized Hindi and Persianized Urdu of the vernacular elite.

Throughout the controversy the participants tended to identify language and religion. In 1868, Babu Shiv Prasad, a prominent advocate of the Nagari script, castigated British language policy, "which thrusts a Semitic element into the bosoms of Hindus and alienates them from their Aryan speech . . . and . . . which is now trying to turn all the Hindus into semi-Muhammadans and destroy our Hindu nationality" (Prasad 1868:5–6). Professor Raj Kumar Sarvadhikari, appearing before the Hunter Education Commission in 1882, remarked that in Awadh "Urdu is the dialect of the Muhammadan inhabitants and Hindi of the Hindus" (Educ Comm Rpt NWP&O:462). Conversely, in 1900, a correspondent of the *Punjab Observer* expressed fears that the recent decision of the provincial government to recognize the Nagari script would eventually lead to the abolition of Urdu, which would in turn cause Muslim boys to become Hindu in thought and expression (Khan 1900:79).

From the very beginning the different parties to the debate consistently confused the names for language and script. "Hindi," "Hindi character," "Nagari," and "Nagari character" seemed interchangeable, as did "Persian," "Persian character," and "Urdu." Sir George Grierson, author of the massive *Linguistic Survey of India,* remarked that "these fanatics have confused alphabet with language. They say *because* a thing is written in Deva-nagari [*sic*] *therefore* it is Hindi, the language of the Hindus, and *because* a thing is written in the Persian character *therefore* it is Urdu, the language of the Musalmans" (Grierson 1903–1928, vol. 9, part 1, xiv, 49). Yet script *was* the critical issue. More than any other linguistic fact, the radically different nature of the two scripts rendered any solution to the Hindi-Urdu controversy intractable.[6] While the grammars of Hindi and Urdu, derived from the regional dialect of Kharī Bolī, were almost identical, and while the vocabularies of the two on the everyday level of discourse overlapped considerably, the two scripts focused and heightened the differences between the Hindu and the Indo-Persian cultures.

Like different channels to different cultural reservoirs, deliberately opened, they allowed the influence of Sanskrit, on the one hand, and of Arabic and Persian, on the other, to pour separately into Hindi and Urdu, bypassing the existing mixture of Indo-Persian culture. The results of this artificial irrigation, highly Sanskritized Hindi and highly Persianized Urdu, not only served to distinguish the rival Hindu and Indo-Muslim cultures from each other, but also sharply differentiated both from the surrounding ocean of popular culture.

6. The Nagari script is syllabic, indicates all vowel sounds, has a chunky and square appearance, has a nearly continuous line across the top, and reads from left to right. The Urdu script (often referred to as the Persian script during our period, though it has several more letters) is alphabetic, does not indicate many vowel sounds, has a curved and flowing appearance, and reads from right to left.

DEFINITION AGAINST INTERNAL RIVALS: HINDUSTANI, BRAJ, AND KAITHI

The processes of separation and rejection, and of definition and affirmation, occurred not only between Hindi and Urdu, but also within the world of Hindi itself. Considerable controversy took place among Hindi supporters over the question of the proper style for literary works. Whatever the merits or demerits of the various styles current among Hindi authors, however, the reading public showed a definite preference for a simple style. The most popular author of the period, Devki Nandan Khatri (1861–1913), wrote in a clear and readable Hindi that made ample use of common Arabic and Persian words. His two best-known series of novels, *Chandrakanta* and *Chandrakanta Santati,* which he started writing in 1888, won him fame and fortune. Within ten years he had earned enough to found his own press in his native city of Banaras. For a few years Khatri became a member of the NPS, but found the atmosphere there uncongenial. From the viewpoint of the Sabha, although Khatri's works (published in the Nagari script) had won more readers than any other author (UP Admin Rpt 1914–1915:72), his style did not deserve to be considered literary Hindi, but rather only merited the designation "Hindustani," a vehicle fit merely for light and frothy creations and too close to Urdu to be respectable (R. C. Shukla 1968:476–77).

In the NPS the whole vexed question of the proper style for Hindi came to a head in a controversy between the Sabha and one of its own officers, Pandit Lakshmi Shankar Mishra, who served as president from 1894 until his resignation in 1902. Mishra possessed impeccable credentials: he held a high position in the provincial Educational Department, he had made efforts for the increased use of Hindi in government schools, and he had published in Hindi on the subject of science before most of his fellow scholars. The heart of the dispute appeared in a letter sent by Mishra to the provincial Text-Book Committee at the time of his resignation. After speaking of a "widening gulf" between Hindi and Urdu, Mishra went on to say:

> As the Grammer of both Urdu and Hindi is identical, they should not be considered as separate languages, and hence for ordinary purposes, in such books as are not technical and which are intended for the common people, [an] attempt should be made to assimilate the two forms into one language, which may be called Hindustani, and may be written either in the Persian script or the Nagari character. (NPS Ann Rpt 1894:35–36, 40 41; UP Educ Progs May 1903:31–32)

Yet the raison d'être of the Sabha was the distinct and separate existence of Hindi vis-à-vis Urdu. Any attempt to combine them or to reduce or eliminate their differences undermined the whole purpose of the organization. Views such as those put forth by Pandit Mishra must have been anathema to the other leaders of the Sabha,[7] and they could hardly tolerate the open expression of such opinions by their own chief officer. The leaders of the Sabha felt obliged both to differentiate their language and script from others and to reject any actual or potential rivals. In Sanskrit plays, characters of loftier social rank speak Sanskrit, while those of lower ranks speak lesser languages. Similarly, the Sabha gave great importance to preserving the Sanskritic purity of an important cultural symbol. In this way, the organization consciously chose to maintain linguistic contact with Hindu vernacular elites in other areas of India, rather than encourage popular culture and enlist the support of the masses of its own area (see Das 1957:251–52).

The Rejection of Braj Bhasha

In its first annual report the Sabha presented a picture of the rise and development of Hindi literature which showed a basic ambiguity (NPS Ann Rpt 1894:1–3). While claiming Braj Bhasha and other literary dialects as part of Hindi literature in the distant past, when speaking of the origins of Hindi prose in the nineteenth century, the Sabha clearly meant only Kharī Bolī Hindi.[8] The Sabha's use of the term "Hindi" expanded while moving toward the "glorious" past and contracted while moving toward the present.

Behind the Sabha's attitude lay the fact that Braj Bhasha remained the most important medium of "Hindi" poetry in large areas of north India until the 1920s. Ironically, several of the leading Braj poets lived in Banaras, some of whom joined the Sabha, and even Bharatendu Harishchandra, widely acclaimed as the father of modern Hindi, had written most of his poetry in Braj. Many members of the Sabha felt that this situation presented a great obstacle to the progress of Hindi; the language of prose and poetry ought to be the same. Instead, most prose appeared in Kharī Bolī Hindi and most poetry in Braj Bhasha or Awadhi. Even primary-level Hindi school books used Braj for their poetic selections, wrote Shyam Sundar Das (one of the founders of the NPS) in 1901, urging the use of Kharī Bolī poetry instead (Misra 1956:209). Nevertheless, Braj remained the language of poetry in Hindi school books for more than another decade (UP SVN 1913:1254).

Years earlier the opening salvo of a controversy between the advocates of Braj Bhasha and those of Kharī Bolī had appeared in a work entitled *Kharī Bolī ka Padya* (Kharī Bolī Prose) by Ayodhya Prasad

7. Decades later Mahatma Gandhi, for a while a leading member of the Hindi Sahitya Sammelan, adopted exactly this approach in his unsuccessful attempt to bring an end to the Hindi-Urdu controversy, an approach ultimately rejected by the Sammelan.

8. Kharī Bolī, the common grammatical basis of both Hindi and Urdu, is also a regional dialect of western U.P. (see n. 3).

Khatri, a resident of Bihar. Khatri published and distributed his book at his own expense to scores of well-known Hindi supporters. He hoped to persuade Urdu poets to use the Nagari script, and Hindi poets to use Kharī Bolī. He wished all concerned to meet on the common ground of Kharī Bolī written in the Nagari script (Misra 1956:158, 179). Although Khatri's efforts met with little success, they did serve to touch off a vigorous debate between two noted Hindi supporters in the pages of *Hindustan,* the province's only Hindi daily at the time.

Shridhar Pathak, the champion of Kharī Bolī, had earned a reputation in both of the rival literary dialects and had authored the first poem of any importance in modern Kharī Bolī Hindi in 1886, only a year before the publication of Khatri's book. Radha Charan Goswami, the defender of the opposing literary dialect, edited a Hindi newspaper in Brindaban in the heart of the Braj area (R. C. Shukla 1968:436, 559). He argued Kharī Bolī and Braj Bhasha were one language; no poetry worthy of the name had appeared in Kharī Bolī; Kharī Bolī did not allow the use of the best Hindi metrical forms; people over a wide area understood Braj; and poetry and prose could never use the same language. Most important, Goswami claimed that should poets accept Kharī Bolī, as Khatri had suggested, their efforts would only serve to spread Urdu. Pathak countered that Kharī Bolī and Braj were two languages; the future possibilities for Kharī Bolī poetry were great; Kharī Bolī did allow the use of a wide variety of metrical forms; many more people understood Kharī Bolī than Braj; and poetry and prose could and should use the same language. Although Pathak did not reply directly to Goswami's most important charge, unlike Khatri he neither spoke of Hindi and Urdu as the same nor excluded Braj Bhasha from the realm of Hindi poetry (Misra 1956:175–82).

Goswami had pinpointed an important issue, namely, Kharī Bolī poetry seemed suspect to many Hindi supporters because almost all of its recent creations were in Persianized Urdu. The real answer to Goswami's imputation appeared in the work of Mahavir Prasad Dwivedi, editor of *Saraswati,* the most influential periodical in the Hindi literary world in the first two decades of the twentieth century. Dwivedi used Sanskrit words and metrical forms in his own Kharī Bolī poetry and encouraged the same approach in those who wrote for his journal (Misra 1956:211; R. C. Shukla 1968:583). After Dwivedi, no one could seriously oppose Kharī Bolī Hindi poetry on the grounds that this would further the spread of Urdu. Dwivedi had succeeded in Sanskritizing the new poetic medium.

More than twenty years later the conveners of the first Hindi Sahitya Sammelan in Banaras in 1910 called on Pathak and Goswami to come forward and reiterate their previous arguments. The situation had changed, for now the question had become not whether Kharī Bolī should become a medium of Hindi poetry, but rather to what extent Braj Bhasha should remain one (Misra 1956:213–24). In the second session of the Sammelan a year later in Allahabad, one advocate of Kharī Bolī had harsh words for Braj. Badrinath Bhatt, later to become professor of Hindi at Lucknow University, told his listeners that in an age when India needed men, the cloying influence of Braj had turned Indians into eunuchs. During the fifth meeting of the Sammelan in 1914, the prominent Hindi poet Maithili Sharan Gupta, a protégé of Dwivedi, spoke even blunter words. He called the supporters of Braj Bhasha enemies of India's national language, Kharī Bolī Hindi (Misra 1956:225, 228–29).

Part of the process of defining "Hindi," then, involved affirming the earlier literary heritage of other regional dialects in the past, but rejecting literary creations in the same dialects in the present. Because they added lustre to Hindi's past, written traditions in these dialects at least merited attention. On the other hand, because they were presumably considered too vulgar and unrefined, oral traditions, such as the *birahā* of the Ahirs of the Bhojpuri-speaking area, received no notice. Thus the records of the NPS (for at least the first twenty years) make no mention of Bhojpuri, although its speakers constitute the great majority in Banaras and environs. Nor do they mention the reputed creator of *birahā*, Bihari Lal Yadav (1857–1926) (see chapter 3).

Nagari Yes, Kaithi No

Script as well as language was subject to these internecine conflicts. The Kaithi script, one of several cursive forms of Nagari used by merchant castes, led a precarious existence in the official infrastructure of British India, though surviving and even thriving in more ordinary surroundings. With a few notable exceptions, British officialdom in the province opposed the use of Kaithi in courts, offices, and schools, even though this script had much greater popularity than Nagari, especially in the eastern districts. Officials in the neighboring province of Bihar, however, displayed very different attitudes. Believing Kaithi to be the most widespread script in the province, as evidenced by the flourishing condition of the indigenous schools teaching it, the government ordered the creation of a font of Kaithi type, and by 1881 had prescribed Kaithi for primary vernacular schools. Kaithi texts soon began to appear, and the schools and courts of Bihar continued to use the script until at least 1913 (see King 1974:162–64, 166–70).

These policies met with bitter criticism from Dr. Rajendralal Mitra, a distinguished Bengali educator, in his testimony before the Hunter Education Commission. He noted that Hindi textbooks for Bihar schools printed in Nagari had previously come from Banaras, and that for every textbook Bihar could produce, the U.P. could produce a hundred.

This flow of books had kept the people of Bihar linguistically united with their fellow Hindus to the west. The use of Kaithi, on the other hand, would eventually deprive Biharis not only of the literature created by their ancestors but also of that more recently created by their kinsmen in the U.P. (Educ Comm Rpt Bengal 1884:334). Mitra spoke of Kaithi as the NPS had written about Hindustani: Kaithi threatened the linguistic and religious identity of Bihari Hindus.

Agreeing with Mitra, the NPS also rejected Nagari's rival. In its ninth year the Sabha, at the suggestion of a member, considered the question of improving Kaithi's shortcomings. After some deliberation, the Sabha declared:

> In the opinion of the Sabha there are no letters more excellent than the Nagari, and in its opinion it is useful and proper for the Aryan languages of India to be written only in their Nagari letters. For this reason the Sabha cannot aid in any way in promoting the progress of Kaithi letters, nor can it display any enthusiasm for this. (NPS Ann Rpt 1903:14–15)

Although the Sabha had earlier expressed the need for a shorthand system for Hindi, it apparently never considered the possibilities of Kaithi for this (NPS Ann Rpt 1895:10; NPS Ann Rpt 1899:20; NPS Ann Rpt 1900:21–22). Moreover, the Sabha made numerous and mostly unsuccessful attempts to establish Nagari court writers in every district of the province, largely because the organization ignored the fact that almost no writers knew Nagari, especially in the eastern districts, though many knew Kaithi, and the indigenous schools teaching this script were thriving.

Contemporary sources indicate that other Hindi supporters thought Kaithi to be as illegible and ambiguous as the Urdu script, no easier or more widely used than Nagari, and unsuitable as a medium of education. Certainly Kaithi lacked the auspicious association with Sanskrit possessed by Nagari; rejecting Kaithi meant indirectly affirming Hindi's close connection with Sanskrit. To Hindi supporters, rejecting Kaithi also meant separating Hindi and Nagari from a more popular but lower level of culture. Thus, a writer in a 1900 issue of the Hindi newspaper *Bharat Jiwan* of Banaras argued that those Hindu trading classes who used the Muria script (another cursive form of Nagari similar to Kaithi) could not hope to better their condition until they received their education through the Nagari script (NWP&O SVN 1900:183). Moreover, a strong association existed between Kaithi and rural life: government policy in Awadh allowed, and in Bihar encouraged, the widespread use of Kaithi by *patwaris* or village record keepers (Educ Comm Rpt Bengal 1884:46–47; NWP&O Educ Rpt 1886–1887:77–78; Oudh Educ Rpt 1873–1874:150).

DEFINITION THROUGH PRINT: THE GROWTH OF PUBLICATIONS

In 1868 several provincial governments began to issue quarterly statements of books and periodicals published or printed in the territories under their jurisdictions. Although these statements had several shortcomings, especially in their earlier years, they constitute by far the most complete and detailed source for the publishing history of India during our period. According to these records, by 1914 Banaras had become the major center for Hindu-heritage languages, well ahead of Allahabad in Hindi and in Sanskrit-Hindi publications, and far ahead of any other center in Sanskrit, while Lucknow led in Islamic-heritage-language publications. Moreover, while the number of Urdu publications had grown substantially in both relative and absolute terms between 1868 and 1914, the number of Hindi publications had grown even more rapidly, so that the latter outnumbered the former by nearly three to one (see table 6.1). Up to 1900 the ratio between Hindi and Urdu publications had remained roughly constant, about fourteen or fifteen books in Hindi for every ten in Urdu. By 1914, however, the ratio had changed dramatically to nearly twenty-seven to ten, almost double the previous ratio. It is not coincidence that this literary expansion

TABLE 6.1 Trends in the Growth Rates of Publications in the United Provinces (1868–1914)

Language	*1868 (No.)*	*1914 (No.)*	*1868 (%)*	*1914 (%)*	*% Change (+ or −)*
Arabic	27,320	3,200	3.2	0.1	−854
Persian	82,913	24,975	9.7	0.7	−332
Urdu	217,153	688,505	25.5	20.3	+317
Islamic-Heritage Languages	327,386	813,655	39.0	23.9	+249
Hindi	392,316	1,868,926	46.0	55.0	+476
Sanskrit	10,866	71,350	1.3	2.1	+657
Sanskrit-Hindi	9,700	190,810	1.1	5.6	+1,967
Hindu-Heritage Languages	412,882	2,131,086	48.4	62.7	+516
Totals	831,304	3,398,888	99.9	99.9	+399

SOURCES: All figures were compiled from the NWP&O SP 1868 and the UP SP 1914.

NOTE: All percentages were calculated to the nearest 0.1%. Besides Arabic, Persian, and Urdu, the Islamic-Heritage Languages total includes works in Arabic-Persian, Arabic-Urdu, Persian-Urdu, and Arabic-Persian-Urdu. The grand total includes other languages, such as English, Urdu-Sanskrit, Urdu-Hindi, English-Arabic, Nepali, Bengali, Punjabi, and several others.

accompanied an increasing articulation of the differences between Hindi and Urdu.

The British-sponsored development of the lower levels of education beginning at about mid-century played a crucial role in this expansion. The new educational system demanded hundreds of thousands of Hindi texts in the Nagari script and created thousands of career opportunities that depended on literacy in Hindi. The government's recognition of Hindi and Urdu as separate subjects in its schools as early as the 1850s, and the printing of textbooks in both the Nagari and the Urdu script, only heightened existing differences and helped to create opposing vernacular elites.

In the nearly five decades between 1868 and 1914 several other trends emerged. Publications in the classical Islamic-heritage languages of Arabic and Persian slowly diminished, with the most rapid decline occurring in the period 1900–1914. Arabic, comprising about 2–3 percent of total publications previously, dropped to 0.1 percent, while Persian publications went from about 10 percent to less than 1 percent. Hindu-heritage languages, on the other hand, after remaining on roughly equal terms with Islamic-heritage languages in the nineteenth century, showed the same striking increase as Hindi in the first years of the twentieth century, especially dual-language works in Sanskrit-Hindi, suggesting a trend toward the popularization of Sanskrit texts. (See also the discussion of the publishing history of the Awadhi *Mānas* in chapter 1.)

The geographical distribution of publication in various languages showed striking shifts during the same period. The proportion of Hindi works in the total output of the eastern part of the province remained practically constant (56–57 percent), as did the proportion of Urdu works (about 29 percent) in the west. After 1900, however, the proportion of Urdu works in the east fell to about half the former level, while that of Hindi works in the west rose to almost twice the previous level. In short, it was as if an increasing tide of Hindi works had pushed a diminishing flow of Urdu works back into the western part of the province. On the level of the vernacular elite, the differences between Hindi and Urdu had become greater. At the same time, the gap between Hindi and Urdu, on the one hand, and the regional dialects, on the other, had widened.

THE WHO OF HINDI SUPPORTERS: PATTERNS IN EDUCATION AND EMPLOYMENT

The Vernaculars and Education

In the mid-1840s the government of the N.W.P. conducted a survey of educational institutions, which presented a clear picture of the social backgrounds of students and teachers in Persian, Hindi, Arabic, and Sanskrit schools in many districts. The distribution of students and teachers in the Persian and Hindi schools (the great majority of the total) of Agra district fairly represented the general situation in other districts. Muslims and Kayasths composed the great majority of teachers and students of Persian, and Brahmins, Baniyas, and Rajputs, of Hindi. Moreover, all but a handful of Muslims studied Persian, while most Hindus (with the notable exception of Kayasths) studied Hindi (NWP Educ Rpt 1844–1845:Appendix I).

Another aspect of language study patterns appears in statistics for government schools in 1859–60. In the western part of the province students learning Islamic-heritage languages were a slight majority, while in the central and eastern parts those learning Hindu-heritage languages were large majorities (NWP Educ Rpt 1859–1860:Appendix A, 2–62). Similar figures for Awadh in 1869 show a pattern very close to that of the western N.W.P., with slightly more than half the students learning Islamic-heritage languages, a little more than a third, Hindu-heritage languages, and the remainder, English (Oudh Educ Rpt 1868–1869:Appendix A). In both Awadh and the N.W.P. another pattern appeared in education statistics during this period: the higher the level of education, the greater the proportion of students taking Islamic-heritage languages and English, and the smaller the proportion taking Hindu-heritage languages (see King 1974:84–91).

When we put these patterns together, a picture emerges which correlates quite well with the distribution of Hindi and Urdu publications discussed above: Hindi in a subordinate position in government institutions, contrasted with Urdu well entrenched in the higher reaches of education and administration; Hindi supported by castes associated with Sanskrit learning and resistance to Muslim rule in the past, versus Urdu upheld by Muslims and those Hindu castes (chiefly Kayasths) with a vested interest in Indo-Persian culture; Hindi whose stronghold lay in the eastern part of the province where the Hindu merchant tradition was more powerful vis-à-vis Urdu, whose strength lay in Awadh and the western part of the province where the Indo-Persian service tradition was more dominant (Bayly 1983); and finally, Hindi and Urdu studied almost entirely by high-caste Hindus and Muslims.

The Vernaculars and Employment

In 1877 the provincial government first prescribed a successful performance in either the Middle Class Vernacular or the Middle Class Anglo-Vernacular Examination as a qualification for government service. By the mid-1880s the sizable increase in the numbers of candidates showed that the order had begun to take effect. Lists of those passing the examinations were sent to each collector or Deputy Commissioner, and in many districts vacancies were filled from them. By the late 1880s these examinations had come to be the educational event of greatest interest to many hopefuls for government service. Their popularity began to wane toward the end of the century, however, as graduates with higher qualifications offered increasing competition. The statistics for these two examinations plainly show the dominance of certain castes, especially Kayasths, in the struggle for government service. They also show that the chief rivals of the Kayasths and Muslims were high-caste Hindus, namely, Brahmins, Rajputs, Khatris, and Baniyas (NWP&O Educ Rpt 1885–1886:Orders of Government, 6; NWP&O Educ Rpt 1886–1887:15–17, 19; King 1974:186–94).

The 1877 order had a significant effect on the numbers of candidates opting to study one or the other of the two vernaculars. In the twenty-year period between 1875 and 1895 the proportions of candidates taking Hindi and Urdu reversed themselves. In the mid-1870s Hindi candidates accounted for more than three-quarters of those taking the examinations; by 1887 Urdu candidates made up more than three-quarters of the total, and this ratio remained nearly the same for the rest of the century (Malaviya 1897:31). The reason for this shift was clear: as a result of the 1877 orders, the candidates chiefly valued the examinations as a means to government service, and naturally preferred to take them in the vernacular language that dominated in courts and offices.

Let us imagine a picture based on the preceding data. A pair of gates labeled Vernacular Middle and Anglo-Vernacular Middle Examinations stands before us. Through them pours a crowd of thousands, moving in the direction of more distant gates. A small portion of the crowd, mainly Muslims and Kayasths, succeeds in passing through one of these more distant gates, labeled Subordinate Judicial and Executive Services, but many others are turned aside. Among these, numbers of Brahmins, Rajputs, Khatris, and Baniyas, as well as a few Muslims, succeed in crossing the portals of a large gate labeled Educational Department. Others, among them many Muslims, manage to enter a smaller gate labeled Police Department. Some of the remaining crowd enter through other, smaller gates, but many fail to pass through any gate and straggle off into the surrounding countryside. Here live millions unacquainted with either Sanskritized Hindi or Persianized Urdu who come from the lower levels of Hindu and Muslim society—Ahirs, Chamars, Bhangis, and many others.

This fanciful portrait is meant to suggest that many non-Kayasth Hindus found that their best hope for government service lay in the newer Educational Department rather than in the older, more prestigious, and more remunerative Revenue or Judicial Departments. From the ranks of such Hindus came many leaders of the Hindi movement. The three founders of the NPS, for example, included a Brahmin, a Rajput, and a Khatri; all three made their careers in education—two in government service, and one in both government and private service. Our portrait also suggests that the great majority of the population, the repository of popular culture, did not share the concerns of the vernacular elite.

Yet another aspect of the relationship between education, language, and employment appeared in the results of an investigation ordered by the provincial lieutenant-governor in May 1900, a month after he had issued a resolution ostensibly granting equal status to the two vernacular languages and scripts. This investigation, which included the courts and offices of the Judicial and Revenue Departments from the highest to the lowest level in each district, aimed at determining the respective numbers of Hindu and Muslim clerks familiar with Hindi or Urdu or both (NWP&O Gen Admin Progs October 1900:111, 119, 122–24).

The results showed that most Hindus knew at least some Hindi, and even more knew at least some Urdu. On the other hand, fewer than half of the Muslims knew at least some Hindi, while all knew at least some Urdu. To put matters differently, almost all the Hindus knew Urdu well, and the majority knew Hindi well too. While almost all the Muslims knew Urdu well, only a small minority knew Hindi well. Contemporary observers suggested with good reason that the results were very likely skewed in favor of Hindi. Even so, the investigation clearly indicated that Muslims had a strong vested interest in Urdu, the dominant language of the courts and offices, while Hindus, though rivaling Muslims in Urdu, could easily turn to Hindi, where they far outstripped Muslims. In sum, Muslims stood to lose much more from any change than did Hindus. For the thousands of Hindus and Muslims educated in the vernaculars—that is, those who constituted the vernacular elite—language identity and economic well-being were bound together inseparably, a fact that intensified the rivalry between supporters of Hindi and Urdu.

THE ROLE OF VOLUNTARY ORGANIZATIONS: THE NAGARI PRACHARINI SABHA

If Pandit Gauri Datta had expressed himself visually, his play might have taken the form of the picture that appeared in the November 1902 issue of *Saraswati* (R. K. Das 1902:359: see figure 14). On the left stood a Muslim prostitute, decked out in all the finery of her profession. On the right, facing her rival, sat a Hindu matron, modestly clothed in an ordinary sari. The caption "Hindi-Urdu" and the verses below made it clear that on the left stood Urdu personified and on the right sat Hindi. The author of the verses was Radha Krishna Das, a member of one of the great merchant families of Banaras, a relative of Bharatendu Harishchandra, and the first president of the Nāgarī Prachārinī Sabhā of Banaras.

As the nexus of relationships embodied in the picture suggests, the Sabha both reflected and contributed to the process of change discussed above. Founded in 1893 by schoolboys of Queen's College in Banaras, the Sabha soon acquired influential patrons such as Madan Mohan Malaviya, played the leading role in mobilizing support for the resolution of May 1900, gave prizes for Nagari handwriting in schools, granted awards for Hindi literature, carried out extensive searches for old Hindi manuscripts and published the results, started two influential journals (the *Nagari Pracharini Patrika* and *Saraswati*), attracted a membership of many hundreds, received donations of thousands of rupees, founded the Hindi Sahitya Sammelan of Allahabad, constructed a major headquarters building, published many important works (including grammars and dictionaries), and lobbied the provincial Text Book Committee and other government organizations for Nagari and Hindi (see King 1974:243–377, 455–79). Through all these activities, the Sabha played the leading role in affirming and defining Hindi during our period, a Hindi separate and distinct from Urdu, other literary dialects, Hindustani, and the popular culture of oral tradition.

The social and geographic origins of the early membership of the Sabha, not surprisingly, showed patterns that strongly correlated with the patterns of publication, education, and employment we have already examined. Brahmins, Khatris, Rajputs, and Baniyās (mainly Agarwals) accounted for more than two thirds of the total membership of 84 in 1894. In the same year provincial residents composed 80 percent of the membership, and residents of Banaras 56 percent. The eastern portion of the province provided 68 percent of the membership, Awadh and the western portion only 6 percent each. The remainder of the membership came from Rajasthan, Punjab, the Central Provinces and Central India, Bihar, and Bengal (King 1974:251–68).

By 1914, the peak year before a prolonged decline in membership, the proportions had shifted. The province had dropped to 64 percent and Banaras to 16 percent of the total of 1,368 members, though the leadership remained firmly in the hands of the same Banaras castes. While the share of the eastern portion of the province fell to about 33 percent, that of the western part rose to 20 percent, and that of Awadh to 12 percent, mostly in the two or three years before 1914. Rajasthan, the Central Provinces and Central India, and Bihar made up 23 percent. The Sabha remained an almost entirely north India and Hindu organization throughout our period: the first of a handful of south Indians joined in 1908, and only tiny numbers of Muslims ever became members (King 1974:445–51).

While much of the financial support for the Sabha came from membership donations and the sale of publications, especially school textbooks, a significant portion came from large donors, many of whom were princes. In the first thirty years the organization's twenty largest donors contributed close to Rs. 100,000, or approximately 30 percent of the total income. Twelve of these donors were princes, seven of whom became official patrons of the Sabha, namely, the Maharajas of Gwalior, Rewah, Baroda, Bikaner, Chatrapur, Alwar, and Banaras (King 1974:452–54, 456–59).

Whereas the Sabha's first decade brought significant successes in both political and literary endeavors, the second decade saw continuing progress in the latter but little or no advance in the former. From about 1914 on, the Sabha devoted most of its energies and funds to literary efforts and turned away from political activities. So politically conservative did the organization become that the government even allowed the Sabha to keep proscribed books. In the decades to come, not the Sabha but the Hindi Sahitya Sammelan played the preeminent political role on both the provincial and the national level in the promotion of Hindi and the Nagari script.[9] The Sabha remained content to embellish Hindi literature.

CONCLUSION: NEW IDENTITIES—THE TERMINUS AD QUEM

The picture in *Saraswati* provides a convenient departure point for summarizing, analyzing, and speculating about what we have learned of the Hindi movement. By the early twentieth century, as the distance between the two women suggests, the Indo-Persian and Hindu cultures had become separate clusters of symbols for many members of what we have called the vernacular elite. From the more extreme Hindu viewpoint, the two figures stood for virtue versus vice; from the more extreme Muslim viewpoint, for barbarism versus refinement (see Rahmat-Ullah 1900). As one scholar of north India has suggested, various symbols of communal identity gradually clustered around the master symbol of religion in a process designated as "multi-symbol congruence" (Brass 1974).

We need not restrict ourselves to models from Western sources to analyze the Hindi movement, however, for the process of linguistic

9. The membership of the NPS and the HSS certainly partially overlapped in the early years of the latter, although how much I do not know. The leadership, however, soon became entirely separate and remained so for decades.

"purification" has a venerable social and cultural history in India. Just as certain standards for social behavior, especially for those castes wishing to elevate their position in the hierarchy, have been embodied in Brahmins for many centuries, so standards for language behavior have resided in Sanskrit, whose very name means "perfected." Thus we can explain much of the Hindi movement as a process of "Sanskritization" in which the excellence of a language was judged by the degree to which it incorporated the standards of Sanskrit. At the same time, we must not overlook the influence of English, which provided a not necessarily antithetical model of a modern language. The supporters of Hindi could choose or reject, and they did; roman letters proved unacceptable, while dictionaries of scientific terms were deemed acceptable.

Through the processes of separation and rejection Hindi supporters determined what Hindi *was not* and what Hindi *should not be.* Through the more positive processes of affirmation and definition they decided what Hindi *was* and what it *should be.* Hindi was certainly not Urdu (separation) nor should it be (rejection). On the other hand, Hindi had descended from Sanskrit (definition), something good for religious and cultural reasons (affirmation). These admittedly imprecise terms suggest the active approach of the vernacular elite to the creation of a new language style, what we might tentatively call the Sanskritization of Kharī Bolī (the common grammatical base of both Hindi and Urdu). From this viewpoint we can argue that the rejection of Hindustani, Kaithi, and popular oral traditions rested primarily on their relatively "impure" natures as compared to a *shuddh* (pure) Hindi. In the cases of Braj Bhasha and Awadhi, however, such an explanation does not suffice. Here more practical reasons seem to have prevailed: though both acted as bearers of a glorious literary tradition and parts of Hindi's past, neither possessed the necessary characteristics for a potential national language. Only Sanskritized Hindi, sharing the same grammatical base as the already widespread Urdu, had both the necessary purity and practicality.

While the vernacular elite played an active, not passive, role in the Sanskritization of Kharī Bolī, they forged Sanskritized Hindi within arenas—the educational system, the press, the publishing industry, voluntary associations, and the government itself—largely introduced through British rule. This external framework displayed fundamental ambiguities, however: thus, a close study of the period reveals that British officials authored language policies with massive contradictions (see, for example, King 1974:383–93) which exacerbated the very conflict they decried and left considerable room for the vernacular elite to maneuver.

By the eve of World War I, then, a class (the Hindi vernacular elite) had appeared in north India, especially in eastern U.P., whose community identity centered on *shuddh* Hindi, Hinduism, and an urban alliance of service and merchant interests. The harmonious working relationship between two leading members of the Sabha, Radha Krishna Das, merchant, and Shyam Sundar Das, educator, beautifully illustrates this alliance. The intensity of the struggle with the Urdu vernacular elite in the province expanded to the national level in the twentieth century. The emphasis on the purity of Hindi widened the gap between Hindi and Urdu as well as between elite and popular culture. The final result came after Independence, when Hindi became one of the two official languages of India, and the only official language of the U.P., thus at last fulfilling the judgment of Maharaja Righteous-Rule in Pandit Gauri Datta's *svāng*. Truly, Queen Nagari, born in Sanskrit-rich Banaras, ruled again.

SEVEN

State and Community: Symbolic Popular Protest in Banaras's Public Arenas

Sandria B. Freitag

Despite its long-lived centrality of place in Indian perceptions, Banaras has not figured prominently in accounts of modern Indian history. This is primarily because it does not lend itself to the approach previously taken by most historians, which focused on the response of a Western-educated elite to the British Empire.

As the richness of subject matter discussed in this volume suggests, such a narrow focal point ignores much that provides texture and significance in the lives of Indians. It also leads to assumptions about popular values and collective motivations that are quite suspect: to the extent that collective protest figures at all in this style of history, it is seen either as popular sentiment manipulated by the elite or as a result of elite loss of control over mass action—the "insensate violence" of the "bazars and mohullas of Indian towns" (Robinson 1974:6). Yet, as the preceding chapters suggest, if the historian's focus shifts from the Western-educated elite (in any case a relatively unimportant identifier in Banaras, even for those who were) to collective activities that express group values and processes of community identity, a very different picture emerges. The historical dynamic captured by this focal point underscores the changing definitions of state and community and their interrelationship. In this view of modern Indian history, Banaras plays a key role.

This essay is meant to suggest the historical interpretations made possible through an analysis of collective activities. It is based on the premise that such actions are not "insensate" but quite rational; that they may be subjected to careful scrutiny to yield evidence about the values and motivating forces of the crowd; and that, moreover, crowd behavior should be seen, not as peripheral to the dynamics of historical change, but at its very heart.[1]

Given the paucity of primary sources that accurately reflect the values and perceptions of participants in collective action, particularly for the nineteenth and early twentieth centuries,[2] those interested in the crowd must analyze its actions. Methodologically, this approach calls for a careful consideration of the full range of actions taken collectively: these possess the potential to speak to us through their shared symbolism, through the general ambiance of the public spaces they occupy, and through their methods of mobilization.[3] As a technique the approach owes much to what Victor Turner has called "comparative symbology," in which the analyst must investigate "the relationships between symbols and the concepts, feelings, values, notions, etc., associated with them by users, interpreters or exegetes." Particularly for the historian, changes over time in the use of these symbols are central to the analysis, for the symbolic actions express "social and cultural dynamic systems, shedding and gathering meaning over time and altering in form" (Turner 1979:12–13).

Collective actions in the public spaces of an urban north Indian environment tended to be of three types: public space performances, collective ceremony, and popular protest. These forms have been dis-

1. The historiographical tradition to which these techniques relate is more developed for European history, particularly that of early modern France and England. See, for instance, the work on "the crowd" of George Rudé, Natalie Z. Davis, E. P. Thompson, et al. More recently, and for South Asia, much of the work of the self-styled "Subalternist school" has attempted a similar historiographical approach.

2. From materials available for the later decades of the twentieth century, we know that the best sources would be the texts of publicly posted placards; folk songs (see lyrics in chap. 3); "popular painting," to use the Archer term (1977), such as illustrations utilized by itinerant storytellers, or even individual paintings depicting local scandals and activities. Unfortunately, although administrators cum amateur anthropologists assiduously collected folk songs and folk tales in the late nineteenth century for the rural areas, we cannot assume that these sources reflect the values or social organization of the urban world. The closest we can come to sources that connect, at least tangentially, to the popular perceptions and values of the city are newspapers, particularly the vernacular press—which, while written by a literate elite, did function to "report" happenings, including collective activities; and petitions submitted to the authorities—which, while written by an elite literate in English as well as in a vernacular language, attempted to "explain" collective action. As is noted below, these sources must be used as judiciously as any primary materials.

3. Sources for such a methodology are somewhat problematic, since they depend not on polemical explanations for crowd behavior (which characterize most vernacular primary sources on a subject), but on accurate descriptions of crowd action. Perversely enough, administrative accounts of protest actions—if detailed enough, written soon after the fact, by someone relatively familiar with the locale—often prove the most valuable sources. The historian must, of course, treat them as any primary source, and take care to use them only for what they *describe,* rather than for what they attempt to *explain.*

cussed in the Introduction to Part 1. Although distinct in significant ways, they developed out of shared cultural assumptions and, taken together, constitute a world that should be considered a coherent whole and analyzed on its own terms. This world may best be described as composed of "public arenas," or activities that represent public expressions of collective values and motivations (Freitag 1989). By analyzing the characteristics shared by the variety of types of collective actions we begin to see a consistent picture of symbolic behavioral expressions. In turn, this consistency of symbols highlights historical change when we compare a series of collective actions over time. In particular, the concept of "public arena" activity is intended to emphasize the "structure-in-process" or "process-ual" elements (to use Turner's terms) that are inherent in this world. That is, it is a world in which changes (in, for instance, the functions of particular groups and the relationships between them) affect, and become reflected in, structure that alters with each iteration. By studying the ritual symbols of this world in conjunction with other expressions of political power and cultural values, we discover what historical change is all about. Turner, too, urges that ritual symbols be studied

> in relation to other "events," for symbols are essentially involved in social process . . . performances of ritual [are] distinct phases in the social processes whereby groups became adjusted to internal changes . . . and adapted to their external environment. . . . From this standpoint the ritual symbol becomes a factor in social action, a positive force in an activity field. (Turner 1979:13)[4]

Several of the chapters in this volume treat the first of these types of public-arena activities. In this chapter I examine in more detail the latter two types, suggesting their significance in constructing a history of north India. At the heart of this processual analysis of symbolic collective behavior are events of 1809–1811. During these two years a style and a symbolic rhetoric of protest emerged in Banaras which differed in important ways from the style that evolved in other U.P. urban centers. After examining the protests of those critical two years, we look, in turn, at collective protests and ceremonials in the 1890s and 1930s in order to chart changes over time. In particular, these changes suggest

4. In this emphasis on "social process" this approach differs from that of Guha (1983) and others of the Subalternist school, who have also interpreted symbolic action. Such action expresses for them a fundamental oppostion of upper and lower class, of oppressor and oppressed (which can, therefore, generally be read backward or forward in time). While I think the evidence shows that, on some occasions, the symbolism did indeed express such opposition, that is not always the case (see chaps. 5 and 6 of Freitag, 1989). Instead, I would argue, the interpretation of symbolic action must be carefully contextualized.

for us the significance of public arenas in accommodating important historical change, expressing through structure-in-process forms the significant alterations in relationships among urban groups, as well as between the state and its constituent communities.

SHARED CULTURE OF PUBLIC ARENAS

Early-nineteenth-century sources refer, albeit briefly, to an array of collectively observed ceremonial activities, most of which were identified by the administration as "religious." Certainly their subject matter was religious, as the observances frequently reenacted stories from sacred texts. Particularly at this time, however, such ceremonials constituted statements of shared civic identity, of "Banarsipan," as much as they did a specific religious identity. The Muslim petition submitted in 1809, for instance, referring to a disputed site, said that "for some years, the lower classes of Hindus and Muhammedans have annually celebrated the marriage of the Laut and have divided the offerings between them" (Board no. 9093:168).[5] Similarly, in referring to a site shared by a temple and a mosque, the Acting Magistrate noted that "the Muslims have frequently participated with the Hindus in the offerings presented to the idols" (Board no. 9093:262A). Even thirty years later, a British observer resident in the city commented that "on most occasions of festive and multitudinous assemblage, the distinctions of religion give way, and the scene bears more the character of a fair than of a religious meeting" (Prinsep 1831, quoted in Eck 1982:254). Indeed, the shared civic sense fostered by such public ceremonials is suggested by Acting Magistrate Bird when he noted in 1809 that "the religious ceremonies of the Muhammedans and Hindus are so inseparably blended" that any attempt to "disunite them" would constitute a "new arrangement" (see fig. 15).[6]

This same source provided a brief description of an observance of Bharat Milāp in 1809, which sketches the nature of these shared cultural activities. The story for the occasion is staged each year on a small field permanently set aside for the purpose in *muḥalla* Nati Imli. After reenacting the reunion of Rāma with his brother Bharat, the observance opens out to become a general celebration shared by thousands of people (see N. Kumar 1984:263). In 1809, although the seeds of conflict had been sown which would soon erupt in a virtually unprecedented riot between groups of Hindus and Muslims, the citywide ceremony was deemed sufficiently important that "it was amicably agreed upon to suppress and conceal their mutual differences during the cele-

5. I have not been able to find a description of this "marriage" ceremony.
6. IOL & R. Board's collections. F/4/365, no. 9093 for 1812-13:269A.

Fig. 15. Drawing of a tazia procession during the Muharram observance, 1831. James Prinsep, *Benares Illustrated* (Calcutta, 1833). Courtesy of Ames Library, University of Minnesota. (Compare with figure 13.)

bration . . . and refer them after the expiration of the holiday to the decision of the Court" (Board no. 9093:44).

Part of a preeminent occasion for collective play,[7] this festival occupied an important place in the inventory of Banaras's public-arena activities. Perhaps the most appropriate documentation of this is found in a vernacular newspaper almost a century later, when the *Bharat Jiwan* commented on "the Bharat Milap of Nati Imli which is famous in this and all nations. . . . None would object perhaps to calling it the foremost of Kashi's melas and festivals, because on that day all Kashivasis—women, aged, children, Hindus, Muslims and the English—feel a rush of Rambhakti [devotion to Rām] in their hearts . . . it would have to be an invalid or disabled person who does not go to see it" (*Bharat Jiwan,* 30 Oct. 1893, 8, quoted in N. Kumar 1984:264). Its eminence can be further attested to by the growth around it of a number of legends (see N. Kumar 1984).

While the occasion was doubtless particularly important to the artisans and other lower-class groups of the city (e.g., Ahirs carried in the *swarups*, or actors, playing Rām, Laxman, and Sītā), the newspaper went on to note by name the important local leaders who participated by observing the event.[8] Even today, one of the measures signifying the importance of the Bharat Milāp observance is participation by the Maharaja of Banaras, who enters first as "*the* king" who then "becomes front rank of the audience, completing the sense of the event as that of a total people, led by their king, witnessing and worshipping the momentary arrival of their God in their midst. . . . The Maharaja, in the words of informants, *is* the people and the kingdom, and his exchange with Rama is symbolic of that of the necessarily anonymous masses [who] throng to the spot" (N. Kumar 1984:266).

By the middle of the nineteenth century this functional role of the Maharaja as symbol of "the people and the kingdom" had become virtually unique in U.P. As the Rohillas, the Nawabi of Awadh, and other successor states gave way to the British Empire, those who performed the integrative function described here were either dispossessed or had their status reduced and trivialized to that of mere large landlords.[9] Nowhere else in U.P. did such a coalition (of merchants, Maharaja, and Gosains) succeed in protecting and extending the shared local culture. How did this unique situation evolve in Banaras? In the remainder of

7. Bharat Milāp provides a pivotal scene in the longer enactment of the Rāmlīlā.

8. Kumar also refers to newspaper advertisements in the 1930s selling tickets for wealthier observers to secure places in nearby gardens and rooftops from which to view the field.

9. Given the right circumstances, some of the taluqdars of Awadh doubtless possessed the potential to expand their control (as the Bhumihar family had) until they possessed kingly attributes (T. Metcalf 1979).

this chapter I will argue that the answer to that question can be found by focusing on public arena activity; this focus points up a series of renegotiations of the relationship between state and community which helped preserve a particular form of local culture even while it accommodated changes in the roles and connections between leaders and followers in Banaras.

The Maharaja's own public ceremonial, as it was elaborated over two centuries, typifies the processual elements of collective observance. As was noted in the Introduction, the Hindu merchant corporation of the city, and the Bhumihar dynasty based in Ramnagar, cosponsored this unique version of Rāmlīlā.[10] By virtue of its thirty-one-day length and its patronage by the dynasty, this Rāmlīlā remains, to the present, "the most extensive, best performed, and draws the largest audience of any" Rāmlīlā in the subcontinent (Schechner and Hess 1977). Its key attributes emphasize expression of the "relationship between government, Maharaja, and ordinary people." Schechner and Hess note that the day-to-day events of the performance follow the outlines of Tulsidas's epic poem, the *Rāmcharitmānas,* "but some events—notably those of great iconographic effect, the processions—are given higher focus: they are good theatre, and especially display the Ramlila's two leading performers, Rama and the Maharaja." This provides the widest possible appeal, incorporating all Banarsis even as it emphasizes the integrative role of the ruler.

Although the Maharaja does not figure in Tulsidas's narrative, or in the other, ubiquitous enactments of it staged throughout north India,[11] "each day's [Ramnagar-sponsored] performance begins only after the Maharaja arrives, either on elephant or horse-drawn carriage or in his 1927 Cadillac limousine." Since the performance ceases and resumes again around the Maharaja's daily *sandhya puja,* it is the Maharaja who imposes, twice a day, a "processional rhythm" on the performance. Indeed, the authors note that "The Maharaja and Rama are mirror images of each other, the twin heroes of the Ramnagar Ramlila. The Maharaja is as much a mythic figure as Rama." Throughout the Rāmlīlā, his actions and attire reflect his mythic kingly role as "upholder of reli-

10. While merchant roles have undoubtedly expanded in the twentieth century, Hess's recent description is worth noting: "Most spectators cross the river [from Banaras to Ramnagar] each day to attend the Lila; a fair number come from the Ramnagar side as well. . . . Though no survey was taken of audience members' caste, occupation, or education, we noticed that small-scale merchants were heavily represented. Almost no one we met in the crowd spoke English. People of different castes and classes appeared to mingle quite freely, though there may have been ways of maintaining separations of which we were unaware" (Hess 1987:3).

11. For a discussion of the political implications of Rāmlīlā performances throughout U.P., see Freitag 1989, chap. 7.

gion, repository of tradition and authority," patron of the arts and learning. At the same time, he has a second mythic role, that of representative of Shiva, the lord of ancient Kashi.

The Ramnagar dynasty quite deliberately pursued certain political ends (see chapter 1) through Rāmlīlā patronage. Important gains were made for Hindu culture in the process—especially noteworthy in the face of the political power of the (Muslim) Nawab of Awadh. But other, internally significant political ends were served as well by this elaboration of a popular observance—ends that reinforced the relations with the lower classes of Banaras, frequently Muslim, through the emphasis on the Maharaja as ruler of all. While Rāma "fulfills his destiny . . . as the bearer of Hindu culture" (Schechner and Hess 1977:54), Tulsidas's equal emphasis on devotion over orthodoxy, of shared brotherhood over community and caste divisions, enabled the dynasty to use this event for integrative purposes, even with Muslim weavers. Thus the observance documents the uniquely Banarsi emphasis on the role of local ruler, with whom all Banarsis could identify. We may speculate, too, that the physical locale of the Ramnagar observance—with its permanent constructions representing various places in the subcontinent located in a space at some remove from the neighborhoods where popular forms of competition were focussed—could function in integrative ways not available to other observances of Rāmlīlā.

EARLY-NINETEENTH-CENTURY STATE AND COMMUNITY

This description of collective ceremonials suggests the structural outlines of the public arena as it existed at the end of the eighteenth century in Banaras. Against this background established by integrative ceremonial, however, the early nineteenth century witnessed two unprecedented occasions of collective protest—a riot in 1809 between groups of Banarsis over sacred space, and a protest in 1810 against an innovative tax imposed by the British on Indian dwellings. By examining these two occasions, we gain a sense both of the process or dynamic that underlay structure and of the turn-of-the-century historical changes that had to be accommodated by that structure.

Sources have always identified the 1809 protest as a religious riot, an accurate characterization in terms of the targets chosen, the symbolic actions of the crowd, and the fact that groups of "Hindus" were generally arrayed against groups of "Muslims." The event left residents much shaken and was perceived at the time and thereafter as extraordinary—for such religious unrest, particularly in terms of the scale of destruction, was unprecedented in Banaras. As a petition from the qadi and *mufti* (the law officers of the Nizamat Adawlut, who resided in Banaras) put it, this was "a disturbance of a more alarming nature than has ever been witnessed in this country . . . for three days this city was filled with rapine, fire and murder" (Board no. 9093:220).

The site of the original dispute was a neutral area between the pillar known as the Lāṭ Bhairava and a neighboring Imāmbārā.[12] To underscore the neutrality of the area, weavers insisted in their 1809 petition that the idols set up on this ground were removed by the Brahmin in charge "when the Muslims met together for the purpose of prayer"; "if there happened to be any which could not be conveniently taken away, they were carefully concealed with grass" (Board no. 9093:169). While this version probably exaggerates the transitoriness of Hindu claims to the ground, it does explain the strong reaction of the weavers to the act of devotion that, in their perception, completely changed the nature of the area. For, into this shared space, came a worshipper of Hanuman who, in fulfillment of a vow, attempted to replace a sheltering mud structure around Hanuman's statue (perceived by Muslims as more "temporary" in nature) with one made of stone.

At first the weavers seemed content to appeal to the qadi, and agreed to continue participating with Hindus in the observance of Bharat Milāp. At the Friday prayers that followed conclusion of Bharat Milāp (October 20, 1809), however, they violently removed the stone structure and damaged nearby sacred objects. Word spread, bringing indignant Rajputs to the site. Kotwal and Acting Magistrate both rushed to the scene; they left again when it seemed that order had been restored. Instead, however, the Rajput crowd "committed some slight injury" (in the words of the Acting Magistrate) to the Imāmbārā. The weavers' reaction drew on both their training in sword-and-stick performances (gained at physical fitness gymnasiums, or *akhāṛās*) and on the symbolic actions they performed during Muharram: "collecting in considerable numbers armed with swords and clubs, [they] hoisted a standard and, exclaiming Imam Hossein and beating their breasts, marched towards the city" (Board no. 9093:45). Continuing their symbolic action, they marched to the temple of Vishveshvara (often transliterated Bisheshwar), which stood next to the mosque Aurangzeb had erected on the site of an older temple. Those left behind invoked religious symbols as well: after pulling down the pillar and breaking it into pieces, they then "slaughtered a [sacred] cow at the foot of the Laut and sprinkled [the broken column] with the blood of the animal" (Board no. 9093:47).

12. The Lat, or "staff," of Bhairava ("popularly known as the police chief of sacred Kashi") is located at the northern end of Banaras. The pillar, removed from a Hindu temple complex when Aurangzeb destroyed it, was left intact, but had once been much taller (Eck 1982:196). An *imāmbārā* is a building used particularly to store the tazias, or floats, paraded during Muharram.

Reaction among Hindu groups in the city varied. The Raja disarmed his men voluntarily and removed them from the city during the violent period. The "brahmins and superior orders" gathered at the ghats and fasted. Rajputs and Gosains, slowly gathering force, invoked symbols appropriate to their own roles in seeking revenge. Late the next morning the Rajputs gathered together again and returned to the Imāmbārā. After destroying it completely and murdering the four or five members of the caretaker's family, they countered the blood symbolism of the slaughtered cow by killing a hog (in Muslim eyes an unclean animal) near the principal tomb. From the Imāmbārā they moved on to destroy the Dargah of Fatima and then turned to the weavers' quarters: they could target domestic quarters and Muslim bodies, for they did not need good relations with the Muslim lower classes of the city. Another crowd, this one composed of Gosains, concentrated instead on Muslim sacred spaces rather than their domestic quarters; it began pulling down the Gyān Vāpī (often transliterated Jnana Vapi) mosque next to the Vishveshvara Temple. "The whole of Benaras," the Acting Magistrate observed, "was in the most dreadful uproar and confusion. The temples were shut, and multitudes of armed Hindus were assembled in every quarter, directing their rage chiefly against the lives and properties of the Joolahers [Julāhās, i.e., weavers] and the Butchers"—indeed, "the whole quarter of the Joolahers was a scene of plunder and violence" (Board no. 9093:48–51). In contrast, the very lack of action by the Raja also proved significant from this vantage point. He remained aloof, withdrawn from the violence, an exemplar of the appropriate behavior by an integrative ruler. In the aftermath of the riot, he worked to restore peace, treating with the British administrators, on the one hand, and working with the leadership of various *muḥalla*s, on the other.[13]

Beyond the overt level of symbolism that classifies this conflict as "religious" lie further meanings. From this vantage point, the specific identification of the combatants, not as "Hindus" and "Muslims," but as Marathas, Rajputs, Gosains, and weavers, becomes significant. Thus, while not denying the religious characterization, we can find much additional meaning by placing these acts in the larger context of the political economy of Banaras at the turn of the century. To begin with, although the British East India Company had formally assumed control from the Raja in 1794, the frailties of the then-reigning Raja may have postponed a perception of finality regarding the transfer of power. By 1809, however, his successor had been agitating unsuccessfully for more than a decade to have the agreement put aside. He had also "lost

13. For a more detailed analysis, see Freitag 1989 chap. 1.

face" in negotiations over changes in structures of rural management.[14] These indicators of loss of power by the Bhumihar dynasty could only have heartened both Marathas and Rajputs.[15] The latter, as landholders who resided in the city but were supported by their holdings located throughout the surrounding district, still occupied "an important position in the district" in the nineteenth century, but they had had "their former predominance" destroyed "by the rise of the Benaras Rajas."

Yet new claims to power and leadership by Marathas and Rajputs necessarily imperiled the relationships already established in the city—both the triumvirate of influence and control exercised by the dynasty, Gosains and merchant-bankers, and the interdependence of the weavers and merchants that was expressed culturally through the figure of the Raja. I would argue that the underlying symbolism of the rioters' actions may be taken to express *these* configurations as much as they expressed conflict between "Hindus" and "Muslims."

During 1809, then, we can discern a first phase in the process by which symbolic structures in the city adjusted to accommodate momentous political change. For this phase, conflicts among those who held power in Banaras—which affected as well the relationship between artisans and their merchant patrons—found expression through a religion-focused symbolic vocabulary. This indicates that the participants, leaders and followers alike, reacted against other Indians perceived as competitors, in the field most open to them—that in which public arena activities were staged.

In this respect what happened in Banaras differed little from the style of urban conflict developing throughout the nineteenth century in U.P. While becoming reified in other urban centers, however, this style of symbolic activities did not come to dominate the public arenas of Banaras. To understand why, we must examine with some care the aftermath of the 1809 riot, as well as the collective protest staged just fourteen months later against imposition of a house tax. For, as the agitation died down in the city, the attendant actions of the various participants—including the British East India Company—reflected changes occurring in Banaras's structures of urban self-rule. The evi-

14. An 1810 document notes: "In the late Tahsildari arrangements . . . the Rajah has been expressively disappointed and chagrined and though he by no means presumes to arraign the orders of government he has fancied himself degraded in dignity and consequently by the little attention paid to his solicitations an opportunity is now afforded . . . of mitigating the Rajah's discontent." IOR. Bengal Revenue Proceedings P/55/vol. 37 (Progs for 11th January 1811).

15. See Introduction to Part 1 for the role of Marathas in the city, particularly in the eighteenth century.

dence is clearest for the kotwal (police) and qadi (courts), but emerges as well for the neighborhoods and the relationship between community and state.

As was noted in the Introduction to Part 1, the functioning of the kotwal and qadi was essential to the well-being of an urban central place. The kotwal required the confidence of all communities resident in the city. In Banaras by the turn of the century, however, evidence strongly suggests that the preexisting relationship between kotwal (as representative of the state) and communities had been eroded. Perhaps the first indicators emerged in 1803 when the British administration instructed the kotwal to become involved in the administration of the *phatakbandi* tax. The measure, we are told by the *Gazetteer,* was "stoutly resisted" (Nevill 1909a:166). Significant further erosion of the kotwal's position is described in some detail in the documentation of the 1809 riots. The kotwal himself acknowledged this diminution in popular recognition of his authority by requesting that he be allowed to retire.

The shape of self-rule in Banaras was most profoundly altered, however, by administrative steps taken after the riot.[16] First, the administration began altering both the composition and the organization of the urban police force. Second and even more significant, the administration decided that certain persons would be "brought to trial not for the outrages each had committed against the other, but one common offence against the peace . . . as an offence against the State." These persons had been selected as appropriate to stand as symbolic representatives for their communities because, "from acts and circumstances which have come to light, [these were the people who] appear to have instigated and encouraged, purely upon religious principle, the disgraceful excesses which were committed, or who were themselves personally concerned in the commission of some overt act of violence and outrage" (Board no. 9093:272–77).[17]

These attempts by the British to alter the relationship of community and state are particularly significant. For evidence suggests that this kind of alteration was at the very heart of the collective protests of these years. The exasperated Acting Magistrate noted, for instance, that "the disturbance is found to have originated in the abuse of that privilege which the Natives have been permitted to enjoy, of assembling among themselves to deliberate on questions of common inter-

16. For details, see Freitag 1989.

17. Qadi and mufti, law officers of the court in which the trials would be conducted, were greatly alarmed at this innovation. Normally, they would have been expected to issue a *fatwā* (decision interpreting the law) on the cases. But this put them, as residents of Banaras, in a particularly awkward position. "These disturbances have been so general that our interference must raise thousands of enemies against us, and as our families reside in the city, we may justly apprehend both their and our total destruction." As a result, the cases were tried without "the intervention of any natives."

est." Further, in condemning the Rajput leader, he notes that "it is clear from the whole tenor of his conduct that he considered this a dispute in which the public authority had no business to interfere. That as the injury had been offered to the Hindus at large it was for them alone to determine the measure of their revenge and unite in the common resolution of inflicting it" (Board no. 9093:261, 295). As the conflict that erupted the following year demonstrated, the ability and inclination of Banarsi communities to gather and decide collectively on courses of action remained strong—and it directly threatened British perceptions of their state authority.

Yet, in the face of these clear messages, the British increased their interference. Thus the administration introduced the changes described earlier in the policing system; passed a proclamation that provided for closer control over collective gatherings;[18] and in December 1810 attempted to introduce a new house-tax that would provide greater revenues for running the municipality, in the process bringing the revenues and administration of the neighborhood-based *chaukidarī* system under closer administrative control.

These intrusions by the imperial state created a new relationship between state and community, one unappealing to the residents of Banaras. Moreover, the style of interaction differed from that demanded by Banarsis. Acting Magistrate Bird willingly worked unceasingly behind the scenes, where he repeatedly relied on personal, face-to-face relationships with the leaders of each community; but they wanted more. They wanted him to act publicly, to place his own person physically in public arena spaces for symbolic purposes. To underscore his perception of the audacity of one protest,[19] for instance, Bird noted that

> on the morning of the 24th the [leaders who became] prisoners assembled with the whole body of goshains and seating themselves upon the ghats remained there in spite of all remonstrance until the agitation occasioned by it, threatening a renewal of those horrors from which the city had recently been rescued, *I was compelled to go in person* to remove them; for this conduct they . . . collected not like the brahmins on the 23rd for religious principles, but for the purpose of obtained concessions. (Board no. 9093:304; emphasis added)

RENEGOTIATING THE RELATIONSHIPS

Reacting to the administrative innovations introduced in the wake of the 1809 riots, the House Tax Protest of 1810 provides a clear symbolic

18. This control operated more in public awareness than in actuality, for the Magistrate was instructed to exercise broad tolerance in permitting collective gatherings.

19. His perception was seconded in London, where the India Office copy has been underlined, with indignant marginal notes.

statement of the second phase in the early-nineteenth-century process during which residents of the city reiterated the distinct Banarsi-styled relationship between state and community. In 1809, the first phase, Indians had acted out symbolic protests against other Indians. In 1810, however, these antagonists turned instead against the British, concentrating on issues that intruded into their preexisting system of urban self-rule. In the first phase, moreover, Banarsis had faced symbolic challenges to the internal relationship established between the ruling group (referred to here as the "triumvirate" of Ramnagar dynasty, merchant-bankers and Gosains) and artisans within the city; the style of the second phase suggests that the participants had resisted these challenges. In 1810, then, it is the underlying continuity of structure and protest that, together, stand out as the principal components of public arena activity.

Pre-British structures of community organization provided critical lines of mobilization to protest the house tax:[20] while "all ranks and description of Banarsis joined in the protest" (Acting Magistrate Bird quoted in Dharampal 1971:6), the initial petitions were submitted by each neighborhood or *muḥalla* (Boards Collections no. 7407:94; Heitler 1972:241). Occupation as well as neighborhood provided organizational networks, as the administration recognized when it tried to negotiate with occupational *chaudhurīs* (headmen).

Forms of protest followed time-honored merchant patterns, described as "sitting dharna." Once again taking oaths to shut down the bazaars and withdraw their services until "the outcry and distress" in the city induced the magistrate to accede, more than twenty thousand inhabitants "sat" in an open field in the city. Caste panchayats not only maintained order, they coerced those whose support was wavering for this "panch" form of protest.[21] Symbolically, the orderly withdrawal to the field demonstrated as well to the British the effectiveness of mechanisms of urban self-rule:

> Vast multitudes came forth in a state of perfect organization: each caste trade and profession occupied a distinct spot of ground, and was regulated in all its acts by the orders of its own punchayat, who invariably punished all instances of misconduct or disobedience on the part of any

20. Regulation XV of 1810 called for a levy for 5 percent on the "annual rent" of all dwellings and 10 percent on all shops. Sources for this protest are contained in IOR. F/4/323, Board's Collections no 7407; and Dharampal 1971 (which, unfortunately, does not contain the texts of any of the petitions). See also the excellent article by Heitler (1972). Where possible I have cited the latter sources, since they will be the most accessible for the readers.

21. Contrary to the impression conveyed by Heitler's article, these tactics are never characterized in the petitions as hartals. Rather, the terms used are "panch" and "sitting dharna."

> of its members. This state of things continued for more than a month; and whilst the authority of the British Government was, in a manner, suspended, the influence of the punchayat was sufficient to maintain the greatest order and tranquility.[22]

As was suggested in the Introduction to Part 2, such "combinations" became possible by working through urban linkages that overarched particular caste- and occupation-specific units. By the early nineteenth century such social integration proved capable of bringing to the field of protest representatives of most families in Banaras and its rural environs (see Dharampal 1971:13, 6). Money was raised through these same networks to support family members whose wage earners had withdrawn to the field: "The individuals of every class, contributed each in proportion to his means, to enable them to persevere, and considerable sums were thus raised."[23]

This was, then, a popular protest, supported by virtually all levels of society and ordered by a variety of mechanisms reflecting local community organization. Even when the government decided to exempt religious buildings and lower-class dwellings, the protest remained general. Moreover, beyond the organizational level, the rhetoric and symbolic action of the protest provides important evidence of the symbolic structures brought to bear during this conflict.

To begin with, as the petitions make clear, Banarsis viewed this new taxation as an intrusion into their customary charitable practices. The city was filled, they noted, with widows, Brahmins, and other poor who were housed in structures that could not be maintained if taxes had to be paid on them as well. Threats to this practice undermined basic tenets on which Banaras had been established: "In this holy city the rajas of ancient times from a principle of virtue and in the hopes of everlasting fame built houses and fixed salaries and settled perpetual donations for the subsistence and residence of brahmins, paupers and mendicants, there are hundreds of such houses appropriated to brahmins" (Boards Collections no. 7407:106–13).

Furthermore, both rhetoric and action deliberately posed their system of self-rule against state perceptions of appropriate behavior. In their final petition to government, the protestors insisted they had not

22. J. D. Erskine, Acting Third Judge of the Court of Appeal and Circuit for the Division of Banaras, included in *Selections of Papers from the Records of the East India House* . . . , Vol. 2:89 (quoted in Heitler 1972:246).

23. Letter from Collector W. O. Salmon, quoted in Dharampal 1971:15. Landlord connections can be inferred from the extensive holdings possessed by Banarsi bankers; see descriptions in Nevill 1909a:117 et seq. Connections in the opposite direction (i.e., from moneylenders located in the countryside who helped contribute to the trading activities centered in Banaras) are discussed in Bayly 1983:103–6. References to fundraising, Bird quoted in Dharampal 1971:13.

created a "disturbance," as the magistrate charged, but had registered a complaint in a legitimate manner. They noted that

> the manner and custom in this country from time immemorial is this: that, whenever any act affecting every one generally is committed by the Government, the poor, the aged, the infirm, the women, all forsake their families and their homes, expose themselves to the inclemency of the seasons and to other kinds of inconveniences, and make known their affliction and distress. (Quoted in Heitler 1972:250)

It is significant, too, that their objections to the tax centered, not on the rate at which it was pitched, but on the very legitimacy of the form of demand. Their petition noted that

> in the Shera and Shaster, together with the customs of Hindostan . . . houses are reckoned one of the principal necessaries of life, and are not accounted disposable property . . . in this country, in the times of Mohamedan and Hindoo princes, houses were never rendered liable to contributions for the service of the state. (Quoted in Heitler 1972:253)

They objected, as well, to the notion that representatives of government should go into their houses to determine the value to be assessed. Finally, they pointed out that already they were paying other taxes, such as stamp, transit, and town duties; in particular they referred to the *phatakbundi.*

The contrast between the new house-tax and the *phatakbundi* was an important one. The *phatakbundi* operation had been organized locally within each *muḥalla;* the substantial sums, collected by the inhabitants themselves, then were used to pay *chaukidars*—also chosen and supervised by the inhabitants. The new taxing arrangements would have represented a very substantial infringement on local self-rule. Thus the antagonists clearly perceived the conflict to be between British authority and Banarsi community control. In early January the government of the East India Company responded to Bird with the observation that Bird should announce the compromise of the *phatakbundi* in the way "best calculated to allay the disposition to riot and resistance to public authority, which appears so generally prevalent among the lower orders in the city of Banaras." Yet three weeks later, Bird despairingly noted that "the people still continue collected as they were," and only fatigue and disappointment were likely to break up the tent city. He was fully aware of the implications of the month-long protest: "I cannot but feel very forcibly, that such a state of things being permitted to continue in defiance of public authority, has already weakened, and weakens daily still more and more, those sentiments of respect, which it is so essential that the community should entertain for the government of the country" (Boards Collections no. 7407:121–24, 185–88).

The tactics with which Banarsi communities fought the state had been carefully designed to protect their legitimacy. The crowd's careful adherence to nonviolence tied Bird's hands, for he felt that only violence would justify use of the military. The tactics, as he noted, thus forced city life to a standstill, leaving the administration little choice but to rescind the tax. Beyond the petition cited above, we have other evidence that the crowd felt itself fully justified in its action. Another petition, with a "style and contents" characterized as "disrespectful" by the judges of the Provincial Court to which it was addressed, baldly declared the "deadly evil" that the tax represented. Indeed, the petitioners continued, "if our bad fortune be such, that you are induced to wish our leaving this for other countries, we trust that you will be pleased to order what we have expended in buildings to be paid to us out of your treasury" (Boards Collections no. 7407:203).

Demands for an appropriate state-community relationship moved beyond the actual issue of taxation, to the increasing reluctance of the new government to symbolically participate in public arenas. The protestors underscored this last grievance by their demand on January 23 that "they were willing to disperse, providing [the Acting Magistrate] *came to them* [in the field where they were residing] *in person* to request it" (Bird, 28.1.1811, quoted in Dharampal 1971:30; emphasis added). After his indignation in 1809, the magistrate flatly refused this time. Instead, he turned to the Raja of Banaras to represent the state in public. The Raja

> proceeded with all the distinctions of his rank to the place where the people were collected, the mob soon listened to his exhortations, and returned to their homes, and the Rajah, selecting from among them, fifty of the persons principally concerned in the disturbance, brought them to [the magistrate] to acknowledge their offences; while the Rajah himself interceded in their behalf and solicited [the magistrate] to endeavour to procure both for themselves and for the subject of their complaint, the indulgence of the Government. (Bird 28.1.1811, quoted in Dharampal 1971:32–33)

The role of the Raja in this process thus proved critical. While his power was doubtless bounded by the British government, his behavior matched public expectations for a traditional ruler. On the one hand, he could represent symbolically the culture shared by upper and lower classes, by Hindus and Muslims alike. On the other hand, he provided the only symbol of authority on which both the Banarsi and the British could agree—the only figure who could operate both in the reformulated system of self-rule emerging in Banaras and as an intermediary figure judged legitimate by British administrators. We might note that his symbolic usefulness continued even after he convinced the residents to abandon their tent city. Once the crowds had dispersed and business and services resumed, the Raja returned to the magistrate. On this visit he again acted on behalf of Banarsi residents, bearing their petition addressed to the Governor General in Council.[24]

In this second phase in Banaras, then, we find that the rituals of protest had resulted in creating a structure in which urban residents—rallied by merchants, Gosains, and Brahmins, and brought together around the figure of the Raja—moved against the imperial government. That they joined together to focus their protest, not against each other but against government measures imposed from above, reflected a society more culturally integrated than that of any other urban center in U.P. Where, in other urban centers public arena activities became increasingly focused on conflicts among communities, in Banaras they focused instead on the relationship between state and community.

This is not to say that Banaras was wracked by collective protest in the nineteenth or early twentieth centuries. On the contrary: for a variety of reasons—relating to its relative economic stability (compared, for instance, with Kanpur) and its Bhojpuri cultural continuity with the surrounding countryside (see Pandey 1983)—very few collective confrontations occurred in Banaras. Those few, however, until the 1930s followed the pattern we saw established early in the nineteenth century. They centered on issues affecting the relationship between state and community. We turn now to an examination of examples of collective protest in Banaras in 1891 and 1931 to discern further shifts in the processual character of public arena activities.

THE CHANGING STYLE OF BANARSI PROTEST: 1891 AND 1913

In the 1890s, while the rest of the province rioted over the issue of Cow Protection, the collective violence in Banaras was directed at state-mandated technology. The administration began introducing a new water-supply scheme into many of the larger cities of U.P.; by 1890 the attendant tax increases to fund the scheme had been levied in Banaras. This municipal taxation, we should not be surprised to learn, was "generally viewed with disfavor by the poorer classes of traders and shopkeepers. The butchers have already [by March 17, 1890] struck

24. Moreover, these representations by the Raja continued to be accompanied by expressions of ongoing public discontent; indeed, householders greeted the assessors with such "sullen silence" that the government could never actually collect the tax. While the administration delayed facing the inevitable, in part to save face and in part to await the decision of the India Office in London, eventually they acceded to public pressure. The tax was finally abandoned in 1811 (Nevill 1909a:166); not until 1860 did the British dare to institute a house tax in Banaras.

work, and other classes are expected to follow suit" (*Raj-ul-Akhbar*, 17 March 1890; *Bharat Jiwan*, 2 March 1890; both in SVN). This intrusion of tax-financed technology exacerbated the perceptions of hardship which had originated with a grain shortage. Particularly hard hit by the great rise in grain prices, Muslim weavers experienced "grave" reductions "in circumstances from the falling off in the demand for those rich fabrics for which Banaras was famous." They had also approached the Collector for financial assistance; as the Officiating Commissioner noted, they suffered more in such circumstances than did others in the city, for "they have no such resources as poor Hindus who are fed in thousands daily at the various chhatras maintained by opulent Hindus from charitable motives."[25]

While not directly related to the waterworks issue, an accompanying act of protest resulted in the city's collective self-denial of pleasure in the face of new taxation and grain scarcity. No observances were held that year of the "Water Carnival," or Burhwa Mangal, a festival in which decorated boats paraded along the river. A crowd predominantly composed of weavers ensured that this ostentatious occasion of play did not occur, by visiting the boatmen (*mallahs*) and warning them against participation.[26]

Actual construction shifted public focus to the waterworks themselves. As a symbol of encroachment, the technology being applied to water proved strikingly apposite.[27] Moreover, Banarsis watched closely the fate of a small temple contiguous to the construction site of the pumping station at Bhadauni, three miles outside of town. Early complaints noted that the engineer repeatedly entered the temple with his shoes on. Soon, however, it became apparent that construction endangered the temple itself. The Municipal Board rather cynically decided to simply permit construction to continue—thus leaving a hole all around the temple some ten feet in depth—so that the temple would "fall down of itself in the monsoon" (White Demi-official). As agitation mounted "the principal pandits and bankers of Banaras" resolved at a public meeting to send a protest memorial to the government and to seek the assistance of the Sujan Samaj of Banaras (*Bharat Jiwan*, 3 November and 1 December 1890, SVN), an organization of Western-

25. Official Report from G. W. Wright, Officiating Commissioner of Banaras District, dated 28 April 1891. IOR. L/P & J/6/301, file 907 for 1891 (hereafter Wright report).

26. Demi-official from Mr. James White, Magistrate of Banaras, to Woodburn, Chief Secy to the Govt NWP & O dated 16 April 1891. L/P & J/6/vol. 301 for 1891, file 907 (hereafter White Demi-official).

27. See Nita Kumar's discussion of the symbolic and practical significance of water in Hindu life (1984, chap. 3); and chapter 8 in this volume on the ecological significance of water for the city.

educated pleaders and clerks opposed to any form of direct taxation (White Demi-official).

Collective activities thereafter combined traditional-styled protest actions and Western-styled argumentation. At February public meetings called by the Samaj, participants protested "against the alleged improper assessment of the house tax and [urged the administration] to consider the subject of electing a better class of men as members of the Municipal Board" (a denial of the legitimacy of those who participated in British-sponsored institutions). Crowds continued to gather each day at the construction site and temple. A similar-sized body "of about 4,000 men" marched on the Collector's house to complain "of hardships caused to them by the scarcity of grain and increase of municipal taxation" (White Demi-official; *Raj-ul-Akhbar* 13 April, 1891, SVN).

Violence finally erupted when the Municipal Board refused to take action to protect the temple. As bankers and shopkeepers closed their storefronts, from five to six thousand people assembled at the temple site. Increasingly agitated, the crowd raised the cry "Destroy the machinery!" and pitched boiler and pump into the river. It is significant that the protest particularly targeted symbols of imperially imported technology. Within two years of major protests that, in the rest of U.P., pitted Hindus against Muslims (i.e., the Cow Protection riots of 1893), Banarsi crowds, instead, tore up water-supply pipes, then rushed through the city to destroy streetlamps, the telegraph office, and the railway station.

Some of these collective activities continued styles used in earlier protests: businesses closed, crowds marched to petition administrators, others gathered at the scene where their values seemed most directly threatened. While the crowd acted in ways somewhat different from those of a century earlier, this symbolic behavior still conveyed concern over shared values represented in public spaces. Crowds concerned with the threatened temple, for instance, included Muslim weavers, lower-class Hindus, and the Brahmins and pandas attached to the temple (White demi-official). That is, within these changing but still culturally continuous modes and alliances of protest, the rioters continued to reflect the two characteristics that distinguished Banarsi protests from those in other U.P. urban centers: (1) the state, rather than a perceived community of "Others," remained the target; and (2) public arena activities still operated in broadly inclusive ways, expressing protest still shared to a significant extent by the mercantile elite of the city and the artisan masses. Comparing this Banarsi protest of 1891 with an ostensibly similar one in Kanpur in 1913, for instance, we can see the importance of these distinguishing characteristics (for full description of Kanpur 1913 riot, see Freitag 1989, chapter 7). Where, in Banaras, a protest that had begun over a temple had been rerouted against the technology of the state, in Kanpur the protest (over the road routed through part of a mosque) evolved into a dramatic and influential statement on the "martyrdom" of Indian Islam. Where in Banaras the symbolic enactments of protest centered on destroying streetlamps and telegraph equipment, in Kanpur they included processions of mourning and the rebuilding of a section of the mosque.

While the Banarsi style of protest remained distinctive over the nineteenth century, however, it was changing as well. The "structure-in-process" elements of symbolic public actions trace these changes. Most important, in contrasts between the agitations of 1809–1811 and that of 1891, we can begin to discern, between the lines of eyewitness descriptions, an increasing gap between the actions of the crowd and those of the Banarsi elite. Unlike 1809, for instance, descriptions of the crowd in 1891 suggest that no upper-caste Hindus joined the lower-class crowds who gathered at the temple or marched on the Collector. While there may still have been hinge individuals or groups who connected protest meetings and these crowd actions, they are less visible by the end of the century (perhaps the most prominent was Raja Shiv Prasad).

The gap between lower-class and upper-class residents of the city widened even more in the early twentieth century. Other chapters in this volume suggest that the period directly preceding the 1930s may have proved critical in this process (see Introduction to Part 1). As Kumar has documented, perhaps the most dramatic example is the Nakkatayya festival (designed around the moment in the Rāmlīlā when Rām cuts off the nose of a demoness). From a festival of reversal in which "antisocial" behavior was expected and condoned for those who marched in the army of the demoness, it first became sanitized, then suffered the withdrawal of elite patronage. Other festivals and events were affected as well, including Burhwa Mangal and even Muharram, which in Banaras had been observed not only by Sunnis and Shias but also by Hindus (N. Kumar 1984).

This process of separation did not begin within a religious frame of reference as it generally did in the rest of U.P. Instead, connected primarily to the growth of nationalism, it was played out in public arenas as a division between upper and lower classes. Yet a large proportion of the lower-class urban population in Banaras was Muslim: most of them weavers, they lived "a hand to mouth existence . . . without exception dependent on the good will of their Hindu employers."[28] The dramatic

28. Copy of a letter No. 118/D.M. dated February 23, 1931, from the District Magistrate, Banaras, to the Commissioner, Banaras Division. IOL & R, L/P & J/7, vol. 75 for 1931, p. 573.

shift in public arena relations, the unprecedented separation of activities patronized by the elite from those participated in by the lower classes, thus had implications for relations between religious groups as well:

> For a period extending beyond the memory of living man Benaras appears to have been free of instances of severe communal disorders although periodically small disturbances have occurred owing to the close proximity of Hindu and Mahomedan sacred places. In 1930, however, signs of increasing [tension] became apparent. In that year two movements came to the fore. On the one hand there was a very pronounced Hindu movement represented by the Congress volunteers and on the other hand there was a Mahomedan movement represented by the Tanzeem organization. A violent clash between the two communities was narrowly averted at the Ram Lila at the end of September.[29]

The ironic and sudden shift in Banaras to an apparently communal style of popular consciousness in 1931 could not be expressed in more symbolically significant terms than the 1931 riot there. The narrative is quickly told. The autumn of 1930 witnessed intense boycotting by Congress of educational establishments, which attracted a strong contingent of student supporters. These, in turn, concentrated on picketing schools, as well as cloth and liquor shops in Banaras. Agitation declined, however, after Congress was declared an illegal association in October, although intermittent pressure continued to be applied to cloth and liquor shopkeepers. In January activity resumed with enthusiasm when the Government of India released the All India Congress Committee. During the picketing in February, Congress volunteers beat a customer in the shop of Agha Muhammad Jan; he called the police in, and the volunteers were arrested. That night Agha Muhammad was severely injured on his way home. Before he died he named as his attacker a student from Banaras Hindu University, head of the Congress student volunteers. Two violent outbursts accompanied Agha Muhammad's funeral procession; one by a crowd awaiting the body near Victoria Park, another by those accompanying the body in procession. The latter had taken offense that Hindu merchants' shops remained open as they passed; their destruction of goods and shops symbolically mirrored the violence exerted by their opposites, the Congress volunteers who had picketed liquor shops. Three days later groups of Hindus retaliated during Friday prayer, choosing as their site of attack the Gyān Vāpī mosque (which had attracted the attention of the Gosains in 1809).

Certainly on the face of it, this conflict looks much the same as ones

29. See IOR. L/P & J/7 vol. 75 for 1931, which includes riot reports and U.P. Legislative Council Proceedings for February and December, 1931.

occurring in these years in Kanpur or Bareilly—involving a Hinduized Congress, alienated Muslims, and sacred spaces (see Freitag 1989, Part 3). What had happened in Banaras in the 1920s to change its own style of collective protest so that it matched, so much more closely, that of other urban centers? I would argue that two simultaneous and complementary processes had altered the relationship of state and community expressed in Banaras's public arenas. First, the question of who possessed the moral authority of the state had become clouded. While in other parts of U.P. the nationalists' claims to state power had led them to attempt to claim authority from the British colonial state, this proved more problematic in Banaras. There, the British had never succeeded in wresting moral authority from the Maharaja and his mercantile supporters. Thus the new nationalist claims challenged the previous integrative understanding achieved between the triumvirate and the lower-class residents of the city. Second, as essays in this volume and Kumar (1984) have documented, a separation of elite and popular culture had developed, which became reflected in public arena activities. The public culture of the lower classes that remained, after elite patronage had been withdrawn, revolved around identities that alternated between class and religion, depending on the particular historical context at the moment.

Not least important in this process was the impact of the depression on the interrelationship between Hindu merchants and lower-class artisans. While we have no detailed studies of this development, we do know, for instance, "that all the ills of the handloom industry . . . came to a head after the world economic crisis of 1929–30" (Fact-Finding Committee 1942:20). "The severe trade depression which has prevailed since 1929 has seriously reduced the average earning capacity of the handloom weaver . . . accentuated by the relative increase in the cost of yarn on account of the protective duty" (Tariff Board Report of 1932:70, quoted in Fact-Finding Committee 1942:20). This materially affected the relationship between weavers and the merchants who functioned as their supply sources and selling agents. To the extent that the relationship had previously included certain protections and benefits for the weavers, we may assume that this economic interdependency was imperiled by the inability of middlemen to protect weavers from economic distress; we certainly have indicators that there were shifts in this period in the shares of the market enjoyed by artisans of particular products (e.g., N. Kumar 1984:45). This social dislocation fortuitously coincided with the reintroduction of Congress nationalist agitations. As Nehru later observed, "The Civil Disobedience movement of 1930 happened to fit in[,] unbeknown to its own leaders at first, with the great world slump in industry and agriculture" (quoted in G. Pandey 1978:155).

Significantly, much of this nationalist agitation in Banaras was expressed in a very particular vocabulary, that of reformism. This development should not surprise us; from the eighteenth century the city had been dominated by a "code of piety and restraint," to use the description of Hindu-Jain merchant culture employed by Bayly (e.g., 1983:385). Banaras Hindu University served as a base for those interested in agitation in the city, hence the prominence accorded to student activists, and a recognition of the collective authority assigned to Hindu scholars in the city. Reflecting reformist values, then, nationalism in Banaras came to be expressed in efforts to curb consumption of alcohol, to remove excess from public festivals: that is, to Sanskritize expressions of Banarsi personal and collective culture. The extent to which elite patronage encouraged this development can be traced, for example, in essays in this volume on drama, the Hindi movement, and religious oratory. Arguments for sanitizing the festivals were sketched out in the pro-Congress *Āj:*

> The aim of Lilas is to educate the public through the teaching of . . . Rama and other pure characters. . . . It is essential for such important Lilas to be pure. Two Lilas are specially splendid here: Bharat Milap and Nakkatayya. . . . Such shameful scenes should be completely stopped. The organizers of Ramlila can stop them in one day. If educated young men would make groups and plead with the makers of floats, these corrupt scenes could be done away with.[30]

Although these values were supported by the elite of the city, they did not appeal to lower-class Muslim artisans, who, as we have noted earlier, made up almost one-fourth of the population. Their search for alternatives led them to public arena activities that focused either on lower-class interests and values (see N. Kumar 1984; chaps. 5 and 6), or on Islam. Fittingly, the form of Islam they supported also reflected reformist influence. Baba Khalil Das "for several months previous to these riots was organizing the Muslims of Banaras, mainly of the lower classes, to adhere more to Islam and to religious practices." In Benin Park and other Muslim quarters of the city, as well as in Victoria Park,[31] the Baba organized his listeners into "processions which paraded the town til late[,] night after night singing and preaching Islam." These followers carried symbols to testify that they belonged to the Tanzim movement, including green badges, distinctive uniforms, and flags. When challenged by the magistrate—who cited Hindu complaints that Tanzim was aimed against them—the Tanzim organizers

30. 17 October 1920, p. 7; quoted in N. Kumar 1984:282.
31. See reference to the group of mourners who attacked from Victoria Park, above.

published a list of "objectives" for the movement that emphasized social and religious reform. The government felt that it could not object.[32]

The economically and socially unsettled context, then, had dislocated the interrelationship of Banarsi communities. These changes were played out in political terms in the competition between Congress agitations and Tanzim, which in Banaras were as much expressions of conflicting class values as they were of conflicting religious identities. Collective violence extended the competition to riots occurring around the murder of Agha Muhammad Jan; these, too, came to be seen as communally motivated. Yet such communally oriented unrest is perceived even now as an aberration in the normal pattern—as is indicated in the oral history cited by residents, who date participation by Hindus in Muharram as being commonplace "'before 1930s,' 'before the Hindu-Muslim riots'" (N. Kumar 1984:316).

Thus the processual shifts in the relationships in Banaras could reflect class or religious differences, depending on the context. But the legacy of the eighteenth century remained. In an effort to nullify such shifts, symbolic acts were organized. Staged in public arenas, these attempted to heal the rift in shared culture. In two town meetings led the following week by Pandit Malaviya, Raja Moti Chand, and others, "resolutions were passed deploring the communal riots, expressing sympathy with the sufferers and deciding to raise funds for repair of temples, mosques, shops and houses that had been damaged and for compensation of the injured." On the following night, "a large number of Mahomedans congregated in the Town Hall grounds where pan, illaichi and garlands were distributed to them by Raja Sir Moti Chand (whose idea this was), Dr. Bhagwan Das and other Hindu gentlemen. This may be regarded as the formal end of an outbreak."[33]

CONCLUSION

In Banaras, then, state and public structures had been integrated symbolically through the person of the Maharaja and, as modern political forms emerged, the merchant elite allied with him. The Hinduized cultural style of the city had been shaped by the values and cultural patronage of merchants and other intermediary groups, who had maintained close ties through the hierarchically structured Banarsi society. Developments in the 1920s and 1930s strained these ties, however: among the most important of these developments were economic dislocation from the world depression, accompanied by an effort to ensure the moral authority of public arena activities through a Sanskritization

32. U.P. Legislative Council Proceedings for December 15, 1931, pp. 146–50.
33. L/P & J/7/75, pp. 580–81.

of popular culture. Alienated lower-class artisans instead developed their own collective activities, which ranged, depending on the context, from festivals staged by and for themselves to Islamic reformist activities such as Tanzim. The change should not be overstated: a shared culture of public arenas still exists in attenuated form today, in which activities featuring the Maharaja of Banaras continue to be seen as "significant" events shared by both elite and lower classes. Nevertheless, many public arena activities are created, organized, and sponsored from within the lower-class culture of the city—a measure of the changes in the processual nature of collective activities which has developed over the last century.

In this context, it is not insignificant that scholars have documented a significant expansion in recent years of a wide variety of collective activities staged publicly in Banarsi neighborhoods. As the welter of festivals around Rāmlīlā attests, the moral authority of the public arena is shared now among competing actors: the Maharaja, the state, and those interested in expressing lower-class community identity.

EIGHT

Land Use and Environmental Change in the Gangetic Plain: Nineteenth-Century Human Activity in the Banaras Region

Robert G. Varady

> *Kashi is not of this earth, they say, no part of the terrestrial globe, for that rests on the thousand headed serpent Ananta; whereas Benares is fixed on the point of Shiva's trident. While it is in the world and at the very center of the world, it is not attached to the earth. No earthquake is ever felt within its holy limits, and in consequence of its peculiar position it escaped destruction during a partial overwhelming of the world.*[1]

According to Brahmin tradition, as illustrated above, Banaras transcends its earthly locale. But in a more temporal sense, this ancient city has been an integral part of its Gangetic environment.

Other chapters in this volume have placed Banaras within a social context and discussed its cultural identity. Preceding chapters have illustrated that the character of modern Banaras has been shaped by its unique institutions, its inhabitants, and their activities. But without an adequate resource base to sustain and nourish urban vitality, the city could not have prospered. Here I shall examine the nature of the relationship and dependence between Banaras and its physical surrounding. During the mid to late nineteenth century these surroundings were subjected to pressures that altered the landscape and affected the ecological balance. The following will identify major agents of change and describe and assess their effects.

HISTORIOGRAPHICAL PERSPECTIVE

Current historical writing on South Asia is richly diverse and broad in scope. But until recently the topics treated often lay within narrow confines. Historical study of environmental change usually remained outside the realm of traditional inquiry. A brief discussion of its antecedents, therefore, can serve as a contextual marker.

1. The passage is a composite of observations by the early nineteenth-century chronicler, Walter Hamilton, and a modern scholar, Diana L. Eck (Hamilton 1820:306; Eck 1982:24).

Historians of South Asia, inheriting the legacy of colonial writers, tended to focus on political might and associated personalities. For some this interest led to studies of the roots of such power. In India with its vast arable terrain and agrarian society, influence required control over land tenure and revenue. Accordingly, during the 1960s numerous historians explored Indian agriculture and reconstructed the dynamics of administration, settlement, and rural economy. The resulting studies, while innovative, still converged on powerful individuals, elites, and institutions and the influence they wielded. Residents, rajas, zamindars, talukdars, *jagirdar*s, and moneylenders; prominent clans, Hindu temples and *math*s, Islamic orders, and British government filled the pages of these works.

More recently, beginning in the early 1970s, some scholars have turned their attention from land *revenue* to land *use*. This new approach has resulted in two noteworthy shifts of emphasis: (1) from affluent elites to peasants and workers, and (2) from wealth and productivity of land to alteration of land and the attendant consequences. These shifts have yielded new historical studies of forest administration; change in the vegetation; development of roads, railways, and irrigation; sanitation and public health; and urbanization. The topics can be categorized as ecological, since in each case a primary concern is the relationship of the environment to social, economic, and political affairs.

During the past dozen years scholars such as Bayly, Clark, Hagen, Haynes, Klein, Ludden, McAlpin, Oldenburg, Richards, Tucker, Whitcombe, and Yang have addressed various aspects of this relationship.[2] In the process, they have created an abundant and fascinating literature, which contributes significantly to our understanding of colonial India. A notable feature of this historical work is that it is rendered from exceptionally scanty resources. Ecology and environmental degradation interested early observers, chroniclers, or administrators only insofar as these processes affected productivity, revenue, and public health. Historians investigating environmental change and its impact, therefore, have needed to examine sources particularly closely and employ them creatively.

2. C. A. Bayly (agriculture, ecology, trade, and politics); Alice W. Clark (demographics, mortality); James R. Hagen (land use, vegetation change); Edward S. Haynes (agriculture, vegetation change); Ira Klein (agriculture, population, public health); David Ludden (ecology, irrigation); Michelle Burge McAlpin (railroads, famine, vegetation change); Veena Talwar Oldenburg (urbanization, sanitation, public health); John F. Richards (cash cropping, vegetation change); Richard P. Tucker (forest administration, devegetation); Elizabeth Whitcombe (public works, irrigation, environmental change); Anand Y. Yang (peasant economy, migration). This list is certainly not exhaustive, but it illustrates the types of subjects being studied. Specific titles are cited in this chapter.

BANARAS: CHARACTERISTIC FEATURES

In nearly all ways the Banaras region has been a prototypical central-Gangetic-plain tract dominated by a large urban center. For centuries Banaras shared many of the characteristics of such relatively nearby locales as Patna, Ghazipur, Allahabad, Faizabad, Lucknow, Kanpur, Agra, and Mathura. In common with these towns, Banaras originated in ancient times, lay on a Gangetic river, exploited a fertile hinterland, developed into a commercial hub, grew to formidable size, and served as an administrative capital during Mughal and British times. And in withstanding the innumerable political changes that followed its establishment, Banaras shared with its neighboring communities a strong sense of survival. For all of northern India, as C. A. Bayly has observed, lay in a zone precariously exposed to variable and volatile climate (Bayly 1983:74).

To facilitate survival in the face of political and environmental uncertainty, Banaras relied on a strong sense of identity. Like Hindu Ayodhya (Faizabad), Prayaga (Allahabad), and Mathura, and Buddhist Pataliputra (Patna), Banaras remained a major center of religious pilgrimage. Accordingly, the city has been associated with Hindu religious sympathies throughout its existence (*Calcutta Review* 1864:256).

But at least two factors distinguished Banaras from its sister pilgrimage sites. First, Banaras was centrally situated astride the Ganges and at the hub of an ancient subcontinental road network, within reach of western, central, and eastern India. More important, Banaras was perceived as the center of the world, the place of creation, the holiest spot on earth, the ultimate destination for all Hindus (Eck 1982:5–6; Havell 1905). Endowed with such authoritative religious sanction, it easily surpassed other centers in importance. And benefiting from ecclesiastical supremacy, Banaras achieved secular prominence. From its alleged founding in the sixth century B.C., the city grew to be one of northern India's largest by the early nineteenth century.[3] The Banaras region, moreover, was one of the most densely populated on the subcontinent, more than twice as dense as any European country.

It is Banaras's religious uniqueness, its resultant preeminence, and its magnetic appeal which set it apart from otherwise similar regions. These features have shaped the development of the city and its envi-

3. Bishop Heber believed that Banaras was at that time larger than any European city (Heber 1828, 1:270). Hamilton grossly exaggerated the population at 582,000 (Hamilton 1820:306). J. Thornton suggested that the district's population was 200,000 (Shakespear 1848:5). The 1872 census enumerated 175,000 in the city (Plowden 1873). Whatever the precise figure, Banaras's population was one of north India's largest throughout the century.

rons. Dense population and continuous pilgrimage have spawned persistent environmental consequences.

ENVIRONMENT AND RESOURCE BASE

Banaras is situated approximately halfway between Delhi and Calcutta, in the heart of Gangetic India. Since Mughal times the city has been within a district (zillah) of the same name. During the nineteenth century the district was the size of Rhode Island (2,600 square kilometers). The district came under British domination by 1781, administered first within the Bengal Presidency, then the North-Western Provinces, and finally, the United Provinces of Agra and Oudh.

Physical Features

The Banaras region lies within the Middle Ganges Plain; more specifically, at the southwestern corner of the lower Ganges-Ghaghara doab (interfluve).[4] The terrain throughout this portion of the Ganges drainage basin is flat and slightly elevated (eighty meters). Banaras city is situated fifteen meters above the Ganges, on its northern bank. The river constitutes the southern border of the district, until just before the city. At that point the Ganges turns northward, bisecting the district before reaching Ghazipur. Within this portion of its course the Ganges has flowed stably for centuries, but seasonal flooding leaves small lakes (*jhīls*), used for irrigating crops. At the eastern extreme of the district the Ganges is joined by the Gomati and then the Karamnasa River.

Thus drained by these three rivers and a number of smaller streams, the district has possessed abundant surface-water resources. One consequence is the region's rich alluvial soils, deposited by the Ganges and its Himalayan tributaries. Textures vary from sandy to loamy to clayey, but virtually all the soils of the region have been fertile and nonsaline. Additionally, alluvial soils tend to be porous and are able to store groundwater. Aquifers exist, and the water table is generally high, permitting exploitation for drinking and irrigation. Nevertheless, in the nineteenth century groundwater surveys did not exist for the region, and tube-well irrigation was infrequent.

In addition to possessing fertile soils, the area lies within a zone of adequate average rainfall. Nevill, writing in the 1909 district gazetteer, listed the mean annual precipitation for 1864 to 1906 as 1,000 millime-

4. Much detailed information exists describing the geography and physical features of Banaras district in the nineteenth and twentieth centuries. This section is not comprehensive, but merely provides a sketch of salient characteristics. For further data, see Hamilton 1820:302–9; Hunter 1881, 1:532–34; Nevill 1909a:1–23; R. L. Singh 1971:183–251; R. N. Mishra 1977:1–22.

ters. But as Bayly has noted, variation was extreme, ranging from a minimum of 540 milimeters to a maximum of 1,620 (Nevill 1909a:22; Bayly 1983:74). There is little evidence to suggest that the region's climate has changed significantly over the past several centuries.[5] Impressed by the soils and water resources of the area, early Europeans traveling through the district and nineteenth-century administrators were uniformly sanguine about the region's agricultural potential.

It is likely that this agricultural potential was in fact intensely exploited. Already by 1820, according to the region's first gazetteer, nearly all arable land was being cropped. Tens of centuries of human occupation and agriculture had stripped most of the original vegetative cover (Hamilton 1820:306–8; R. L. Singh 1971:204–5). According to Nevill, by the turn of the century no forest remained, only jungles. In the remaining jungles, wildlife population and diversity has been reduced appreciably. Banaras, Nevill wrote, had become one of the province's poorest districts in regard to fauna. Once abounding in predators, deer, and antelope, the area retained only a rich bird population (Nevill 1909a:14, 17–18).

As for nonrenewable natural resources, the Banaras region has been poorly endowed. The alluvial plain is devoid of all rock but limestone (*kankar*) and contains no minerals. *Kankar,* gravel, sand, and clay were the only useful products. These were employed in road building, construction, brick making, and the manufacture of lime. The nearest commercial stone quarries were in nearby Ghazipur, Chunar, and Mirzapur (Hamilton 1820:303; Purser 1859:563; Nevill 1909a:15–16).

Agriculture

As was indicated above, Banaras is situated in a zone that Bayly has termed agriculturally "stable."[6] During Akbar's time the region was known to be productive, and records indicated that urbanization induced substantial increases in cultivated area during the seventeenth century. In the 1820s Hamilton and Heber noted continued extension of cultivation, increased demand and high prices of cropland, and shortage of grazing land. By 1848 Shakespear reported in his statistical survey that 71 percent of the district's area (181,000 hectare) was culti-

5. Climatologists and social scientists continue to debate whether climatic change or human activity has been primarily responsible for desertification and other forms of environmental degradation over the past century.

6. There is ample documentation on agricultural conditions in the Banaras area, so this section simply summarizes important characteristics. As with all statistics on nineteenth-century India, figures must be treated skeptically, owing to faulty enumeration techniques and reporting. For additional figures, see Hamilton 1820:302–5; Shakespear 1848:154–62; Colvin 1872; Nevill 1909a:31–49; Administration Reports 1896–1900; Ganguli 1938:1–110; Whitcombe 1972: A. Siddiqi 1973.

vated (Shakespear 1848:154; Heber 1828:255; Bayly 1983:76; Sinha 1974). Although Hamilton's and Shakespear's figures can hardly be considered accurate, it is probable that cultivation did increase throughout the region during this period.

Given the high proportion of sown acreage, further extension was limited. A survey in 1878–1882 showed a mere 2.4 percent increase in sown area.[7] In the district gazetteer Nevill considered even this small gain illusory, attributing it to previous underreporting of terrains in the Ganges floodplain. The reported total remained essentially stable through the rest of the century, prompting speculation that the limits of cultivation had been attained. As late as 1931 cultivated area stood officially at 74.7 percent of total area (Nevill 1909a:31–32; Ganguli 1938:6).

From the beginning of British rule, then, agriculture seemingly occupied most of the arable terrain. Cultivation, as was shown, was being extended to its limits. Two additional developments may be noted; irrigated area was increasing, and more and more land was being double-cropped. Heber, on his approach to Banaras, observed that the country was "imperfectly" irrigated. Certainly he saw no canals, for there were none. The topography of this portion of the Gangetic plain has not been conducive to canal irrigation. First, the large rivers lay too far below their adjoining banks. And in some places outlying water-deficient areas were at higher elevations than the rivers. In the absence of canals, growers employed floodwater, *jhīls*, tanks, and wells to irrigate their crops. The earliest semireliable estimates of irrigated area are from the late 1880s. From then to the end of the century, one-quarter to two-fifths of cultivated land (40,000 to 64,000 hectares) reportedly was irrigated, depending on annual rainfall—the less rain, the more irrigation (Nevill 1909a:42–43; Administration Report 1896–97:6).

In contrast to the early extension of cultivation and irrigation, double-cropping remained uncommon until the latter part of the century. Shakespear fails to mention this mode of farming. Nevill, without indicating the source for his estimates, lists the 1840 double-cropped area as a mere 2,700 hectares (1.7 percent of cultivated area). By 1886, according to his data, the acreage had risen twelvefold, to 34,000 hectares (21.3 percent of cultivated area). If subsequent figures are indicative of general trends, this area fluctuated widely each year. In the four growing years beginning in 1896–97, 31,000, 24,000, 37,000 and 35,000 hectares were reported to be double-cropped. Like irrigated areas,

7. The actual acreage figures appeared to decrease (from 180 to 161,000 hectares), indicating earlier overestimation of cultivation. The amount of land cultivated reportedly increased from 71 to 72.7 percent of total (Nevill 1909a:31).

these areas varied in proportion to annual rainfall, and observers have noted a close correspondence between irrigation and double-cropping (Nevill 1909a:32–33; Administration Reports 1896–1900:6; Ganguli 1938:45). Since both practices were associated with improved yields, exaggerated reported increases may have served to illustrate progress under British rule.

The crops grown in Banaras were typical for the region. Fertile soil, good drainage, and adequate rainfall enabled rice cultivation. Rice remained the leading crop throughout the century, covering as much as two-fifths of the terrain sown in the autumn (*kharīf*). Barley was the next most common superior grain, followed by inferior grains and pulses (*jowār, bajrā,* peas, *gram,* and *arhar*). In addition to grains and pulses, major crops were sugarcane, which decreased in importance, opium, fodder, fruits, and vegetables (Nevill 1909a:34–41; Administration Reports 1896–1900:6).

Livestock, an important component of the agricultural system, were not generally bred locally, but were imported and purchased at fairs. Although pastureland was limited, the numbers were nevertheless great. Cattle were not enumerated until the end of the century; by then the census listed some quarter million bulls, bullocks, cows, buffalos, and calves. Another 100,000 sheep, goats, mules, donkeys, and horses made up the remaining livestock population. Changes in this population are difficult to estimate, but Nevill believed that the number of goats and sheep had declined, mostly because of extended cultivation (Nevill 1909a:19–21; Administration Report 1896–1900:6).

Human Population

Human population size in the various districts greatly interested British administrators. Yet for most of the nineteenth century census figures remained quite unreliable, often suggesting puzzling or contradictory trends. Recently developed techniques have permitted historians to adjust these figures in order to estimate more accurately some characteristic features of population. Alice Clark employs some of these methods to analyze fertility and mortality trends in Banaras (Clark 1986).

Of interest here are the effects of population pressure on environmental resources. As was noted above, the population of Banaras city was one of northern India's largest throughout the nineteenth century. As a result, the district's population density was listed as the highest in the province. In 1872 it was estimated at more than 300 persons per square kilometer, a representative figure for most of the century. As in much of north India, the measured population of Banaras remained stable, having attained a relative maximum by mid-century. In fact the low variation in this measure (300 to 350 per square kilometer) seems to mirror the stability of cultivated acreage, which was also reported to have achieved a relative maximum at that time (Shakespear 1848: 12–13, 154; Plowden 1873:xxv, 2–3; Hunter 1881:532; Nevill 1909a: 83–85).

It would be deceptive, however, to suppose that stability in population size and cultivated acreage precluded pressure on land. On the contrary, population increase may have been limited by poverty-induced high mortality, rather than by prosperity. Crowding, land scarcity, and low productivity likely exerted continuous pressure on available resources (Klein 1974:194–99).

ENVIRONMENTAL ALTERATIONS

Physical environment is subject to continuous modification from natural causes, such as tectonic forces, temperature extremes, fire, wind and river erosion, vegetation processes, and animal action. No less than natural agents, human actions can result in widespread and irreversible environmental change. Many of these processes occur insidiously over prolonged periods. In such instances, the effects often are cumulative. Other human actions may be more sudden and concentrated, resulting in immediate and noticeable change.

Whether continuous or precipitous, these human actions frequently have degraded the affected environment. The nineteenth century, a time of British consolidation in Gangetic India, witnessed both types of phenomena. Traditional environmental alterations continued, while imported technologies introduced new, more threatening agents of change.[8]

Agents of Continuous Change

The Banaras region, like most of the Gangetic plain, has been continuously populated for some twenty-five hundred years. In the process local residents established an important urban center, maintained its streets and buildings, connected it to other communities, supplied its industrial needs, and fed its population. Throughout this time human occupation affected the surroundings in a variety of ways.

Land Use and Resource Depletion. Over the centuries while Banaras city grew, its inhabitants exploited the adjoining terrain and its resources.

8. For similar analyses of environmental change in Africa, see, for example, Advisory Committee on the Sahel 1983; and Gritzner 1981.

They cultivated the land to near capacity; hunted wildlife; raised livestock; and extracted timber, fuel, stone, sand, clay, and groundwater. Those materials and supplies which were unavailable locally were imported and brought in by road or stream.[9]

As Banaras continued to grow and prosper, surrounding lands strained to supply the rising needs of the city and its visitors. By 1800 the region's resource base was becoming strained. The town itself was built on the site of the legendary Forest of Bliss. But by the nineteenth century, according to Diana Eck, townspeople retained only memories of the once luxuriant woods. One central neighborhood came to be known as the "Cut-Down Forest" (Eck 1982:29).

In the countryside, too, large tracts had been cleared for farming, leaving only isolated trees and planted groves. The extensive fields in place by 1800 blanketed what was once a natural habitat of dense forest. The original cover included stands of valuable trees, such as sal (*Shorea robusta*) shisham (*Dalbergia sissoo*), jaman (*Eugenia jambolana*), mahua (*Bassia latifolia*), ber (*Ziziphus jujuba*), pipal (*Ficus religiosa*), neem (*Azadirachta indica*), *pāgun* (*Bombax ceiba*), banyan (*Ficus bengalensis*), tamarind (*Tamarindus indica*), and babul (*Acacia arabica*). Apart from isolated stands near villages, few of these trees remained in the nineteenth century. Grasses and shrubs, too were continuously grazed and harvested for manufacturing bricks (Troup 1921, 2:8; 3:4, 147, 231; Stebbing 1922–26:glossary; R. L. Singh 1971:204).

This large-scale devegetation of the countryside put an enormous strain on the soil resources. No longer compacted by broad root systems, topsoils were swept away by floods and blown off by winds. And depletion of leguminous trees and shrubs deprived the earth of the nitrogen-fixing action of roots, leaving soils deficient in bacterial content. The stresses of repeated cropping and traditional shallow tillage minimized soil rotation, accelerated nutrient depletion, and reduced fertility. Finally, with firewood growing scarcer owing to devegetation, manure was employed as fuel, reducing the input of fertilizer (Crooke 1897:322–34).

The familiar cycle of deforestation, reduction of biotic diversity, soil erosion, reduction of fertility, and decline in productivity certainly was manifest in the Banaras region. The responses to this process were equally common: extension of cultivation to terrains previously considered "wastelands" or "barren" lands; increased irrigation; or multiple cropping.

9. For discussions of land-use changes elsewhere in colonial India, see Richards and McAlpin 1983:68–94; Tucker 1983:146–66; Richards, Hagen, and Haynes 1985: 699–732.

As was noted above, British observers asserted that Banarsi cultivators increasingly adopted irrigation and multiple cropping techniques. Reclamation of barren land also occurred but was severely limited by availability. Already by the end of the eighteenth century most such land had been plowed and sown. Although varying perceptions of what constitutes wasteland render that term ambiguous, figures confirm that little such terrain was available by the 1840s. It appears that the amount may have decreased somewhat between 1848 and 1872 (from 19 to 15 percent), but stabilized at the latter level through the rest of the century. There is some evidence, meanwhile, that farmers were simultaneously abandoning previously productive lands. In 1788 Jonathan Duncan had already noted the desertion of formerly productive fields. Nearly a hundred years later the provincial land-settlement report of 1872 estimated that 5 percent of cultivated land had been recently abandoned (Shakespear 1848:169–70; Colvin 1872, Appendix:16; K. P. Mishra 1975:85).

In sum, despite an ostensibly stable population, pressure on farmland was demonstrably heightening. The measures taken to compensate for erosion and soil depletion aggravated the situation. Each of the three alternatives employed—reclamation, irrigation, and multiple cropping—was intensive, adding further stresses on finite resources.

Religious Activity and Environmental Pollution. The processes described above were principally rural and resulted from land use intensification. Their effects were to degrade a limited resource base. Such phenomena have been common to many societies and typical for much of agrarian north India.

Considerably less typical and far more controversial have been the alleged ecological consequences of religious activity in Banaras. As the principal focal point of Hindu pilgrimage and the leading center of Brahmin ritual observance, Banaras has drawn enormous numbers of visitors throughout the year and on special occasions. It is principally the Ganges that affords this distinction, and it is on its banks that most activity occurs.

Primarily as a result of the vast number of participants, the riparian environment has been affected. Crowding, sewage generation, and the influx of ill visitors have caused serious public health concern since the beginning of the colonial period. Other actions may have contributed in small ways to riverine pollution, but their effects have been consistently overstated. Throughout British rule, Hindu religious practices were termed responsible for the pollution of the river and the adjoining areas.

For centuries throngs of pilgrims have converged on Banaras. In addition to the daily arrival of Hindus seeking personal salvation, seasonal fairs or eclipses drew occasional crowds of a hundred thousand or more. These congregants required food, drink, and other substantive needs, adding further pressure on overtaxed resources (Hamilton 1820:301; Nevill 1909a:66–67; 1909b:85; Oude and Rohilkund Railway 1875:1169; 1878:1057; K. P. Mishra 1975:67). Their contribution to local degradation has been notable, but environmental pollution due to their presence has been a lingering concern. This is particularly ironic given the religious function of Banaras: to purify and cleanse ritual pollution. Diana Eck notes the importance of running water in general, and of Ganges water in particular, in purification. But this notion, as she recognizes, is unrelated to microbial purity (Eck 1982:216–17).

To colonial observers, eager to introduce Western hygienic principles, Hindu practices appeared unclean. Perceiving a real threat to their own health and well-being, Europeans eagerly condemned certain ritual acts. With the advent of the germ theory, objections that had been merely moral were accorded scientific sanction. By the 1850s a burgeoning body of literature joined religious criticism with social outrage and fear (*Calcutta Review* 1848:404–36; 1851:156–230; 1864: 253–94).

Foreign observers repeatedly cited the infectious nature of practices they found deplorable. Of these, perhaps the most shocking to British sensibilities was the Hindu custom of cremating the deceased and casting the remains into the Ganges. In theory cremation itself was not objectionable. In practice, however, it was noted that scarcity of fuel often resulted in incomplete cremation.[10] The consequences of partial consumption aroused an outpouring of righteous anger among British residents and administrators. They were appalled by "scorched trunks" thrown into the Ganges to float toward the sea "in a state of horrible decomposition, poisoning the water of narrow streams, or sickening the eye, whilst tumbled in the torrents of the Ganges" (*Calcutta Review* 1848:416; 1851:222). Additional concern was aroused by other aspects of cremation: decomposing corpses awaiting cremation, and burial of incompletely burned bones and dead animals.

On several occasions colonial officials attempted to intervene, citing public health considerations. In one such action in 1868 the Banaras Municipal Board asserted its right to close burning ghats or cemeteries deemed problematic. Within days, after reassessing the effective threat posed by the ghats and gauging popular feeling, the Magistrate repealed the proclamation (*Bharat Jiwan* [23 September] in SVN for 1912:898).

10. Perhaps the earliest Western notice of this phenomenon was by Jean-Baptiste Tavernier (1676, 2:231).

Disposal of human and animal bodies in the Ganges was another source of English consternation. Although these acts occurred, it is unlikely that their volume could have appreciably affected the quality of the water. Modern residents of Banaras, including the present Maharaja, insist that the above allegations are inaccurate and overstated (N. Kumar communication, March 1986).

But if the burning ghats were unlikely sources of pollution, other long-term human actions measurably affected the quality of the Ganges and its banks. The dumping of waste, sewage, and industrial effluent into the river; the bathing of persons and cattle; the washing of clothes and vessels; and emissions of noxious smoke represented real hazards. In addition, poor drainage allowed accumulation of stagnant waters in ponds (*Bharat Jiwan* [1 May] in SVN for 1893:191; Gopalkrishnan 1985:3–4). As early as 1864 the *Calcutta Review* noted that the "water is of deadly influence, and the vapour from which fills the air with fever-breeding and cholera-breeding miasma." The journal called for immediate steps to improve drainage in the vicinity of the ghats (*Calcutta Review* 1864:293).

Sensitized by the press, authorities and local residents feared the percolation of toxins and pollutants into the groundwater. In response, in 1886 concerned citizens formed a local pollution-prevention society, the Kashi Ganga Prasadini Sabha. The Sabha's primary objective was to eliminate river contamination, undertake a drainage scheme, and purify drinking water. Nevill reported that the project was completed in 1892. But in February 1893 the *Bharat Jiwan* of Banaras complained that drains had yet to be constructed and that wastewater continued to flow through city streets. And K. S. Muthiah, writing in 1911, confirmed the failure to implement its scheme (Nevill 1909a:262–63; Administration Report 1896–97:167; *Bharat Jiwan* [6 February] in SVN for 1893:69; Muthiah 1911:164).

Perhaps the greatest immediate threat to public health was posed by the streams of crowds from throughout India, whose mere presence acted as a universal disseminator of infection. Since Banaras has been a magnet for persons wishing to die in the holy city, many visitors have been aged and generally in poor health. Accordingly, the city has been subjected to epidemics of cholera, typhus, and plague, and to chronic outbreaks of malaria and dysentery. The mortality rate from disease remained one of the province's highest through most of the century (*Shola-i-Tur* in SVN for 1871:704; Administration Report 1896–97: 6–7; Klein 1974:210).

One supposed factor contributing to epidemics was cited in an 1848 issue of the *Calcutta Review*. According to the author, sick and infirm individuals, "anxious for their rewards in the next life," were being encouraged to set up residence in crowded, damp, unsanitary huts by the river. The article decried this practice, which it termed "ghat murders." Certain that the custom hastened death, the author warned against the "unsalutary" effects of the vicinity (*Calcutta Review* 1848:404–36).

While similar issues surfaced in other cities, the status of Banaras as the country's leading pilgrimage center heightened British sensitivity to the polluting aspects of religious activity. Sentiments shared by Europeans elsewhere in India found clear expression in Banaras. Certainly, fears of contamination and deadly disease were not baseless. But many observers were unable to distinguish between the real dangers to public health resulting from unsanitary practices and assumed threats posed by certain ritual acts. The resulting mix of missionary righteousness and scientific theory directed unexpected attention to the environment, but the attendant rhetoric often obscured the nature of the problem.

Modern Agents of Change

The processes described in the preceding section resulted from ongoing practices, not from any sudden changes. Ninteenth-century improvements in transportation facilitated travel and thus increased pilgrimage to Banaras. The greater traffic placed additional stress on local resources and accelerated riverfront pollution. The modern transportation network and other newly established public works also had a more direct impact on regional environment. Roads and railways were superimposed on the rural landscape. First their construction, then their operation and maintenance, resulted in pronounced and usually permanent modifications of the terrain (Varady 1981, 1985a, 1985b).

Public Works Construction. From the 1830s to the end of the century northern India underwent a period of intense public-works construction. Cognizant of the benefits of improved communications, the ruling East India Company initiated a vigorous program for road improvement. Even earlier, in the first years of British administration, Collector Jonathan Duncan had authorized road improvements near the city. The first major project was a complete renovation of the old imperial highway connecting Bengal to the Punjab. Renamed the Grand Trunk Road, this throughfare was graded, then metaled (paved) with crushed limestone. Other provincial roads to Ghazipur, Jaunpur, Allahabad, Mirzapur, and Sasaram soon received similar attention. During the decade 1840–1850 alone the British constructed some fifty thousand kilometers of roads throughout their Indian territories (Abbott 1846:56–74; Sanyal 1930:3).

Even before the provincial road network was completed, the government turned its attention to railways. By the mid-1840s entrepreneurs and administrators had discussed the idea in England, and soon they took the first steps to actuate their decisions. By 1854 the first train of the East Indian Railway Company (EIR) left Howrah to initiate the line that would parallel the Grand Trunk Road to Delhi and the Punjab.

For the next eight years the tracks crept toward Banaras. Construction continued northward through Bengal up to the Ganges, and then via Bhagalpur and Patna along the southern bank to Mughal Sarai, across the river from Banaras. After the completion in 1862 of the 860-kilometer route from Calcutta, construction continued on to Mirzapur, eventually to join the branch descending from Kanpur (East Indian Railways 1853–63; *Bengal Past and Present* 1908:55–61; Varady 1981:51).

Building roads and railway lines was both labor intensive and resource intensive. In each case, after rights of ways were secured the surface needed preparation. Gangs of thousands of *bēldār*s (laborers) from the nearby countryside were hired. Housed in meager shacks, underfed, and overworked, these laborers commonly were ill. Epidemics among road and rail gangs were frequent and destructive. There are records of camps of ten thousand losing up to a third of the workers to cholera and other diseases. Worse, the contagion often spread to nearby towns (Varady 1981:188–89; United Provinces Public Health Dept. 1903).

The work teams were employed to clear jungles of vegetation, excavate tree roots, flatten roadbeds, lay gravel or limestone, dig drainage ditches, construct embankments and berms, and bridge streams and *nalla*s. Additionally, railways required placement of creosoted sleepers (ties) every seventy-five centimeters (Bingham 1858:3–21; Muir 1858: 277–79).

The quantities of materials required were prodigious. To complete eighty kilometers of railway tracks in Banaras district, the contractor executed 1.2 million cubic meters of earthwork and 6,000 cubic meters of brickwork; in addition, 210,000 cubic meters of ballast were used. Limestone, gravel, and sand were obtained from neighboring floodplains and carted to the sites. The effects of such large-scale removal have not been studied, but elsewhere quarrying of stream beds has seriously affected flow and drainage patterns (Purser 1859:563; Davis 1985:1–5).

In the case of rail lines, vast amounts of timber were used for sleepers. Based on figures used by Tucker for the Rajputana Railway, tracks in Banaras district alone would have required a hundred thousand sleepers. Although some hardwood sal remained available in the region, stands were too depleted to furnish the railways's needs. Instead, the wood was imported, either from England or from the upper

Gangetic tracts northeast of Delhi, forested with deodar (*Cedrus deodara*). The demand on Himalayan timber resources was thus considerable, especially since sleepers needed replacement every five years (Tucker 1983:160–61; East Indian Railways 1856:505; 1859a:531).

Although timber was not available in Banaras, local firewood and charcoal supplies were employed to make burnt-clay ballast and to bake the bricks used for bridges, stations, and culverts. In any case, as a Calcutta correspondent wrote to the *Times* in 1862, "the want of India is daily becoming more and more a want of wood." In the Banaras region, as in the rest of northern India, the railways clearly were agents of deforestation (East Indian Railways 1859a:531; 1862:555).

Road and Railway Operation and Maintenance. Devegetation and resource depletion were two important results of road and rail construction. Once in place, the networks continued to affect the surrounding environment. First, roads and railways, by their very presence, interrupted natural landscape. In the interest of efficiency and directness, they both sought linearity. Rather than skirting streams, it was cheaper to cross them. In nearby Son district the EIR alone constructed 240 bridges and culverts in 1860. Primary and secondary roadways also crossed rivers and streams whenever they were encountered. These interruptions interfered with drainage and flow patterns. Runoff characteristics, already altered by devegetation, were further disturbed. Instead of being stored in soils, water was lost to agriculture. Puddles and ponds were formed alongside thoroughfares, providing breeding habitats for disease vectors. Similarly, culverts silted up with lost topsoil. After heavy monsoon rains rushing waters created gullies and arroyos, further hastening soil erosion (East Indian Railways 1859b:1189–90; *Colvin Gazette* [15 April] in SVN for 1890:251; *Hindostan* [15 August] in SVN for 1902:527; Varady 1985b:2–3: Whitcombe 1972:12).

Partly from weather extremes, and partly from the relentless action of hoofed, wheeled, or rail traffic, surfaces needed constant repair and maintenance. Like the original construction, this activity required extensive labor and supplies. Metaled roads were paved smooth with ten centimeters of pounded limestone. Before long the road rutted and became impassable, demanding full resurfacing. Railbeds were similarly affected by rain, flooding, and heavy wear. Patrolling work crews added ballast and replaced broken and rotten sleepers. Upkeep of the nineteenth-century transportation network placed a continual drain on stone, sand, and timber resources.

Locomotives, moreover, required fuel. For much of the century engines burned wood, procured wherever it was sold, preferably in the vicinity of the route. So serious was the problem of supply that in the early 1860s, the *Calcutta Review* reported, "a great cry arose that the Railway must soon stop for want of fuel." Though perhaps exaggerated, the concern was valid, as Indian railway operation consumed enormous amounts of firewood (50,000 kilograms per kilometer per year, according to one estimate). In some areas roots were burned as fuel. And by the mid-1860s some railway firms were calling for private fuel-wood plantations to meet growing demand. Only the advent of cheap coal enabled the EIR and other lines to continue operating (*Calcutta Review* 1867:262–327).

CONCLUSION

During the nineteenth century the area surrounding Banaras was rich in renewable natural resources and remained one of northern India's relatively prosperous areas. In most ways it typified the Gangetic plain. The region's one outstanding feature, its appeal to pilgrims, magnified similar conditions manifest elsewhere. A look at human-induced environmental change in Banaras, therefore, offers some insight into the processes of resource degradation and environmental pollution throughout the Gangetic belt.

Like other urban centers, Banaras relied heavily on local production of food, fuel, and building materials. The perpetual requirements of the resident population, coupled with the need to provide for millions of visitors, strained the capacity of the countryside to respond to the demand. Colonial agricultural officers, seeking to modernize farming and increase yields, introduced techniques that intensified cultivation. Production rose, but by the end of the century fertility was being depleted, and available cropland was diminishing. In the process, vegetation was being cleared to permit sowing, and soil erosion accelerated, threatening to reverse recent gains in productivity.

Other modern innovations brought further degradation of the rural environment. Road and rail construction scarred the watersheds and altered drainage patterns. And once in place, the new transportation systems continued to exact a toll from the surrounding terrain. Maintenance materials and fuel wood were constantly required, and the action of traffic hastened erosion.

Nearer the city, the presence of festival-goers, pilgrims, and residents affected the riparian environment. The quality of the river and of groundwater deteriorated, and epidemic disease vectors found hospitable habitats. Environmental health became a widely discussed issue among Europeans. Fear of disease prompted concerted attacks on religious practices seen as morally and hygienically unacceptable.

In sum, the effects of human activity in the Banaras region underlined the city's dependence on local resources and ecological stability. The prosperity and physical well-being of Banarsis required abundant agricultural production, a steady supply of construction materials, and a relatively disease-free environment. As this chapter has suggested, these conditions generally deteriorated during the nineteenth century.

NINE

The Ecology and Cosmology of Disease in the Banaras Region

David Arnold

The cities of northern India have begun to engage the attention of historians at several levels of enquiry and analysis—as centers of trade and political activity, for example, or as focal points for the cultural and religious life of the region. Some interest has been shown, too, in the nature of the colonial impact upon these cities and how British ideas and policies affected their physical form and social order. Anthony D. King in his study of "colonial urban development" in Old and New Delhi, J. B. Harrison in his "sanitary history" of Allahabad, and Veena Talwar Oldenburg in her account of the "making of colonial Lucknow" have pointed, inter alia, to the importance of Western ideas of health and sanitation in the transformation, or attempted transformation, of urban north India during the colonial period (King 1976, Harrison 1980, Oldenburg 1984). As Oldenburg in particular shows, the British determination that the city "must be clean" was a matter of more than simply sanitary significance: it revealed underlying colonial attitudes and preoccupations; it touched upon political cultural concerns that were central to colonial control in the urban setting.

There is much to be gained from such an approach, not least for the political insights it gives to a subject too often regarded as obscurely municipal and dry as dust and for the depth of the colonial divide it displays. In a modest way this essay attempts a similar line of enquiry for another north Indian city, Banaras. But there is a danger in concentrating on a single city or artificially divorcing it from its natural hinterland, and this would seem especially constrictive in discussing diseases and epidemics that commonly ignored municipal limits and city boundaries. The health of Banaras was, like that of other cities of the north Indian plain, closely bound up with the region as a whole and with extensive networks of pilgrimage, trade, communications, and migration, as well as with its status as a major Indian city.

Like cities elsewhere in India, those of the upper and middle Gangetic plain were, no doubt, subjected to a greater degree of medical and sanitary intervention during the colonial period than was the countryside around them. One crude index of this was the far higher level of expenditure by municipalities than district boards on public health in the late colonial era. Upwards of 35 percent of municipal income in the United Provinces (U.P.) was spent in this way, compared with a bare 3 percent of the considerably smaller funds available to the district boards (ARDPH 1925:49; ARDPH 1947:8–9). The cities of the region also maintained political and cultural traditions that could be strongly resistant to Western medicine and sanitation. Anticipated hostility from the urban centers of the North-Western Provinces—from Lucknow and Kanpur especially—and from Delhi forced the moderation in 1898 of the government's proposed antiplague measures, even though similar ones had already been imposed upon the towns and cities of western India.[1] Clearly, then, there were respects in which cities stood apart from their hinterland, and the cities of the north were distinctive even in colonial eyes. What is important, however, is to set this distinctiveness against or alongside the aspects of disease and medicine which tied a city like Banaras to its wider environment.

Diseases, and especially the epidemic diseases on which the first half of this essay concentrates, thus help to locate Banaras within a series of interlocking temporal, spatial, and cultural relationships. To some extent, this might be called a Braudelian approach, in that it gives emphasis to the long-term trends, as well as identifying some of the shorter-term cycles and fluctuations to which Banaras and the region were exposed. There are some evident parallels here with C. A. Bayly's broad perspective on north Indian trade and politics in the "age of British expansion," though the nature of the sources available forces one to concentrate mainly on the years after 1870, rather than, as in Bayly's book, on the earlier period (Bayly 1983). But I share the reservations of those critics of the Braudelian *longue durée* who, like Jean Chesneaux, feel that such "massive history is in reality a passive history," resulting in a "depoliticized long run" (1978:98). Where Braudel sets out with only a "dialectic of space and time (geography and history" (1975:16), this essay sees a need to juxtapose the long-term trends and influences with more immediate consequences of human activity and will. If people are to be understood as active agents in the making

1. Government of India, Home (Sanitary), May 1898, nos. 421–567, National Archives of India (NAI); Home, August 1898, nos. 777–813, NAI.

of their own history, and not merely as the inert recipients of whatever long-term changes might be forced upon them, it is necessary to consider the perceptions that they bring to their own situation. It is one of the arguments of this chapter that both the ecology and the cosmology of disease have a place in the social history of health in the Banaras region.

THE SEASONALITY AND PERIODICITY OF EPIDEMIC DISEASE

As a major urban center, Banaras under British rule shared many of the problems and consequences of overcrowded and insanitary conditions, contaminated water supplies, inadequate sewage disposal, and deficient public health services which were the lot of other colonial cities in India and indeed of cities throughout the world during the period. Although by the 1930s Banaras and similar Indian cities were better equipped with hospitals and dispensaries, piped water and sewers, vaccinators and sanitary inspectors than the rural populations around them, urban morbidity and mortality rates remained, nonetheless, disproportionately high. This was particularly so in the case of Banaras. In U.P. as a whole during the quarter-century 1901–1925, urban mortality averaged 45.08 per thousand inhabitants: for the province generally (the towns included) the rate was 37.44. The figure for Banaras district, 33.74, was slightly below the provincial average, but for its principal city the mortality rate was a startling 57.88, considerably above even the average urban level in U.P. (calculated from five-year averages in ARSC 1906, 1911, 1916; ARDPH 1921, 1926). Banaras was one of the most deadly cities in northern India. The explanation for this was not just that Banaras was a populous and insanitary city: it was also a consequence of its geographical, cultural, and epidemiological context.

Never a purely random occurrence, disease reflected the material conditions of human existence, the influences of climate, vegetation, and landscape, and the characteristics of social organization and cultural behavior. Each disease enjoyed its own distinctive, if to human eyes enigmatic, relationship to the human environment. In a region where the seasons were well marked and the advent or failure of the monsoon rains had such momentous consequences, the incidence of disease (especially epidemic disease) bore a striking correspondence with the annual and seasonal variations in rainfall, temperature, and humidity.

Seasonality was more evident in some diseases than in others. In Banaras district, as in much of eastern U.P., the period following the onset of the monsoon in mid to late June was generally the unhealthiest time of the year, with mortality from "fevers" (a vague description but probably including a preponderance of deaths from malaria)[2] and dysentery particularly high. In general, the dry months from December through March and April were the healthier part of the year. But it was during the dry season that smallpox, a disease widely prevalent in eastern U.P.,[3] made its annual appearance. Smallpox flourished with the spring—so much so that further east in Bengal it was known as *basanta rog*, the "spring disease" (Wadley 1980:38). It reached its greatest intensity between March and June, fading rapidly with the arrival of the monsoon, though in and around Banaras, with its year-round pilgrim traffic, this seasonality was not as extreme as in most rural areas. Temperature and low humidity influenced the activity and contagiousness of the smallpox virus, but social and cultural factors had some effect too. In a display of physical mobility rarely associated with a predominantly peasant society, the early months of the year were a time for travel and festivity—the time for Holi, pilgrimages, and weddings. These elaborate and intersecting networks of human mobility created social conditions conducive to the spread of a disease dependent upon human contact for its survival and transmission. Commenting upon this aspect of smallpox seasonality, the provincial Sanitary Commissioner observed in 1886 that

> those who travel much about the country, cannot but be struck with the continual movement going on amongst the population of the country at this time of year. When the rains set in, smallpox diminishes in severity, partly, no doubt, from the cessation of intercourse which follows the increased difficulties of communication, and perhaps partly owing to the influence of moisture upon smallpox contagion. (ARSC 1886:26)

Despite increasing medical intervention—the number of vaccinations in U.P. rose from under three-quarters of a million in the 1870s to two million in the 1940s, with about a third of the population of Banaras district so protected by 1939 (ARSC 1878:27; ARDPH 1939:55)—the seasonality of the disease remained unaffected. In 1871, 70 percent of smallpox deaths occurred between March and June; figures for 1940 show 50 percent of deaths during the second quarter of the year with a further 25 percent in the first quarter (ARSC 1871:9; ARDPH 1940:7). During the ten years 1925–1934, 54 percent of smallpox deaths in Banaras district fell in the months of April to June and 21 percent between January and March (table 9.1). Although the city of

2. E.g., in 1925, when 765,799 of 875,594 "fever" deaths were attributed to malaria (ARDPH 1925:14).

3. In 1940, 44 percent of smallpox deaths in U.P. occurred in the Banaras and Gorakhpur divisions (ARDPH 1940:7).

TABLE 9.1 Average Monthly Mortality in Banaras District, 1925–34

	Jan.	*Feb.*	*Mar.*	*Apr.*	*May*	*June*	*July*	*Aug.*	*Sept.*	*Oct.*	*Nov.*	*Dec.*
Cholera	1	5	20	87	110	164	141	140	56	26	31	14
Smallpox	21	20	36	64	67	71	44	18	4	3	7	20
Plague	50	74	97	31	6	–	–	1	3	2	6	16
Fever	1,022	978	1,167	1,436	1,474	1,539	1,430	1,577	1,592	1,556	1,519	1,311
Dysentery/Diarrhoea	48	43	61	81	79	68	72	123	96	73	78	77
Respiratory Diseases	157	149	166	181	184	162	138	186	171	144	169	165
Totals	1,299	1,269	1,547	1,880	1,919	2,004	1,825	2,045	1,922	1,804	1,810	1,603

SOURCE: *Annual Reports of the Director of Public Health of the United Provinces,* 1925–34; appendix B.

Banaras held only a fifth of the district population at this time, it was responsible for nearly 44 percent of the total smallpox mortality. Even in years when smallpox became epidemic in the countryside, the city's share remained disproportionately high.

Smallpox had a distinctive place, too, in the human life-cycle. In a land where the disease was endemic as well as periodically epidemic, few Indians reached adulthood without either surviving an attack of the disease or receiving the protection conferred by inoculation (variolation) or cowpox vaccination. The buildup of a pool of unprotected infants was thus one of the determinants of smallpox epidemicity. Across U.P. as whole major epidemics erupted every three or four years, but within a single locality the incidence was more irregular. Banaras and its environs suffered severe epidemics in 1878, 1884, 1889, 1897, 1926, 1930, 1934, 1942–45 and 1951–52 (Joshi 1965:353). Fifty percent or more of the deaths from smallpox were among children under twelve years, indicating its importance as a childhood disease. Years of smallpox epidemics were likely to be years of high infant mortality. In the interwar period, 1918–1939, about 72 percent of recorded smallpox deaths in U.P. were among those under ten, 28 percent of them among infants under one year old. However, as vaccination (and by the 1930s revaccination) became common and the disease passed through a period of low incidence between 1898 and 1925, so a large percentage of the adult population was left unprotected by either natural or artificial means. The result was a recrudescence of the disease after 1925 and a higher rate of adult mortality. In 1932, for example, the proportion of fatalities in those over ten reached as high as 40 percent (ARDPH 1932:14). Smallpox was losing something of its customary status as a childhood disease.

Like cholera, a disease with which it shared certain characteristics in the Indian context, smallpox not only followed a seasonal cycle but also formed part of the multiple crises occasioned by war, drought, flood, and famine. A disease that thrived in a dry climate and possibly profited from the undernourishment and debility of its human hosts, smallpox became particularly widespread in famine years or in the season following the failure of a monsoon (Rogers 1926:6; ARSC 1878: 23a). The wanderings of the famine-struck in their search for food, work, and water, their congregation at relief centers and in towns like Banaras (where religious and princely charity, as in the famine year 1878, could confidently be expected),[4] further favored the spread of the disease. Although the Banaras division escaped relatively lightly

4. *Report on the Scarcity and Relief Operations in the North-Western Provinces* 1880:76. Banaras was also the city of the goddess Annapurna, "She of Plenteous Food" (Eck 1983:161, 163–64).

from the famines of the late nineteenth and the early twentieth century, conditions of scarcity or famine in 1877–1879 and 1896–1897 contributed to the high smallpox mortality in those years. Conversely, the virtual absence of famine after 1908 was a factor in the marked decline in smallpox epidemics until the Bengal famine of 1943 helped fuel a later resurgence. The disruption caused by the two world wars and their political sequels was similarly registered in high levels of smallpox mortality, whereas the depression years, perhaps because they were a time of low grain prices with little administrative and social dislocation, were remarkably free from major epidemics.

Taking an even longer perspective, it is possible that smallpox and cholera, despite their certain antiquity in India, became especially prevalent as a result of the political disruption of the eighteenth and nineteenth centuries, with the accompanying invasions, large-scale troop movements, and economic disorganization (cf. Nicholas 1981: 33–34; Arnold 1986). If this was so—and the evidence is as yet too patchy to be more than suggestive—then the advent of colonial rule in northern India may have caused or coincided with a significant upturn in epidemic mortality similar to that attributed to colonial intervention in sub-Saharan Africa in the late nineteenth century (Kjekshus 1977). The growth of international and internal trade, the establishment of new and more rapid forms of transportation, and the increased mobility of wage labor, as well as the part British economic policies may have played in accentuating the effects of famines in the late nineteenth century, may all have contributed to making the colonial period a time of abnormally high epidemic mortality, a trend only gradually and partially countered by increasing medical and sanitary intervention (Klein 1972, 1973; Whitcombe 1972; but cf. Stone 1984). Viewed in this broad perspective the colonial era in northern India might itself be regarded as constituting a single epidemiological cycle.

SPATIAL AND SOCIAL ASPECTS OF EPIDEMICS

Smallpox maintained a relatively direct and straightforward relationship with its human hosts, one factor that aided its containment and eventual eradication in the 1970s. But other diseases had a more complex relationship, closely linked to environmental and sanitary conditions or mediated through insect and animal vectors. Plague offers one example of this. The spread of plague across northern India in 1899–1901 has been identified with the distribution of the rat flea *Xenopsylla cheopis,* thought to have originated in Egypt's Nile valley and to have been introduced into India through the expanding traffic between the two countries which followed the opening of the Suez Canal in 1869. Plague tended to be most intense in areas like eastern U.P.—Banaras and Gorakhpur divisions were among the worst affected localities in rural India (Rogers 1928:45)—where *X. cheopis* had become naturalized: it was less prevalent in much of eastern and southern India where *X. astia* remained more common (Hirst 1953:348–71). Reaching eastern U.P. in 1901–2, plague at first caused heavy mortality in urban areas. There were two thousand plague deaths in Banaras city alone in the years 1901, 1903, 1905 and 1911. Thereafter, however, urban mortality from the disease fell, rising above a hundred deaths only in 1912, 1917–18 and 1947, while in the countryside it became firmly entrenched. This can be read as evidence of the greater effectiveness of antiplague measures in urban Banaras, but *X. cheopis* also found a securer ecological niche among the rodent population of the densely inhabited, grain-rich countryside. Like smallpox, plague had an annual as well as an epidemic cycle, though one more regionally variable. In U.P. as a whole, about 60 percent of plague deaths occurred between April and June: in eastern U.P. and Banaras, January to April was the main period (table 9.1). The reasons for this variation were linked to climatic factors and to the breeding cycles of the rats and their fleas (Rogers 1928:42–43, 58–60; Hirst 1953:260–80). The timing of the year's grain harvest had a bearing, too, providing food for rats as well as humans and, through the transportation of grain, contributing to the fleas' mobility. One factor behind the resurgence of plague in eastern U.P. between 1942 and 1947 (apart from the breakdown of control measures during wartime) may have been the massive grain movements caused by the 1943 famine in Bengal.

But plague also illustrates the importance of human vectors. The epidemic arrived in eastern U.P. in November 1899 with the return of three Muslim Julāhā weavers whose employment in the cotton mills of Bombay had ceased with the closure of the factories in that plague-stricken city. From the weavers' homes in the small town of Mau-Aima in Allahabad district, plague spread to Banaras and from there to other towns and villages in the area. Plague had also established itself in rural Bihar and was encroaching on Banaras and Gorakhpur divisions from the east. Market towns were among the first to be affected, with grain traders and handlers among the earliest victims. Subsequently, as plague moved into the villages a disproportionate number of deaths occurred among women, whose housebound lives made them more vulnerable than adult males to a disease borne by domestic rats' fleas (ARSC 1900:6a;ARSC 1901:16; Blunt 1912:43–44).

Migration from eastern U.P. to Bombay, Calcutta, Assam, and Bihar,[5] and the counter flow of pilgrims, traders, and professional men

5. "It is said . . . that there is not a single family in the Benares division which has not at least one member in the provinces of Bengal, Assam, Bihar and Orissa" (Blunt 1912:49).

from Bengal were also human factors of great epidemiological consequence. The advent and progress of the plague epidemic was but one illustration of this. The severe epidemic of dengue ("breakbone") fever that struck eastern U.P. in the early months of 1872 was traced to importation from Calcutta where it was already rampant. The first recorded cases were among passengers on a Ganges River steamer which arrived at Mirzapur on March 14, 1872; they infected coolies unloading the vessel and the disease spread rapidly. The first case in Banaras was reported on April 27, 1872—a Bengali who had come by rail from Calcutta two days earlier. From these two points of entry, dengue fever raced through the eastern districts, advancing mainly along the lines of rail and river traffic. An estimated 75 percent of the inhabitants of Banaras city were affected, though only two deaths resulted (ARSC 1872:15–16). By contrast, the influenza epidemic of 1918 reached Banaras from the west, causing rather less mortality than at Agra or Allahabad, but still raising the city's death rate to the highest annual figure (81.31 per thousand) on record (ARSC 1918:18a). Another disease, the protozoan infection known as kala-azar, spread by sand fleas, was becoming increasingly common in the Banaras area in the 1930s and 1940s, partly as a result of inroads from Bihar, but also through the return of migrant laborers from Assam where the disease was endemic (Joshi 1965:348). Cholera epidemics, too, were often attributed to seasonal labor movements between Nepal and the adjacent districts of eastern U.P. This was one explanation of the perennially high levels of mortality from cholera along U.P.'s northeastern border (ARDPH 1926:41; Banerjea 1951: 25).

Cholera offers striking evidence of the close connection between human mobility and epidemic disease. Unlike smallpox, cholera has no uniform season. In Bengal it was most widespread between October and January and again in March and April. In Bihar, Orissa, and eastern U.P. the main season fell between April and August; in Punjab it was June to August (Pollitzer 1959:55). The disease thus appeared to move westward each year along what Bryden (1869) described as the "northern epidemic highway." Banaras lay in the path of the advancing epidemics; the first cases appeared early in the year, and mortality rose steadily between April and June, before waning in September and October. Although temperature and relative humidity were important factors (Rastogi, Prasad, and Bhatnagar 1967:844–50), the curious character of cholera epidemicity also bore some relation to human mobility and especially to Hindu pilgrimage routes and seasons.

Banaras stood at a critical juncture between the pilgrimage places of eastern India—Puri, Baidyanath, and Gaya especially—and the sacred sites of the upper Ganges valley and was one of the key centers in the all-India network of temples, shrines, and religious festivals. Few pilgrims from the east or northwest failed to pass through Banaras, to visit its temples and bathe from its celebrated ghats. One party of pilgrims from Naini Tal journeyed in 1899 to Allahabad, Banaras, Gaya, Baidyanath, Calcutta, and Puri before some of their number fell victim to cholera (ARSC 1889:21). Bimla Devi, who died from the disease at Hardwar in March 1927, came from Burdwan in Bengal, visiting Gaya, Banaras, Ayodhya, and Nimsar en route to the Hardwar mela (ARDPH 1927:27A). The direction and duration of the pilgrims' journey was contingent upon many factors, including their means and devotional objectives. But the pilgrimages bore the imprint, too, of the agricultural cycle: the dry months were the period when agricultural work was slackest and thus pilgrimage most opportune. The timing of the major fairs and festivals (itself perhaps showing the influence of the agrarian calendar) was a further factor. Many pilgrims from Bengal and Bihar passed through Banaras at the start of the year to reach Allahabad in time for the Magh Mela in January–February and to arrive at Hardwar for the main bathing festival in March or early April. Many continued from there to Badrinath and Kedarnath, returning home for the monsoon and the resumption of agricultural activity (Bhardwaj 1973:219). There was a second period of festivals later in the year, during the month of Karttike (October–November), with melas at Garmuktesar near Meerut and, closer to Banaras, at Ballia, where the Dadri fair drew many hundreds of thousands of worshippers (ARSC 1901:16). But these later festivals attracted local rather than long-distance pilgrims.

From the 1860s the colonial authorities began to collect evidence linking cholera epidemics in northern India to the timing and direction of the main pilgrim flows. Banaras appeared doubly affected. Although it did not have such popular bathing festivals as those at Allahabad and Hardwar, its smaller fairs still acted as major epidemic foci, with infected pilgrims returning, as in 1924 following the lunar-eclipse fair, to such places as Deoria, Gorakhpur, and Azamgarh (ARDPH 1924:29; see also ARDPH 1927:46). Banaras was subject, too, to wider patterns of pilgrim mobility and disease dissemination. Cholera was unwittingly brought by pilgrims from Bengal to Banaras and to other religious centers in eastern U.P., such as Allahabad, and from there spread by dispersing pilgrims throughout the region. (See fig. 16 for one illustration of this.) Railroad junction as well as pilgrim town, Banaras could also be hit by cholera epidemics emanating from more distant sites, such as Puri and Hardwar. The Kumbh Melas, held at Allahabad and Hardwar at twelve-year intervals, and the intervening Ardh Kumbh Melas, by bringing together as many as a million pilgrims at a single time and place, created conditions peculiarly conducive to cholera outbreaks. The Kumbh Melas at Hardwar in 1867 and 1891 and those at Allaha-

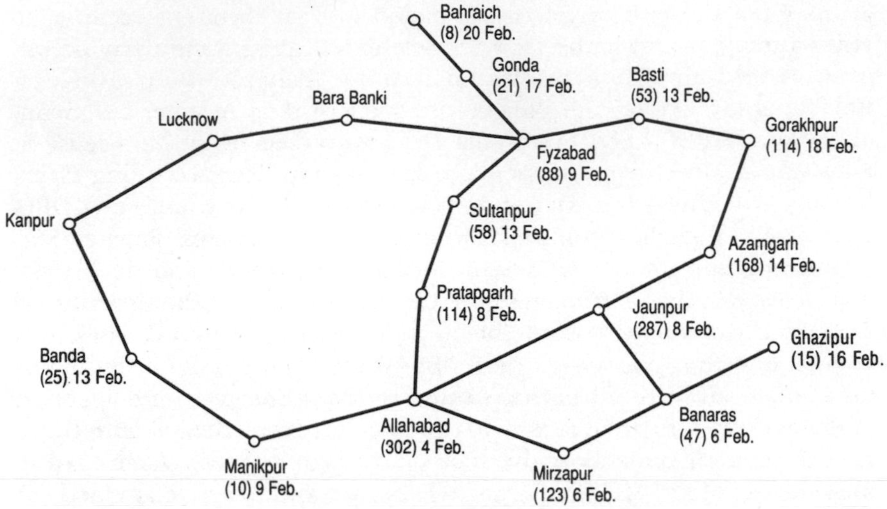

Fig. 16. Cholera deaths among pilgrims dispersing from Allahabad Kumbh Mela February 1894. Numbers after town names indicate fatalities; the date is of the first reported cholera death. Source: Annual Report of the Sanitary Commissioner of the North-Western Provinces and Oudh, 1894:30.

bad in 1894 and 1906 were seen as clear examples of the epidemic hazards of these periodic mass gatherings (Pollitzer 1959:882–85; Banerjea 1951; 28–31). As figure 17 indicates, cholera mortality in Banaras district reflected the incidence of these fairs, though it should be borne in mind that in some cases the correlation was fortuitous and the melas were not directly responsible.

As Banaras came to be recognized as a major turnpike along the "northern epidemic highway" special measures were introduced to prevent pilgrims from introducing cholera into eastern U.P. From 1927, health officials were posted at Mughal Serai (as well as at Ballia and Gorakhpur) to intercept and detain pilgrims suspected of suffering from cholera and other serious diseases. In this way fifty-seven cholera cases were detected in 1929 and sixty-one in 1930, the year of the Allahabad Kumbh Mela (ARDPH 1929:12; ARDPH 1930:21A).

Examples could be multiplied, but I hope that enough evidence has been given to suggest some of the ways in which the city of Banaras was subject to wider patterns of human mobility and mortality, or seasonal and cyclical change, and of epidemiological incidence and variation. In these respects one is struck not by the uniqueness of Banaras or by the significance of a rural-urban divide, but by the extent to which the city reflected or accentuated the characteristics of the regional society and the environment as a whole.

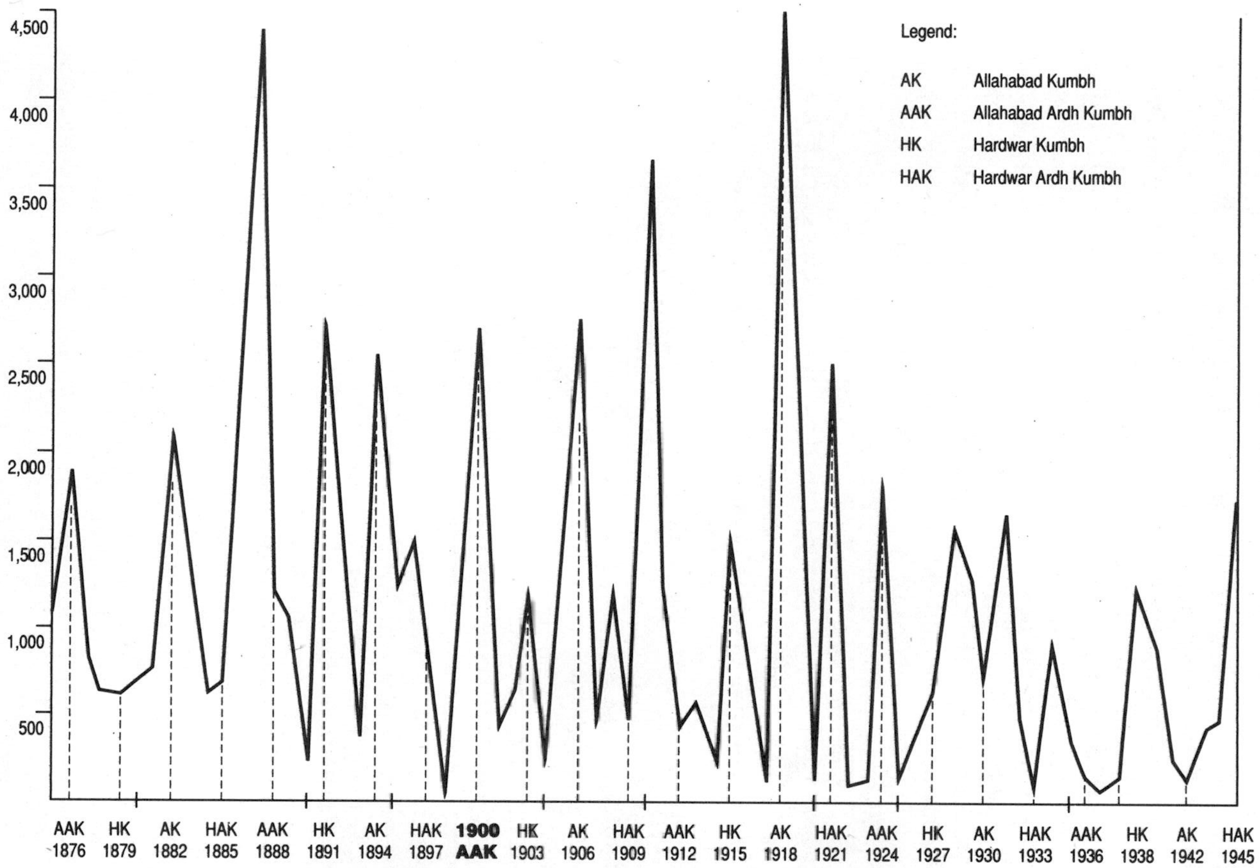

Fig. 17. Cholera mortality in Banaras district, 1875–1945. Source: Annual Reports of the Sanitary Commissioner and Director of Public Health, 1875–1945.

DISEASE, DEATH, AND CURING

Banaras had, however, a special place in Indian and even British thinking about disease, death, and curing. In the traditions of Ayurveda, Banaras enjoyed particular eminence. It was reputedly there that Dhanvantari, "physician of the gods" and "father of Indian medical science" (Stutley and Stutley 1977:75; Sukul 1974:93–94), imparted his knowledge and skills to Sushruta, the author or compiler of the *Sushruta Samhitta.* Other works of classical Ayurveda, such as *Chikitsa Kaumudi* and *Chikitsa Darshan,* were also said to have been written at Banaras during the reigns of the early kings of Kashi. From an early date, probably even before the time of Buddha, Banaras was renowned for its physicians (Joshi 1965:344). With the rise of Muslim power in northern India from the twelfth century, Banaras also became a center for the Unani system of medicine, itself evolving through interaction with Ayurveda. Fashions in medicine, at least among the elite, tended to reflect changes in political supremacy, and the advent of British rule in the late eighteenth century was soon followed by the introduction of Western, allopathic medicine. At first the British showed some tolerance, even respect, for the indigenous medical systems, but as British power grew in confidence and strength attitudes became more openly disdainful. In the Anglicization of the 1830s the East India Company withdrew its former patronage for indigenous learning, including Ayurveda (B. Gupta 1976:370); but the Rajas of Banaras, like the Kings of Delhi and the Nawabs of Awadh until the mid-1850s (Sharar 1975:97–98), remained important patrons, enabling Indian medicine to survive into the late nineteenth century, when it began to be taken up again by the middle classes. As guardians and patrons of Vedic scholarship, the Rajas of Banaras extended their support to Ayurveda as well. Though in a manner indicative of the pluralistic nature of elite culture in Banaras (Saraswati 1975:31, 52), they also employed, indeed seemed to show a preference for, Unani practitioners. The district gazetteer lists among those who served the Rajas the *vaidya* Trimbak Shastri and the hakims Muhammad Hadi (born 1825), Muhammad Jaffar (born 1854), and Mazhar-ul-Hasan (born 1867), each of whom served in turn as court physician (*tabib-i-khas*) (Joshi 1965:34–35). With the establishment of the Banaras Hindu University in 1916 (with its own Medical College and Institute of Medical Sciences) and with the accession of the Congress to ministerial power in U.P. in 1937 and again in 1946, there was a revival of Ayurveda, yet Western medical education and practice remained in the ascendant (Joshi 1965:360; Sukul 1974:102, 115).

But Ayurveda and Unani by no means exhausted the medical specialists of whom Banaras could boast. Hindu and Muslim astrologers, for example, were consulted about the cause of physical and mental ailments and recommended various charms and observances to free their clients of their afflictions (Pugh 1981). Clearly, popular ideas about disease and curing were intimately bound up with wider beliefs about malevolent and benevolent forces affecting human fortunes, health, and happiness. Banaras and eastern U.P. also produced specialists of a more evidently practical kind, such as Jarrahs, or barbers, who performed minor surgical operations (Joshi 1965:345). The region was also one where smallpox inoculation had long been practiced: indeed, the Brahmins of Banaras seem to have been celebrated practitioners of the art (Holwell 1767:8). One early-nineteenth-century report (interestingly, by a Muslim, Nawab Mirza Mehadi Ali Khan) tells of a Brahmin at Banaras who performed a kind of pre-Jennerian cowpox inoculation in the name of Sitala, the smallpox deity; but this cannot have been common (*Asiatic Annual Register* 1804:98–99). In eastern U.P. generally, inoculators were commonly men of the Mali, or gardener, caste who traveled about the countryside plying their trade during the smallpox season and then returned to their agricultural pursuits as the disease waned—another example of the connection between the agrarian and the disease cycle. Despite British attempts to suppress inoculation in favor of Western vaccination, the practice continued in and around Banaras until at least the 1880s and probably, more discretely, for some time thereafter.[6]

In Banaras, however, curing or preventing disease was not the province of medical specialists alone. The city itself, with its temples, shrines, ghats, and wells, was widely believed to possess a special capacity to cure, protect, and assuage suffering. To some extent this was the mark of the eminence of Kashi as one of the most sacred places of Hindu India. The abode of Shiva as Vishvanatha, the point where the Ganges flowed north toward the Himalayas, Kashi was an exceptionally auspicious place to die or to be cremated. "Death, which elsewhere is feared, is there welcomed as a long-expected guest. Death, which elsewhere is polluting, is there holy and auspicious" (Eck 1978:191). One path of "curing" offered by Banaras was thus escape from physical and earthly suffering through the certain salvation (moksha) that death in the city conferred. Since disease and suffering were associated with sin and divine displeasure, spiritual and ritual solutions were as commonly sought as any medical therapy. The waters of the Ganges, which could cleanse the soul of all sin, could also by association free the body of its physical afflictions. Pilgrims bathed in the Ganges and took the water home with them from a belief in its curative and protective properties,

6. For Brahman inoculators at Banaras in the early nineteenth century, see correspondence in the Board's Collections, F/4/186, no. 3906, India Office Records, London (IOR); and for further discussion of inoculation, see ARSC 1878:30, 24A; ARSC 1885:47; Greenough 1980; Nicholas 1981:27–29.

as well as for its ritual uses. The sick traveled to Banaras in the hope of being cured or at least of dying in the holy city. Others visited it in fulfillment of vows made during illness. Like Allahabad, Baidyanath, and a number of other sacred places in northern India, Banaras was a site where lepers congregated, whether in the hope of finding charity or from a belief that the holiness of the place would rid them of their disease. It was also to Kashi that thousands fled from eastern India and the Deccan to escape the plague in 1900–1, believing that the dreaded disease could never enter so sacred a place (Nevill 1909a:27). The religious reasons that made Banaras such a magnet for the sick and dying also help to explain why the mortality rate in the city was so perennially high.

In addition to its all-India prominence as a center for pilgrimage and worship, Banaras was also a "microcosm of Indian life, customs and popular beliefs" (Havell 1905:80). As such it attracted to itself ideas about disease and curing which belonged to a wider Hindu or Indian cosmology of belief and explanation. The "disease godlings" (Crooke 1926:114f.) of the folk tradition here commingled with the Sanskritic deities and Ayurveda of the literati and the elite (the so-called Great Tradition) in ways that defied neat division and compartmentalization. The worship of Sitala could be taken as one illustration of this. The Brahmin inoculators of Banaras invoked the goddess for the success of their operations; and the city seems to have long been important as a center for her worship (Wadley 1980:51–53; Nicholas 1981:30–31). As one of the shakti (female) forms of Shiva, Sitala was perhaps thought deserving of special representation in Shiva's city, and shrines to the goddess were often to be found in close association with Shaivite temples in Banaras (Havell 1905:113). But Sitala also remained part of the folk tradition from which she had originated (Eck 1983:171–72), and her popularity as an object of worship in the city may have reflected the prevalence of smallpox in the region and the reverence with which the goddess was widely regarded.[7]

Other forms of popular disease propitiation and curing were to be found in Banaras. Vidyarthi in his recent study of the "sacred complex" of Kashi (1979:39, 54) lists thirteen deities with special attributes, including healing and protective powers. Apart from Sitala, these include Khokhi Devi for coughs and colds, Jwarharneshwar Mahadeo for

7. But again the exceptionality of Banaras should not be overdrawn. The worship of Sitala was widely observed in northern India in the spring months, and festivals and pilgrimages to Sitala shrines occurred in a number of different places. See Jackson and Fisher 1883:104; ARSC 1881:25; *North Indian Notes and Queries* 1891, I (1):5; 1895, IV (12):202.

fevers, and Kal-Bhairava for warding off ghosts and malevolent spirits. Eck (1983:194) also identifies Bhairava as a popular protector against illness and misfortune. Other sources list tanks, wells, and shrines with similar properties. The Amrit Kupa (or "well of immortality") was said to be associated with the cure of skin diseases, including leprosy. It was also called after Dhanvantari, who was said to have thrown his medical bag into the waters, giving them their curative powers—an interesting link between Ayurveda and popular belief (Joshi 1965:345; Sherring 1868:219; cf. Eck's description of the Kala Kupa, "the well of time," 1983:262–63). At the Nag Kupa, or "serpent's well," an annual festival was held at the time of the Naga Panchami in Shravana (July–August) partly in order to obtain protection from snakebite (Fisher and Hewett 1884:139; Eck 1983:264).

Some of these protective or curative rites had their place in the annual cycle of the seasons, when a particular disease, like smallpox (Wadley 1980:37–38, 42–43), or when snakebite (Eck 1983:264), was most feared. But the annual cycle was interrupted or punctuated by the greater calamities of major epidemics when special measures were employed. On such occasions in eastern U.P., "scapegoats" were used to drive out epidemic disease, or offerings dedicated to a disease deity were passed on from village to village in the hope that the pestilence would move away with them. Sometimes as much noise and clamor as possible was made in a bid to scare off the demon of disease (*North Indian Notes and Queries* 1891, I (6): 111, 119; I (8): 127; Crooke 1968, chap. 3). Disease-driving rituals at times occasioned local clashes, for the inhabitants of contiguous neighborhoods did not always take kindly to the disease deity or demon being driven into their territory. On the night of March 10, 1901, as the plague epidemic closed in on Banaras, gangs of "rowdies" gathered in Dashashvamedha and Sigra in the south of the city to repulse the "scapegoat" of the disease driven out from Chaitganj (*Bharat Jiwan* [11 March] in SVN for 1901).

Such rituals gave emphasis to the continuing gulf between popular Indian beliefs concerning disease and the ideas held by the colonial administration. The depth of that divide, and its political as well as cultural connotations, was further exemplified by the rumor widespread in Banaras and other towns of northern India at the time that the British were deliberately spreading the plague through the poisoning of the municipal water supplies in order to rid themselves of a troublesome populace or to break down caste and religion (*Kalidas* [2 June] in SVN for 1900). But it is also indicative of the variety of responses provoked by epidemic disease that other Hindus and Muslims offered up prayers for protection in the city's temples and mosques and that the editor of the Banaras newspaper *Bharat Jiwan* turned to the Ayurveda to find sanction for the British policy of evacuating infected towns and villages (*Bharat Jiwan* [11 March] in SVN for 1901).

A COLONIAL COSMOLOGY OF DISEASE

Disease and medicine were also powerful and enduring influences in British attitudes toward Banaras, though the nature of their influence varied over the long period of British involvement with the city and, to some extent, with the professional outlook of the individuals concerned. There was a disposition among European observers, medical men and missionaries especially, to denigrate Banaras as a Hindu sacred place by pointing to the contrast between its alleged sanctity and purity and its actual squalor and want of sanitation. Typical of this attitude was the following diatribe from the Reverend M. A. Sherring in the 1860s:

> Threaded with narrow streets, above which rise the many storied edifices for which the city is famous, it is, without doubt, a problem of considerable difficulty, how to preserve the health of its teeming population. But, when we reflect on the foul wells and tanks in some parts of the city, whose water is of deadly influence, and the vapour from which fills the air with fever-fraught and cholera-breeding miasma; when we consider the loathsome and disgusting state of the popular temples, owing to the rapid decomposition of the offerings, from the intense heat of the sun; when we call to mind the filthy condition of nearly all the by-streets, due to stagnant cesspools, accumulated refuse, and dead bodies of animals; and, when, in addition, we remember how utterly regardless of these matters, and incompetent to correct them, is the police force scattered over the city, the difficulty becomes overwhelming. (Sherring 1868: 181–82)

One can see in this description the almost total reversal of the Hindu understanding of Banaras. Even its sacred and curative waters have become "foul wells and tanks" whose effects are described as "deadly" rather than life-giving or life-preserving. The Ganges at Banaras was subjected to a similar sanitary critique (cf. Eck 1983:216–17). It was also characteristic of Sherring's late-nineteenth-century British standpoint that he believed that the solution to the city's insanitary and insalubrious state lay in the creation of an efficient and purposeful municipal corporation. Under such a body, he claimed, "we should soon see a thorough transformation of the city," and the execution of "radical changes, so imperatively demanded in this region of palaces and filth, in this hot-bed of periodical disease" (Sherring 1868:183).

The British attack upon the insanitary, disease-ridden nature of Hindu pilgrimage centers and sacred places like Banaras was in part an assault on Hinduism itself and an expression of the disgust, loathing, and incomprehension many nineteenth-century Europeans felt for Hindu India (Arnold 1986). Representing their own ideas and methods as rational and scientific, they characterized the whole of Indian medicine, religion, and popular belief as superstitious and irrational. Medicine and sanitation were among the means by which they sought to demonstrate and to implement their belief in the innate superiority of Western civilization. Through medicine and sanitation the West constituted itself the rival and the antithesis of Indian modes of thought and action.

But, for all the strength of their convictions, the British were forced to recognize the force of Indian cultural and social resistance to Western innovation and intervention. They could not simply ignore the importance of Banaras as a Hindu place of pilgrimage and worship. And, as an alien regime, in a vast and populous land, they were alert to the political risks in attempting too forcefully to impose their own ideas upon a wary population. At first, however, because Banaras was one of the earliest and largest Indian cities to pass under British control, and because it was such an important center for the Hindu religion, the British were keen to make the city a showpiece of their benevolence and enlightenment. Among the first institutions established at Banaras were those twin temples to the healing arts—a hospital (originating with subscriptions collected by Jonathan Duncan, the Resident, in 1787) and a lunatic asylum (1809). By 1814 the "native hospital" was one of three in the Bengal Presidency, but the other two, at Calcutta and Murshidabad, appear to have been more successful propagandists for the virtues of Western medicine. W. W. Bird, one of the governors of the Banaras hospital, observed stoically that the "rise and progress of every benevolent purpose has been a perpetual struggle against opposition and difficulty, but enlightened zeal and perseverance have always prevailed, and doubtless will in the present instance."[8]

Vaccination was another of the boons conferred by Western science and benevolence which it was at first hoped Hindus would embrace with alacrity and gratitude. In practice, in and around Banaras, inoculation continued to be more popular while vaccination was viewed with great suspicion. One of the rumors that circulated about it in eastern U.P. was that it was an attempt by the British to find a child with white blood (or milk) in its veins, the Mahdi or the Kalki, who would otherwise drive the British out of India (*North Indian Notes and Queries* 1891, I (2):32; I (8):120; Hopkins 1983:147). But the British continued to

8. Bird to Secretary, Government of Bengal, 17 October 1814, Board's Collections, F/4/513, no. 12337, IOR.

think of the benefits of medicine as helping to complement or balance out the more openly coercive aspects of their rule. It was, significantly, at the opening of the Victoria Hospital at Banaras in December 1889 that the lieutenant-governor, Sir Auckland Colvin, possibly with the Mutiny more in mind than medicine, observed that "our empire in India to be secure must rest not on physical force only, but on the goodwill of the people" (*Hindustan* [28 December] in SVN for 1889). But to many of "the people" Western medicine, through such practices as vaccination, appeared to be just another aspect of colonial coercion (Arnold 1985, 1987).

But from self-interest and from the strength of the resistance encountered, the British were obliged to make frequent concessions to Indian sentiment, placing political pragmatism before medical idealism, and thus tending to confirm their own view of Indian ingratitude, ignorance, and immutable conservatism. When Duncan in 1790 tried to improve upon the primitive state of sanitation in Banaras a "vast multitude of persons" gathered on the outskirts of the city and forced the shopkeepers and traders to observe a *hartal* (a closure of shops and workplaces as a protest). A petition presented to Duncan complained that his measures were "a novelty" that made the people "apprehensive and disturbed them." He explained that there had been no sinister motive behind his action and that the changes had been intended to benefit the citizens of Banaras. With this reassurance, the people dispersed, "shouting their thanks and rejoicing, to their homes." But Duncan concluded from this and similar experiences that "all innovations, even for evident advantages, should be cautiously attempted, as far as they may affect the various classes and sects who inhabit the local centre of the Hindu faith" (Oldham 1876:208).

The British in Banaras (and to varying degrees elsewhere in colonial India) accordingly pursued a cautious policy, pressing what were seen to be the benefits of Western medicine when they could, but otherwise acknowledging political, cultural, and financial restraints. Early in the nineteenth century they elicited from the pandits of Banaras a statement that vaccination was not in contravention of the shastras (*Report of the Smallpox Commissioners* 1850:29). By the late 1870s smallpox inoculation had been formally outlawed within the municipalities of Banaras, Ghazipur, and Ballia, and in 1881 vaccination was made compulsory in the municipality of Banaras, followed two years later by the cantonment (colonial Banaras, it should be remembered, was also a military station). But as late as the 1920s the government refrained from making vaccination obligatory throughout Banaras district, fearing the strength of the opposition from the higher castes in the countryside

(ARSC 1879:31A; ARSC 1889:47; ARDPH 1925:44; Nevill, 1909a:26). Similarly, in 1900–1 the Collector of Banaras was at pains to impress the city's inhabitants that the government would not be enforcing the more extreme antiplague provisions, such as compulsory segregation and hospitalization of suspected cases (*Indian Appeal,* 8 February 1901; *Bharat Jiwan* [18 February] in SVN for 1901).

In a fashion that echoed the policies of the "Oudh School" of colonial administration, medical and civilian officers in eastern U.P. in the second half of the nineteenth century also sought to overcome or bypass popular resistance to Western medical measures by looking to local elites as intermediaries and leaders. In discussing the prospects for vaccination in the area, J. MacGregor, the regional Superintendent of Vaccination, remarked in 1878 that "an alteration in social customs to be successful in India, as in other countries, must take firm root in the upper strata before it penetrates downwards to the masses." It had been found from experience, he continued, "that when a zamindar's child is vaccinated, the *ryots* [peasants] submit their children with only the slender amount of pressure required to remove the *vis inertia* of apathy." When, however, the landholder was "an absentee or malcontent," the vaccinator "was obliged to find his recruits among those outcasts who live in the slums, or in the outskirts, of the village," a course of action likely to further prejudice the higher castes against vaccination (ARSC 1878:20A). Vaccination officers accordingly sought the assistance of Indian government servants, newspaper editors, municipal councillors, zamindars, and the Raja of Banaras to try to persuade townsfolk and villagers to accept vaccination (ARSC 1877:41; ARSC 1878:20A, 24A).

By the 1880s Western medical and sanitary ideas were gaining at least partial acceptance among many of these traditional and more recent elites (though not, it should be stressed, necessarily to the exclusion of indigenous beliefs and therapies). It was, for example, on the initiative of the Raja of Banaras and his diwan (chief minister) that the Kashi Ganga Prashadini Sabha was formed in 1886 to redirect the sewage of Banaras, keeping the bathing ghats free from pollution. Veneration for the Ganges, the traditional leadership of the Raja, and Western (rather than Hindu) notions of cleanliness and pollution were in this cojoined (*Bharat Jiwan* [22 November] in SVN for 1886; Nevill 1909a:262). It is striking, too, how many newspaper editors in Banaras and neighboring towns associated themselves with the government's often unpopular vaccination and antiplague policies and were critical of what they, too, saw as the prejudices of the "ignorant masses" (e.g., *Hindustan* [24 March] in SVN for 1901). Despite the earlier antipathy and divergence between Western and Indian medical belief and practice, by the late nineteenth and the early twentieth century there were signs of a growing accommodation and compatibility between the two.

CONCLUSION

For the social historian of modern India the study of disease opens up several inviting lines of enquiry. By looking at the incidence of disease, especially epidemics, one can gain insights into the material conditions and social organization of the population as a whole and of the subordinate classes in particular, for whom there is often otherwise a paucity of information. Disease morbidity and mortality can tell us a great deal about the temporal rhythms and spatial dimensions of rural life, and about the periodic crises brought about by drought and famine, war and political disruption. There is, too, a subjective domain to be considered—the cultural precepts that shaped the understanding of different social groups in their approaches and responses to particular diseases and afflictions. These reactions and perceptions in their turn may be revealing of wider social and political identities and divisions. For the colonial period especially, disease and medicine are richly informative about the nature and depth of the division between the British and their Indian subjects and about the growing penetration of state power, as well as about the practical and political limits to colonial intervention. These lines of enquiry may well lead in different directions, but ideally it ought to be possible to combine an awareness of the material aspects of disease causation and incidence with its social, cultural, and political dimensions.

For the purposes of this essay, Banaras—the city and its wider hinterland—has been the focus of attention. Banaras certainly possessed some features, not least its importance as a sacred place of all-India stature, that made it distinctive. But Banaras was also subject to and representative of wider patterns and influences. It shared many of its characteristics with other north India cities; it was bound in with the larger region through trade, transport, labor migration, pilgrimage, and numerous other factors of medical epidemiological significance.

A study of disease and medicine in Banaras also illustrates the pluralistic nature of its society and culture—folk and elite, Hindu, Muslim, and Western. At times the divisions appear so sharp as to be almost unbridgeable: such was the case most strikingly with certain aspects of British medical ideas and practice during the nineteenth century. But at other times and in other contexts, although the divisions remained important, there were significant linkages established. The Hindu Rajas of Banaras could be patrons of Ayurveda, have Unani hakims for their court physicians, and fund Western-styled hospitals and dispensaries. Muslim astrologers could follow beliefs and prescribe cures not vastly dissimilar from their Hindu counterparts (Pugh 1981). Muslims might participate in the propitiation of Sitala and receive inoculation from Hindu practitioners of the art (Vidyarthi 1979:58), while Hindus might pray at Muslim tombs for health, wealth, and progeny (Sukul 1974:159). Even Western ideas and therapies, so often viewed with deep suspicion, could gradually find their way into elite culture and into the medical treatment of the poorer townsfolk and peasantry. Banaras provides some striking examples of this complex process of borrowing and intertwining, but it is doubtful whether in this regard the city can be said to be exceptional.

LIST OF ABBREVIATIONS

Administration Reports	Reports on the administration of the North-Western Provinces and Oudh
ARDPH	Annual Report of the Director of Public Health of the United Provinces
ARSC	Annual Report of the Sanitary Commissioner of the North-Western Provinces and Oudh
Board	IOL & R. [Revenue] Board's Collections
Educ Comm Rpt	Report of the Indian Education Commission
Educ Comm Rpt Bengal	Education Commission. Report by the Bengal Provincial Committee
Educ Comm Rpt NWP&O	Education Commission. Report by the North-Western Provinces and Oudh Provincial Committee
GAD	General Administration files (located in provincial archives, India)
IOL & R	India Office Library and Records
Ind	Industries
NPS Ann Report	Nagari Pracharini Sabha Annual Report (Varshika Vivarana)
NWP Educ Rpt	Report on the State of Popular Education in the North-Western Provinces
NWP Gen Admin Progs	Proceedings of the Government of the North-Western Provinces and Oudh in the General Administration Department
NWP Lt-Gov Progs SBRD	North-Western Pronvinces Lieutenant-Governor's Proceedings in the Sudder Board of Revenue Department
NWP&O Educ Rpt	Report on the Progress of Education in the North-Western Provinces and Oudh
Oudh Educ Rpt	Report on Public Instruction in Oudh IOL & R. Political and Secret Files
SP	Statement of Particulars Regarding Books and Periodicals Published in the North-Western Provinces and Oudh, Registered under Act XXV of 1867
SVN	Selections from the Vernacular Newspapers of the North-Western Provinces for the Years . . .
TFR	Thana Festival Register (Banaras)
TR	Thana Register (Banaras)

UP Admin Rpt	United Provinces of Agra and Oudh Administration Report
UP Educ Progs	Proceedings of the Government of the United Provinces in the Educational Department
UP Educ Rpt	General Report on Public Instruction in the United Provinces of Agra and Oudh
White Demi-official	IOL & R. L/P & J/6/vol. 301 for 1891, file 907

BIBLIOGRAPHY

(Sources are given by original dates of publications, as this information is historically useful. Reprint information is included as necessary.)

I. ARCHIVAL SOURCES

Banaras. Thana Festival Registers (TFR).

———. Thana Registers (TR).

IOL & R. Bengal Revenue Proceedings P/55/vol. 37 [Progs for 11 January 1811].

———. F/4/365, [Revenue] Board's Collections no. 9093 [for 1812–13].

———. F/4/323, [Revenue] Board's Collections no. 7407 [for 1812].

———. 1873. "A History of the Province of Benares." Part I. London: India Office.

———. L/P & J/6/vol. 301 file 907 [for 1891].

———. L/P & J/7/vol. 75 [for 1931].

———. L/PS/10, vol. 173 for 1910, file 876; Winter to Dale, pp. 6–7.

———. NWP Judicial A Proceedings, nos. 48–108 for 19 January 1865.

———. NWP & O General Proceedings for June 1890.

United Provinces of Agra and Oudh. 1903. "Plague in Unao," Public Health Dept. Bundle 30, S1 26, File 663B. Uttar Pradesh State Archives.

Uttar Pradesh State Archives. General Department, File no. 173 for 1921, Keepwiths: Petition from Ahirs of Banaras Division.

II. PRINTED BOOKS AND OTHER SOURCES

Abbott, F. 1846. "Grand Trunk Road." *Selections from the Public Correspondence published by Authority, N.W.P.* Part I. Agra: Government Press.

Advisory Committee on the Sahel. 1983. *Environmental Change in the West African Sahel.* Washington, D.C.: National Academy Press.

Ahmad, Imtiaz, ed. 1981. *Ritual and Religion Among Muslims in India.* Delhi: Manohar.

Ā.j. 1920–1957.

Ali, A. Yusuf. 1900. *A Monograph on Silk Fabrics Produced in the North-Western Provinces and Oudh.* Allahabad: N.W. Provinces & Oudh Government Press.

———. 1917. "The Modern Hindustani Drama." In *Transactions of the Royal Society of Literature,* 2nd ser., vol. 35, pp. 79–99. London: Oxford University Press.

All India Handloom Board. 1965. *Weavers' Service Centre.* Delhi.

Anand, Mahesh. 1978. "Bhāratenduyugīn rangmanch." In *Ādhunik Hindī nātak aur rangmanch,* ed. Nemichandra Jain. Delhi: Macmillan.

Annual Report of the Director of Public Health of the United Provinces. Allahabad: Government Press.

Annual Report of the Sanitary Commissioner of the North-Western Provinces and Oudh. Allahabad: Government Press.

Ansari, Ghaus. 1960. *Muslim Caste in Uttar Pradesh.* Lucknow: The Ethnographic and Folk Culture Society, U.P.

Archer, Mildred. 1977. *Indian Popular Painting.* London: Her Majesty's Stationery Office.

Arnold, David. 1985. "Medical Priorities and Practice in Nineteenth-Century British India." *South Asia Research* 5:167–83.

———. 1986. "Cholera and Colonialism in British India." *Past and Present* 113:118–51.

———. 1987. "Touching the Body: Perspectives on the Indian Plague, 1896–1900." In *Subaltern Studies V,* ed. Ranajit Guha. Delhi: Oxford University Press.

Asiatic Annual Register 1804. London: T. Caddell and W. Davies.

Avasthi, Induja. 1979. *Rāmlīlā: paramparā aur shailiyā̃.* Delhi: Radhakrishna Prakashan.

Babcock, Barbara A. 1978. *The Reversible World: Symbolic Inversion in Art and Society.* Ithaca, N.Y.: Cornell University Press.

Banerjea, A. C. 1951. "Note on Cholera in the United Provinces." *Indian Journal of Medical Research* 39:17–40.

Barish, Jonas. 1981. *The Antitheatrical Prejudice.* Berkeley and Los Angeles: University of California Press.

Basu, Dilip. n.d. "Mallabir: Life History of A Calcutta Killer." Unpublished paper in author's possession.

Bayly, C. A. 1975. *The Local Roots of Indian Politics: Allahabad, 1880–1920.* Oxford: Clarendon Press.

———. 1978. "Indian Merchants in a 'Traditional' Setting; Banaras, 1780–1830." In *Imperial Impact: Studies in the Economic History of Africa and India,* ed. C. Dewey and A. G. Hopkins. London: University of London.

———. 1983. *Rulers, Townsmen and Bazaars: North Indian Society in the Age of British Expansion, 1770–1870.* Cambridge: Cambridge University Press.

———. 1986. "Delhi and Other Cities of North India During the 'Twilight.'" In Frykenberg 1986.

Bedi, Susham. 1984. *Hindī nātya: prayog ke sandarbh mẽ.* Delhi: Parag Prakashan.

Bengal Past and Present. 1908. "The Opening of the East Indian Railway." Vol. 2, pp. 55–61.

Bharat Jiwan. 1884–1922.

Bhardwaj, Surinder Mohan. 1973. *Hindu Places of Pilgrimage in India: A Study in Cultural Geography.* Berkeley and Los Angeles: University of California Press.

Bhushan, Jamila Brij. 1958. *The Costumes and Textiles of India.* Bombay: Taraporewala Sons & Co.

Bingham, L. H. 1858. "Notes on Road Making." Roorkee: Thomason College.

Bismillah, Abdul. 1986. *Jhini Jhini Bini Chadariya.* New Delhi: Rajkamal Prakashan.

Blackburn, Stuart. 1981. "Oral Performance: Narrative and Ritual in a Tamil Folk Tradition." *Journal of American Folklore* 94:207–27.

Blake, Stephen P. 1974. "Dar-ul-Khilafat-i-Shahjahanabad: The Padshahi Shahar in Mughal India: 1556–1739." Ph.D. dissertation, University of Chicago.

———. 1986. "Cityscape of an Imperial Capital." In Frykenberg 1986.

Blumhardt, James Fuller. 1893. *Catalogues of the Hindi, Punjabi, Sindhi, and Pushtu Printed Books in the Library of the British Museum.* London: British Museum.

———. 1902. *Catalogue of the Library of the India Office.* Vol. 2, pt. 2: Hindustani Books. London: India Office Library.

Blunt, E. A. H. 1912. *Census of India, 1911: volume XV; United Provinces of Agra and Oudh, Part I: Report.* Allahabad: Government Press.

Bonazzoli, Giorgio. 1983. "Composition, Transmission, and Recitation of the Puranas." *Purāna* 25, no. 2:254–80.

Brass, Paul R. 1974. *Language, Religion, and Politics in North India.* London: Cambridge University Press.

Braudel, Fernand. 1975. *The Mediterranean and the Mediterranean World in the Age of Philip II.* 2 vols. London: Fontana.

Briggs, George Weston. 1938. *Gorakhnath and the Kanphata Yogis.* Reprint. Delhi: Motilal Banarsidass, 1973.

Bryden, James L. 1869. *Epidemic Cholera in the Bengal Presidency.* Calcutta: Superintendent of Government Printing.

Burghart, Richard. 1978. "The Founding of the Rāmānandī Sect." *Ethnohistory* 25, no. 2:121–39.

Burke, Peter. 1978. *Popular Culture in Early Modern Europe.* New York: Harper and Row.

Calcutta Review. 1848. "Exposure of the Sick on the Banks of the Ganges." Vol. 10, no. 20, pp. 404–36.

———. 1851. "Indian Epidemics and Mofussil Sanatory Reform." Vol. 16, no. 31, pp. 156–230.

———. 1864. "Benares Past and Present." Vol. 40, no. 40, p. 256.

———. 1867. "Railway Fuel in the Punjab." Vol. 46, pp. 262–327.

Chakrabarty, Dipesh. 1976. *Communal Riots and Labour: Bengal's Jute Mill Hands in the 1890s.* Calcutta: Centre for Studies in Social Sciences, Occasional Paper No. 11.

Chandavarkar, Raj. 1981. "Workers' Politics and the Mill Districts in Bombay Between the Wars." *Modern Asian Studies* 15, no. 3:603–47.

Chartier, Roger. 1984. "Culture as Appropriation: Popular Cultural Uses in Early Modern France." In Steven L. Kaplan, ed., *Understanding Popular Culture.* New York: Mouton Publishers. Pp. 229–53.

Chatterji, A. C. 1908. *Notes on the Industries of the United Provinces.* Allahabad: Government Press.

Chaube, Ramgharib. 1910. "Note on Origin of Swang." *Indian Antiquary* 39 (January): 32.

Chaube, Shambhunarayan. 1976. "Rāmcharitmānas." In *Tulsī granthāvalī,* vol. 3. Banaras: Nāgarī Prachārinī Sabhā.

Chaudhuri, Nirad. 1951. *Autobiography of an Unknown Indian.* New York: MacMillan.

Chesneaux, Jean. 1978. *Pasts and Futures, Or What Is History For?* London: Thames and Hudson.

Chiranjilal-Natharam. 1897. *Sāngīt Chandrāvalī kā jhūlā.* Kanpur: La[w] Press.

Clark, Alice. 1986. "Mortality and Fertility in the Gangetic Plain, 1881–1931." Paper presented to the Southeastern Regional AAS, Raleigh.

Coccari, Diane Marjorie. 1986. "The Bir Babas of Banaras: An Analysis of a Folk Deity in North Indian Hinduism." Ph.D. dissertation, University of Wisconsin at Madison.

Cohn, Bernard. 1960. "The Initial British Impact on India: A Case Study of the Benares Region." *Journal of Asian Studies* 19, no. 4:418–31.

———. 1962. "Political Systems in Eighteenth Century India: The Banaras Region." *Journal of the American Oriental Society* 82:312–20.

———. 1964. "The Role of the Gosains in the Economy of Eighteenth and Nineteenth Century Upper India." *Indian Economic and Social History Review* 1, no. 4:175–82.

Colvin, Auckland. 1872. *Memorandum on the Revision of Land Revenue Settlements in the North-Western Provinces, A.D. 1860–1872.* Allahabad: Government Press.

Crooke, William. 1896. *The Popular Religion and Folk-lore of Northern India.* Reprint. 2 vols. Delhi: Munshiram Manoharlal, 1968.

———. 1897. *The North-Western Provinces of India: Their History, Ethnology, and Administration.* Reprint. Karachi: Oxford University Press, 1972.

———. 1926. *Religion and Folklore of Northern India.* 3rd ed. London: Oxford University Press.

Damle, Y. B. 1960. "Harikathā—A Study in Communication." *Bulletin of the Deccan College Research Institute* 20:63–107.

Das, Radha Krishna. 1902. "Hindī-Urdū." In *Sarasvatī* 3:359.

Das, Raghunath, ed. 1873. *Rāmāyan satīk.* Lucknow: Naval Kishor Press.

Das, Ramkumar. n.d. *Mānas shankā samādhān ratnāvalī.* 3 vols. Ayodhya.

Das, Shyam Sundar. 1957. *Merī Ātmakahānī* (The Story of My Life). Prayag (Allahabad): Indian Press.

Das, Veena. 1984. "For a Folk-technology and Theological Anthropology of Islam." *Contributions to Indian Sociology* 18, no. 2:293–300.

Das, Vrajratna, ed. 1953. *Bhāratendu granthāvalī: tīsrā khand.* Varanasi: Nāgarī Prachārinī Sabhā.

Das Gupta, Jyotirindra. 1970. *Language Conflict and National Development.* Berkeley and Los Angeles: University of California Press.

Datta, Pandit Gauri. 188?. *Nāgarī aur Urdū kā Svāng arthāt Nāgarī aur Urdū kā ek Nātak* (A Mime of Nagari and Urdu, or, A Play of Nagari and Urdu). Meerut: n.p.

Davis, Kenneth H. 1985. "Gravel Pits in Flood Plains, FHWA Perspective." *Proceedings of the Roads and Streets Conference,* Tucson, April 25–26, pp. 1–5.

Dharampal. 1971. *Civil Disobedience and Indian Tradition.* Varanasi: Sarva Seva Sangh Prakashan.

Din, Jayramdas. 1942. *Mānas shankā samādhān.* Gorakhpur, U.P.: Gita Press.

Dodwell, H. H., ed. 1929. *Cambridge History of India.* Vol. 5. Cambridge: Cambridge University Press.

DuBois, Emily. 1986. "Banaras Brocade Weaving." *Ars Textrina*, vol. 3 (May). Charles Babbage Research Centre, Winnipeg, Canada.

———. 1987. "Banaras Brocade Weaving." Unpublished paper.

Dvivedi, Sudhakar, ed. 1903. *Rāmcharitmānas*. Allahabad: Indian Press.

East Indian Railways. 1853–1863. "Half-yearly Meetings." *Railway Times*.

———. 1856. "Report of the Directors." *Railway Times* 19, no. 17 (26 April): 505.

———. 1859a. "Progress of Works." *Railway Times* 22, no. 19 (7 May): 531.

———. 1859b. "Half-yearly Meeting." *Railway Times* 22, no. 44 (29 Oct.): 1189–90.

———. 1878. "Report." *Railway Times* 41 (14 December): 1057.

Eck, Diana L. 1978. "Kasi, City and Symbol." *Purāna* 20:169–92.

———. 1982. *Banaras: City of Light*. New York: Knopf (other eds. by Routledge and Kegan Paul, 1983, and Princeton University Press, 1982).

Ellickson, Jean. 1976. "Islamic Institutions: Perception and Practice in a Village in Bangladesh." In T. N. Madan, ed., *Muslim Communities of South Asia*. Delhi: Vikas.

Elwin, Verrier. 1946. "The Ballad of Lorik and Chandaini." In *Folk-songs of Chhattisgarh*. Madras: Oxford University Press.

Fact-Finding Committee (Handlooms and Mills). 1942. *Report*. Delhi: Government of India Press.

Fisher, F. H., and J. P. Hewett. 1884. *Statistical, Descriptive, and Historical Account of the North-Western Provinces of India*, volume XIV, Part I, *Benares*. Allahabad: Government Press.

Fox, Richard G. 1969. *Kin, Clan, Raja, and Rule*. Berkeley and Los Angeles: University of California Press.

Freitag, Sandria B. 1980. "Religious Rites and Riots: From Community Identity to Communalism in North India, 1870–1940." Ph.D. dissertation, University of California, Berkeley.

———. 1985. "Collective Crime and Authority in North India." In *Crime and Criminality in British India*, ed. Anand Yang. Tucson: University of Arizona Press (for Association of Asian Studies, Monograph No. XLII).

———. 1989. *Collective Action and Community: Public Arenas in the Emergence of Communalism in North India*. Berkeley: University of California Press.

Fruzzetti, Lina. 1981. "Muslim Rituals: The Household Rites versus the Public Festivals in Rural India." In Imtiaz Ahmad 1981.

Frykenberg, R. E., ed. 1986. *Delhi Through the Ages: Essays in Urban History, Culture, and Society*. Delhi: Oxford University Press.

Ganguli, Birendranath. 1938. *Trends of Agriculture and Population in the Ganges Valley: A Study in Agricultural Economics*. London: Methuen & Co.

Gargi, Balwant. 1966. *Folk Theater of India*. Seattle: University of Washington Press.

Ginzburg, Carlo. 1982. *The Cheese and the Worms: The Cosmos of a Sixteenth Century Miller*. Trans. John and Anne Tedeschi. New York: Penguin Books.

Gopalkrishnan, K. 1985. "The Ganga: India's Poisonous Pilgrimage." *Hindustan Times*. In *Earthscan Bulletin* 8, no. 4:3–4.

Gopal, Madan. 1953. *This Hindi and Dev Nagri*. Delhi: Metropolitan Book.

———. 1972. *The Bharatendu: His Life and Times.* Delhi: Sagar Publications.
———. 1977. *Tulasi Das, A Literary Biography.* New Delhi: The Bookabode.
Gordon, Stewart N. 1971. "Comment." *Indian Economic and Social History Review* 8:219–20.
Greenough, Paul R. 1980. "Variolation and Vaccination in South Asia, c. 1700–1865: A Preliminary Note." *Social Science and Medicine* 14:345–47.
Grierson, George A. 1884. "Some Bihari Folk-Songs." *Journal of the Royal Asiatic Society* 16:196–246.
———. 1885. "Two Versions of the Song of Gopichand." *Journal of the Asiatic Society of Bengal* 54:35–55.
———. 1886. "Some Bhojpuri Folk-Songs." *Journal of the Royal Asiatic Society* 18:207–67.
———. 1889. *The Modern Vernacular Literature of Hindustan.* Calcutta: Asiatic Society.
———. 1903–1928. *Linguistic Survey of India.* Calcutta: Superintendent of Government Printing.
———. 1929. "The Birth of Lorik." In *Studies in Honor of Charles Rockwell Lanman.* Cambridge: Harvard University Press.
Gritzner, Jeffrey A. 1981. *Staff Report: Environmental Degradation in Mauritania.* Washington, D.C.: National Academy Press.
Grout, Donald Jay. 1973. *A History of Western Music.* Rev. ed. New York: W. W. Norton.
Growse, Frederick Salmon, trans. 1887. *The Rāmāyana of Tulasīdāsa.* Reprint. Delhi: Motilal Banarasidass, 1978.
Guha, Ranajit, ed. 1982. *Subaltern Studies I: Writings on South Asian History and Society.* Delhi: Oxford University Press.
———. 1983. *Elementary Aspects of Peasant Insurgency.* Delhi: Oxford University Press.
———. 1984. *Subaltern Studies III: Writings on South Asian History and Society.* Delhi: Oxford University Press.
Gupta, Brahmananda. 1976. "Indigenous Medicine in Nineteenth- and Twentieth-Century Bengal." In *Asian Medical Systems: A Comparative Study,* ed. Charles Leslie, pp. 368–78. Berkeley and Los Angeles: University of California Press.
Gupta, Mataprasad. 1945. *Hindī pustak sāhitya.* Allahabad: Hindustani Academy.
Gupta, Somnath. 1958. *Hindī nātak sāhitya kā vikās.* 4th ed. Jalandhar: Hindi Bhavan.
———. 1981. *Pārsī thiyetar: udbhav aur vikās.* Allahabad: Lokbharti Prakashan.
Haberman, David. 1984. "Acting as a Way of Salvation." Ph.D. dissertation, University of Chicago.
Hamilton, Walter. 1820. *A Geographical, Statistical, and Historical Description of Hindostan and the Adjacent Countries.* Vol. 1. Reprint. Delhi: Oriental Publishers, 1971.
Hansen, Kathryn. 1983a. "Sultana the Dacoit and Harischandra: Two Popular Dramas of the Nautanki Tradition of North India." *Modern Asian Studies* 17, no. 2.

———. 1983b. "Indian Folk Traditions and the Modern Theatre." *Asian Folklore Studies* 42, no. 1:77–89.

———. 1986. "Nautanki Chapbooks: Written Traditions of a Folk Form." *India Magazine*, January, pp. 65–72.

Harrison, J. B. 1980. "Allahabad: A Sanitary History." In *The City in South Asia*, ed. K. Ballhatchet and J. B. Harrison, pp. 166–95. London: Curzon Press.

Harrison, Selig S. 1960. *India: The Most Dangerous Decades*. Princeton: Princeton University Press.

Havell, E. B. 1905. *Benares, the Sacred City: Sketches of Hindu Life and Religion*. London: Blackie & Son.

Heber, Reginald. 1828. *Narrative of a Journey through the Upper Provinces of India, from Calcutta to Bombay, 1824–1825*. 2 Vols. Philadelphia: Carey, Lea, and Carey.

Hein, Norvin. 1972. *Miracle Plays of Mathura*. New Haven: Yale University Press.

Heitler, Richard. 1972. "The Varanasi House Tax Hartal of 1810–11." *Indian Economic and Social History Review* 10, no. 3:239–57.

Henry, Edward O. 1988. *Chant the Names of God: The Musical Culture of a North Indian Village*. San Diego: San Diego State University Press.

Hess, Linda. 1987. "The Poet and the People." Revised version of a paper presented at the University of Washington, Winter 1986.

Hirst, L. Fabian. 1953. *The Conquest of Plague*. Oxford: Clarendon Press.

Hobsbawm, Eric, and Terence Ranger, eds. 1983. *The Invention of Tradition*. Cambridge: Cambridge University Press.

Holwell, J. Z. 1767. *An Account of the Manner of Inoculating for the Small Pox in the East Indies*. London: T. Becket and P. A. De Hondt.

Hopkins, Donald R. 1983. *Princes and Peasants: Smallpox in History*. Chicago: University of Chicago Press.

Hunter, W. W. 1881. *The Imperial Gazetteer of India*. Vol. 1. London: Trubner & Co.

Imperial Gazetteer of India: United Provinces of Agra and Oudh. 1984. 2 vols. Reprint of 1908 ed. New Delhi: Usha Jain.

Jayakar, Pupul. 1967. "Naksha Bandhas of Banares." *Journal of Indian Textile History*, no. 7:22.

Jhingaran, P. N. 1976. "Ham sevak sab ati bar bhāgī." *Sāptāhik Hindustān* 26, no. 28:20–25.

Jiya Lal. 1877. *Sānīt Rājā Harischandra kā*. Banaras: Munshi Ambe Prasad.

Johnson, Francis. 1852. *Dictionary of Persian, Arabic, and English*. London: W. H. Allen.

Jones, Kenneth W. 1976. *Ārya Dharm: Hindu Consciousness in Nineteenth-Century Punjab*. Berkeley and Los Angeles: University of California Press; and New Delhi: Manohar.

Joshi, Esha Basanti, ed. 1965. *Uttar Pradesh District Gazetteers: Varanasi*. Allahabad: Government Press.

Juergensmeyer, Mark. 1982. *Religion as Social Vision*. Berkeley and Los Angeles: University of California Press.

Kane, Pandurang Vaman. 1973. *History of Dharmasastra.* Poona: Bhandarkar Oriental Research Institute.

Kashthajihva Swami et al. 1896–1898. *Rāmāyan paricharyā parishisht prakāsh.* Bankipur, Bihar: Khadgavilas Press.

Keay, F. E. 1931. *Kabir and His Followers.* Calcutta: Association Press.

Kesari, Arjundas. 1980. *Lorikayan.* Mirzapur: Lokruchi Prakashan.

Khan, Hamid Ali. 1900. *The Vernacular Controversy: An Account and Criticism of the Equalisation of Nagri and Urdu* . . . under the Resolution no. 585/III-343c-68 of Sir A. P. MacDonnell . . . dated 18 April 1900. n.p.

King, Anthony D. 1976. *Colonial Urban Development.* London: Routledge and Kegan Paul.

King, Christopher R. 1974. "The Nāgarī Prachārinī Sabhā (Society for the Promotion of the Nagari Script and Language) of Benares, 1893–1914: A Study in the Social and Political History of the Hindi Language." Ph.D. dissertation, University of Wisconsin.

Kjekshus, Helge. 1977. *Ecology Control and Economic Development in East African History.* London: Heinemann.

Klein, Ira. 1972. "Malaria and Mortality in Bengal, 1840–1921." *Indian Economic and Social History Review* 9:132–60.

———. 1973. "Death in India, 1871–1921." *Journal of Asian Studies* 32:639–59.

———. 1974. "Population and Agriculture in Northern India, 1872–1921." *Modern Asian Studies* 8, no. 2:191–216.

Kluyev, Boris I. 1981. *India: National and Language Problem.* New Delhi: Sterling Publishers.

Kolff, D. H. A. 1971. "Sannyasi Trader-Soldiers." *Indian Economic and Social History Review* 8:213–18.

Krishna, Rai Anand, and Vijay Krishna. 1966. *Banaras Brocades.* New Delhi: Crafts Museum.

Kumar, Nita. 1984. "Popular Culture in Urban India: The Artisans of Banaras c. 1884–1984." Ph.D. dissertation, University of Chicago.

———. 1985. "Urban Culture in Modern India." Amritsar: Urban History Association of India Occasional Papers series, no. 7.

———. 1986. "Open Space and Free Time: Pleasure for the People of Banaras." *Contributions to Indian Sociology* 20, no. 1:41–60.

———. 1987. "The Mazars of Banaras: A New Perspective on the City's Sacred Geography." *National Geographical Journal of India* 33, no. 3:263–67.

———. 1988. *The Artisans of Banaras: Popular Culture and Identity, 1880–1986.* Princeton: Princeton University Press.

Kumar, Ravinder. 1978–1979. "The Changing Structure of Urban Society in Colonial India." *Indian Historical Review* 5, nos. 1–2:200–15.

Lal, Shrikrishna. 1965. *Ādhunik hindī sāhitya kā vikās.* 4th ed. Allahabad: Hindi Parishad.

LeClercq, Jean. 1961. *The Love of Learning and the Desire for God.* New York: Fordham University Press.

List of Leading Officials, Nobles, and Personages, 1925. Allahabad: Government Press.

Lutgendorf, Philip. 1987. "The Life of a Text: Tulsīdās' *Rāmcharitmānas* in Performance." Ph.D. dissertation, University of Chicago.

Lutt, Jurgen. 1970. *Hindu-Nationalismus in Uttar Pradesh, 1867–1900.* Stuttgart: Ernst Klett.

McGregor, Ronald Stuart. 1972. "Bengal and the Development of Hindi, 1850–1880." *South Asian Review* 5, no. 2:137–46.

———. 1974. *Hindi Literature of the Nineteenth and Early Twentieth Centuries.* Weisbaden: Otto Harrasowitz.

Madan, T. N. 1981. "Religious Ideology and Social Structure: The Hindus and Muslims of Kashmir." In Imtiaz Ahmad 1981.

Mahābhārata.

Malaviya, Madan Mohan. 1897. *Court Character and Primary Education in N.W.P. and Oudh.* Allahabad: Indian Press.

Masselos, Jim. 1987. "The Discourse From the Other Side: Perceptions of Science and Technology in Western India." Paper presented to the Association for Asian Studies, March 1987.

Mathur, Poonam. 1978. "Observations on the Enactment of the Ramlila during October 1977." *N. K. Bose Memorial Foundation Newsletter* 1:1.

———. 1979. "Notes on Banaras 'Ramlila.'" *N. K. Bose Memorial Foundation Newsletter* 2, no. 1:2.

Metcalf, Barbara Daly. 1982. *Islamic Revival in British India: Deoband, 1860–1900.* Princeton: Princeton University Press.

———. 1986. "Hakim Ajmal Khan: *Rais* of Delhi and Muslim Leader." In Frykenberg 1986, pp. 299–315.

Metcalf, Thomas R. 1979. *Land, Landlords, and the British Raj.* Berkeley and Los Angeles: University of California Press.

Mishra, Jvalaprasad, ed. 1906. *Shrī Gosvāmī Tulsīdās-jī krit Rāmāyan.* Bombay: Shri Venkateshvar Steam Press.

Mishra, Kamala Prasad. 1975. *Banaras in Transition (1738–1795): A Socioeconomic Study.* New Delhi: Munshiram Manoharlal.

Mishra, R. N. 1977. *The Lower Ganga-Ghaghra Doab: A Study in Population and Settlement.* Agra: Sahitya Bhawan.

Mishra, Shivprasad, ed. 1974. *Bhāratendu granthāvalī: pahlā khand.* Varanasi: Nāgarī Prachārinī Sabhā.

Misra, Shitikantha. 1956. *Kharībolī kā Āndolan* (The Khari Boli Movement). Kashi (Banaras): Nāgarī Prachārinī Sabhā.

Monier-Williams, Monier. 1899. *Sanskrit-English Dictionary.* Oxford: Clarendon Press.

Muir, W. 1858. "Course of the Railway through the N.W.P." *Selections from the Records of Government, N.W.P.* 2:277–79. Calcutta: Baptist Mission Press.

Mukharji, T. N. 1888. *Art Manufactures of India (Specially Compiled for the Glascow International Exhibition).* Reprint. New Delhi, 1972.

Muthiah, K. S. 1911. *Smiling Benaras.* Madras: Raithby & Co.

Naqvi, H. K. 1968. *Mughal Hindustan: Cities and Industries, 1556–1903.* Karachi: National Book Foundation.

Narayan, Pitambar. 1971. *Hindī sāhitya sārinī.* Hoshiarpur: Vishveshvaranand Institute.

Narayana, Birendra. 1981. *Hindi Drama and Stage.* Delhi: Bansal & Co.

Narula, S. S. 1955. *Scientific History of the Hindi Language.* New Delhi: Hindi Academy.

Nayar, B. R. 1969. *National Communication and Language Policy in India.* New York: F. A. Praeger.

Nesfield, John C. 1885. *Brief View of the Caste System of the N.W. Provinces and Oudh.* Allahabad: Government Press.

Neuman, Daniel M. 1980. *The Life of Music in North India: The Organization of an Artistic Tradition.* New Delhi: Manohar.

Nevill, H. R. 1909a. *Benares: A Gazetteer,* being Volume XXVI of the *District Gazetteers of the United Provinces of Agra and Oudh.* Allahabad: Government Press.

———. 1909b. *Cawnpore: A Gazetteer,* being Volume XXIX of the *District Gazetteers of the United Provinces of Agra and Oudh.* Allahabad: Government Press.

Nicholas, Ralph W. 1981. "The Goddess Sitala and Epidemic Smallpox in Bengal." *Journal of Asian Studies* 41, no. 1:21–44.

Nomani, Abdus Salam. 1963. *Tarikh Asar-i-Banaras.* Banaras: Makhtab Nadvatulma ᶜarif.

North Indian Notes and Queries. 1891.

Oldenburg, Veena Talwar. 1984. *The Making of Colonial Lucknow, 1856–1877.* Princeton: Princeton University Press.

———. 1987. "Lifestyle As Resistance: The Case of the Courtesans of Lucknow." Paper presented to the American Historical Association, December 1987.

Oldham, Wilton. 1876. *Historical and Statistical Memoir of the Ghazeepoor District.* Part Two. Allahabad: Government Press.

Oman, John Campbell. 1908. *Cults, Customs, and Superstitions of India.* London: T. Fisher Unwin.

Oude and Rohilkund Railway. 1875. "Report." *Railway Times* 38 (11 December): 1169.

Pandey, B. P. 1981. *Banaras Brocades: Structure and Functioning.* Varanasi: Gandhian Institute of Studies.

Pandey, Gyanendra. 1978. *The Ascendancy of the Congress in Uttar Pradesh, 1926–34.* Delhi: Oxford University Press.

———. 1982. "Peasant Revolt and Indian Nationalism." In Guha 1982.

———. 1983a. "Rallying Round the Cow: Sectarian Strife in the Bhojpuri Region, c. 1888–1917." In *Subaltern Studies II,* ed. Ranajit Guha. Delhi: Oxford University Press.

———. 1983b. "'The Bigoted Julaha.'" *Economic and Political Weekly* 18, no. 5:19–28.

———. 1984. "'Encounters and Calamities': The History of a North Indian *Qasba* in the Nineteenth Century." In Guha 1984, pp. 231–70.

Pandey, Shyam Manohar. 1979. *The Hindi Oral Epic Loriki.* Allahabad: Sahitya Bhawan.

———. 1982. *The Hindi Oral Epic Canaini.* Allahabad: Sahitya Bhawan.

Parry, J. P. 1980. "Ghosts, Greed, and Sin: The Occupational Identity of the Benares Funeral Priests." *Man* 15:88–111.

———. 1981. "Death and Cosmogony in Kashi." *Contributions to Indian Sociology* 15, nos. 1–2:337–65.

———. 1982. "Sacrificial Death and the Necrophagous Ascetic." In *Death and the Regeneration of Life,* ed. M. Block and J. P. Parry. Cambridge: Cambridge University Press.

Planalp, Jack M. 1956. "Religious Life and Values in a North Indian Village." Ph.D. dissertation, University of Chicago.

Platts, John Thompson. 1960. *A Dictionary of Urdu, Classical Hindi, and English.* London: Oxford University Press.

Plowden, W. C. 1873. *Census of the N.-W. Provinces, 1872,* Vol. I, *General Report.* Allahabad: Government Press.

Poddar, Hanuman Prasad, ed. 1938a. *Shrī Rāmcharitmānas.* Gorakhpur, U.P.: Gita Press.

———. 1938b. *Kalyān: Mānasānk.* Gorakhpur, U.P.: Gita Press.

Pollitzer, R. 1959. *Cholera.* Geneva: World Health Organization.

Prakash, Gyan. 1987. "Empowered Resistance and Contested Power in South Asia: The State of Its Historiography." Paper presented to the American Historical Association, December 1987.

Prasad, Shiv. 1868. "Memorandum: Court Characters in The Upper Provinces of India." Banaras: no publisher (located in the library of the Nāgarī Prachārinī Sabhā).

Pritchett, Frances W. 1983. "Sit Basant: Oral Tale, Sangit, and Kissa." *Asian Folklore Studies* 42, no. 1:45–62.

———. 1985. *Marvelous Encounters: Folk Romance in Urdu and Hindi.* Riverdale, Md.: Riverdale Company, Inc.

Pugh, Judy F. 1981. "Person and Experience: The Astrological System of North India." Ph.D. dissertation, University of Chicago.

Purser, Edward. 1859. "East Indian Railway—Progress of Works." *Railway Times* 22, no. 20 (14 May): 563.

Raghunathji, K. 1880–1882. "Bombay Beggars and Criers." *Indian Antiquary* 9:247–50, 278–80; 10:71–75, 145–47, 286–87; 11:22–24, 44–47, 141–46, 172–74.

Rahmat-Ullah, M. 1900. *A Defence of the Urdu Language and Character. (Being a reply to the pamphlet called "Court Character and Primary Education in N.-W. P. and Oudh"*). Allahabad: Liddel's N.-W. P. Printing Works Press.

Rao, M. S. A. 1964. "Caste and the Indian Army." *Economic Weekly* 16 (29 August): 1439–43.

———. 1979. *Social Movements and Social Transformations: A Study of Two Backward Classes Movements in India.* Delhi: Macmillan.

Rao, V. Narayana. 1988. "A Ramayana of Their Own: Woman's Oral Traditions in Telegu." Paper presented to the 1988 Association of Asian Studies.

Rastogi, S. N., B. G. Prasad, and J. K. Bhatnagar. 1967. "A Study of Epidemiology of Cholera in Uttar Pradesh: A Study in Retrospect." *Indian Journal of Medical Research* 55:843–59.

Report of the Smallpox Commissioners. 1850. Calcutta: Military Orphan Press.

Report on the Scarcity and Relief Operations in the North-Western Provinces and Oudh (During the Years 1877–78 and 1889). Allahabad: Government Press.

Reports on the Administration of the North-Western Provinces and Oudh. 1896–1900. Allahabad: Government Press.

Richards, J. F., James R. Hagen, and Edward S. Haynes. 1985. "Changing Land Use in Bihar, Punjab, and Haryana, 1850–1970." *Modern Asian Studies* 19, no. 3:699–732.

Richards, J. F., and Michelle Burge McAlpin. 1983. "Cotton Cultivating and Land Clearing in the Bombay Deccan and Karnatak: 1818–1920." In *Global Deforestation and the Nineteenth-Century World Economy,* ed. Richard P. Tucker and J. F. Richards, pp. 68–94. Durham: Duke University Press.

Ridgeway, William. 1915. *The Dramas and Dramatic Dances of Non-European Races, in Special Reference to the Origin of Greek Tragedy.* Cambridge: Cambridge University Press.

Robinson, F. C. R. 1974. *Separatism Among Indian Muslims.* Cambridge: Cambridge University Press.

———. 1983. "Islam and Muslim Society in South Asia." *Contributions to Indian Sociology* 17, no. 2:185–203.

Robson, John. 1866. *A Selection of Khyals or Marwari Plays with an Introduction and Glossary.* Beawar: Beawar Mission Press.

Rocher, Ludo. 1985. *The Purānas.* Weisbaden: Otto Harrasowitz.

Rupkala, Sitaramsharan Bhagvanprasad, ed. 1909. *Shrī Bhaktamāl.* Lucknow: Naval Kishor Press.

Russell, Ralph, and Khurshidul Islam. 1968. *Three Mughal Poets.* Cambridge: Harvard University Press.

Sadiq, Muhammad. 1984. *History of Urdu Literature.* Delhi: Oxford University Press.

Sahay, Babu Shivnandan. 1905. *Harishchandra.* Reprint. Lucknow: Hindi Samiti, Uttar Pradesh Samiti, 1975.

Saksena, Krishna Mohan. 1977. *Bhāratenduyugīn nātya-sāhitya mẽ loktattva.* Allahabad: Abhinav Bharati.

Saksena, Ram Babu. 1940. *A History of Urdu Literature.* 2nd ed. Allahabad: Ram Narain Lal.

Sanyal, Nalinaksha. 1930. *Indian Railways.* Calcutta: University of Calcutta.

Saraswati, Bsidyanath. 1975. *Kashi: Myth and Reality of a Classical Cultural Tradition.* Simla: Indian Institute of Advanced Study.

Schechner, Richard, and Linda Hess. 1977. "The Ramlila of Ramnagar." *Drama Review* 21, no.3:51–82.

Schimmel, Annemarie. 1975. *Classical Urdu Literature from the Beginning to Iqbal.* Wiesbaden: Otto Harrasowitz.

———. 1985. *And Muhammad Is His Messenger.* Chapel Hill: University of North Carolina Press.

Schwartzberg, Joseph E., ed. 1978. *A Historical Atlas of South Asia.* Chicago: University of Chicago Press.

Seiler-Baldinger, Annemarie. 1979. *Classification of Textile Techniques.* Ahmedabad: Calico Museum of Textiles.

Selections from the Vernacular Newspapers of the North Western Provinces for the years. . . . Allahabad: Government Press.

Sen, Rajani Rajan. 1912. *The Holy City (Benares).* Chittagong: M. R. Sen.

Shakespear, A. 1848. *Memoir on the Statistics of the North Western Provinces of the*

Bengal Presidency. Calcutta: Baptist Mission Press.
———. 1873. *Selections from the Duncan Records*. Vol. 2. London: India Office.
Sharan, Anjaninandan. 1938. "*Mānas* ke prāchīn tīkākār." In Poddar 1938b, pp. 908–28.
Sharar, Abdul Halim. 1975. *Lucknow: The Last Phase of an Oriental Culture*. Trans. and ed. E. S. Harcourt and Fakkir Hussain. London: Paul Elek.
Sharma, Ramvilas. 1973. "Bhāratendu yug aur Urdū." *Ālochanā* 24:18–26.
Sherring, M. A. 1868. *The Sacred City of the Hindus: An Account of Benares*. London: Trubner and Co.
———. 1872. *Hindu Tribes and Castes, as Represented in Benares*. Vol. 1. Reprint. Delhi: Cosmo Publications, 1974.
Shrīmad Bhāgavata Mahāpurāṇa. 1964. 2 vols. Gorakhpur, U.P.: Gita Press.
Shrimati Chhoti Maharajkumari. 1979. "Rāmnagar kī rāmlīlā Maharāj Chetsimh ke purva bhī?" *Vidhyā Mandir Patrikā*, pp. 43–45.
Shukla, Bhanudev. 1972. *Bhāratendu ke nātak*. Kanpur: Grantham.
Shukla, Pandit Manoharlal. 1922. *Rāshtrīya Sāngīt Julmī Dāyar yā Jaliyānvālā Bāg*. Kanpur: Manoharlal Shukla.
Shukla, Ram Chandra. 1968. *Hindī Sāhitya kā Itibās* (The History of Hindi Literature). Kashi (Banaras): Nāgarī Prachārinī Sabhā.
Siddiqi, Asiya. 1973. *Agrarian Change in a North Indian State: Uttar Pradesh 1819–1833*. Oxford: Clarendon Press.
Siddiqi, M. I. n.d. "History of Weavers." Unpublished paper.
Singh, B. N. 1941. *Benares, a Handbook: Prepared for the Indian Science Congress 28th Session*.
Singh, Bhagavati Prasad, 1957. *Rāmbhakti mē rasik sampradāy*. Balrampur, U.P.: Avadh Sahitya Mandir.
Singh, Jang Bahadur. 1918. *Mānas shankā mochan*. Banaras, n.p.
Singh, R. L., ed. 1971. *India: A Regional Geography*. Varanasi: National Geographic Society of India.
Singh, Ramadhar. 1973. "Bhāratendu aur Hindī." *Ālochanā* 26:65–70.
Singh, Ram Sevak, "Birahā Book, 1950–55." Unpublished paper in author's possession.
Sinha, S. N. 1974. *Subah of Allahabad under the Great Mughals*. Delhi: n.p.
Smith, Donald E. 1963. *India as a Secular State*. Princeton: Princeton University Press.
Sontheimer, Gunther-Dietz. 1976. *Birobā, Mhaskobā und Khandobā: Ursprung, Geschichte und Umwelt von Pastoralen Gottheiten in Mahārāstra*. Wiesbaden: Franz Steiner.
Stebbing, E. P. 1922–1926. *The Forests of India*. 3 Vols. London: John Lane.
Stone, Ian. 1984. *Canal Irrigation in British India: Perspectives on Technological Change in a Peasant Economy*. Cambridge: Cambridge University Press.
Stutley, Margaret, and James Stutley. 1977. *A Dictionary of Hinduism: Its Mythology, Folklore, and Development, 1500 B.C.–A.D. 1500*. London: Routledge and Kegan Paul.
Sukul, Kuber Nath. 1974. *Varanasi Down the Ages*. Patna: K. N. Sukul.

Sundardas, Shyam, ed. 1965. *Hindi Sabdsagar.* Kashi (Banaras): Nāgarī Prachārinī Sabhā.

Taneja, Satyendra Kumar. 1976. *Nātakkār Bhāratendu kī rangparikalpanā.* Delhi: Bharti Bhasha Prakashan.

Tavernier, Jean-Baptiste. 1676. *Travels in India.* 2 Vols. Reprint. Lahore: Al-Biruni, 1976.

Temple, Richard Carnac. 1884. *The Legends of the Panjab.* Vols. 1–3. Reprint. Patiala: Language Department, Panjab, 1962.

Thapar, Romila. 1978. *Ancient Indian Social History.* New Delhi: Orient Longman. Especially "Renunciation: The Making of a Counter-Culture."

Thiel-Horstmann, Monika. 1985. "Warrior Ascetics in 18th Century Rajasthan." Unpublished paper.

Timberg, Thomas A. 1978. *The Marwaris.* New Delhi: Vikas.

Tivari, Bholanath. 1982. *Rājbhāshā Hindī* (Hindi: the National Language). Delhi: Prabhat Prakashan.

Tivari, Gopinath. 1959. *Bhāratendukālīn nātak sāhitya.* Jalandhar: Hindi Bhavan.

Troup, R. S. 1921. *The Silviculture of Indian Trees.* 3 Vols. Reprint. Delhi: Government of India Press, 1975–1981.

Tucker, Richard P. 1983. "The British Colonial System and the Forests of the Western Himalayas, 1815–1914." In *Global Deforestation and the Nineteenth-Century World Economy,* ed. Richard P. Tucker and J. F. Richards, pp. 146–66. Durham: Duke University Press.

Tulpule, Shankar Gopal. 1979. *Classical Marathi Literature.* Wiesbaden: Otto Harrasowitz.

Turner, Victor. 1974. *Dramas, Fields, and Metaphors: Symbolic Action in Human Society.* Ithaca: Cornell University Press.

———. 1979. *Process, Performance, and Pilgrimage.* New Delhi: Concept Publishing.

Upadhyay, Rajeshkumar. 1984. "Surīle svar mẽ tairtī Rām kathā kī gunj." *Dharmyug* 35, no. 15:16–17.

Varady, Robert G. 1981. "Rail and Road Transport in Nineteenth Century Awadh: Competition in a North Indian Province." Ph.D. dissertation, University of Arizona.

———. 1985a. "Harvesting Natural Resources: A Century of Mining and Lumbering." Paper presented at symposium, "Desert Dialogue: Humanistic and Scientific Views of Land Use in the Southwest," Tucson.

———. 1985b. "Infrastructure and Environment: Speeding Deliveries through a Fragile Landscape." Paper presented at "Desert Dialogue," Tucson.

Varma, Lakshmikanta, ed. 1964. *Hindī-Āndolan* (The Hindi Movement). Prayag (Allahabad): Hindi Sahitya Sammelan.

Varma, Ram Chandra, ed. 1966. *Mānak Hindi Kosh* V. Prayag (Allahabad): Hindi Sahitya Sammelan.

Vatuk, Ved Prakash, and Sylvia Vatuk. 1967. "The Ethnography of *Sang,* A North Indian Folk Opera." *Asian Folklore Studies* 26, no. 1:29–51.

Verma, Ganeshilal. 1974. "Hindi Journalism and Socio-Political Awakening in the North West Provinces and Oudh in the Last Three Decades of the 19th Century." *Journal of Indian History* 52 (April): 377–87.

Vidyarthi, L. P. 1979. *The Sacred Complex of Kashi: A Microcosm of Indian Civilization*. New Delhi: Concept Publishing.

Wadley, Susan S. 1980. "Sitala: The Cool One." *Asian Folklore Studies* 39:33–62.

Watts, Sir George. 1904. *Indian Art at New Delhi 1903*. Calcutta, n.p.

Weiner, Myron. 1957. *Party Politics in India*. Princeton: Princeton University Press.

Whitcombe, Elizabeth. 1972. *Agrarian Conditions in Northern India*. Volume I: *The United Provinces under British Rule, 1860–1900*. Berkeley and Los Angeles: University of California Press.

Wilson, Horace Hayman. 1862. *Religious Sects of the Hindus*. Reprint. Calcutta: Sushil Gupta Pvt. Ltd, 1958.

Yadav, Laksmi Narayan. 1975. "Birahā ke Bihari tathā Lok Gītok kā Vikās." Unpublished paper in author's possession.

Yadav, Mangal. 1982–1983. "Lok Gīt Sangrah." Unpublished paper in author's possession.

Yadav, Ram Sakal. n.d. Unpublished song text in author's possession.

Yajnik, R. K. 1933. *The Indian Theatre*. London: George Allen & Unwin.

Yang, Anand A. 1980. "Sacred Symbols and Sacred Space in Rural India: Community Mobilization in the 'Anti-Cow Killing' Riot of 1893." *Comparative Studies in Society and History* 22, no. 4:576–96.

———. 1987. "The Many Faces of Sati in Early Nineteenth Century India." Unpublished paper.

Yeo, Eileen, and Stephen Yeo, eds. 1981. *Popular Culture and Class Conflict, 1590–1914: Explorations in the History of Labour and Leisure*. Atlantic Highlands, N.J.: Humanities Press.

INDEX

Ahirs. *See* Yādavs
Akhāṛās, 32, 70, 96–97, 121; and *Banārsipan,* 166; and communalism, 120; and competition, 32; in 1809 riot, 211; and mobilization, xiii; in Muharram, 159; as patrons, 32; and popular culture, 120; in *qaṣba* life, 121; in *shringārs,* 143
Ansaris. *See* Weavers
Artisans, 169. *See also* Weavers; Yādavs
Arya Samāj, 47, 90, 136
Ascetics, 135. *See also* Gosains
Audience, 29–32; judging in *birahā,* 105; participation in *kathā,* 35, 37; role in Svāng, 71

Banaras region: disease ecology of, 248–57; ecology of, 231–39
Banārsipan, 166, 206
Bankers, 5–8. *See also* Hindu merchant culture
Barawafat, 159–61, 163
Bharat Milāp, 206, 211
Bhojpuri, xvii, 1, 3, 93, 111, 186
Bhumihars, 7, 8n, 213
Bihari Lal Yadav, 95–96
Birahā, 93–113
Bīrs, 130–46
Braj Bhasha, 62, 190–92

Cholera, 251–52, 254, 257
Cities, movement of population, 18. *See also* Urban centers
Collective action, 205, 239; of corporations, 19
Community: constructions of, xii; invoked in *birahā,* 118; varying for Muslims, 147
Competition: and *birahā,* 97, 105–6; and community, 33; over disease, 261; in 1809 riot, 213; and language identity, 186; in Muharram, 158; and nationalism, 227; among neighborhoods, 106; in neighborhood, 161; occupation, 123; in popular culture, 32–33; in Svāng, 70
Corporations, role of in cities, 19

Devotional cults, 26, 37, 38
Devotionalism, 156–57

East India Company, 10
Ecology, 175, 230–33, 248–57
Education, and language controversy, 195; and caste, language, 196
Education Department, and language training, 197
Elites: and medical practices, 265; rejection of Parsi theatre, 77; theatre societies, 83; values inverted in Svāng, 73; withdrawal from popular culture activities, 163; withdrawal from protests, 223; withdrawal from *shringārs,* 106–7
Epidemics, 240–41

Compositor: Interactive Composition Corporation
Text: 10/13 Sabon
Display: Sabon
Printer: Braun-Brumfield, Inc.
Binder: Braun-Brumfield, Inc.